THE ESSENTIAL GUIDE TO PSYCHOACTIVE DRUGS IN CANADA

THE ESSENTIAL GUIDE TO PSYCHOACTIVE DRUGS IN CANADA

A Resource for Counselling Professionals

Second Edition

Rick Csiernik

The Essential Guide to Psychoactive Drugs in Canada: A Resource for Counselling Professionals, Second Edition
Rick Csiernik

First published in 2019 by
Canadian Scholars, an imprint of CSP Books Inc.
425 Adelaide Street West, Suite 200
Toronto, Ontario
M5V 3C1

www.canadianscholars.ca

Library and Archives Canada Cataloguing in Publication

Title: The essential guide to psychoactive drugs in Canada : a resource for counselling professionals / Rick Csiernik.
Other titles: Just say know
Names: Csiernik, Rick, author.
Description: Second edition. | Originally published under the title: Just say know. | Includes bibliographical references and index.
Identifiers: Canadiana (print) 20190156155 | Canadiana (ebook) 20190156163 | ISBN 9781773381602 (softcover) | ISBN 9781773381619 (PDF) | ISBN 9781773381626 (EPUB)
Subjects: LCSH: Psychotropic drugs—Canada—Handbooks, manuals, etc. | LCSH: Psychopharmacology—Canada—Handbooks, manuals, etc. | LCSH: Drugs of abuse—Canada—Handbooks, manuals, etc. | LCSH: Substance abuse—Canada—Handbooks, manuals, etc. | LCGFT: Handbooks and manuals.
Classification: LCC RM315 .C75 2019 | DDC 615.7/80971—dc23

Page layout by S4Carlisle Publishing Services
Cover design by Em Dash

Printed and bound in Ontario, Canada

Canada

TABLE OF CONTENTS

PREFACE

The first edition of this book was published in 2014, and in just a few short years our knowledge of and relationship with psychoactive drugs have changed in many ways, in some instances quite dramatically. We have gone from charging, fining, and even incarcerating cannabis users at a cost to taxpayers, to courting these same individuals to create taxation revenue. Fentanyl went from an obscure, minimally used, therapeutic opioid to a daily media story, altering public health policy and treatment practices, and we were introduced to novel psychoactive substances, learning new drug names such as flakka, BZP, and JWH-018. Upwards of 1,000 Canadians a year die needlessly of drug overdoses, and while the Supreme Court of Canada has upheld the right for communities to establish safe injection sites, in 2015, under the leadership of Prime Minister Stephen Harper, the Canadian Parliament passed Bill C-2, An Act to amend the Controlled Drugs and Substances Act, using the Orwellian title of the Respect for Communities Act, making it more difficult to establish such agencies (Dhalla et al., 2009; Fischer & Rehm, 2009; Bill C-2, 2015). The association between illicit drugs and crime has been well documented, consistently indicating that not only are many offences committed by those who are under the influence of psychoactive drugs, but also that crime is often fuelled by the need to obtain money to purchase these substances. The justice- and enforcement-related costs associated with illicit drug use alone, including expenses for police, courts, and correctional services, in 1996 were estimated at over $2 billion annually in Canada, four times more than what is spent on health care responses (Rehm et al., 2006; Single et al., 1996). By 2014, less than two decades later, this estimate had more than quadrupled to $9 billion (Canadian Substance Use Costs and Harms Scientific Working Group, 2018). However, of those incarcerated in Canada, a disproportionate number come from vulnerable, poor, and marginalized communities, including far too many from First Nations, Métis, and

Inuit groups, just as in the United States a disproportionate number are young African Americans (Kellen, Powers, & Birnbaum, 2017).

Psychoactive drugs have been linked to and identified as the cause of deaths of celebrities across the generations, from Tommy Dorsey, to Marilyn Monroe and Judy Garland, to Jimi Hendrix, Janis Joplin, Michael Jackson, and Prince, to Lenny Bruce, John Belushi, and Chris Farley, to Heath Ledger, Cory Monteith, and Philip Seymour Hoffman. However, the World Health Organization (WHO; 2014b) estimates that the deadliest drug on the planet remains tobacco; 100 million people died prematurely due to tobacco-related illnesses in the 20th century, and among those, 37,000 Canadians a year. That means that between the publication of the first and second editions of this book it would be as if everyone, of all ages, in New Glasgow, Nova Scotia; Joliette, Quebec; Woodstock, Ontario; Moose Jaw, Saskatchewan; and Campbell River, British Columbia died. All five communites across Canada would be ghost towns due to deaths directly due to tobacco. Though of course in their place we do have tobacco sales that bring in approximately $5 billion a year in tax revenue.

Psychoactive substance use touches every facet of our lives. One in four families is directly affected (Alaggia & Csiernik, 2017), and in any given year one in five Canadians experiences a mental health or addiction problem, and of those, one in five is a concurrent disorder (Rush et al., 2008; Smetanin et al., 2011). Addiction has an impact on all dimensions of human wellness: our physical health, our psychological health, our social health, our intellectual/vocational health, and our spiritual health. There is not a nation on earth that has not been affected by the trauma that psychoactive substance use creates, or the ripples that the integration of drugs into civil society brings until civil society itself is threatened, as we have seen from Colombia to Mexico to Afghanistan to Guinea-Bissau. Psychoactive drugs have been part of horrific historical events, such as the colonial slave trade (Jankowiak & Bradburd, 2003), and continue to be part of the human trafficking economy in the 21st century (Wheaton, Schauer, & Galli, 2010). The direct and indirect harm that psychoactive drugs bring to individuals and their families, the workplace, and the global economy is incalculable.

However, the good that psychoactive drugs bring to individuals and their families, the workplace, and the global economy is likewise incalculable, for without the trade in prescription, recreational, and illicit drugs, the world's economy would be in tatters (African Union, 2012; Gresser, 2013; Khaled, 2013; United Nations Office on Drug and Crime [UNODC], 2018). Without the use of psychoactive drugs, people would die both prematurely and in terrible pain. Without psychoactive drugs, many of the leisure activities we engage in would not occur, be it through alcohol companies sponsoring sports, including hockey, football, and darts, or soft drink conglomerates sponsoring the Olympics. This book is not an examination of the social evils or social benefits that psychoactive drugs bring. What it does present is the biological facts pertaining to psychoactive drugs, including both risks and benefits, and an understanding of how and why psychoactive drugs produce their effects. In essence, this book is a study of the pharmacology of psychoactive drugs. In Greek, *pharmakon* means remedy, but it can also mean poison or magical charm. In order to address this global issue rationally, as well as to be able to address the needs of each individual from an evidence-informed basis, a core understanding of what a psychoactive drug is actually doing is required. Most counselling professionals already have an excellent understanding of how to help service users. This book simply provides one additional tool: an understanding of what the drugs are actually doing inside the person, and how. This information will be invaluable both for yourself and your service users as you plan the most appropriate, evidence-informed treatment plan. This is the future of the addiction field; one based in fact and no longer in fear.

Be the fish that sees the water you swim in!

Rick Csiernik
Hamilton, Ontario
February 2019

CHAPTER 1

Pharmacological Principles

OVERVIEW

The opening section of the chapter begins with an examination of the most problematic and commonly misunderstood term in the entire addiction field: the idea of *addiction* itself; what it actually is and what it entails. This is followed by a brief overview of the various families of psychoactive drugs that the remainder of the book will examine in depth, along with some of the costs to Canadian society of drug use and addiction. The main focus of this chapter, however, is the brain and how it functions to better allow us to understand how psychoactive drugs alter substance users' physiology and perceptions, changing how they view and interact with the physical world. Core pharmacokinetic and pharmacodynamic concepts are then reviewed to provide you with foundational knowledge of the biological aspects related to the process of addiction. The chapter concludes with one of the most neglected areas of knowledge, the relationship between substance use, sleeping, and dreaming.

1.1 UNDERSTANDING ADDICTION

Psychoactive Drugs

What distinguishes psychoactive drugs from other substances is their ability to alter the central nervous system (CNS). A psychoactive drug is any substance, natural, semi-synthetic, or wholly synthesized, that by its chemical nature alters the structure or function of the mind and body of a living organism (Le Dain Commission, 1972). When ingested, psychoactive drugs work by altering an individual's mental processes, including cognition, and affect by decreasing, increasing, disrupting, or balancing CNS activity. This in turn produces changes in mood, perception, sensation, need, consciousness, and other psychological functions, and ultimately produces changes in behaviour (Special Committee on Non-Medical Use of Drugs, 2002). As well, all psychoactive drugs have additional effects upon the larger peripheral nervous system (PNS), primarily the autonomic nervous system (ANS) component. The ANS is divided into two parts: the sympathetic nervous system produces an excitatory response, while the parasympathetic nervous system produces the opposite reaction. This means that consuming a psychoactive drug can, and does, depending upon the drug, also affect respiration, cardiovascular function, digestion, salivation, perspiration, urination, hormonal balance, and sexual arousal. It is also now known that using psychoactive drugs alters sleep, and even more importantly, dreaming, and this in turn has profound effects upon both physical and mental health (Raman-Wilms, 2014).

Psychoactive drug use occurs along a continuum, with most individuals who use these drugs never becoming physically or psychologically dependent upon them. Use of a psychoactive agent implies a minimal level of impairment when the drug is used to socialize and slightly alter one's CNS. Typically, no negative consequences arise and there are no lingering thoughts of needing to use again or when the drug will next be accessed. Use may not appear abusive and typically does not lead to dependence; however, the circumstances under which a person uses may still put them at risk during the time the drug is being used or lead to a temporary misuse. The idea of abuse relates to more chronic consumption, which can interfere with obligations at work, home, or school, increasing the likelihood of substance-related legal problems and/or recurrent social or interpersonal problems. Abuse is typically associated with the ideas of physical dependency, psychological dependency, and addiction (Beshears, Yeh, & Young, 2005; Csiernik & Rowe, 2017; National Institute on Drug Abuse, 2012b).

Physical Dependency

Physical dependency is a biological change that occurs in the body at the cellular level. It happens when a drug has been administered for an extended time period, and the body's homeostatic level, its balance point, is altered such that the body functions best when the drug is present. When the psychoactive drug is not present in the body at a sufficient level, the individual will become physically ill. This physical state is termed *being in withdrawal.* Withdrawal symptoms are typically the opposite reactions of those that the use of the drug initially produces upon administration. If a person were using a psychoactive substance to relax or sleep, the expected withdrawal reaction would be agitation and insomnia. Likewise, if a person were using an energy drink to stay awake, withdrawal would be extended and even excessive tiredness. Withdrawal can be prevented by using more of the same psychoactive drug or a pharmacologically related substance. This process of withdrawal avoidance plays a crucial part in the development of an addiction (see section 1.6).

Psychological Dependency

Psychological dependency typically develops alongside physical dependency but can also occur independently. In contrast, physical dependency rarely occurs without psychological dependency ensuing. Psychological dependency is the belief that a drug must be taken for the individual to be able to function. It is evident when the psychoactive agent becomes the central organizing principle of a user's life. The person literally cannot function if they do not possess or have ready access to the psychoactive drug. Unlike physical dependency, psychological dependency can also occur with behaviours such as gambling, Internet use, and even sex, though there is a significant biological distinction between compulsive behaviours and addiction (Csiernik, 2016).

Psychological dependency tends to be more problematic than physical dependency and is more apt to trigger lapse or relapse, a return to drug use, more readily and for a far longer period of time. Psychological dependency can range from a mild wish to a compelling emotional need for periodic or continuous use of a drug, including becoming quite desperate when the drug is not available. When a person is psychologically dependent upon a psychoactive drug, they believe that the drug is needed to cope, and drug use eventually supersedes all other coping mechanisms they draw upon.

Addiction

It is no small irony that the term *addiction* is likely the most misused term in the field of addiction. It is typically used as a synonym for *dependency*, though here too most people associate it more with physical dependency than with psychological dependency. However, addiction is more than just physical or psychological dependency or the combination of the two, though it contains both. Addiction also considers the social context of the user, at the micro, mezzo, and macro levels. Thus, when discussing addiction, not only must the psychoactive drug being administered be considered, but also what the social function of the drug is. Critical to fully understanding addiction is examining what social issues led to and allowed the drug to be used, be they physical availability or cultural accessibility; important social considerations include not only who sells it and at what price, but also the customs or taboos that support or diminish acceptance of the drug. Larger social factors, such as societal status, income level, sex, gender, sexual orientation, age, and level of ability, along with race and culture, also factor into the social dimension of addiction, and, interestingly, contribute to whether a nation deems a psychoactive drug licit or illicit as much as do the physical effects upon users. Thus, addiction is a distinct concept from dependency and should be viewed in a holistic manner as a bio-psycho-social phenomenon (figure 1.1).

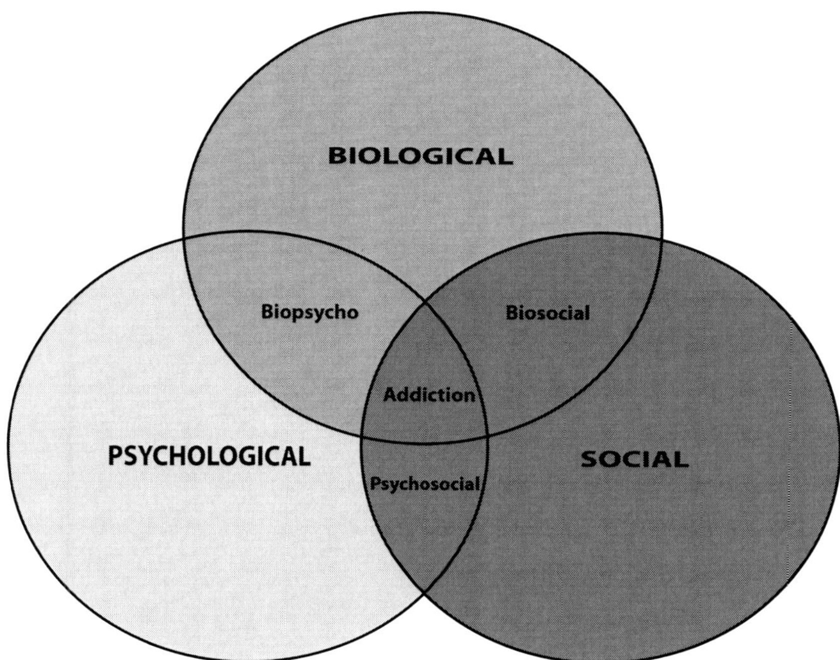

Figure 1.1: Holistic View of Addiction

1.2 PSYCHOACTIVE DRUG GROUPS[1]

Psychoactive drugs are categorized based on how they alter the central nervous system and thus in turn alter the peripheral and autonomic nervous system. There are four possible changes to the central nervous system that a psychoactive drug can produce. The CNS can be

- slowed down, or depressed;
- sped up, or stimulated;
- disrupted so that the brain does not perceive what is actually occurring in the physical world, producing hallucinations; or
- brought back into a more homeostatic balance when it is not perceiving the external world accurately.

Depressants

Psychoactive drugs in the depressant family produce a reduction of arousal and activity in the central nervous system, primarily through altering the neurotransmitter gamma-aminobutyric acid (GABA). These drugs have a range of therapeutic uses revolving around sedation and reducing anxiety and enhancing sleep, though while doing so they also typically negatively affect the dream cycle, which in turn has a negative impact on mental health. Depressants slow the body's metabolism and the functioning of autonomic nervous systems, along with the CNS. Mood enhancement occurs because of the disinhibiting properties of this drug group. While central nervous system depressants slow brain activity, they do not necessarily depress a person's mood. The members of this group are barbiturates, non-barbiturate sedative-hypnotics (NBSH), benzodiazepines, inhalants (including solvents, aerosols, and anaesthetics), antihistamines, and alcohol. Alcohol is a unique member of the depressant family, for while it has its primary effect upon GABA, it also indirectly impacts more neurotransmitters than any other psychoactive agent (see appendix A).

Opioids

Opioids are a specific subgroup of CNS depressants. Unlike the other members of this group, their primary effect at the neuron level is upon endorphins, with a secondary effect upon GABA, as well as upon dopamine, histamine, and norepinephrine. Opioids are primarily used to treat pain, though they are all also able to suppress cough and resolve issues with diarrhea. Like all CNS depressants, opioids also slow brain and peripheral nervous system activity. Opioid antagonists are drugs that are not psychoactive but that are important to be aware of, as they are able to reverse the respiratory depressant effects of opioids, which can be fatal, and have been used as pharmacological therapies for treating physical dependency on both opioids and alcohol.

Stimulants

Stimulants enhance the activity of the central nervous system, producing enhanced mood, increased vigilance, and the postponement of fatigue.

Stimulants also suppress the appetite, are used as decongestants, and can be used to treat attention-deficit/hyperactivity disorder (ADHD) in children and adults. Members of this drug family include cocaine, amphetamine, methamphetamine, methylphenidate (Ritalin and Concerta), anorexiants, decongestants, khat, bath salts, betel, nicotine, and caffeine. Stimulants primarily alter the neurotransmitter dopamine, with many also having secondary effects upon norepinephrine and/or serotonin. The two major exceptions are caffeine, where the primary effect is upon adenosine, and nicotine, with a primary alteration of acetylcholine. With both of these psychoactive agents, consumption also produces a secondary effect upon dopamine.

Hallucinogens

Hallucinogens affect the central nervous system in a distinct manner when compared to both CNS depressants and stimulants. Rather than decreasing or increasing CNS activity to produce euphoria, hallucinogens disrupt the way in which the brain perceives stimuli, thus creating a disconnect between the physical world and the user's perception of the physical world. Hallucinogens, except for cannabis and phencyclidine (PCP), all alter serotonin, the same neurotransmitter a majority of antidepressants alter.

Hallucinogens are divided into four groups. Indolealkylamines, such as LSD and psilocybin, have no secondary psychoactive effects, whereas phenylethylamines, such as mescaline, ecstasy, and jimson weed, have structural similarities to amphetamines, producing secondary stimulant effects upon the body by altering dopamine and norepinephrine as well as serotonin. A third category, dissociative anaesthetics—psychoactive drugs such as PCP and ketamine—are members of the arylcycloalkylamine family and possess depressant properties along with their hallucinatory effects, and primarily affect glutamate and acetylcholine. The final member of this family, cannabis, affects a distinct neurotransmitter from all other hallucinogens: endocannabinoid. Unlike other hallucinogens, physical dependency to cannabis does develop, and thus it is the only hallucinogen that is a fully addicting substance.

Psychotherapeutic Agents

The primary purpose of these psychoactive drugs is to treat people with specific forms of mental health issues. Rather than increasing, decreasing, or disrupting central nervous system activity as other psychoactive agents do, the function of psychotherapeutic agents is to return the user to a balanced, homeostatic level of functioning. In general, psychotherapeutic drugs take far longer to alter CNS functioning compared to other psychoactive drug groups. That, combined with the fact that they often produce quite unpleasant side effects, means there is typically little recreational use, and thus these substances are generally not misused or abused to the extent that other psychoactive drugs are.

There are three distinct groupings of psychotherapeutic agents. Antipsychotic drugs are used to treat individuals whose behaviour disconnects them from reality, which at times can lead to actions that harm the individual or others. These drugs affect dopamine, histamine, and serotonin. Mood stabilizers, such as lithium, are used by individuals who fluctuate between a balanced homeostatic state, a manic state, and a depressed state. Mood stabilizers also affect dopamine as well as GABA, glutamate, norepinephrine, and serotonin. The most common form of psychotherapeutic agent is used by individuals suffering from depression, with the majority of these psychoactive drugs altering serotonin and norepinephrine levels, though several monoamine oxidase inhibitors (MAOIs), tricyclic antidepressants, and norepinephrine-dopamine reuptake inhibitors (NDRIs) also alter dopamine levels.

1.3 THE COSTS OF PSYCHOACTIVE DRUG USE

Substance use disorders are a significant health issue and a leading preventable cause of disability and death globally (Büttner, 2011; UNODC, 2018). The World Health Organization (2018) reported that 2.3 billion people were alcohol consumers and that alcohol is the seventh leading risk factor for both deaths and disability-adjusted life years (DALYs) lost, accounting for 2.2% of female deaths and 6.8% of male deaths (GBD

2016 Alcohol Collaborators, 2018). An estimated 4.9% of the world's adult population suffer from alcohol use disorders alone, with alcohol causing an estimated 257 DALYs lost per 100,000 people globally. An estimated 22.5% of adults in the world, one billion people, use products containing nicotine, with an estimated 11% of deaths in males and 6% in females each year due to tobacco consumption. Tobacco ranks among the world's top three leading causes of premature death alongside heart disease and conflict/violence. There were 15.5 million opioid-dependent people globally in 2010. Opioid dependence was estimated to account for 9.2 million DALYs lost globally in 2010, a 73% increase compared to 1990. Regions with the greatest opioid dependence DALY lost rates were North America (292.1 per 100,000), eastern Europe (288.4 per 100,000), Australasia (278.6 per 100,000) and southern sub-Saharan Africa (263.5 per 100,000) (Degenhardt et al., 2014). Illicit drug use, which is more difficult to quantify, accounts for roughly an additional 83 lost DALYs and 17.3 deaths per million population aged 15 to 64 (Gowing et al., 2015).

The most recent comprehensive and empirically supported figures we have for the cost of addiction in Canada come from the Canadian Substance Use Costs and Harms Scientific Working Group (2018). They reported that in 2014, the cost of substance use in Canada was $38.4 billion. This is actually a conservative amount, as Quebec health care costs were not available, though the Working Group estimated this would have added another $750 million to the overall total. Table 1.1 provides of summary of the findings by province.

Of the total cost, $14.6 billion (38.1%) was alcohol related, $12.0 billion (31.2%) tobacco related, $3.5 billion (9.1%) linked to licit and illicit opioid use, and $2.8 billion (7.3%) to cannabis use. The three primary cost areas were lost productivity (lost value of work due to premature mortality, long-term disability, short-term disability, absenteeism, and impaired job performance; $15.7 billion [40.8%]), health care costs ($11.1 billion [29.0%]), and costs for criminal justice system services ranging from enforcement to incarceration ($9.0 billion [23.3%]). More Canadians are hospitalized for alcohol-related issues alone than for heart attacks, though of course a good number of those hospitalized

Table 1.1: Cost of Substance Use by Province (2014)

Province or Territory	Population in Millions	Cost of Substance Use in Billions ($)	Most Costly Substance	Approximate Cost in Millions ($)
Newfoundland and Labrador	519,716	$0.726	tobacco	$300
Prince Edward Island	142,907	$0.178	alcohol	$67
Nova Scotia	923,598	$1.2	tobacco	$434
New Brunswick	747,101	$0.93	tobacco	$350
Ontario	13,448,494	$14	alcohol	$5,344
Manitoba	1,278,365	$1.4	alcohol	$577
Saskatchewan	1,098,352	$1.3	alcohol	$563
Alberta	4,067,175	$5.4	alcohol	$2,396
British Columbia	4,648,055	$4.8	alcohol	$1,935
Yukon	35,874	$0.071	alcohol	$41
Northwest Territories	41,462	$0.102	alcohol	$56
Nunavut	35,944	$0.096	alcohol	$56

Source: Canadian Substance Use Costs and Harms Scientific Working Group, 2018

for heart attacks are there because of their alcohol misuse. The Conference Board of Canada (2017), in an independent study, found that 45,464 deaths annually in Canada were attributable to smoking, leading to 599,390 potential years of life lost from premature mortality. This represents approximately 18.4% of all deaths in Canada in a year, or 125 persons per day.

Between 2007 and 2014 the Working Group (2018) conservatively estimated that cost per person per year, regardless of age, had increased by 5.5% from $1,025 to $1,081, with the majority of this increased cost attributed to licit psychoactive drug use. The report stated that 43% of crimes, not including impaired driving, would not have been committed if the perpetrator had not been under the influence of or seeking alcohol or other psychoactive drugs. Almost one in five violent crimes would not have occurred if the perpetrator had not been under the influence of or seeking alcohol. Interestingly, only 11% of criminal justice costs were associated with drug possession and trafficking. While there is no single Canadian source that summarizes deaths due to psychoactive drug use, and the way a death is classified is open to a degree of interpretation, figure 1.2 employs multiple sources to provide a relative comparative examination of the lethal consequences of psychoactive drug consumption in Canada. Though substantively more individuals die prematurely due to tobacco (nicotine) and alcohol use, more than 9,000 people died in Canada between January 2016 and June 2018 because of their use of opioids. As well, the rate of hospitalization due to opioid poisoning increased by 8% in Canada between 2016 and 2017, averaging 17 people per day. In the first half of 2018 there were 2,066 deaths linked to opioid use in Canada, with 94% ruled accidental (Government of Canada, 2018).

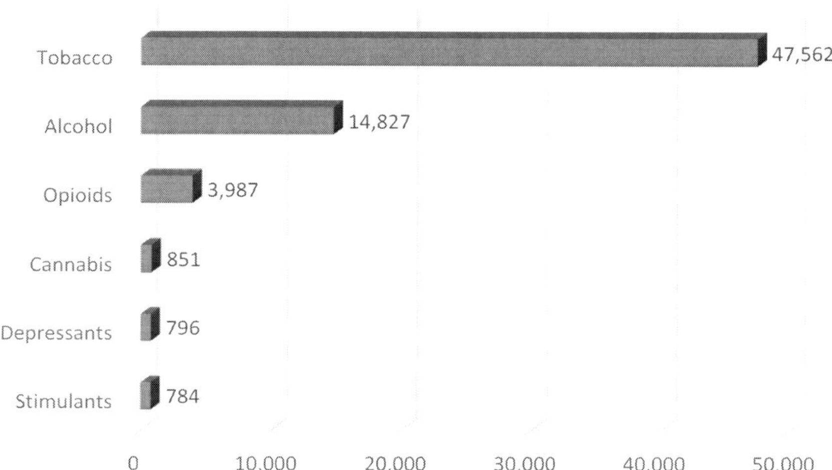

Figure 1.2: Premature Death by Drug (Canada)

Sources: Canadian Institute for Health Information, 2017; Dobrescu et al., 2017; Special Advisory Committee on the Epidemic of Opioid Overdoses, 2018

1.4 THE NERVOUS SYSTEM

Overview of the Human Nervous System

The central nervous system (CNS) is part of the overall nervous system of the human body (figure 1.3) and is divided into two components: the brain and the spinal cord. The peripheral nervous system (PNS), composed of sensory receptors and motor effectors, consists of nerve cells that lie outside the brain and spinal cord, but unlike the CNS, it is not protected by bones, leaving it more vulnerable to injury and toxins. The sensory component of the PNS detects changes in the external environment using the range of human senses—sight, sound, touch, taste, and smell—and communicates them to the CNS through afferent sensory nerves. The motor component of the PNS, like the CNS, is divided into two distinct components: the autonomic nervous system (ANS) and the somatic nervous system (SoNS), which is also referred to as the voluntary nervous system. The SoNS is responsible for voluntary body movements through efferent nerves (motor nerve fibres that carry impulses away from the CNS) that stimulate muscle contractions of both muscle and skin. Efferent nerves also carry ANS signals from the CNS to organs through two complementary systems: the sympathetic

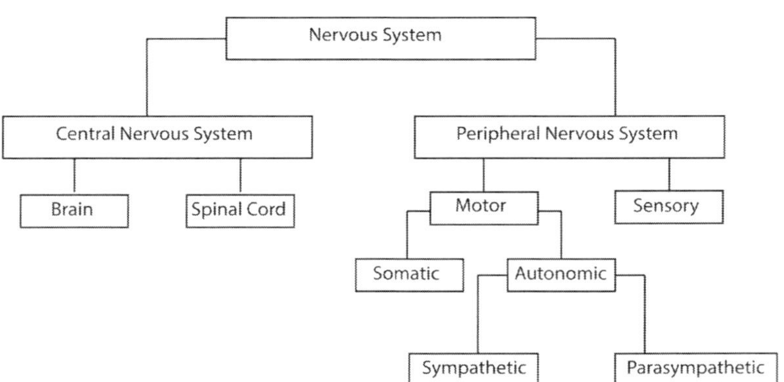

Figure 1.3: Organization of the Human Nervous System

Source: Adapted from *Neuroscience Tutorial* (http://www.columbia.edu/cu/psychology/courses/1010/mangels/neuro/neurotutorial.html, 2003)

nervous system, which governs the human fight-flight response, and the parasympathetic nervous system, which is responsible for maintaining the homeostatic level within the body. However, what distinguishes psychoactive drugs from all other substances is their direct and substantive impact on the CNS (Goldstein, 2010).

Overview of the Brain

Who we are, our essence, our being, is dependent upon our brain and our central nervous system. The typical human brain weighs about 1.5 kilograms, of which less than one-third is grey matter, which is responsible for higher-order thought. The CNS consists of nerve cells called neurons, found in both the brain and the spinal cord, while, as discussed above, the peripheral nervous system is composed of the nerves extending outward to the rest of the body. The CNS works by perceiving the stimuli collected through our five senses by the PNS. This information is processed by the brain, leading to some action, an output, based on how the information is decoded. The processing occurs on both a conscious and subconscious level, leading to each individual person's behaviour. This behaviour can be altered by psychoactive drugs that have the capacity to structurally change the brain (Cadet, Bisagno, & Milroy, 2014).

The cerebral cortex is the largest and most developed part of the human brain, making up more than 75% of the brain's size. It controls thinking, perception, and understanding language. The cerebral cortex is divided into a right and a left hemisphere. The right hemisphere controls the left side of the body and is responsible for artistic expression and for understanding relationships in space such as reading a map. The left hemisphere controls the right side of the body and is primarily responsible for mathematical ability, problem solving, and comparing information needed to make decisions. It is also the brain's language centre. The two hemispheres communicate with one another through a bundle of fibres connecting the two halves called the corpus callosum (Brick & Erickson, 2013).

While the brain itself does not grow much after the age of six, it does undergo a massive reorganization between the ages of 12 and 25. The cerebrum is the largest component of the human brain and is responsible

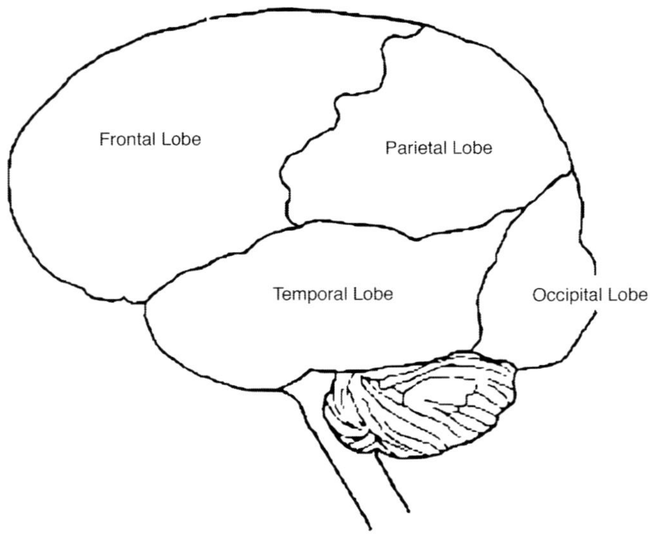

Figure 1.4: The Brain's Lobes

Source: Adapted from the Epilepsy Foundation

for higher function, primarily thought and action. It is divided into four parts, or lobes, each with its own unique function (figure 1.4):

- **Frontal** is responsible for initiating and coordinating motor movements and higher cognitive skills. It functions to regulate attention, judgment, and emotional response. The frontal lobe is involved in reasoning, thought, long-term planning, imagination, speech, emotions, learning, decision making, problem solving, memory, and behaviours that generally involve discipline and higher reasoning. It is one of the last brain regions to fully mature, which usually does not occur until the early to mid-20s.
- **Occipital** is involved in processing and creating visual information.
- **Parietal** is responsible for movement, orientation, recognition, perception, and integration of auditory, visual, and tactile signals contributing to touch and language. The parietal lobe continues to develop until the mid-teens.

- **Temporal** is involved in hearing, memory, emotion, and language comprehension, and additional processing of visual information. Development of the temporal lobe occurs until the mid- to late teens.

The activities of each lobe of the brain are not exclusive, as the brain is interconnected, interdependent, and flexible. This means that even though each lobe carries its own activities, functions are routinely shared; thus, if damage occurs to one part of the brain, other parts have the ability to compensate to some degree (Brick & Erickson, 2013).

As well as being divided into four lobes, the brain is composed of three core components: the forebrain, the midbrain, and the hindbrain (figure 1.5). The forebrain consists of the cerebrum, where the majority of information processing occurs; the thalamus, whose function includes relaying sensory and motor signals to the thin layer of cells covering the brain; the cerebral cortex, where the regulation of consciousness, sleep, and alertness occurs; and the limbic system. The limbic system, located within the cerebrum, just under the cortex, includes the hippocampus, which is involved in the formation of new memories and is also associated with learning and emotions, and the amygdala, which integrates and processes incoming information pertinent to reward, motivation, and emotional behaviour such as fear and anxiety, promoting survival by warning of potential danger (figure 1.6) (Lowinson et al., 2011).

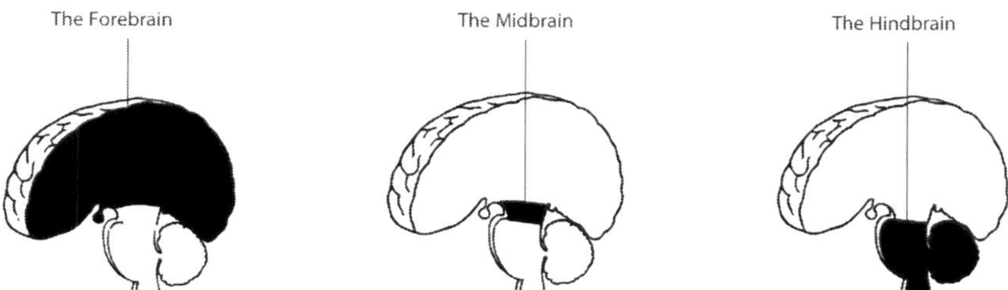

Figure 1.5: Core Components of the Brain

Source: Adapted from National Institute of Neurological Disorders and Stroke, *Brain Basics: Know Your Brain* (http://www.ninds.nih.gov/disorders/brain_basics/know_your_brain.htm, 2014)

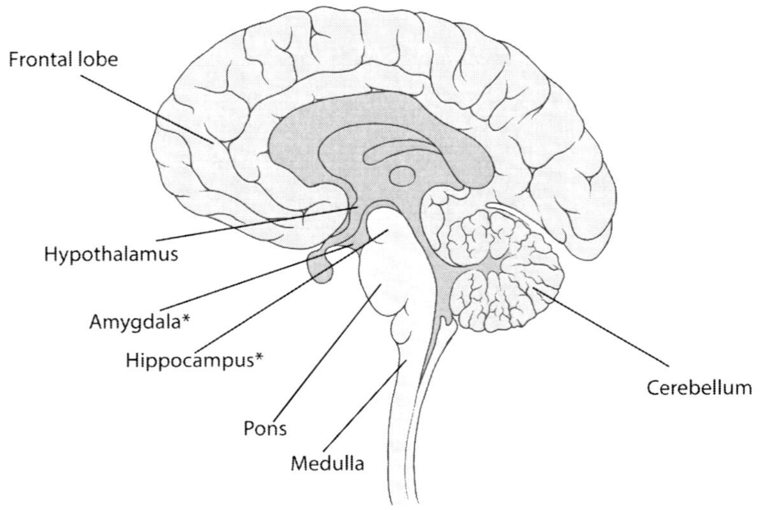

Figure 1.6: Cross-Section of the Brain
Source: Adapted from Wikimedia Commons

Also called the emotional brain, the limbic system is evolutionarily very old, and it is within the limbic system that the core structures of the brain reward pathway are located. This part of the brain is responsible for the experiencing of emotion, behaviour, motivation, long-term memory, learning, and monitoring the internal homeostasis of the body. It also drives important aspects of feeding and sexual behaviour. Also important in the functioning of the limbic system is the nucleus accumbens (NAc), which is an important structure of the brain reward pathway that psychoactive drugs directly activate. Likewise, the endocrine and autonomic nervous systems also interact via the hypothalamus to influence the limbic system, and thus the primary brain reward pathway. The hypothalamus is involved in every aspect of endocrine, visceral, and autonomic functions, influencing eating, drinking, sexual activity, aversion, rage, and pleasure. The hypothalamus regulates not only food but also alcohol intake (Barson & Leibowitz, 2016).

The basal ganglia is another component of the forebrain. The role of the basal ganglia is to control voluntary motor movements and eye movement, and to facilitate learning, cognition, and affect. The basal ganglia contributes to processing information, including sensations of reward and motivation, and is altered by a host of psychoactive drugs (Lowinson et al., 2011).

The midbrain, which connects the hindbrain and the forebrain, consists of two components: the tegmentum (Latin for "covering") and tectum (Latin for "roof"). It is involved in auditory and visual responses, as well as motor function. Within this area is found the ventral tegmental area (VTA), a grouping of neurons where the critically important mesocorticolimbic dopamine system is found. The medial forebrain bundle (MFB), connecting the VTA to the NAc, is the primary neural pathway within the brain responsible for the regulation of human reward. The NAc is a major input structure of the basal ganglia and integrates information from cortical and limbic structures to regulate goal-directed behaviours. This pathway is altered by most psychoactive drugs, specifically those creating euphoria by directly or indirectly affecting dopamine (Scofield et al., 2016).

Craving in the addiction process is both intense and painful because there is both a physical and a psychological component, and because the midbrain associates psychoactive drugs with survival. As the craving intensifies, becomes more painful, and is prolonged, the risk of compulsive use to seek relief increases. The midbrain is also one part of the brain stem, which is found at the base of the brain and connects the brain's cerebrum to the spinal cord. The brain stem controls the flow of messages between the brain and the rest of the body, including the key autonomic functions of breathing, swallowing, heart rate, blood pressure, arousal, vigilance, and wakefulness (Tomkins & Sellers, 2001). Research on the neurobiology of addiction argues that the reinforcing properties of most psychoactive drugs are mediated by activation of the mesolimbic dopamine system, the orbitofrontal cortex, and the amygdala (Büttner, 2011). This means that biologically, a key aspect of addiction involves the transmission of neurotransmitters between the synapses in the mesolimbic and mesocorticol pathways of the brain (Huang et al., 2017).

The hindbrain consists of the cerebellum, pons, and medulla. The cerebellum, or little brain, developed early in the evolution of the human brain and has two hemispheres and a highly folded surface. The cerebellum controls movement coordination, balance, equilibrium, and muscle tone, helping to produce a sense of balance. Like the cerebral cortex, it is composed of white matter and a thin outer layer of densely folded grey matter. The folded outer layer of the cerebellum, the cerebellar cortex, has smaller and more compact folds than those of the cerebral cortex; however, both contain hundreds of millions of neurons for processing sensory input. The cerebellum is situated at the base of the skull, above the brain stem and beneath the occipital lobes of the cerebral cortex. The brain stem, which, as previously noted, connects the brain to the spinal cord, controls simple reflexes such as coughing and sneezing. The two main parts of the brain stem are the pons and the medulla. The pons contains nerve fibres that connect the cerebral cortex with the cerebellum and the spinal cord. The pons relays signals from the forebrain to the cerebellum that regulate a vast range of functions, including respiration, swallowing, bladder control, hearing, equilibrium, taste, eye movement, facial expressions, facial sensation, and posture. The pons also controls sleep, awakening, and dream onset. The medulla aids in regulating breathing, heart and blood vessel function, digestion, sneezing, and swallowing (Goldstein, 2010).

The reticular activating system (RAS) is a set of interconnected nuclei located throughout the brain stem that is critical in regulating autonomic nervous system functions. When activity in the RAS is reduced, there is a lessening of anxiety. The RAS connects the lower brain to the upper brain; the ascending portion of the RAS is connected to the cortex, hypothalamus, and thalamus, while the descending portion is connected to the nerves essential to the sleep cycle. Combined, the midbrain, pons, medulla oblongata, and lower brain stem are responsible for basic autonomic life functions below the level of consciousness. These include breathing, heart rate, digestion, salivation, perspiration, body temperature regulation, pupillary dilation, urination, and sexual arousal. While the majority of autonomous functions are involuntary, several do have some degree of conscious control, including breathing, swallowing, and sexual arousal (Dorland, 2012).

Neurons

The brain consists of a variety of cells, each of which has a unique and critical function:

- astrocytes, which function to provide protection and maintenance of the brain's chemical environment
- oligodendrocytes, which form a myelin sheath around neurons. This sheath acts as an electrical insulator for neurons to increase the speed at which signals are sent between them, allowing the body to function much more quickly and efficiently in all its processes
- microglia, the smallest of cells in the brain, which are involved in injury repair and cell debris and waste removal
- ependymal cells that line the ventricles of the brain, which contain cerebrospinal fluid that acts as a protective cushion for the brain, as well as a transport system for nutrients and wastes
- neurons, nervous system cells that carry, process, and transmit electrical signals at incredible speeds throughout the brain

Of these, it is only the neuron that has the capacity to process information, and thus it is neurons that are affected by the consumption of psychoactive drugs (Brick & Erickson, 2013).

It is estimated that the brain has upwards of 15 billion neurons. Messages travel within each cell as electrical transmissions, but as one neuron has no direct physical contact with another, electrical transmission between cells cannot occur. Thus, information between nerve cells must be communicated chemically, through neurotransmitters such as dopamine, serotonin, or GABA. A neuron consists of the cell body, or soma, where metabolic activity occurs, featuring the nucleus and dendrites. Dendrites are the extension of the soma and receive messages from the axons of adjoining cells. The axon, a long projection from the cell body, is the part of the neuron along which signals are transmitted to adjoining cells that terminate in axon terminals. It is in the axon terminals where the various neurotransmitters are stored in synaptic vesicles (figure 1.7).

Messages travel within the nervous system electrically, but chemically between neurons. Each neuron is bound by a semi-permeable membrane, allowing transfer across the cell membrane. The fluid surrounding the neurons contains different ions, which are not evenly distributed. The three most important ions in terms of creating a message within the brain are sodium, which has a positive charge, potassium, and chlorine. Sodium is more heavily concentrated outside the cells and is pushed out of cells, whereas potassium and chlorine are more heavily concentrated within neurons. Outside the cell, there is a more positive electrical charge, and then, like a battery, there is a potential difference across a cell membrane of –70mV. When an electrical signal is received within a neuron, it is immediately translated by the cell's receiving areas on the dendrites into tiny electrical signals. The signals either excite the membrane (stimulatory) or decrease the excitability of the cell (inhibitory). Each minute signal, excitatory or inhibitory, travels along the membrane of the dendrite until it reaches the soma. In the soma, the hundreds of messages arrive simultaneously from different receptor sites and are integrated, with excitatory signals being added together and inhibitory signals subtracting from the total. If the overall total of signals exceeds the threshold level, a new message is generated by the soma

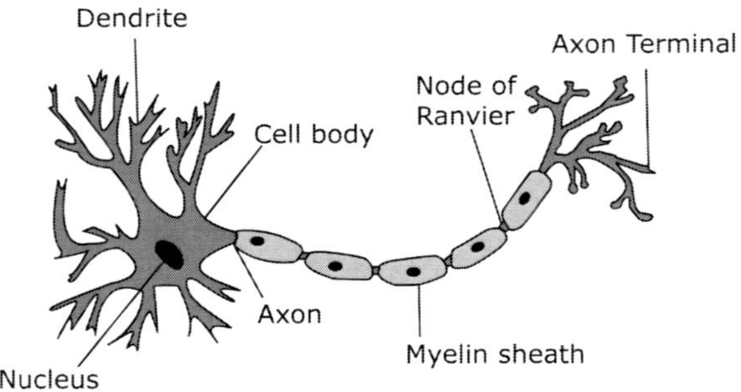

Figure 1.7: A Neuron

Source: Adapted from Wikimedia Commons

and is transmitted along the axon to the axon terminal. This signal is called the action potential, and when the action potential is sufficiently strong, the signal is sent to the terminal buttons, where the synapses are located, and the neuron secretes the designated neurotransmitter, depending on what type of signal is being transmitted to the synapses (Dorland, 2012; Goldstein, 2010).

As noted above, neurons do not physically touch each other, and neurotransmitters are required to bridge the minute gap between them in order to send a message from one neuron to the next. This gap, called the synaptic cleft, is typically 10 to 20 nanometres across. This space is so incredibly small that it takes only 0.1 milliseconds for a neurotransmitter to drift, or diffuse, across the gap to the next axon. This also explains why even small amounts of psychoactive drugs can have a profound impact on CNS functioning, and thus human behaviour (Giordano, 2013; Goldstein, 2010).

Neurotransmitters

Neurotransmitters are chemical-signalling molecules in the brain that are used to relay, amplify, and modulate signals between a neuron and another cell. They have been grouped into three categories:

- monoamines, including acetylcholine, norepinephrine, dopamine, histamine, and serotonin
- peptides and hormones, including endorphins, cortisone, and nitric oxide
- amino acids, including GABA and glutamate (Inaba & Cohen, 2011)

All the approximately 100 identified neurotransmitters that carry chemical information between cells follow the same chemical transmission pathway. However, they can act in different ways upon this pathway. First, a neurotransmitter is released from the sending neuron into the synaptic cleft from a storage vesicle located in the axon terminal. The neurotransmitter then diffuses (travels) across the synaptic cleft. This is a process of random movement from an area of high concentration, near the sending neuron, toward an area of low concentration, the receiving neuron. On the receiving neuron, there are specialized receptor areas that are designed to receive one type of neurotransmitter and bind with it. As more and more binding occurs, an electrical signal begins to form in the receiving neuron, and when a sufficient amount of the neurotransmitter is bound, an internal electric charge is generated and the message is sent forward, following the same pattern of transmission. Once the charge is generated, the neurotransmitter may be broken down by enzymes in the cleft and thus deactivated or actively transported back to its point of origin, the axon terminal of the sending neuron (figure 1.8).

If neurotransmitters are unable to bind to receptor sites, the message will not be passed along to the next neuron. Also, if the enzymes in the synaptic cleft break down the neurotransmitters faster than they can bind in sufficient numbers, the message will be blocked. However, if the enzymes are blocked or if additional neurotransmitters are pushed into the synaptic cleft beyond the enzymes' ability to process them, then the message will not only be sent, but will be intensified and/or prolonged. If the reuptake process that brings neurotransmitters back to

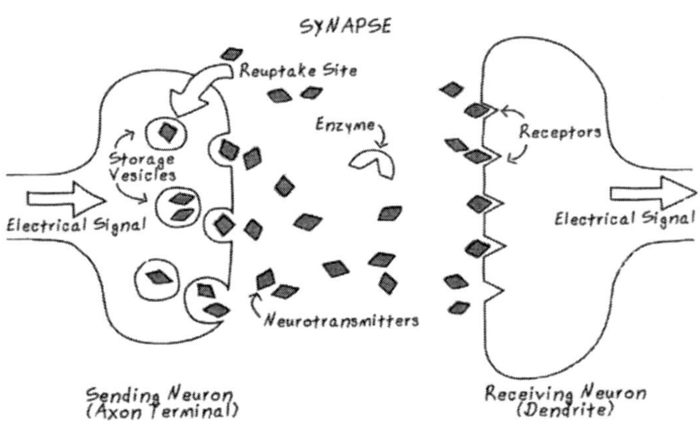

Figure 1.8: Chemical Transmission between Cells

Source: B. Sproule, *Pharmacology and Drug Abuse*, 2nd edition (Toronto: Centre for Addiction and Mental Health, 2004)

the sending neuron is blocked or if a neurotransmitter is aided in binding better to a receptor site, then, again, there is a greater likelihood that the message will be passed on to the next neuron.

The chemical structure of many psychoactive drugs is like that of neurotransmitters. Similarity in structure allows them to be recognized by neurons and to alter normal brain messaging. This leads to six chemical processes produced by psychoactive drugs to influence the CNS and change behaviour, which are termed *pharmacodynamic* interactions:

- blocking the reuptake of a neurotransmitter back into the axon terminal, allowing more of the neurotransmitter to be available for binding, thus enhancing the message (Prozac)
- pushing more neurotransmitters out of the storage vesicles into the synaptic cleft, increasing the opportunity for binding and thus enhancing the message (amphetamines)
- enhancing the binding ability of the neurotransmitters, acting like glue, to further enhance binding to the receptor site to enhance the message (diazepam)
- blocking the enzyme from breaking down the drug in the synaptic cleft, allowing more neurotransmitters to bind to their receptors to enhance the message (MAOIs, which are antidepressants, such as phenelzine [Nardil] and tranylcypromine [Parnate])
- blocking neurotransmitters from binding and thus diminishing the message (methadone)
- mimicking neurotransmitters and binding directly to receptor sites, enhancing the message (morphine)

Of the known neurotransmitters, only a few are significantly affected by psychoactive drugs, leading to changes in the CNS, ANS, and ultimately behaviour. The most prominent neurotransmitters are discussed below. Appendix A provides an overview of which psychoactive agents interact with which specific neurotransmitters.

Acetylcholine (ACh)

Acetylcholine was the first neurotransmitter to be discovered, isolated in 1921, nearly four decades before dopamine. Acetylcholine receptors, also known as cholinergic receptors, function to regulate nervous system transmission through the binding of the neurotransmitter acetylcholine. While cholinergic receptors are found throughout both the CNS and PNS, they are prominent in the hippocampus, cerebral cortex, thalamus, basal ganglia, and cerebellum, functioning to coordinate voluntary movements including posture, balance, coordination, and speech. Like GABA, acetylcholine produces anti-excitatory effects. Cholinergic receptor activation affects learning, memory formation, attention, endocrine and exocrine secretion, heart rate control, and blood pressure (Pandey et al., 2018; Queiroz et al., 2013). Acetylcholine is one of the most important neurotransmitters controlling sleep-wake patterns, as cholinergic neurons form the core of the brain stem's reticular activating system. These neurotransmitters also play a prominent role in producing REM sleep (chapter 1.7) (Krystal, 2010).

Acetylcholine is also the primary neurotransmitter for the transmission of information in the parasympathetic nervous system. Acetylcholine deficiency has been associated with Alzheimer's and Parkinson's diseases. It has also been demonstrated that some antihistamines block the production of acetylcholine, and if used for a prolonged period, can affect episodic memory, produce vertigo, and mimic or even induce symptoms of dementia, particularly among older adults already prone to reduced levels of this neurotransmitter (Papenberg et al., 2017; Phillips et al., 2018). Increasing acetylcholine in the brain is thought to be able to aid in treating schizophrenia (Haydar & Dunlop, 2010), while excessive amounts of acetylcholine can lead to sneezing, sweating, vomiting, and diarrhea (Kocherlakota, 2014).

Acetylcholine receptors are classified into two groups: muscarinic and nicotinic. Muscarinic receptors are influenced in part by specific hallucinogens such as scopolamine and belladonna. Acetylcholine activation has been linked to dependency to tobacco as nicotine binds specifically to nicotinic receptors, with repeated binding requiring increased levels of acetylcholine, which is believed to be the major cause of physical dependency to nicotine (Pandey et al., 2018). There is also evidence that the nicotinic acetylcholine receptors play a role in major depressive disease development and physical dependency to alcohol (Rahman, 2015).

Adenosine (Ado)

Adenosine is an inhibitory neurotransmitter, acting as a natural CNS depressant, promoting sleep and suppressing arousal. Levels of adenosine rise each hour a person is awake, contributing to the development of fatigue during the course of a day. Adenosine is the primary neurotransmitter inhibited when you consume caffeine. When adenosine release is impeded, arousal is produced and fatigue is postponed. In contrast, when alcohol is consumed, adenosine production is enhanced, producing sedation. Decreased levels of adenosine increase muscle activity and can relieve migraine headaches; however, when levels are too low, jitteriness, increased anxiety, and insomnia result. Adenosine can also depress the release of acetylcholine from neurotransmitters (Fredholm et al., 1983) while increasing dopamine release (Zheng & Hasegawa, 2016). Adenosine receptors are associated not only with the development of physical dependency but also with Parkinson's disease, sleep disorders, and pain (Ferré et al., 2007).

Anandamide (AEA)

The endocannabinoid system is a complicated biological system involved in regulating movement, mood, memory, appetite, fertility, pain, and physiological homeostasis. It consists of cannabinoid receptors and cannabinoid receptor proteins that are active throughout both the central and peripheral nervous systems. Two endogenous molecules, meaning internal or natural to the body, that activate the endocannabinoid system have been found. The first, 2-arachidonoyl glycerol (2-AG), occurs in peripheral tissues, while anandamide (Sanskrit for "supreme joy") is a neurotransmitter. Likewise, two primary endocannabinoid receptors have been identified: CB_1, first cloned in 1990, and CB_2, cloned three years later. CB_1 receptors are found primarily in the CNS, specifically in the cerebral cortex, cerebellum, thalamus, basal ganglia, and hippocampus, which explains why cannabis affects cognition, memory, and movement. CB_1 receptors are also found in peripheral organs and tissues. CB_2 receptors are less densely located in the CNS and are more abundant in the immune and gastrointestinal systems. CB_1 is the main molecular target of anandamide, whereas 2-AG is active at both sites. The psychoactive component of cannabis, Δ9-tetrahydrocannabinol (THC), mimics the actions of anandamide, whereas the main therapeutic component of cannabis, cannabidiol (CBD), mimics 2-AG (Mechoulan & Parker, 2013). Interestingly, 2-AG is found in both human and cow's milk (Fride, Bregman, & Kirkham, 2005).

While the psychoactive constituent in cannabis, THC, was isolated in the mid-1960s, CB_1, CB_2, anandamide, and 2-AG were not identified until a quarter of a century later. Unlike neurotransmitters such as acetylcholine, dopamine, and serotonin, anandamide and 2-AG are not stored in vesicles but rather are synthesized when and where they are needed. Additionally, contrary to THC, which is metabolized over several hours and excreted, or stored as one of its metabolites, endocannabinoids are rapidly removed from the body. CB_1 receptors are widely expressed on almost all neuronal types in the brain, including GABA, glutamate, serotonin, noradrenaline, and dopamine terminals, though the primary effects of CB_1 receptor activation appear to be linked to their interaction with GABA and glutamate (Hill et al., 2018; Mechoulan & Parker, 2013).

Endocannabinoids serve as signalling molecules at many synapses in the brain, and in turn regulate reward seeking by affecting dopamine, particularly in the VTA. Likewise, THC is also able to bind to dopamine neurons, sending signals to the dopamine terminal to release more dopamine into the synaptic cleft (figure 1.9), which explains why cannabis both relaxes users, as does anandamide, and also produces euphoria. Endocannabinoids have also been linked to regulating the physiological and behavioural effects of emotional states and stress exposure, particularly with respect to biochemical aspects of the stress response (Hill et al., 2018; Hua et al., 2016; Joy, Watson, & Benson, 1999; Navari & Province, 2006).

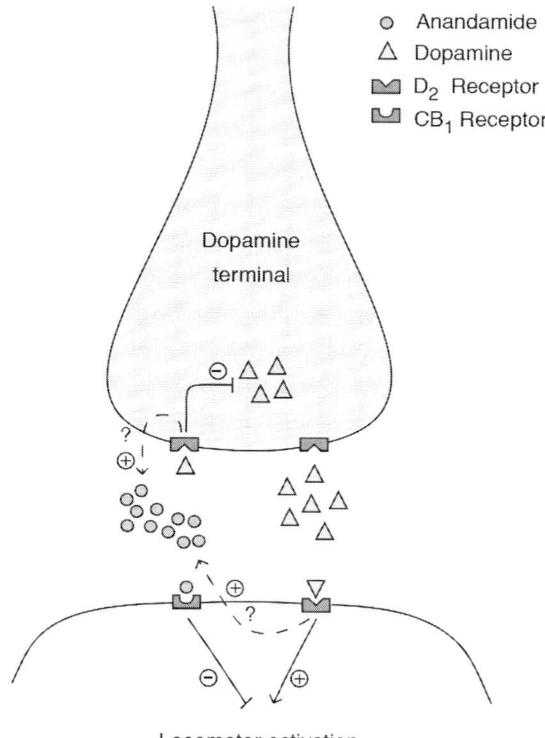

Figure 1.9: Cannabis Neurotransmission

Source: D. Self, Anandamide: A candidate neurotransmitter heads for the big leagues (*Nature Neuroscience*, 2[4], 304–305, 1999)

Dopamine (DA)

This neurotransmitter, discovered in 1958, is a member of the monoamine catecholamine family of neurotransmitters, which also includes epinephrine, serotonin, and norepinephrine. Dopamine receptors are most common in the midbrain, VTA, cerebral cortex, and hypothalamus. Dopamine stimulates the nerve receptors in these parts of the brain, regulating mood and playing a prominent role in motivation and reward through its ability to create sensations of power, energy, and, most importantly, euphoria (figure 1.10). Dopamine, through its different neuronal systems and receptor subtypes, also plays a significant role in the control of sexual behaviour (Holder, Veichweg, & Mong, 2015; Melis & Argiolas, 1995). The dopaminergic (DAergic) system also plays an important part in human cognition, which includes attention, memory, language comprehension and expression, problem solving, and decision making; thus, the way we learn. The role of dopamine follows a U-shape pattern, which means either too little or too much signalling impairs cognitive performance (Nakajima et al., 2013). Excessive amounts of dopamine can lead to psychotic-like behaviour

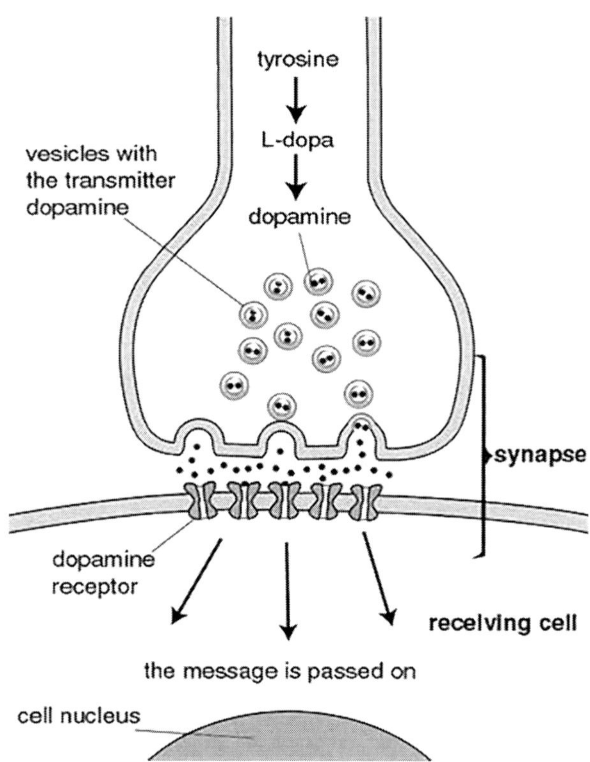

Figure 1.10: Dopamine Chemical Transmission Process

Source: The Nobel Committee for Physiology or Medicine, *Physiology or Medicine for 2000—Press Release* (Nobelprize.org, April 30, 2014). © The Nobel Committee for Physiology or Medicine, 2000

including schizophrenia, while having too-low levels produces hyperirritability and anxiety (Kocherlakota, 2014).

There are several dopamine systems in the brain, with the mesolimbic dopamine system located in the VTA appearing to be the most important for motivational processes, positive and negative reinforcement, and self-regulation of behaviour. It is also the system upon which most psychoactive drugs produce their euphoric effects (Volkow, Wise, & Baler, 2017). There are five major dopamine receptors, divided into two classes: D_1-like (D_1 and D_5 receptors) and D_2-like (D_2, D_3, and D_4 receptors). Both D_1 and D_2 have been linked to the development of physical dependency (Krawczyk et al., 2013; Trifilieff et al., 2017), while D_2 is associated with the development of schizophrenia (Seeman, 2013a). D_3 receptors have the highest density in the limbic areas of the brain, which are associated with cognitive and emotional functions. Dysregulation of the D_3 receptor may contribute to mental health issues such as the development of depression and schizophrenia (Stahl, 2017). Excessive stimulation of the D_4 receptor gene has been associated with attention-deficit/hyperactivity disorder as well as the personality trait of novelty seeking (Ding et al., 2002), while D_5 receptors function to regulate working memory, attention, and recency memory (Carr et al., 2017).

The circuit model of addiction focuses on how different psychoactive drugs affect dopamine. There are those drugs, such as nicotine, that can directly depolarize (change the chemical charge of the molecule) dopamine neurons. Other psychoactive agents interfere with reuptake of dopamine, including cocaine, amphetamines, and ecstasy (MDMA), while a third group leads to disinhibition and includes opioids, cannabis, benzodiazepines, and the solvent GHB. Interesting, there is still no consensus on exactly how alcohol fits into this model, though it is known to both stimulate and increase dopamine (Luscher, 2016) (appendix A).

Endorphins

Endorphin is an abbreviation of the term *endogenous* (natural) *morphine*. Endogenous morphine in the body is mimicked in nature and through synthesis by the opioid family of psychoactive drugs. Endorphins bind to opioid receptors, which are located on post-synaptic cells as well as on the terminals of other neurons. In addition to blocking the perception of pain, endorphins modulate dopamine transmission in the brain. While this neurotransmitter does not directly stimulate the VTA, as dopamine does, there is an indirect interaction involving GABA. Thus, opioid users not only obtain the sensation of pain-masking by taking drugs such as Demerol, OxyContin, and heroin, but also obtain an artificially induced sense of euphoria (Katzung, 2007).

Four types of opioid receptors have been identified: mu_1, mu_2, delta, and kappa, named after letters in the Greek alphabet. All opioids exert their effects by activating one or more of these receptors (figure 1.11). Each of the four identified receptors is involved in different functions, though it is mu_1 that most psychoactive agents activate, as analgesia (relief from pain) involves the direct activation of this receptor (table 1.2). Interestingly, alcohol, cannabinoids, and nicotine also indirectly influence mu_1. Mu_1 receptors are also involved in the creation of a sense of euphoria, respiratory depression, and decreased gastrointestinal activity. Mu_2 receptors play a role in respiratory

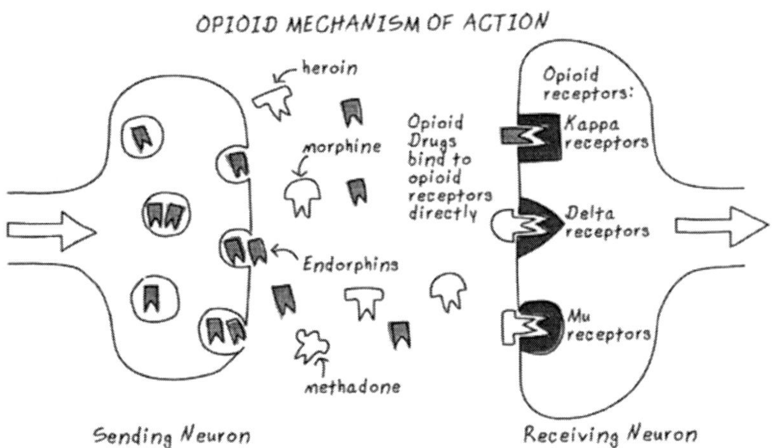

Figure 1.11: Opioid Mechanism of Action

Source: B. Sproule, *Pharmacology and Drug Abuse*, 2nd edition (Toronto: Centre for Addiction and Mental Health, 2004)

Table 1.2: Features of Opioid Receptors

Receptors	Mu_1	Mu_2	Kappa	Delta
Effects	Analgesia (supraspinal, spinal) Euphoria Low abuse potential Miosis Bradycardia Hypothermia Urinary retention Emesis	Analgesia (spinal) Physical dependence Constipation (marked) Depression of ventilation Emesis	Analgesia (supraspinal, spinal) Dysphoria Low abuse potential Miosis Sedation Diuresis	Analgesia (supra-spinal, spinal) Physical dependence Constipation (minimal) Depression of ventilation Urinary retention
Agonists	Endorphins Morphine Synthetic opioids	Endorphins Morphine Synthetic opioids	Dynorphins	Enkephalins
Antagonists	Naloxone Naltrexone	Naloxone Naltrexone	Naloxone Naltrexone	Naloxone Naltrexone

Source: Malaysia Ministry of Health, 2013

depression and intestinal constipation, as well as drowsiness, nausea, mental clouding, and the production of physical dependency associated with the chronic use of opioids (Contet, Kieffer, & Befort, 2004). Both mu_1 and mu_2 have also been shown to play a role in the development of social attachment and hedonia, the ability to perceive pleasure (Lutz & Kieffer, 2013). Delta receptors appear to be involved with higher-order cognitive processes, motor function, mood, and emotional responses, as well as delusions and hallucinations that occur from administering more potent opioids (Pellissier et al., 2016). Finally, kappa opioid receptors are associated with the creation of analgesia in the spinal cord, sedation, and respiratory depression, and have been postulated to be involved in the mediation of negative affective states associated with stress, including anxiety and depression, promoting drug dependency and relapse, and not only with opioids but also with nicotine (Grella et al., 2014; Lalanne et al., 2014).

All endorphin receptor types are located throughout the brain, but with greater concentrations in and activation of

- the limbic system, which controls emotions, producing feelings of pleasure, relaxation, and contentment;
- the brain stem, interacting with the autonomous nervous system and in turn slowing breathing, inhibiting the cough reflex, and masking the perception of pain; and
- the dorsal root ganglion located just outside the spinal cord and the spinal cord itself, leading to the lessening of the sensation of pain (figure 1.12) (Prahham et al., 2011).

Recent findings indicate that opioids not only activate cells faster and to a greater extent than do the body's natural endorphins, but also affect other cells that natural endorphins do not activate at all (Stoeber et al., 2018).

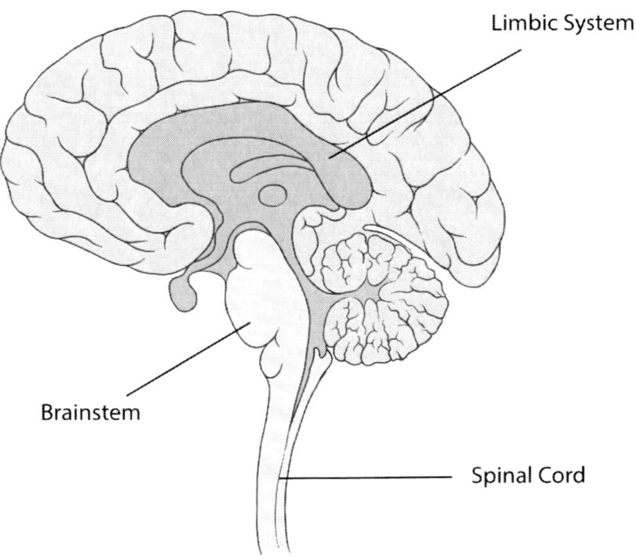

Figure 1.12: Sites of Endorphin Action

Source: Adapted from Wikimedia Commons

Gamma-Aminobutyric Acid (GABA)

GABA is an amino acid that acts as a depressant transmitter that also contributes to the reduction of anxiety. It works by occupying receptor sites and preventing their stimulation (figure 1.13). The message that GABA transmits is an inhibitory one: it tells the neurons it contacts to slow down or stop firing. As approximately 40% of the billions of neurons throughout the brain respond to GABA, this means that GABA has a general quieting influence on the brain, serving as the body's natural tranquilizer. GABA acts on the limbic, thalamic, and hypothalamic systems in producing sedation and hypnotic effects, reduction of anxiety, anticonvulsant effects, and skeletal muscle relaxation. GABA also has a particularly powerful effect upon the reticular activating system (RAS), which not only affects the degree of anxiety a person perceives but is also vital in regulating wakefulness and attention as well as sleep and dreaming (Iqbal, Sobhan, & Ryals, 2002).

GABA is considered the principal neurotransmitter of the body's circadian system. When these processes are inhibited by GABA, sedation and a lack of focus result, along with a decrease in anxiety. When GABA molecules are inhibited by CNS depressants, such as alcohol, barbiturates, and benzodiazepines, an increased amount of dopamine is released, adding a sense of euphoria to the sedation. When external sources of GABA are introduced, the body decreases the amount of GABA it produces, intensifying feelings of anxiety when the psychoactive drug is metabolized and leaves the body. Withdrawal is in part a result of temporarily curtailed GABA production by the brain. This can lead to the use of additional psychoactive drugs to compensate. When GABA is not produced in adequate quantities due to environmental stress, a person's anxiety levels will rise, which can be beneficial in the short term, such as when preparing for a presentation, but extremely negative on a long-term basis (Golan, 2016).

Glutamate (Glu)

Glutamate, or glutamic acid, is the body's most prominent excitatory neurotransmitter and the source from which GABA is synthesized, though interestingly, as discussed above, GABA is an inhibitory

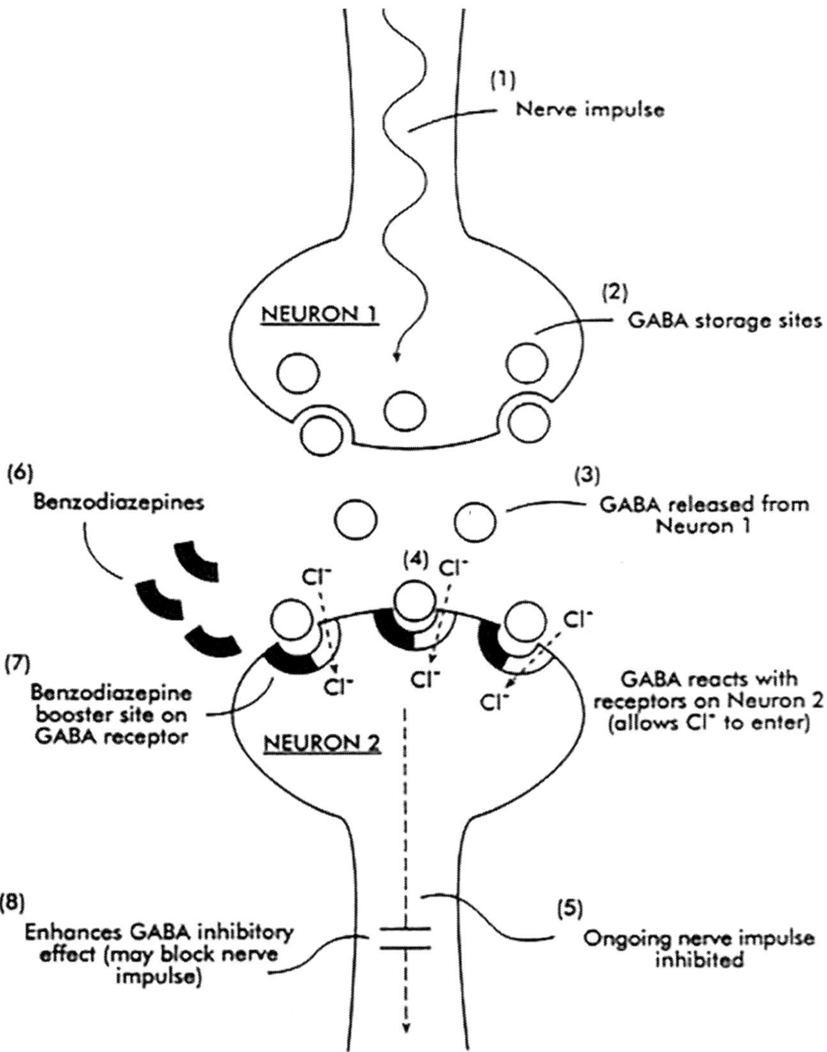

Figure 1.13: GABA Transmission Process

Source: H. Ashton, Diagram of Mechanism of Action of the Natural Neurotransmitter GABA (Gamma Aminobutyric Acid) and Benzodiazepines on Nerve Cells (Neurons) in the Brain (http://www.benzo.org.uk/manual/bzcha01.htm, 2013)

neurotransmitter. Glutamate is associated with every major excitatory function, accounting for over 90% of the synaptic connections in the human brain (Petroff, 2002). The brain, from a perspective of chemical neurotransmission, is largely a glutamatergic excitatory machine, regulated by a relatively smaller GABA inhibitory component and modulated by a far fewer number of monoamine neurons releasing other neurotransmitters, including dopamine and serotonin (Sanacora, Treccani, & Popoli, 2012).

Biochemical receptors for glutamate fall into three major classes: AMPA receptors, NMDA receptors, and metabotropic glutamate receptors plus kainate receptors, which are the least abundant. Glutamate itself is linked to memory and learning, thus any alteration to glutamate will affect both. This includes environmental stressors that can enhance glutamate release and transmission in the limbic/cortical areas of the brain, which in turn can structurally change the brain through remodelling of dendrities and reduction of synapses (Sanacora et al., 2012). There is an association between glutamate modulation and the development of attention deficit/hyperactivity disorder, Parkinson's and Huntington's diseases (Bellone & Gardoni, 2015), and mood and anxiety disorders (Terbeck et al., 2015).

Psychoactive drugs remodel the brain's reward circuitry, specifically the mesocorticolimbic dopamine (DA) system, which contributes to both the development and the persistence of addiction. While increased dopamine levels produced by psychoactive drugs are the foundation for the development of physical dependency, dopamine signalling alone does not explain the changes in behaviour that continue to occur after the drugs have been cleared from the brain. It is now hypothesized that an imbalance between synaptic and non-synaptic glutamate increases vulnerability to relapse by inducing widespread adaptations of glutamate synapses. When excessive glutamate is produced, the brain is unable to regulate itself, which can produce permanent damage. Two distinct roles for glutamate have been forwarded: slow and enduring changes produced by the chronic drug use, which are a major regulator of the addictive behaviour; and rapid transient increases in synaptic strength of glutamate synapses that reflect rapid changes that can occur to the brain due to drug use (Márquez et al., 2017). Additional research has demonstrated that glutamate plays a role in alcohol metabolism, intoxication, and craving (Cheng et al., 2018; Gainetdinov et al., 2001), as well as cocaine self-administration, with cocaine use for longer than six months decreasing cortical glutamine levels (Hulka et al., 2016). Clinical research has also found that individuals suffering from major depressive disorder (chapter 5.1) can have dysfunction in glutamate (Hillhouse & Porter, 2015).

Histamine (H)

Histamine is a member of the small molecule neurotransmitter substances group, which also includes dopamine and serotonin. While there is always histamine circulating in the brain and body, extra histamine is produced in response to an attack by an outside irritant such as food, dust, pollen, or insect bites. An excessive histamine response can produce skin, nose, throat, and lung irritation including itchiness, redness, swelling, rash, cough, and development of excessive mucus. These reactions are part of the inflammatory response to the foreign object, which is a core immune response. Histamine plays a role in arousal, attention, vigilance, recognition and spatial memory, memory consolidation, regulation of gastric acid and the function of the gut, control of pituitary hormone secretion, suppression of eating and cognitive functions, and sexual response. Brain histamine levels are decreased in Alzheimer's disease patients, whereas abnormally high histamine concentrations are found in the brains of those with Parkinson's disease and schizophrenia. Low histamine levels are associated with convulsions and seizures. The release of histamine is also altered in response to different types of brain injury. Morphine-induced pruritus syndrome (ongoing itching) may also be caused by release of histamine from mast cells in the skin (Esbenshade et al., 2008; Nuutinen & Panula 2010).

There are four distinct histamine receptor subtypes (H_1, H_2, H_3, and H_4), all of which function as excitatory neurotransmitters. Blocking H_1 sites will reduce allergenic responses, while blocking H_2 receptors reduces the production of gastric acid secretion. Blocking H_3 receptors is believed to have a positive impact on several cognitive disorders, including attention deficit/hyperactivity disorder and schizophrenia (Esbenshade et al., 2008). H_4 seems to have two distinct roles, affecting pruritic responses as well as mediating the immune system, specifically lung inflammation associated with asthma (Thurmond, 2015). Histamine is also one of the most important wake-promoting neurotransmitter systems in the brain, which is why antihistamines produce drowsiness among users and why it has drawn interest to treating sleep-wake disorders, such as narcolepsy. Low histamine levels are associated with convulsions and seizures (Chikahisa et al., 2013; Krystal, 2010).

Norepinephrine (NE)

Norepinephrine, a monoamine catecholamine that is synthesized from dopamine, plays an important role in attentional processing and affective behaviours, including depression. It is released by the adrenal gland and acts not only as a neurotransmitter, but also as a hormone. It is essential in the transmission of information in the sympathetic nervous system. In its hormonal form, it works in conjunction with adrenaline and epinephrine to boost the body under stressful situations, underlying the human fight-flight response: increasing heart rate, blood pressure, and blood flow to the muscles, as well as leading to the release of glucose from the body's energy stores (Katzung, 2007). Norepinephrine is released in the brain during sexual activity, though its hormonal activity is also associated with decrease in appetite; thus, too much norepinephrine can create anorectic outcomes upon the body (Meston & Frohlich, 2000). Its function as a neurotransmitter relates to both depression and mania and is linked with arousal, stress, mental illness, learning, and sleep. Inhibiting the reuptake of norepinephrine aids in alleviating depression, while elevated levels of this neurotransmitter can lead to mania. It interacts with and enhances the effects of both dopamine and serotonin (figure 1.14). Norepinephrine receptor sites are prominent in the midbrain, VTA, cerebral cortex, and hypothalamus (Katzung, 2007).

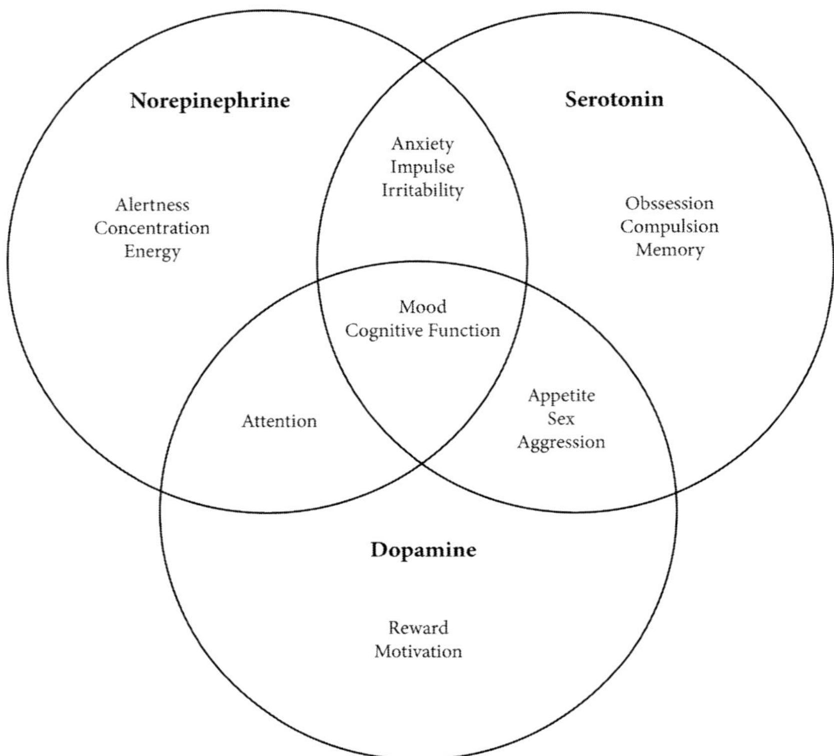

Figure 1.14: Effects of Norepinephrine, Dopamine, and Serotonin

Serotonin (5-hydroxytryptamine, or 5-HT)

Serotonin is an ancient chemical, evolving at least one billion years ago, that is present not only in animals but also in fungi and plants (Andrews et al., 2012). It is referred to by some as the "happiness transmitter." Serotonin is the third crucial monoamine, like dopamine and norepinephrine, though it belongs to the indolamine group, with 14 known receptor sites. The serotonin system, specifically 5-hydroxytryptamine (5-HT), is known to alter human affect, reducing feelings of depression, alleviating anxiety, elevating mood, and increasing feelings of self-worth. It also plays an important role in mood, appetite, and libido. In limbic regions, 5-HT is vital in regulating dopamine and norepinephrine signalling (Ketcherside, Matthews, & Filbey, 2013). If 5-HT transmission is reduced in the brain, increases in impulsiveness and aggressive behaviours occur (Carhart-Harris & Nutt, 2017), while reduced serotonin transporter availability is linked to cognitive impairment (Smith et al., 2017). Serotonin is also important in controlling memory, learning, attention, digestion, insulin levels, electrolyte balance, cerebral blood flow, and body temperature. Inadequate amounts of serotonin are associated with sleep fragmentation and deprivation, for as a person enters the REM stages of the sleep cycle (figure 1.20), the amount of serotonin in the body drops (Kirby, Zeeb, & Winstanley, 2011; Kocherlakota, 2014; National Institute on Drug Abuse, 2008).

The 5-HT system is affected by all major psychoactive drug groups. Both stimulants and alcohol increase serotonin; opioids enhance both synthesis and release of 5-HT in parts of the brain while inhibiting serotonin firing in other parts, though this also relates to acute (increased activity) or chronic (decreased activity) use of opioids. The serotonin system is closely associated with the group of antidepressants that includes Prozac, Paxil, Zoloft, Luvox, Lexapro, and Celexa. However, disrupting serotonin is also linked to the effects produced by hallucinogens. Serotonin and dopamine are viewed as the most significant neurotransmitters in terms of mental health (figure 1.15).

While increased dopamine in the brain reward system is believed to be the final pathway for the reinforcing properties of psychoactive drugs, serotonin is also involved in the regulation of both drug self-administration and dopamine levels. Serotonin may be important in modulating motivational factors, or the amount of work an individual is willing to perform to obtain a drug. Serotonergic neurons project to both the nucleus accumbens (NAc) and the ventral tegmental area (VTA) and appear to regulate dopamine release at the NAc. However, the relationship between serotonin and dopamine release is complex in that serotonin has numerous receptor types, and its regulation of dopamine release is at times inhibitory and at other times excitatory (Lowinson et al., 2011). Despite the importance of serotonin for human functioning, it has been estimated that, of the approximately one hundred billion neurons in the brain, only about two to three hundred thousand are serotonergic, which, like norepinephrine, are prominent in the midbrain, VTA, cerebral cortex, and hypothalamus (Baker et al., 1991).

Serotonin syndrome is a potentially life-threatening reaction from the administration of two or more psychoactive substances that enhance serotonin production and/or activity resulting in a range of cognitive, autonomic, and somatic effects. Onset is typically rapid, with initial symptoms consisting of increased heart rate, shivering, sweating, dilated pupils, headache, hallucinations, and intermittent tremor or twitching, as well as hypervigilance and overresponsive reflexes. This can be followed by agitation, nausea, vomiting, increased blood pressure, and a body temperature in excess of 40°C (106.0°F) that can lead to a coma state. Because so many psychoactive drugs, both licit and illicit, including alcohol, antidepressants, hallucinogens, opioids, and stimulants, alter serotonin, the occurrence of serotonin syndrome is a

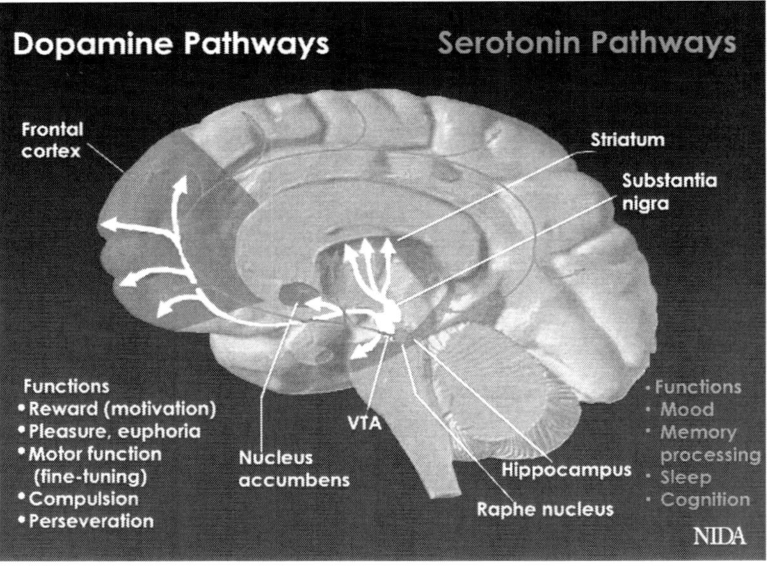

Figure 1.15: Serotonin and Dopamine Pathways

Source: National Institute on Drug Abuse, *Brain pathways are affected by drugs of abuse* (http://www.drugabuse.gov/publications/addiction-science/why-do-people-abuse-drugs/brain-pathways-are-affected-by-drugs-abuse, 2008)

risk with any polydrug usage of these substances (Birmes et al., 2003; Boyer & Shannon, 2005).

1.5 PHARMACOKINETICS

Pharmacokinetics is the study of what the body does to drugs. It examines how the human body absorbs, distributes, and eliminates drugs. The effect of a psychoactive drug depends on the amount administered, the extent and rate of absorption, the extent and rate of distribution, the binding and localization in tissues, metabolism, and the bio-transformation of the drug so that it can be excreted.

Absorption and Administration

How much, how often, and how fast a drug reaches the brain determines the behavioural and structural changes associated with the addiction process. Central to understanding pharmacokinetics is understanding how drugs get into and move throughout the body, as the shorter the time between drug administration and changes to the CNS, the greater the reinforcement power of the drug. Absorption simply refers to the process of getting the drug from outside the body into the bloodstream, from which the drug is transported to the CNS, where it can produce a change to the brain. There are five means through which drugs can be administered so that they can be absorbed by the body:

1. Orally: through the mouth and stomach to the intestines, where the drug is absorbed into the bloodstream, but only after first passing through the liver and undergoing partial (first pass) metabolism
2. Across mucous membranes: via the nasal lining, gums, vaginal walls, or rectum
3. Injection: through a vein or muscle, or under the skin
4. Inhalation: through the lungs
5. Transdermal: across the skin (table 1.3)

Oral Administration

Oral administration entails swallowing a psychoactive drug. If a drug is in a solid state, pill or powder, then it must first be turned into a fluid state in the stomach so that it can be absorbed through the lining of the small intestine and into the bloodstream, where it is distributed to the central nervous system once processed by the liver. How much of the drug is absorbed depends on its solubility, how well it is turned into liquid in the stomach, and its permeability—how well it passes through the lining of the intestine—as well as by the presence or absence of food in the digestive tract. The more food present, the slower the entire operation proceeds.

Across Mucous Membranes

Fewer layers of cells exist in mucous membrane areas than in other parts of the body, allowing for a quicker absorption of psychoactive agents. Mucous membrane is found in the nose, lips, gums, vaginal walls, and rectum. Drugs that can be sniffed, such as cocaine hydrochloride, stick to the nasal membranes and are transferred into the bloodstream, and then to the central nervous system. Betel, khat, and nicotine from chewing tobacco all cross the mucous membrane of the mouth into the blood and then move to alter neurotransmitters in the CNS. Psychoactive drugs in the form of suppositories are useful if a person is vomiting, unconscious, or unable to swallow. While there is no first-pass metabolization with this method of administration, meaning this too offers a high level of bioavailability, there can be erratic absorption as the drug passes through different mucous membranes in the body at different speeds. *Sublingual administration* is the specific term used when a drug is placed under the tongue to be absorbed, while *buccal administration* refers to placing a tablet between the teeth or gums and the mucous membrane of the cheek.

Injection

When a drug is injected directly into the body, the natural biological barriers are bypassed. There are three ways in which to inject drugs (figure 1.16):

1. Intravenously (IV): injecting the drug directly into a vein. This is the fastest of the three injection options, with the

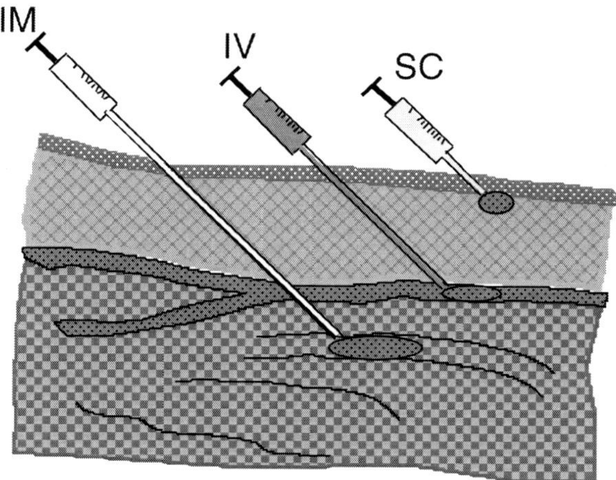

Figure 1.16: Drug Injection Options

Note: IM = intramuscular; IV = intravenous; SC = subcutaneous
Source: D. Bourne, *A First Course in Pharmacokinetics and Biopharmaceutics* (https://www.boomer.org/c/p4/c07/c0705.php, 2001)

initial effect generally perceived in the CNS within 10 to 15 seconds. This allows you to administer large amounts of the drug with no metabolization before it reaches the brain (100% bioavailability). However, as with all three injection options, the only way to reverse the effects is to administer an antagonistic drug, such as injecting a person overdosing on heroin with naloxone.

2. Subcutaneous (SC): injecting the drug just under the skin; also referred to as skin popping. When a drug is administered subcutaneously, it is absorbed beneath the skin into the connective tissue or into fat under the dermis. Drug solubility and constriction of blood vessels may cause delays in drug absorption when psychoactive drugs are given using this injection option. However, the subcutaneous route can provide easier and still somewhat rapid onset of effect without requiring finding a vein. The psychoactive effect begins to take place five to ten minutes after the injection, depending on how quickly the drug

penetrates the walls of the blood vessels and the rate of blood flow through the skin. Some users have been known to inject the drug between their toes to minimize others being able to see the puncture marks that accumulate with multiple injections to the arms.

3. Intramuscular (IM): injecting the drug into skeletal muscle: arms, legs, or buttocks. This method of injection takes between 10 and 15 minutes to begin producing a psychoactive effect. The absorption rate in this method of administration is also dependent upon the rate of blood flow to that muscle and is not a preferred route, as intramuscular injections are often painful and drug absorption is variable and unpredictable. This method does require less precision, and a greater amount can be administered compared to the other two injection options.

Inhalation

Gases such as nitrous oxide or ketamine pass through the lung membranes and into the blood extremely quickly, in as little as eight to ten seconds. The almost immediate effect is a direct result of the large surface area of the lung. Nicotine in cigarettes and Δ9-tetrahydrocannabinol (THC), the psychoactive agent found in cannabis smoke, act somewhat differently. These drugs are contained in small particles carried in the smoke, and although absorption is still quick, it is not as efficient as with anaesthetic gases, as not all of the drug particles get through to the brain.

Transdermal

Transdermal drug delivery systems (TDDS), also known as patches, are dosage forms designed to deliver a therapeutically effective amount of drug across a person's skin. This is a comparatively slow means of producing an effect in the CNS, and as such, it is not a primary means of ingesting psychoactive drugs recreationally. However, it does have therapeutic use for individuals who require a slow, steady administration of a drug, and who often prefer it over regular injections or swallowing pills on an ongoing basis. Transdermal administration provides a controlled, constant administration of a drug, as well as allowing for

Table 1.3: Routes of Administration

Method	Example of Drug	Time Needed for Effect	Advantages of Route	Disadvantages of Route
oral	methadone	20–60 minutes	convenient	slow, irregular
across mucous membranes	chewing tobacco	1–2 minutes	convenient	local tissue damage
inhalation	crack cocaine	8 seconds	fast	lung damage
intravenous injection	Dilaudid	15 seconds	fast	overdose, infections
subcutaneous injection	heroin	15–20 minutes	safer and easier than intravenous; provides an option when no vein access	infections
intramuscular injection	haloperidol	10–15 minutes	controlled	painful
transdermal	LSD	15–20 minutes	convenient	limited application

continuous input of drugs with short biological half-lives. Nicotine patches as a mechanism of drug substitution, and opioid patches, such as fentanyl for those with chronic pain, are two examples of this practice (Krishnarajan et al., 2016).

A summary of the various methods of administration is presented in table 1.3. Using cocaine as an example, figure 1.17 illustrates the difference in intensity of action and duration of action produced by different routes of administration.

Distribution

Substances are distributed throughout the body by the circulation of the blood. Once a psychoactive drug is absorbed into the blood, a balance is established between the drug that binds to the protein in the blood and that which floats freely. All psychoactive drugs, save alcohol and lithium, bind to this protein. As protein molecules are too large to

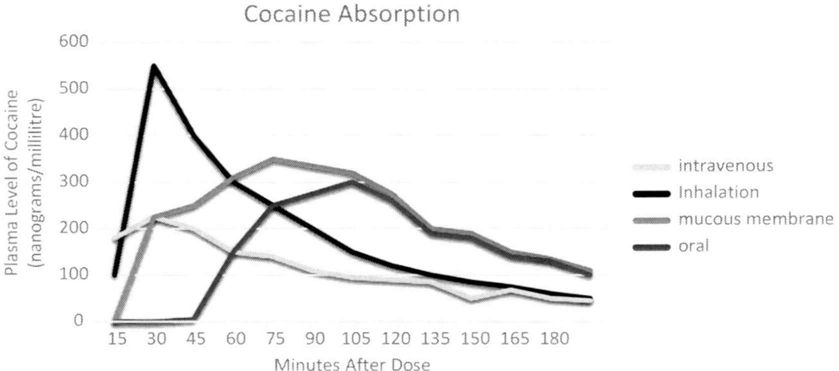

Figure 1.17: Drug Intensity and Duration Based upon Method of Administration

Source: R. Jones, The Pharmacology of Cocaine Smoking in Humans (in C. Chiang & R. Hawks (Eds.), *Research Findings on Smoking of Abused Substances*, Rockville, MD: United States Department of Health and Human Services, 1990)

leave the bloodstream, it is only unbound drug molecules that can alter the central nervous system in the blood; those that are bound remain inactive until released. As the unbound drug moves into the brain or is eliminated, more of the bound drug is released to maintain the bound/unbound balance in the bloodstream, until the drug is fully metabolized and eliminated. However, the distribution of most drugs in the body is far from even. This makes it difficult to correlate blood levels and the pharmacological effects of the drugs used. Psychoactive drugs create their effects by reaching specific cells within the CNS; however, cells the drugs affect are also found throughout the body, such as in the digestive, cardiovascular, immune, and endocrine systems, which explains many of the side effects produced by psychoactive drugs (Sproule, 2004).

For a drug to be distributed throughout the body, it must be small enough to pass through the pores in capillaries from the veins, and smaller still to pass through the cell walls. Drug molecules must also be lipid (fat) soluble. Cells in the body are surrounded by a membrane containing a double layer of fatty molecules, which limits the movement of substances in and out of the cell. If a substance is lipid soluble, it can more easily pass through the cell membrane. This is critical in that any substance administered in any way other than injection must be able to cross the membranes of the small intestine (oral administration), the lungs (inhalation), or the mucous membrane. In addition, the greater the lipid solubility of a drug, the easier the drug passes from the blood into the brain across the appropriately named blood-brain barrier. The blood-brain barrier (BBB) is a unique membrane that tightly segregates the brain from the circulating blood, regulating the entry of all small and large molecules entering the brain and thus limiting the uptake of most drugs by the brain. This makes the BBB of immense importance to the brain in terms of safety. However, the vast majority of psychoactive drugs are highly lipid soluble, meaning they pass easily into the brain to produce their effects; that said, some synthetic drugs are made to have low lipid solubility so that they circulate in the blood longer and thus extend the effects they produce on the CNS. Yet another factor related to distribution is ionization, which is the positive or negative charge a drug carries. The greater the positive charge, the less fat soluble the drug is, and the slower it can pass through lipids to alter the CNS (Alberts et al., 2007).

Metabolization and Elimination

Once it enters the body, a psychoactive drug divides into two parts: the part that remains unchanged and the part that changes, the latter having undergone metabolization. Drugs are metabolized by compounds called enzymes, primarily in the liver. For a drug to be removed from the bloodstream, and thus no longer affect the CNS, it must be metabolized by the liver into compounds that are more water soluble than the parent drug. It can then be eliminated from the body, primarily in the form of urine and, to a lesser degree, feces. Drugs must first be metabolized so that they cannot pass back from the kidney into the blood. The conversion of fat-soluble drugs to water-soluble substances may involve several chemical steps, each step yielding a slightly more soluble substance, for eventual excretion by the kidneys. One drug can therefore yield many different metabolites, which are the substances formed when a drug is biologically altered by the liver. This process is necessary to eliminate a drug from the body. Most metabolites are inactive, but some remain active, meaning they still have psychoactive properties and need to be further metabolized to become inactive. An example of this is heroin; when metabolized by the liver, it becomes morphine, which continues to exert a psychoactive influence on the CNS. When morphine molecules, metabolized from heroin, pass through the liver, they are metaboilized into morphine-3-glucuronide (M3G) and morphine-6-glucuronide (M6G). M6G is an active metabolite that needs to be metabolized yet again to become inactive, whereas M3G is an inactive metabolite that cannot pass through the BBB and is unable to influence either the CNS or PNS.

As a psychoactive drug becomes progressively less fat soluble, it loses both its ability to cross the BBB and its strength to alter the functioning of the brain. Intermediate metabolites are generally less potent than the parent drug, with some being completely devoid of any pharmacological activity. Some metabolites can produce a completely different activity from the parent drug, such as when methyl alcohol, a partially poisonous intoxicant, is metabolized into formaldehyde, which is lethal to the human body. Anaesthetic gases and volatile drugs are eliminated through the lungs, as is approximately 5% of all beverage alcohol consumed. Other sites of elimination for some drugs are the sweat glands, through saliva, and in breast milk.

Another factor that needs to be considered is bioavailability. This is the term used to indicate the amount of a drug that reaches the target site, which in the case of psychoactive drugs is the brain. For example, a drug that is absorbed from the stomach and intestine will pass through the liver before it reaches the circulatory system. If the drug is metabolized in the liver or excreted in the bile, some of the active drug will be destroyed before it can be distributed to its site of action. If the metabolic capacity of the liver for a given psychoactive agent is substantial, bioavailability will be substantially decreased. This is called the first-pass effect. The decrease in availability of the drug is also partly a function of how the drug is administered (Alberts et al., 2007).

After a drug is totally absorbed into the body, the concentration in the blood soon starts to fall. This drop is initially rapid because of the movement of the drug from the bloodstream into the body's tissues.

The rate of decline slows as excretion begins and depends on both the type of drug and the concentration of the drug in the blood. The higher the drug concentration, the faster metabolism and excretion will proceed. This variability makes it difficult to compare the rate of metabolism of one drug with that of another. To get around this difficulty, the concept of half-life was borrowed from nuclear physics. Half-life is a way to measure the rate of metabolism of a drug. It indicates the length of time required for a drug's blood concentration to fall by one-half. By knowing the half-life of a drug, one can better assess the appropriate dosage, frequency, and amount required to treat a specific medical condition. In the later stages of metabolism and excretion, the half-life of a drug is constant, no matter how great the initial concentration was. The half-life of many drugs increases with the user's age. This may be due to increased amounts of body fat, which acts as a reservoir for highly lipid-soluble drugs, or from impaired liver or kidney function. In most situations, it takes about six half-lives to eliminate a drug from the body. The most familiar drug that does not have a half-life, but rather is eliminated at a constant rate from the body, is ethyl alcohol (Hancock & McKim, 2018).

1.6 PHARMACODYNAMICS

Tolerance

After repeated use of a drug, the user may become more resistant to its effects. This loss of sensitivity is known as tolerance. Tolerance simply means that the body has adapted to the presence of the drug. With many chemical agents, the brain becomes used to the substance, and the original effects of the drug diminish over time. Tolerant individuals may appear to walk and talk with no impairment, but more complex and less observable behaviours, such as precise judgment or fine motor skills, will still be negatively affected, as will memory. Tolerance may occur to both the desired effects of the drug of choice, as well as to its adverse effects. Tolerance may also occur after a period of chronic exposure or after a single dose. This is referred to as acute tolerance, and is evidenced in persons who appear to become less intoxicated the longer they drink. For these individuals, there is more impairment at the start of a drinking session than at its conclusion (Harris & Buck, 1990). For drugs such as alcohol, the liver also becomes slightly more efficient in breaking down the substance, requiring more to be consumed to obtain the desired effect. The most common example of tolerance is someone who can "really hold their liquor." This is merely one indication of an individual who consumes alcohol on a regular and ongoing basis.

Tolerance can also be categorized as either dispositional—when the liver is able to process the drug more efficiently and excrete it faster from the body, also referred to as metabolic—or functional, also called pharmacodynamic, tolerance. Functional tolerance occurs when actual physical changes take place in the body's receptors, or when receptor sensitivity is altered. Drug sensitivity may also decrease over the course of a small number of administrations (Sproule, 2004).

Functional tolerance development depends on a variety of factors, including

- the drug that is administered;
- the effect being measured;
- the selected dose (generally, the greater the dose, the faster the rate of tolerance development);
- previous drug history (if a person has been tolerant in the past, tolerance will develop much more quickly on subsequent drug exposures to members of the same family of psychoactive drugs);
- behavioural demands (if drug users are required to handle complex tasks during periods of intoxication, they will quickly develop tolerance to those drug effects that affect their performance of that task adversely); and
- the setting in which use takes place (if a person administers a drug in the same room each day, their body learns to expect the substance in that room; conditioned compensatory changes occur in the brain that reduce the intensity of the experienced effect. If the same amount is consumed in a different environment, the person can overdose) (Dziegielewski, 2005).

In many instances, after an individual becomes tolerant to the effects of one drug, that person will also show tolerance to other psychoactive drugs with similar effects upon the central nervous system. This is called cross-tolerance. A phenomenon often referred to as reverse tolerance or sensitization has been noted with some drugs, notably hallucinogens, in which the desired effects may reportedly be achieved with smaller doses after the initial experience with the drug. Learning, environmental, and pharmacological mechanisms have been suggested to underlie this process.

A most interesting pharmacological process is tachyphylaxis. This is a rapid reduction in the effect produced by the drug, regardless of how much of the drug is consumed. It is the development of total tolerance that occurs in a short period of time, such that there is no physical withdrawal to the drug. If a drug is taken for consecutive days, after three or four days, no psychoactive effects of any type are perceived. This occurs almost exclusively with hallucinogenic drugs, though for those that have secondary effects, such as methylenedioxymethamphetamine (MDMA/ecstasy) or ketamine, those secondary effects will be perceived even if the primary hallucinogenic effect is not. Tachyphylaxis has also been noted with longer use of some psychotherapeutic agents and is what occurs when someone experiences "Prozac poop-out" or a similar cessation of the effectiveness of their medication without warning (Procyshyn, Bezchlibnyk-Butler, & Jeffies, 2017).

Withdrawal

Withdrawal is the development of physical disturbances or physical illness when drug use is suddenly discontinued. It is the rebound effect of physical dependence, though a person need not be physically dependent to suffer withdrawal. Hangovers are the classic example of minor withdrawal effects resulting from overindulgence in ethyl alcohol. When a drug ceases to be administered, the compensatory mechanisms cause a temporary overactivity of the cells; this overactivity, rebounding, is the basis of withdrawal symptoms. The severity of the withdrawal reaction after stopping drug use is not necessarily related to the severity of dependence. Withdrawal from depressants generally results in

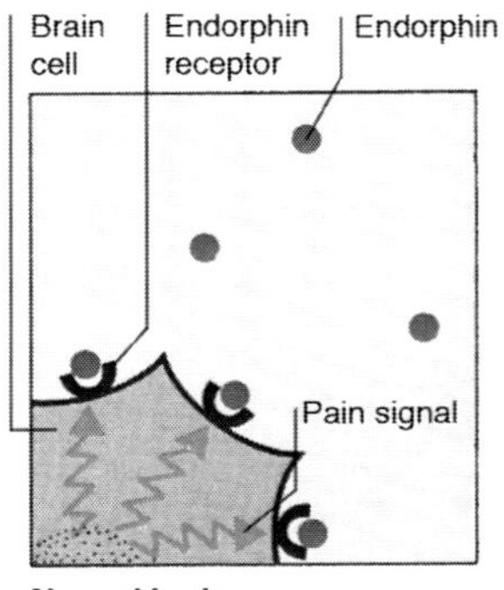

Normal brain
When no drug is present, natural substances called endorphins inhibit the transmission of pain signals.

Effect of heroin
Heroin occupies the same receptors in the brain as endorphins, suppressing production of endorphins.

Heroin withdrawal
Abrupt withdrawal of heroin leaves the brain without a buffer to pain signals, even from minor stimuli.

Figure 1.18: Process of Heroin Withdrawal

Source: L. Raman-Wilms, *Canadian Pharmacists Association Guide to Drugs in Canada*, 4th edition (Dorling Kindersley Ltd., 2014)

symptoms of acute and toxic hyperactivation and physiological arousal, while the pattern following intense stimulant use usually involves sedation, CNS depression, and sleep. Withdrawal symptoms can be prevented or promptly relieved by reusing the original drug, or one that is pharmacologically equivalent: the "hair of the dog" (Brands, Sproule, & Marshman, 1998). The process of heroin withdrawal is illustrated in figure 1.18.

Drug Interaction

A pharmacodynamic drug interaction occurs when the pharmacologic response of one drug is modified by another drug without the effects being the result of a change in drug concentration. There are four possible pharmacodynamic drug-interaction outcomes. The first is a synergistic effect, which is when each individual drug's effects are increased when the two drugs are administered together. This is the 1 + 1 = 3 effect. An example of this is when two depressants are taken together, such as alcohol and a benzodiazepine (e.g., Xanax). The synergistic effect is to produce more sedation than either drug could on its own. This type of effect can lead to a drug overdose at lower dose levels than one would expect given each individual drug's impact on the CNS and PNS.

The second type of effect is antagonistic, when a drug's effect is decreased. An example of this is mixing alcohol and caffeine. In this instance, despite the depressant effect of alcohol, the user's CNS and PNS do not slow down as much as they otherwise would because of the opposite effect the caffeine produces.

The third possible outcome is a new effect that neither of the two drugs would produce on their own. An example of this is when a person consumes alcohol and cocaine at the same time. When these two drugs interact, a new chemical is formed in the body that exists nowhere else in nature: cocaethylene. Cocaethylene is more toxic to the body than is either alcohol or cocaine.

The fourth possible outcome is when there is no interaction and the two drugs just act on the body independently. An example of this is nicotine and LSD. Nicotine exerts minor stimulant effects and LSD produces hallucinogenic effects, but nothing more would happen to the user when the two were taken simultaneously than if they were administered independently of one another.

Drug Lethality

The median lethal dose of any drug is known as its LD_{50}. This is the amount of a substance that is required to kill half the members of a population after a test period. The LD_{50} value is used as a general indicator of a substance's acute toxicity. The smaller the LD_{50} value, the more hazardous a drug is and the less of it is required to produce a fatal overdose. A drug's LD_{50} is typically written as the mass of the drug administered per unit mass of the test subject, typically as milligrams of substance per kilogram of body mass (Canadian Centre for Occupational Health and Safety, 2018).

Safety ratio is the difference between the effective dose—the amount of a drug required to produce a psychoactive or therapeutic reaction—and the drug's LD_{50}. Table 1.4 provides a comparison of various psychoactive drugs and their safety ratios. A major caveat that must be considered here, and as you review the various psychoactive drugs

Table 1.4: Estimated Effective and Lethal Dose Levels of Psychoactive Substances

Substance	Category	Effective Dose	Lethal Dose	Safety Ratio
Cannabis	Hallucinogen	15 milligrams	15 grams	1,000
LSD	Hallucinogen	100 micrograms	100 milligrams	1,000
Psilocybin	Hallucinogen	6 milligrams	6 grams	1,000
Ativan	Depressant (benzodiazepine)	5 milligrams	1,850 milligrams	370
Nitrous Oxide	Depressant (inhalant)	3.5 litres	525 litres	150
Caffeine	Stimulant	100 milligrams	10 grams	100
Fluoxetine (Prozac)	Psychotherapeutic	20 milligrams	2 grams	100
Phenobarbital	Depressant (barbiturate)	100 milligrams	5 grams	50
Ketamine	Hallucinogen	70 milligrams	2.7 grams	38
Rohypnol	Depressant (benzodiazepine)	1 milligram	30 milligrams	30
Mescaline	Hallucinogen	350 milligrams	8.4 grams	24
Codeine	Opioid	40 milligrams	800 milligrams	20
DMT (ayahuasca)	Hallucinogen	27 milligrams	540 milligrams	20
Methadone	Opioid	5 milligrams	100 milligrams	20
Quaaludes	Depressant (NBSH)	300 milligrams	5.4 grams	18
MDMA	Hallucinogen	125 milligrams	2 grams	16
Cocaine	Stimulant	80 milligrams	1,200 milligrams	15
Alcohol	Depressant	33 grams	330 grams	10
Amobarbital	Depressant (barbiturate)	200 milligrams	2 grams	10
Methamphetamine	Stimulant	15 milligrams	150 milligrams	10
Pentobarbital	Depressant (barbiturate)	200 milligrams	2 grams	10
GHB	Depressant (inhalant)	2 grams	16 grams	8
Isobutyl Nitrite	Depressant (inhalant)	0.2 millilitres	1.6 millilitres	8
Heroin	Opioid	8 milligrams	50 milligrams	6

Source: Gable, 2004; 2006

described later, as well as when working with service users, is that sex and weight truly matter, and matter immensely. Safety ratio is based on lean weight, and thus the less you weigh, the less drug is required for both the effective dose and the lethal dose. However, water-to-fat ratio of the body also matters. Women have a higher fat-to-water ratio than men do. What this means is that a woman of equal lean body weight to a man will be more readily affected by a psychoactive drug than the man will. This is relevant not only for safety ratio but also for recreational and therapeutic use of any psychoactive substance, be it benzodiazepines, alcohol, opioids, stimulants, hallucinogens, or psychotherapeutic agents. Another pharmacodynamic factor to consider is tolerance; individuals who have been long-term users of a psychoactive drug will require more of a substance over time to achieve a psychoactive effect. Likewise, tolerant individuals may be able to administer a higher dose than a stated LD_{50}, as this value represents the median lethal dose level. Finally, when considering illicit drugs there is always the question of purity. There is a vast difference between the quality of drugs that are tested in highly controlled laboratory conditions and drugs that are illicitly manufactured and sold.

Paradoxical Drug Effects

A paradoxical drug reaction or paradoxical drug effect is when the opposite reaction occurs than is expected. There is no way in which to anticipate when a person will react in an opposite direction except through observation once the drug has been administered. The exact cause for a paradoxical reaction in any given individual cannot be determined in advance, and the effect is typically specific to a drug group and even a specific drug within a pharmacological family. Paradoxical effects may be the result of

- a gene mutation (Heisler & Tecott, 2000);
- the amount of drug consumed (Robbins & Sahakian, 1979);
- the pharmacological complexity of the drug (White, Sklar, & Amit, 1977);
- drug interactions (Perucca et al., 1998); or
- the user's age, physical condition, and environmental context (Hall & Zisook, 1981).

Paradoxical effects have been documented for a range of psychoactive substances: stimulants that produce drowsiness in users; individuals who receive an opioid and who either do not feel any pain relief or become agitated; antipsychotic drugs that produce more seizure activity; and benzodiazpeines that lead to a heightened state of anxiety and agitation (Dunleavy et al., 1972; Hall & Zisook, 1981; Perucca et al., 1998; Tecce & Cole, 1974; White et al., 1977). This phenomenon further speaks to the complexity of pharmacology, and while we need to be cognizant of patterns and trends that drug groups produce, we must always view each person distinctly.

1.7 SLEEPING AND DREAMING

Sleeping is an integral part of our lives, and yet the scope of its importance is typically not fully appreciated. Insomnia is a major public health issue, as it has a significant negative impact on individuals' physical and social performance, their ability to work, and their quality of life (Atalay, 2011; Crain & Barber, 2018). While most people realize sleep is necessary for physical health, what is not as readily acknowledged is the importance of dreaming for mental health and how sleep deprivation negatively affects psychological well-being (figure 1.19). It has been empirically demonstrated that almost all substance-related disorders and psychiatric disturbances, from anxiety to depression (Lyall et al., 2018) to the risk of dementia (Pase et al., 2017) to schizophrenia (Cohrs, 2008) and suicidality (Drapeau & Nadorff, 2017), are associated with sleep disruption.

The process of dreaming is essential in helping individuals to understand unconscious mental processes and experience feelings, memories, wishes, fantasies, conflicts, impulses, and defenses, as well as images of themselves and others. Dreams also provide a psychological space where complex, unbearable affects can be experienced, helping to maintain waking homeostasis. The need for sleep is so essential that if a person misses one night of sleep, their body tries to recover what was lost in subsequent nights. Sleep appears to be universal in that virtually every species engages in some type of sleep. There are various theories behind

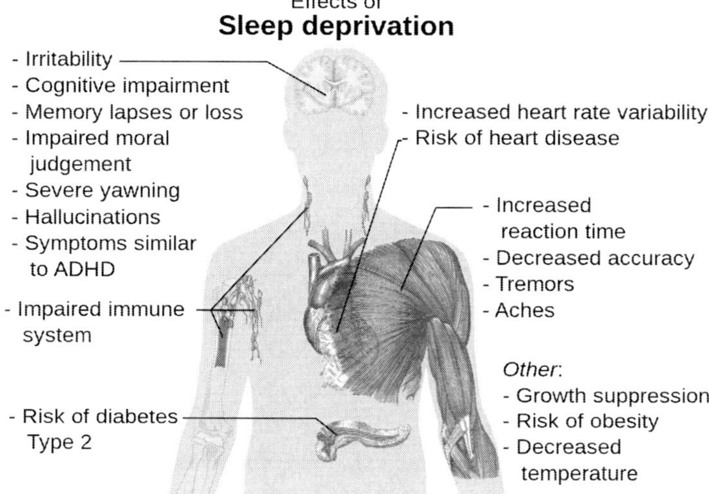

Figure 1.19: Effects of Sleep Deprivation

Source: Wikimedia Commons

why we must sleep, with physical rest being only one explanation. There is no argument that sleep allows our bodies to save and restore energy, and that while we sleep our metabolism is much slower than when we are awake. It is also believed that neurotransmitter levels are replenished while we sleep, as brain activity is generally lower than when we are awake. The parts of the CNS that are most active while we are awake are generally much less active during sleep (Steiger, 2010). While we are asleep, our brains also reorganize and store information, something for which dreaming is crucial. The rapid eye movement (REM) stage of sleep plays a role in memory retention and consolidation; even one night without REM sleep decreases the ability to retain newly learned information, and the retention of complex information is greatly reduced when a person is deprived of the REM stage of sleep. It has also been hypothesized that REM sleep is designed to remove useless and unneeded information from memory (Diekelmann & Born, 2010).

While awake, the brain's pattern of electrical activity is rapid and irregular, with a relatively low level of electrical output, indicating that neurons are firing at different intervals, at different times, and with different strengths. Figure 1.20 illustrates a typical eight-hour sleep cycle, though the reality is that few North Americans actually sleep eight consecutive hours on a regular basis. Stages 1 and 2 are the initial stages of sleep, from which we are most easily roused. During Stage 1, a person is in a twilight stage, half asleep and half awake. It entails a progressive reduction of the awareness of self and of one's environment, when breathing becomes more regular and gradually deepens. Stage 1 constitutes approximately 5% of the total duration of sleep on any given night and is dominated by theta brain waves. During Stage 2, which constitutes 40–50% of the sleep cycle, sleep deepens, and one is slowly removed from perceiving stimuli in the outside world. The beginning of Stage 2 sleep is characterized by the appearance of the K-complex, a single high-voltage negative wave, followed by a single slow positive wave, and then the spindle—oscillating waves that last one to two seconds each in their respective cycles. Stages 3 and 4 are deeper stages of sleep, dominated by slow delta waves, that are physically restorative as natural growth hormone is released during this period, which aids in muscle and tissue repair. Upon entering Stage 3 of the sleep cycle, brain activity becomes more synchronized. Cells are

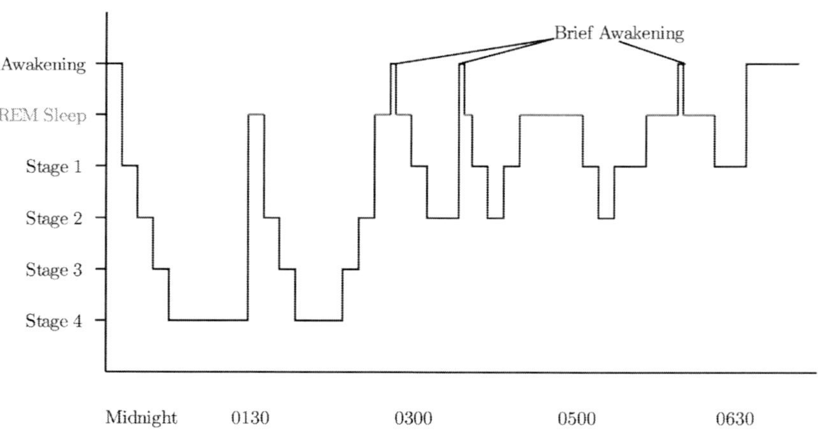

Figure 1.20: Stages of Sleep

Source: Adapted from Wikimedia Commons

firing far more in unison than when a person is awake. If awakened at this point in the sleep cycle, individuals respond slowly and are usually momentarily confused and uncertain of their surroundings. Stages 1 through 4 are collectively referred to as NREM sleep, non-REM sleep, to clearly distinguish the two distinct cycles that occur during sleeping. During NREM sleep, brain waves typically become synchronized, dominated by slow-frequency and high-voltage waves, in contrast to the fast-frequency and low-voltage waves typical of wakefulness (Berteotti et al., 2015; Steiger, 2010).

At the top of the sleep cycle (figure 1.20) is REM sleep, which constitutes 20–25% of our time asleep. REM is the dreaming state where our mind is active, replaying recent events and reliving past events, both pleasant and traumatic, while recalling non-events that, while they never occurred, arise in the sleep patterns of people universally. These include flying, falling from a great height, being unprepared for a test or important event, and appearing in public in inappropriate or no clothing. A healthy human being can go upwards of 60 days without food, whereas as little as 10 days without sleeping or dreaming can be fatal. Likewise, disrupted sleep leads to a range of physical health issues. If a person is allowed to sleep but not enter REM sleep, their mental health will rapidly deteriorate (Everson, 1993; Everson & Szabo, 2009).

The first REM cycle typically begins approximately 90 minutes after a person has entered Stage 1 of sleep. The initial REM cycle lasts upwards of 10 minutes, with subsequent episodes each being longer, some lasting upwards of an hour at the end of a night. During REM sleep, the synchronized pattern that emerges in Stages 3 and 4 is interrupted and brain wave patterns become desynchronized, looking much more like that of a waking state. At this stage, the CNS is intensely active, but the skeletal motor system is paradoxically forced into a state of muscle paralysis, though the eyes remain active. Although their muscles are not able to work, a person still experiences the sensation of moving while dreaming, which means that they feel the dream as though it were real. Eye movement during REM sleep is related to the scanning of the visual scene of a dream. In other words, the dreamer looks at the surroundings in the dream the same way they observe their surroundings when they are awake. Although in this phase of the sleep cycle a person remains mostly disconnected from the outside world, they are very easily roused if their name is called or if a loud sound is heard. During eight hours of sleep, a person can experience four or even five REM cycles, with each successive REM cycle lasting longer than the one before. However, if a person had shortened sleep the previous evening, the mind will work to increase the amount of REM sleep relative to the other stages. In order to conserve energy, body temperature drops to its lowest point of the night during REM, which can be as low as 96.5°F (Steiger, 2010).

While brain activity is lessened during a normal night of sleep, various parts of the CNS remain active. The hypothalamus, just above the brain stem, regulates the chemicals that promote sleep and then arousal. The thalamus, located in the forebrain, blocks input from the senses during sleep, allowing the brain to focus on processing sensory inputs perceived during the preceding day. The hippocampus, part of the limbic system, replays memories that will be stored by the brain. It is also hypothesized that the cerebral cortex is active during dreaming, and that it is the cerebral cortex that attempts to interpret and make sense of all the information gathered during waking hours. During Stages 3 and 4 of the sleep cycle, growth hormone is secreted from the pineal gland, which encourages bone and muscle growth in children and aids in tissue repair in adults (Reinoso-Suarez et al., 1999).

Neurotransmitters that promote wakefulness are the monoamines, dopamine, norepinephrine, and serotonin (5-HT), along with acetylcholine and histamine. Neurotransmitters that promote sleep are adenosine and GABA, as well as two neurotransmitters not previously discussed, galanin and melatonin. Thus, it is not surprising that psychoactive drugs would have a direct and profound impact on all activities of the brain associated with the sleep cycle, especially dreaming. The association between substance use and sleep appears to be bidirectional, meaning that psychoactive drugs directly cause sleep disturbances, while difficulty sleeping may be a trigger for lapse and relapse of drug use. There is also increasing evidence that links substance use to disturbances in circadian rhythms, one's internal body clock that tells the body when to sleep, wake, and eat and that underlies most autonomic physiological processes (Becker-Krail & McClung, 2016; Hasler et al., 2012; Parekh, Ozburn, & McClung, 2015). Circadian disruption and insomnia have been hypothesized to be partly related to a hyperactivity of the dopamine system and dysfunction within regulation of the GABA system (Monti et al., 2013). Disturbed sleep during late childhood and adolescence appears to accelerate not only the onset of initial substance use but also the development of clinically defined substance use disorders (Hasler, Kirisci, & Clark, 2016; Logan et al., 2018; Mike et al., 2016).

Many of the drugs discussed in the next chapters that promote sedation also limit and disrupt the sleep cycle, restricting the amount of time spent in Stages 3 and 4 while also having significant effects on REM sleep. Likewise, stimulants minimize the need for sleep, creating additional health and mental health issues along with their physical and psychological dependency (Chan et al., 2013). One study found that nearly 70% of individuals admitted for detoxification reported sleep problems prior to admission, while 80% in the study who reported sleep problems related them to their substance use (Roncero et al., 2012), though long-term abstinence can reverse sleep issues (Angarita et al., 2016). Having dreams about using drugs has been found to correspondingly increase cravings during waking hours (Tanguay et al., 2015), as has insomnia (Kaplan et al., 2014). Thus, recalled dreams have the potential to act as a trigger, further contributing to the argument that more emphasis should be placed on discussing sleeping and dreaming during addiction treatment.

QUIZ

1. What is the quickest way to administer a drug to produce a change to the central nervous system?
2. When a person requires more and more of the psychoactive drug to produce the same feeling of euphoria, what have they developed?
3. Which organ is responsible for metabolizing psychoactive drugs?

4. More commonly associated with physics, what is the term used to measure the time it takes for a drug to clear the body?
5. Which neurotransmitter is responsible for producing the sensation of pleasure?
6. The process of addiction consists of three separate but integrated dimensions. Pharmacology is primarily concerned with which of these?
7. What must psychoactive drugs pass through in order to alter the functioning of the central nervous system?
8. Which neurotransmitter do OxyContin, codeine, and methadone affect in the central nervous system?
9. What is the most common means through which the body eliminates a psychoactive drug?
10. While the majority of hallucinogens affect one neurotransmitter, cannabis affects a totally different one. What are these two neurotransmitters?

LEARNING ACTIVITIES

Choose one psychoactive drug, either one you are already familiar with or one you have been wanting to learn more about, and answer the following questions:

1. Your drug
   a. What psychoactive drug did you choose?
   b. Why did you choose it?
   c. Provide its:
      - Generic name
      - Trade name(s), if any
      - Slang name(s), if any
      - Systemic name
      - Molecular formula
   d. To what class/family does the psychoactive drug belong?
   e. For what purpose is the psychoactive drug generally administered?

2. Dosage and pharmacokinetics
    a. What is a typical therapeutic (or non-medical) dose of this psychoactive drug in a non-tolerant user?
    b. In what forms (tablets, capsules, liquid) and strengths is the psychoactive drug available?
    c. List the routes by which the psychoactive drug is commonly consumed and explain why each route is used.
    d. How lipid soluble is this psychoactive drug?
    e. What effects does the degree of lipid solubility have on the drug's pharmacokinetics?
    f. How quickly is the psychoactive drug metabolized?
    g. Where in the body is it metabolized?
    h. Are there any active metabolites? If so, what are they called?
    i. By what route(s) is the psychoactive drug primarily excreted?
    j. What is the half-life of the drug?
    k. How long do the effects of a typical therapeutic or non-medical dose of the drug generally last?
3. Mechanism of action and effects
    a. Does the psychoactive drug act on a specific receptor/neurotransmitter? Which one(s)?
    b. Draw a diagram indicating the process of interaction at the neuron level.
    c. What are this psychoactive drug's most important desired effects?
    d. What are its most prominent side effects?
    e. How does taking the drug affect sleeping and dreaming?
    f. Weigh the potential benefits of taking this psychoactive drug against the risk of adverse consequences and determine the utility of your drug compared to its associated risks.
4. Drug interactions
    a. Identify one psychoactive drug from each of the following four groupings:
        - CNS depressant
        - CNS stimulant

- Hallucinogen
- Psychotherapeutic agent

b. Describe what would occur if the psychoactive drug you have been describing were taken with each of these other psychoactive substances.

NOTE

1. Appendix A provides a detailed summary of which neurotransmitters each drug family affects.

CHAPTER 2

Depressants

OVERVIEW

The common feature of all drugs placed into the large pharmacological family of depressants is that they slow down the functioning of the central nervous system (CNS). The majority do so by affecting GABA; however, a special subgroup, opioids, do so by initially directly affecting endorphins, and in turn indirectly affecting GABA and dopamine. Other members of this group that work in unique manners are antihistamines, inhalants, and the world's most misused psychoactive substance, alcohol.

2.1 SEDATIVE-HYPNOTICS

Four types of CNS depressants are found in this subcategory: barbiturates, non-barbiturate sedative-hypnotics, benzodiazepines, and cyclopyrrolones (Z-drugs). However, these drugs not only produce sedation, inducing sleep though not enhancing dreaming, they most importantly also act as anxiolytics, reducing anxiety. They are all synthetic psychoactive drugs that produce their effects by inhibiting neurotransmission and thus decreasing the likelihood of an action potential occurring within the CNS, which means that there is less likelihood of a message being passed from one neuron to the next. All four act as bonding agents, allowing the GABA being released from the sending neuron (axon terminal) to adhere better to receptor sites at the receiving end of other neurons (dendrite), increasing the likelihood that the message received will produce an inhibiting effect on the brain. These drugs do not lead to an increased production of GABA, but rather increase the likelihood that the natural GABA individuals have in their brains will move across the synapse and create the cascade effect needed to slow the CNS. This is referred to as increasing GABA affinity to the GABA receptor. This process also leads to a change in dopamine, producing feelings of euphoria along with sedation (Luscher, 2016).

Barbiturates

slang: *general:* abbots, barbs, barbies, downers, goofballs, seekies, sleepers, stumblers

amobarbital (Amytal): blues, blue angels, blue clouds, blue devils

amobarbital (Tuinal): Christmas trees, double trouble, rainbows

pentobarbital (Nembutal): nebbies, yellows, yellow dolls, yellow jackets

secobarbital (Seconal): reds, red birds, red bullets, red devils, seccy

The synthesis of all barbiturates is based upon barbituric acid (figure 2.1), which was named for Saint Barbara, the patron saint of artillerymen, miners, and others who work with explosives and military hardware (New Advent, 2009). Barbituric acid was first synthesized in 1864 by Adolf von Baeyer, though it was not used medicinally until 1904, followed soon after by phenobarbital in 1912. The sedative effects of phenobarbital are such that it was used as "truth serum" to produce a sense of relaxation, allowing queries to be answered by otherwise unwilling respondents. Other members of this group of sedative-hypnotics include amobarbital (Amytal), secobarbital (Seconal), pentobarbital (Nembutal), and Tuinal (see table 2.1). While over 2,000 barbiturate

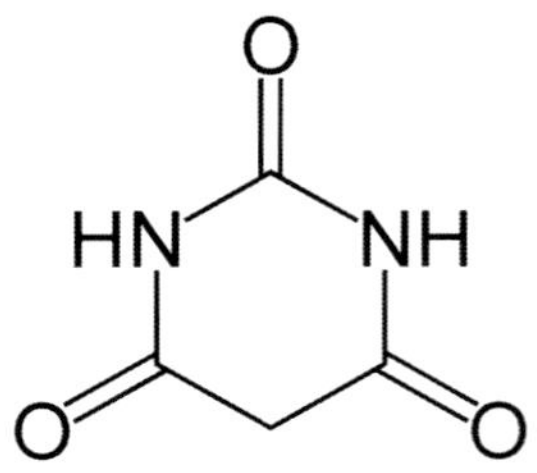

O
HN NH
O O

Figure 2.1: Chemical Structure of Barbituric Acid[1]

Source: Wikimedia Commons

Table 2.1: Major Barbiturates

Name	Chemical Name	Chemical Formula	Medical Use	Brand Name
Allobarbital	5,5-diallylbarbituric acid	$C_{10}H_{12}N_2O_3$	insomnia	Dialog
Amobarbital	5-ethyl-5-isopentylbarbituric acid	$C_{11}H_{18}N_2O_3$	insomnia, sedation, seizures	Amytal Tuinal
Barbital	5,5-diethylbarbituric acid	$C_8H_{12}N_2O_3$	insomnia	Malonal Veronal
Butalbital	5-allyl-5-isobutylbarbituric acid	$C_{11}H_{16}N_2O_3$	tension headaches	Fiorinal Lanorinal
Butobarbital	5-butyl-5-ethylbarbituric acid	$C_{10}H_{16}N_2O_3$	insomnia, sedation	Soneryl
Methylphenobarbital	5-ethyl-1-methyl-5-phenylbarbituric acid	$C_{13}H_{14}N_2O_3$	epilepsy, daytime sedation	Prominal
Pentobarbital	5-ethyl-5-(1-methylbutyl)barbituric acid	$C_{11}H_{18}N_2O_3$	insomnia, sedation, seizures	Nembutal
Phenobarbital	5-ethyl-5-phenylbarbituric acid	$C_{12}H_{12}N_2O_3$	epilepsy	Luminal Gardenal
Secobarbital	5-allyl-5-(1-methylbutyl)barbituric acid	$C_{12}H_{18}N_2O_3$	insomnia, sedation, seizures	Quinalbarbitone Seconal Tuinal

Source: European Monitoring Centre for Drugs and Drug Addiction, 2015a

derivatives have been synthesized, only about 50 have ever been used medically (European Monitoring Centre for Drugs and Drug Addiction [EMCDDA], 2015a).

Barbiturates were created with the goal of aiding sleep, but it was also discovered that in small doses, barbiturates were able to relieve anxiety, tension, convulsions, and high blood pressure by producing calmness and muscular relaxation through enhancing the bonding of GABA. Barbiturates were among the first psychoactive agents used to treat individuals with expressed mental health issues entailing excessive anxiety and psychosis. However, it was soon realized that individuals not requiring this drug for therapeutic use would experience a significant sense of euphoria when self-administering. Presently, the most common use for barbiturates is to induce a medical coma when a person has suffered traumatic injuries and needs to be sedated, as an anaesthetic, or to prevent epileptic seizures (Hancock & McKim, 2018).

Intoxication from barbiturates is characterized by deficits in attention, memory, judgment, cognitive ability, and fine and gross psychomotor skills, along with change in affect, producing mood swings, emotional depression, and/or hostility. Physical signs of barbiturate use include glazed eyes, dry skin, rapid breathing, rapid pulse, high blood pressure, cramps, nausea, tremors, and mild to severe convulsions. As is the case with most psychoactive drugs, it was readily noted that after ongoing use, physical dependency to the drug developed. As well, larger doses of barbiturates produce impaired judgment, loss of coordination, delayed reaction time, slurred speech, decreased respiration, and impaired short-term memory. These effects make it dangerous to drive a car or perform other complex tasks while consuming barbiturates (Desmond et al., 1972). The use of barbiturates during pregnancy has been linked to birth defects and behavioural abnormalities in newborns (appendix B).

Barbiturates disrupt both the sleep and dream cycles; thus, while historically people often took these drugs to aid in sleeping, it is now known that they do not produce normal sleep patterns, with users feeling tired and irritable upon waking, regardless of what early advertising of the drugs promoted. In a study involving 40 individuals with epilepsy, the use of phenobarbital led to an increase in light sleep (Stages 1 and 2), while REM sleep was decreased (Wolf, Roder-Wanner, & Brede, 1984).

Barbiturates are among the few psychoactive agents that are not readily flushed from the human body, as they accumulate in body fat. With regular use, tolerance develops to their effects; it develops more slowly to the harmful effects than to the sleep-inducing or intoxicating effects. Barbiturates bind to receptors adjacent to GABA receptors on chloride channels (figure 2.3), leading to the retention of GABA, which increases the flux of chloride. At high doses or when mixed with other CNS depressants, particularly alcohol, respiratory depression and/or cardiovascular depression leading to death are possible. Overdose for a healthy, 170-pound male varies from two grams for amobarbital and pentobarbital to five grams for phenobarbital (table 1.4), though the lethal dose level is lower if the individual is consuming any other CNS depressant due to the synergetic pharmacodynamic effect. Also, with continued heavy use, the difference between the effective dose and the fatal dose narrows, and the risk of fatal overdose increases (EMCDDA, 2015a). Symptoms of an overdose include incoordination, slurred speech, difficulty in thinking, coma, and respiratory and cardiovascular depression with hypotension and shock, leading to renal failure and death. If barbiturate poisoning or overdose occurs, medical intervention is always required. This is one substance for which non-medical withdrawal management is typically not a viable option. If overdose occurs, the first step is to remove any unabsorbed drug through vomiting, and then work to maintain respiration through the administration of oxygen, and if that is not effective, intubation or tracheostomy (Hancock & McKim, 2018).

Physical and psychological dependency are common with all barbiturates. Not only is overdose a risk, but withdrawal is also potentially life threatening, and the recommended process is therefore always a taper, often using another barbiturate that has a longer half-life. Abrupt withdrawal for a person who is physically dependent leads to progressive restlessness, anxiety, and possible delirium, delusions, grand mal seizures, and potentially death. Withdrawal symptoms will appear shortly after abrupt discontinuation and, if not fatal, can last upwards of two weeks. Temporary sleep disturbances may lead a user to incorrectly decide that more of the drug is required, leading to further risk of overdose. There is a high cross-tolerance between barbiturates and other depressants, particularly alcohol (Hancock & McKim, 2018). Barbiturates have been used as part of drug cocktails both for lethal injections for individuals who have committed a capital crime and for those who have chosen a medically assisted death.

Non-Barbiturate Sedative-Hypnotics (NBSHs)

slang: *general:* knockout drops

chloral hydrate mixed with alcohol: Mickey Finn

Doriden: doors

Quaaludes: Joe Fridays, lemons, lewds, lovers, Q, Quads, Vitamin Q, soapers, wallbangers

Non-barbiturate sedative-hypnotics are a group of drugs with actions very similar to those of barbiturates, but they do not contain the barbituric acid molecule. Given the utility, but also the risk, of synthetic barbiturates, pharmaceutical companies attempted to find a new drug group that would be a "safe, non-addicting" alternative to barbiturates. The group of drugs that emerged included glutethimide (Doriden), methyprylon (Noludar), methaqualone (Dormutil, Mandrax, Parest, Quaalude, Somnafac), and ethchlorvynol (Placidyl). Like barbiturates, they inhibit GABA in the CNS; however, despite the lack of barituric acid as part of their chemical structure, they also quickly produce physical dependency and have the same withdrawal and overdose risks as traditional barbiturates. Case studies have suggested that methaqualone may possess an abuse potential exceeding that of any of the barbiturates (Morgan, 1990). Like barbiturates, NBSHs produce sedation, but again, REM sleep patterns are disrupted. While Quaaludes and other NBSHs allow a person to obtain the physical rest required while asleep, they can decrease Stage 4 sleep and suppress REM sleep, leading to psychotic-like behaviour in as little as three weeks. For an individual recovering from NBSH use, REM sleep significantly increases over time (Mirmiran et al., 1983). Additionally, tolerance is quick to develop, and sleep, initially produced by 300 milligrams of the drug, can eventually require up to 2,000 milligrams. For a typical 120-pound woman, the lethal range begins at 5,400 to 5,500 milligrams (Carroll & Gallo, 1985).

At low doses, glutethimide and methaqualone are likely to produce calmness, sedation, drowsiness, relaxation, and lethargy, and they are just as likely to cause nausea, gastrointestinal discomfort, and disruption of eating patterns. Large doses of these drugs produce a barbiturate-like intoxication. NBSHs are associated with the rapid deterioration of vital signs during overdose. However, at high doses, respiratory depression is less marked than with barbiturates, and the risk of accidental overdose is therefore somewhat lessened. Respiratory depression can be intensified by the simultaneous administration of other CNS depressants. Cardiovascular complications and seizures with these psychoactive agents can be quite severe, with cardiovascular collapse and coma resulting from misuse. Other common effects include dizziness, visual impairment, lethargy, and the exacerbation of existing pain, as well as the previously discussed reduction of REM sleep, resulting in less dreaming. The effects of long-term use are primarily continuations of short-term effects because of the accumulation of the drug in the body. Even after discontinuing drug use, a lack of motor coordination, unsteadiness, muscle weakness, visual difficulties, thinking and memory impairment, slurring of speech, tremors, irritability, and apathy may remain (Gass, 2008).

Tolerance to the sleep-inducing effects and to the euphoric and sedative effects of NBSHs develops rapidly, as it does with barbiturates. If the user wishes to maintain the original intensity of any of these desired effects, the size of the daily dose must be increased. A high degree of cross-tolerance occurs between these drugs and both alcohol and barbiturates, and both physical and psychological dependency can occur quickly. Withdrawal, while not as severe as with barbiturates, may also be life threatening and must be medically monitored. Early withdrawal symptoms tend to occur within 24 hours after the last dose and may include sweating and fever alternating with chills, nausea and vomiting, abdominal cramps, abnormally rapid heart rate, headache, tremors, muscle twitches and spasms, agitation and hyperactivity, insomnia, or brief periods of agitated sleep accompanied by nightmares, uncontrollable facial grimaces, psychosis-like syndromes characterized by disorientation, delirium, hallucinations and paranoid delusions, and grand mal seizures. Some of these symptoms, including grand mal seizures, have abruptly occurred in regular users without their abstaining from the drug. The caution necessary in using barbiturates also applies to the use of all NBSHs (Gass, 2008).

Benzodiazepines

slang: *general:* benzos, downers, sleep away, tranqs, Z's

Librium: libbys

Rohypnol: forget-me, Mexican valium, roachies, roofies

Valium: foofoo, howards, mother's little helpers, V's, vals, vallies, yellows

Xanax: dogbones, footballs, four bars, X-box, xanny, zanis, zanibars

Benzodiazepines were the third type of sedative-hypnotics to be synthesized. While the first benzodiazepines were marketed not long after non-barbiturate sedative-hypnotics, their chemical formula was radically different, making them far safer in terms of both withdrawal and overdose (figure 2.2).

The pharmaceutical industry synthesized an estimated 2,000 benzodiazepines worldwide over the course of the 20th century, all differing to various degrees in terms of their potency, speed of onset, and duration of effects. Of these, currently 35 are subject to international control under the Convention on Psychotropic Substances of 1971 (UNODC, 2016). Benzodiazepines also act upon gamma-aminobutyric acid; however, they do not increase the brain's creation of GABA in any way. Benzodiazepines have receptor sites distinct

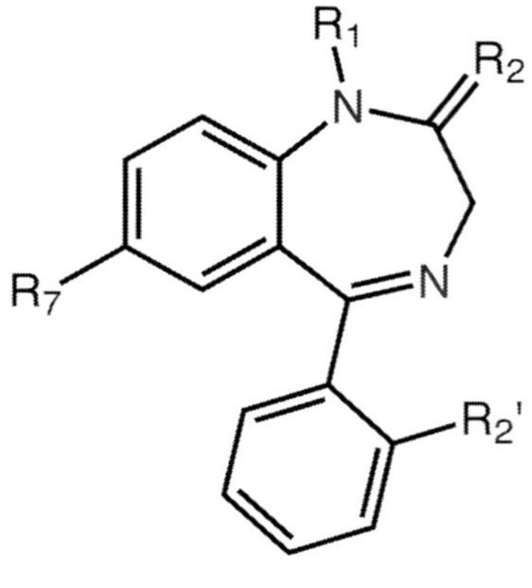

Figure 2.2: Benzodiazepine Chemical Structure

Source: Wikimedia Commons

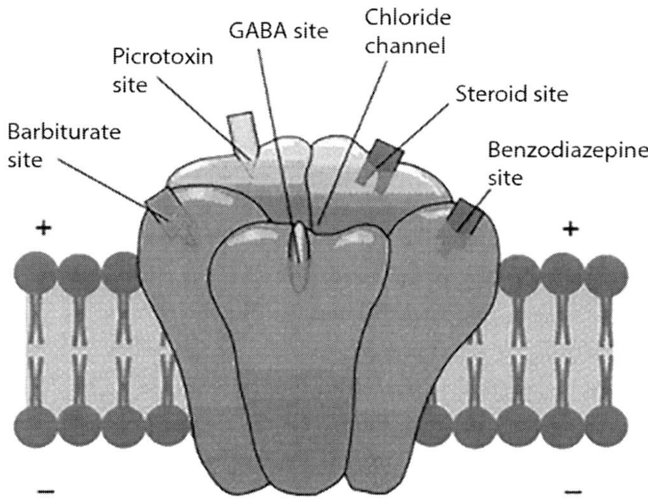

Figure 2.3: Barbiturate and Benzodiazepine Receptor Sites

Source: International Federation of Clinical Chemistry and Laboratory Medicine (IFCC), Neurotransmitters and Their Receptors (http://www.ifcc.org/media/476986/ejifcc2004vol15no3pp061-067.pdf, 2004)

from those of barbiturates (figure 2.3). It is known that benzodiazepines enhance GABA-mediated chloride influx, which inhibits neural activity (figure 2.4). When this occurs in the reticular activating system, anxiety along with general mental activity in the brain is reduced. However, extended use of benzodiazepines decreases the synthesis of GABA in certain areas of the brain (Advokat, Comtay, & Julien, 2018).

Benzodiazepines were introduced to replace barbiturates and NBSHs in the treatment of anxiety and insomnia. These drugs are much safer, as they rarely cause a fatal overdose. The typical lethal range for a 170-pound male is anywhere from approximately 1,000 to 7,500 five-milligram tablets, though it can take less for some members of this drug family, such as Serax and Halcion, to produce an overdose. While benzodiazepines are much less likely to produce an overdose than either barbiturates or NBSHs, overdose is still possible, particularly when benzodiazepines are mixed with another CNS depressant, such as alcohol (Hancock & McKim, 2018).

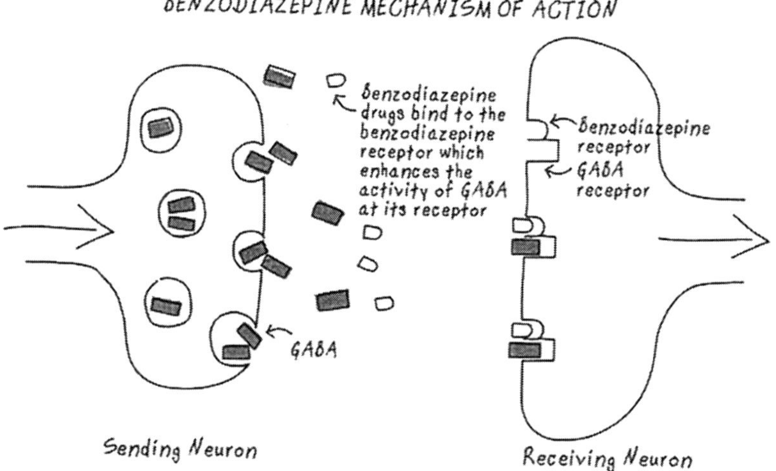

Figure 2.4: Benzodiazepine Mechanism of Action

Source: B. Sproule, *Pharmacology and Drug Abuse*, 2nd edition (Toronto: Centre for Addiction and Mental Health, 2004)

The short-term effects of benzodiazepines are variable, depending upon the dose, the personality of the user, and the user's anxiety level. They include

- calming hyperactivity tension and agitation;
- relaxing muscles and relieving anxiety;
- combatting withdrawal effects of other depressant drugs, primarily alcohol;
- impairing muscle coordination;
- producing dizziness, low blood pressure, and/or fainting; and,
- inhibiting short-term memory.

While a normal therapeutic dose produces relaxation and a feeling of psychological well-being, higher doses may produce a state similar to that of intoxication from other sedative-hypnotics. Excessive use results in cognitive impairment, drowsiness, lethargy, disorientation, confusion, memory impairment, trance-like episodes, double vision, personality alterations, and other symptoms resembling those of drunkenness, including contributing to traffic collisions and falls in the elderly (Sylvestre et al., 2012). Benzodiazepines can also sometimes produce unexpected paradoxical effects, such as agitation, insomnia, aggression, rage, and hostility—the very symptoms they have been prescribed to alleviate. High doses can lead to over-sedation, and in seniors they can contribute to erroneous diagnosis of Alzheimer's or other forms of dementia (Centre for Addiction and Mental Health, 2012), though prolonged use of benzodiazepines does increase the risk of developing Alzheimer's disease (Tapiainen et al., 2018).

Use of benzodiazepines for as little as three to four weeks can lead to both physical and psychological dependency, and use for as little as six months has been linked to increased risks of both suicidal ideation and suicide attempts (McCall et al., 2016). Withdrawal from minor tranquilizers is like that from other sedative-hypnotics. Commonly observed effects include tremors, sweating, hypersensitivity to sensory stimuli, blurred vision, tingling sensations, tinnitus (ringing of the ears), insomnia, headache, difficulties in concentration, anorexia, increased lethargy, indifference to one's surroundings, irritability and emotional flatness, disorientation and confusion, gastrointestinal upsets, sexual dysfunction, increased anxiety, panic attacks, insomnia, menstrual irregularities, and memory, cognitive, and psychomotor impairment. Withdrawal symptoms range in intensity from progressive anxiety, restlessness, insomnia, and irritability in mild cases, to delirium and convulsions in severe cases. As with other psychoactive drugs, the intensity of the reaction depends on the dose level, the duration of use, and individual user differences. However, there is not the risk of seizure as occurs with barbiturates and NBSHs (Baldwin et al., 2013; Lader, 2011).

Benzodiazepines impact all activities of the brain associated with the sleep cycle. In general, while they induce Stages 1 and 2 sleep cycles, they reduce the amount of time a person spends in Stages 3 and 4. Their major negative effect, however, is suppressing REM sleep (Cascade & Kalali, 2008; Pagel & Parnes, 2001). For example, Xanax (table 2.2) has been demonstrated to drastically reduce the amount of time spent in Stage 3 sleep and produces delays in moving into REM. In one study, during the first three nights, use of Xanax led to rapid sedation and prolonged sleep throughout the night. However, by the end of the first week of regular use the drug had lost about 40% of its efficacy, and within three days of drug termination, there was a significant degree of rebound insomnia (Kales et al., 1987). Lorazepam has been shown to decrease Stage 1 sleep and increase Stage 2 sleep while having no impact on Stages 3 or 4, but it significantly decreases the amount of time spent in REM sleep, affecting the mind's ability to process memory (Roth et al., 1980).

Licit benzodiazepines available in Canada are summarized in table 2.2. Flunitrazepam (Rohypnol), which is not legally available in Canada, is the benzodiazepine media reports most commonly link to drug-facilitated sexual assaults, commonly referred to as date rape. However, forensic toxicology shows that only a very small number of such assaults involve the use of "roofies." A number of European studies suggest that alcohol and other licit benzodiazepines are an underestimated problem in such cases, rather than Rohypnol, which is much less readily accessible (EMCDDA, 2008b).

The risk–benefit ratio of benzodiazepines remains positive for most users if used only for a brief time period of two to four weeks. However, after that short window for therapeutic use, issues arise as the risk of dependency increases the longer the drug is administered (Lader, 2011). Whitaker (2005) summarized the findings of several studies that examined the use of Xanax to assist individuals who suffered from panic attacks. The Cross-National Collaborative Panic Study, which involved 1,700 patients in 14 countries, reported that at the end of four weeks, 82% of individuals receiving Xanax were moderately improved or better, compared with 42% of those receiving a placebo. However, by the end of eight weeks, there was no difference among the individuals who remained in the study. In a six-month Canadian study, participants again improved for the first four weeks, with no increased changes over the next month followed by a worsening of symptoms. Even more problematic was that as participants were weaned from the drugs, after six months they were worse off than those treated without drugs. One-quarter of the individuals who had received a treatment

Table 2.2: Regulated Benzodiazepines Available in Canada

Name	Duration of Action (Half-Life in Hours)	Major Trade Name
Sedative-Hypnotics		
Brotizolam	Short (3.5–8)	Lendormin
Estazolam	Intermediate (10–24)	Pro-Som
Flurazepam	Long (25–100)	Dalmane
Loprazolam	Intermediate (12–16)	Dormonoct
Lormetazepam	Short (8–12)	Noctamid
Midazolam	Short (1.5–2.5)	Versed
Nimetazepam	Long (8–27)	Erinin
Nitrazepam	Intermediate (18–24)	Mogadon
Temazepam	Short (7–11)	Restoril
Triazolam	Short (2–4)	Halcion
Anxiolytics		
Alprazolam	Short (4–6)	Xanax
Bromazepam	Long (11–22)	Lexotan, Lectopam
Camazepam	Intermediate (6.5–10.5)	Albego
Chlordiazepoxide	Long (6–30)	Librium
Clobazam	Long (18–50)	Frisium
Clonazepam	Long (30–40)	Rivotril
Clorazepate	Long (40–50)	Tranxene
Clotiazepam	Short (6.5–18)	Trecalmo
Cloxazolam	Long (60–70)	Sepazon
Delorazepam	Long (80–115)	En
Diazepam	Long (25–100)	Valium
Ethyl hoflazepate	Long (50–100)	Meilax
Fludiazepam	Short (2–3)	Erispan
Ketazolam	Long (26–200)	Anseren
Lorazepam	Short/Intermediate (12–16)	Ativan
Medazepam	Long (36–200)	Nobrium
Nordazepam	Long (36–200)	Stilny
Oxazepam	Short (7–20)	Serax
Oxazolam	Long (50–70)	Tranquit
Pinazepam	Long (60–72)	Domar
Prazepam	Long (36–200)	Centrax
Tetrazepam	Short (3–26)	Clinoxan

Sources: European Monitoring Centre for Drugs and Drug Addiction, 2015b; Government of Canada, 2009

with Xanax, after drug use was terminated, suffered from rebound anxiety while suffering on average four times as many panic attacks as those not taking the benzodiazepine. It should be noted that counselling in parallel with drug administration was not part of this clinical trial.

Cyclopyrrolones (Z-Drugs)

slang: sleepers, Zim-Zims

In the late 1980s, a new chemically distinct group of non-benzodiazepine sedative-hypnotic GABA receptor agonists were introduced to treat insomnia: Z-drugs. Cyclopyrrolones include zaleplon (Andante, Sonata, Starnoc), zolpidem (Ambien, Edluar, Intermezzo, Zolpimis), zopiclone (Dopareel, Imovane, Zimovane), and eszopiclone (Lunesta). This group of drugs is molecularly distinct from benzodiazepines as they lack fused benzene and diazepine rings, though they are still able to bind to GABA receptor sites. This subgroup of sedative-hypnotics has a quick onset and short duration of action due to having shorter half-lives than traditional benzodiazepines. This distinct pharmacology led to Z-drugs being purported to be safer than benzodiazepines, and as such they were quickly adopted for therapeutic use with individuals who had difficulty falling asleep or experienced nocturnal

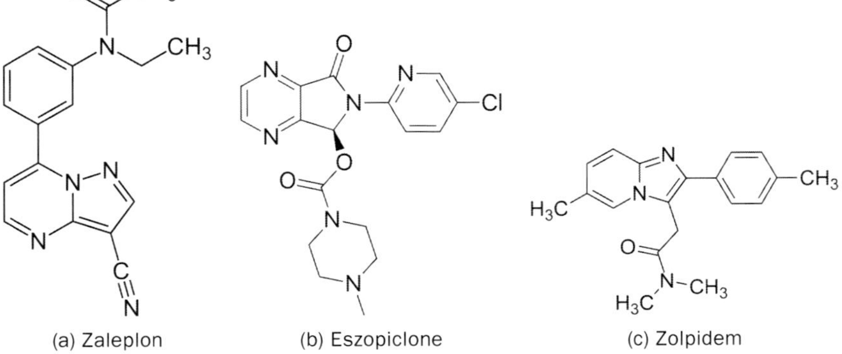

(a) Zaleplon (b) Eszopiclone (c) Zolpidem

Figure 2.5: Cyclopyrrolones

Source: Wikimedia Commons

awakening and/or early morning awakening, as well as to counter anxiety (Ciraulo & Oldham, 2014).

However, as in the past when other new types of sedative-hypnotics were first synthesized and were promised to be non-addicting, it was quickly learned that cyclopyrrolones produce both physical and psychological dependency, which means cessation even after short periods of use produces withdrawal symptoms. Withdrawal, while typically not severe, consists of restlessness, anxiety, and of course, increased insomnia (Pottie et al., 2018). Z-drugs were thought to be associated with significantly fewer accidents and better daytime functioning, total sleep, quality of sleep, and tolerability in older people. However, these perceptions are not based on current evidence or national guidance. As with the benzodiazepines listed in table 2.2, these drugs impair cognition and psychomotor performance, which means that the degree of sedation they produce can also produce confusion and impair a person's ability to operate a motor vehicle or any other type of machinery. While these drugs do produce fewer side effects than traditional benzodiazepines, research indicates that their use increases the risk of developing depression. Recommended length of use is 14 days (Umbricht & Velez, 2015), so any use should be accompanied by counselling to address the underlying reasons the prescription was written.

The most prominent feature of Z-drugs is that they decrease sleep latency and increase the duration of sleep. The duration of Stage 1 sleep is shortened, and the time spent in Stage 2 sleep increased. In most studies, Stages 3 and 4 sleep tended to be increased, but no change and actual decreases have also been observed in clinical trials. The effect of zopiclone on Stages 3 and 4 sleep differs from that of benzodiazepines, which suppress slow-wave sleep. While the onset of REM sleep can be delayed by cyclopyrrolones, they do not appear to reduce the total duration of REM sleep, which is a positive (Nu-Pharm, 2009; Sanofi-Aventis, 2018). In 2014 Health Canada put a recommended dosage on zopiclone due to the adverse behaviours its users were experiencing, including impairment lasting for up to two days. Amnesia can result from using this drug, as highlighted by reports of people getting out of bed while not fully awake after taking cyclopyrrolones and unknowingly engaging in activities, with no memory of the action the next day (Sanofi-Aventis, 2018).

2.2 ANTIHISTAMINES

slang: T's and blues: Tripelennamine when mixed with pentazocine (Talwin)

Antihistamines are synthetic central nervous system depressants whose initial and primary therapeutic utility remains in counteracting allergy symptoms produced by excessive histamine activity (H_1-receptor site) along with regulation of stomach acid (H_2-receptor site), though their potential use has greatly expanded with the relatively recent discovery of H_3- and H_4-receptor sites (table 2.3). Histamine, an organic amine that also serves as a neurotransmitter, was discovered in 1910 by Henry Dale and Patrick Laidlaw. Histamine has the capacity to mediate a range of physiologic functions through its ability to stimulate a range of smooth muscles, including those in the bronchi, gastrointestinal tract, and uterus. However, the most prominent function of histamine is to increase the permeability of capillaries to white blood cells and proteins to allow them to respond to foreign pathogens in infected tissues. Large amounts of histamine are produced in mast cells, which are part of the immune system, in places where the body encounters the outside environment, such as the nose, throat, lungs, and skin. Figure 2.6 illustrates an antihistamine blocking the receptor site so that histamine cells produced by an allergen (mast cell) cannot interact with the receptor, which prevents them from producing any symptoms (Raman-Wilms, 2014).

Antihistamines are structurally similar to histamine and act to prevent histamine-receptor interaction through competition with histamine for histamine receptors. The function of antihistamines is to reduce or block histamines, so they stop the excessive reaction by the body to the allergen. Immune system cells monitor the blood and mucosae for foreign substances, and if either the skin is damaged or the immune system detects a foreign substance, histamine is released from mast cells. Allergens such as pollen, dust mites, mould, and animal dander all work

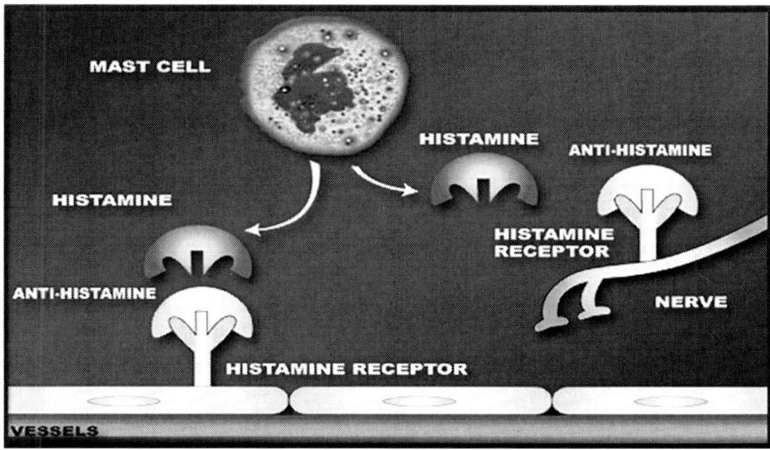

Figure 2.6: Antihistamine Blocking Histamine-Receptor Site

Source: Wikimedia Commons

in the same manner, creating a change in the intracellular calcium and causing the production of large amounts of histamine and other chemical mediators known as leukotrienes. It is the release of these chemicals into the bloodstream that causes inflammatory symptoms such as sneezing, runny nose and eyes, itching, hives, nausea, cramps, diarrhea, bronchoconstriction, edema, sleep disorders, and even stomach ulcers and anaphylactic shock in extreme cases. Allergic reactions are caused by an oversensitivity or exaggerated reaction of the immune system to a specific allergen. Histamine made by cells that line the stomach helps to produce acid for food digestion, while in the CNS histamine also triggers the release of excitatory neurotransmitters such as glutamate and acetylcholine in the cerebral cortex. In this way histamine plays a key role in attention and vigilance and it may have a potential role in mediating health issues as diverse as attention-deficit/hyperactivity disorder, Alzheimer's, and schizophrenia (Esbenshade et al., 2008; Leurs et al., 2009).

Current antihistaminic drugs can inhibit histaminic action at only one of the four distinct histamine-receptor sites. The first antihistamines that were introduced bound at H_1 and worked by inhibiting histamine-induced hay fever, decreasing the allergic inflammation of the mucous membrane inside the nose. They are also used to decrease hives as well as the itch and swelling of insect bites, and to treat the skin condition atopic eczema, allergic conjunctivitis (pink eye), and mild or moderate allergic reactions caused by food allergies, though more severe allergic reactions (anaphylaxis) typically require treatment with adrenaline. H_1-antihistamines tend to be more successful in controlling acute rather than chronic conditions, meaning that they are most useful at the beginning of the hay fever season, when the allergens are present in low concentration, but are of less value with non-seasonal, non-allergic inflammation of the mucous membranes of the nose brought on by environmental or emotional stimuli. Other H_1-antihistamines that have an important antimuscarinic activity (inhibiting the action of acetylcholine), like diphenhydramine (Benadryl, Sominex) and dimenhydrinate (Dramamine, Gravol), are used in preventing or minimizing motion sickness. Diphenhydramine may also be used with Parkinson's sufferers to decrease stiffness and tremors, and the liquid form can be used to relieve the cough due to colds or hay fever, while hydroxyzine has been used to assist in controlling anxiety. Additionally, although these uses are not included in product labelling, cyproheptadine (Periactin) is used as an appetite stimulant in children and adults as well as a vascular headache treatment, promethazine (Histantil) has a local anaesthetic effect, and loratadine (Claritin) and cetirizine (Zyrtec) can be used in combination with asthma medicines before and during exposure to substances that cause the reactions to prevent or reduce bronchospasm. In addition, as all first-generation antihistamines have the capacity to produce drowsiness as a side effect, they are often used as a sleep aid for both adults and children (Chow et al., 2012; Meltzer & Hamilos, 2011; Simons, 2003).

First-generation H_1-antihistamines have poor receptor selectivity and thus readily cross the blood-brain barrier (BBB). In contrast, second- and third-generation H_1-antihistamines have been formulated to be more highly selective and do not cross the BBB as readily, and thus have far fewer adverse side effects. Because they do not produce sedation and have a very low incidence of drowsiness, longer-lasting effects, and increased efficacy, second- and third-generation antihistamines have become the most popular medications for treating the symptoms of allergic rhinitis and chronic urticaria (hives). H_1-antihistamines are not an effective remedy for upper respiratory track infections, as they do not have any ability to mitigate symptoms of the common cold; however, it is primarily because of their ability to induce sedation that they are regularly added to cold medications (Arroll, 2005; Kalpakioglu & Baccioglu, 2012; Leurs, Church, & Tagliatatela, 2002).

In general, when used as recommended, antihistamines are relatively safe over-the-counter psychoactive medications. However, as first-generation antihistamines do cross the BBB into the CNS, and because there are few controls on their purchase, a range of unintended side effects beyond sedation are possible, including decreasing both sympathetic nervous system and serotonin activation in the CNS. Side effects of first-generation H_1-antihistamines include drowsiness; dizziness; mild impairment of CNS function, including perception, concentration, and psychomotor abilities, which is further enhanced by alcohol or other CNS depressants; lethargy; mood enhancement; gastrointestinal discomfort; and appetite suppression. Higher doses can further enhance mood or cause minor hallucinatory effects, especially when mixed with alcohol or other CNS depressant drugs (Hancock & McKim, 2018).

First-generation H_1-antihistamines can also produce confusion and disorientation through their blocking of the neurotransmitter acetylcholine, which in older users resembles the onset of dementia symptoms. Confusion, difficult or painful urination, dizziness, drowsiness, feeling faint, or dryness of mouth, nose, or throat may be more likely to occur in elderly users. Also, nightmares or unusual excitement, nervousness, restlessness, or irritability may be more likely to occur in this population (Levine et al., 2007), as well as a negative impact on episodic memory (Papenberg et al., 2017).

Tolerance to the sedative effects of antihistamines develops with regular use as the liver increases its ability to metabolize the drug. If an antihistamine is regularly used for its psychoactive effects, users may become both psychologically and physically dependent. While first-generation H_1-antihistamines produce less euphoria than other CNS depressants, these drugs do alter CNS functioning and their abuse potential remains moderate because of their easy availability. While antihistamines are used as sleep-inducing agents, and they do assist in producing sedation, this does not necessarily produce high-quality sleep as antihistamines block acetylcholine. This leads to more time spent in Stages 1 and 2 sleep and less in Stages 3 and 4. H_1-antihistamines also reduce REM sleep, impair learning, and reduce work efficiency. They have been implicated in civil aviation, motor vehicle, and boating accidents; deaths resulting from accidental or intentional overdosing in infants and young children; and suicide in teenagers and adults. Some exhibit cardiotoxicity in overdose (Church et al., 2010).

Second-generation histamine H_1-receptor antagonists were developed in the 1980s to reduce or eliminate the sedation and anticholinergic adverse effects that occur with older H_1-antihistamines. They produce fewer negative side effects because of their more limited penetration of the BBB due to being larger in size and their increased binding to the protein in the blood. In addition, these drugs are highly selective for H_1-receptors while also having some anti-inflammatory properties. Thus, second-generation H_1-antihistamines, as well as even newer, third-generation ones, should be used instead of first-generation antihistamines unless sedation is a desired outcome (Church & Church, 2011; Slater, Zechnich, & Haxby, 1999).

Histamine also has a distinct physiological function in regulating the secretion of acid in the stomach, where it stimulates the parietal cells to produce hydrochloric acid, which controls the local bacterial population and therefore serves a protective function for the human body. In the 1970s a new class of synthetic drugs was invented that blocked the action of histamine at its H_2-receptors, the first of these being cimetidine (Tagamet). These drugs are extremely effective in inhibiting histamine-induced gastric acid secretion. H_2-receptor antagonist drugs like cimetidine and ranitidine (Zantac) rapidly established a place in the treatment of conditions involving the hypersecretion of gastric acid, such as peptic ulcers. By reducing acid secretions in the stomach, H_2-receptors are useful in treating heartburn, gastric reflux, and esophagitis stress ulcers of the stomach and digestive tract. They can also reduce the effects of Zollinger-Ellison syndrome, which produces tumour cells that release large amounts of gastric acid secretions, and can also promote healing of the syndrome. Most side effects of H_2-antihistamines are due to cross-reactivity with unintended receptors. For example, cimetidine has been identified as antagonizing testosterone receptors at high doses (Leurs et al., 2009; Raman-Wilms, 2014).

H_3-receptor antagonists are a newer classification first categorized in 1999 that block the action of histamine at H_3-receptor sites. H_3-receptor expression is prominent in the basal ganglia, hippocampus, hypothalamus, and frontal cortex in humans, though receptor sites have been found throughout the brain. The precise signalling events that contribute to neurotransmitter release by H_3-receptors is still not well understood, but it is known that they have neurological and cognitive enhancing effects. This has made them of great interest for their potential in addressing neurodegenerative conditions such as Alzheimer's disease, attention-deficit/hyperactivity disorder, and schizophrenia (Esbenshade et al., 2008).

H_4-antagonists were only discovered in 2000 as an outcome of the human genome project. Initial studies describing the expression of the H_4-receptor suggest that it has a moderating role in the immune system in relation to asthma, allergic rhinitis, and pruritus (itching). H_4-receptors have become labelled as the histamine receptor of the immune system due to their association with blood cells and lymphoid tissues. H_4-receptors have also been linked to a range of inflammatory responses mediated by histamine, including chemotaxis (cell movement in response to environmental stimuli), cell recruitment, mobilization of intracellular calcium, and upregulation of adhesion molecule expression. There is substantial evidence that many of the actions of histamine not explained by either H_1-receptors or H_2-receptors can be attributed to H_4-receptors. Therefore, there is great potential for H_4-receptor antagonists to serve as therapeutic agents in treating a range of conditions, including allergic

Table 2.3: Antihistamines and Their Trade Names by Type and Generation

Substance	Trade Name
First-Generation H_1-Antihistamines	
Alimemazine	Nedeltran, Panectyl, Repeltin, Temaril, Therafene, Theralene, Theraligene, Vallergan, Vanectyl
Antazoline	Otrivine-Antistin, Refresh Eye Allergy Relief, Vasocon-A
Azatadine	Optimine
Brompheniramine	Bromfed, Bromfenex, Dimetapp, Lodrane
Buclizine	Buclina, Migraleve, Upanta
Carbinoxamine	Clistin, Histex PD, Palgic, Rhinopront, Rondec
Chlorcyclizine	Di-Paralene, Mantadil, Pruresidine, Trihistan
Chlorpheniramine	Aller-Chlor, Allergy Relief, Chlo-Amine, Chlor-Mal, ChlorTan, Chlor-Trimeton, Ed ChlorPed, Ed-Chlortan, PediaTan, Triaminic Allergy
Cinnarizine	Stugeron, Stunarone
Clemastine	Allerhist-1, Tavist-1
Cyclizine	Bonine, Emoquil, Marezine, Valoid
Cyproheptadine	Periactin, Peritol
Dexbrompheniramine	Conex, Desihist, Dexaphen Dexophed, Disobrom, Disophrol, Dixaphedrine, Drexophed, Drixomed, Drixoral Cold and Allergy, Pharmadrine
Dexchlorpheniramine	Polaramine
Dimetindene	Fenistil
Diphenhydramine	Benadryl, Nytol, Sominex, Valdrene
Diphenylpyraline	Allergen, Arbid, Belfene, Diafen, Hispril, Histyn, Lergobine, Lyssipol, Mepiben, Neargal
Doxylamine	Diclectin, Extra Strength Tylenol Sinus Nighttime Caplet, Neocitran Cold & Flu Syrup
Hydroxyzine	Atrasx, Hyzine, Vistaril
Meclizine (dimenhydrinate)	Antivert, Bonamine, Dramamine, Postafen, Sea Legs
Mepyramine (pyrilamine)	Maximum Strength MIDOL PMS
Methdilazine	Dilosyn, Tacaryl
Pheniramine	Avil, Delhistine D, Visine-A
Phenyltoloxamine	Aceta-Gesic, Dologesic, Duraxin, Ed-Flex, Flextra-650, Novagesic, Pain-gesic, Phenylgesic

Substance	Trade Name
Promethazine	Atosil, Avomine, Farganesse, Lergigan, Phenergan, Promethegan, Prothiazine, Receptozine, Romergan
Thonzylamine	Nasopen, Poly Hist
Trimeprazine	Nedeltran, Panectyl, Repeltin, Temaril, Therafene, Theralene, Theraligene, Vallergan, Vanectyl
Tripelennamine	Di-Delmaine, Pyribenzamine (PBZ), Vaginex
Second-Generation H_1-Antihistamines	
Cetirizine	Reactine, Zyrtec
Dexchlorpheniramine	Polaramine
Fexofenadine	Allegra, Telfast
Kettotifen	Alaway, Claritin Eye, Zadien, Zaditor
Mequitazine	Primalan
Mizolastine	Mizollen
Rupatadine	Alergoliber, Painure, Ralif, Rinialer, Rupafin, Rupax
Terfenadine	Seldane
Third-Generation H_1-Antihistamines	
Desloratidine	Aerius, Claramax, Clarinex, Dazit, Delot, Deselex, Neoclarityn
Levocetirizine	Xyzal
Loratadine	Claritin
First-Generation H_2-Antihistamines	
Cimetidine	Tagamet
Ranitidine	Zantac
Second-Generation H_2-Antihistamines	
Famotidine	Gaster, Pepcid, Pepcidine
Lafutidine	Lafaxid, Lemeiting, Stogar
Nizatidine	Axid, Tazac
Roxatidine	Roxit
H_3-Antihistamines	
Ciproxifan	
Clobenpropit	
Conessine	
H_4-Antihistamines	
Thioperamide	

and inflammatory conditions affecting the lungs, skin, and gastrointestinal system; inflammatory and neuropathic pain; acute and chronic pruritus; hearing disorders; rheumatoid arthritis; and inflammatory bowel disease. The recent identification of H_4-receptors in the nervous system and certain regions of the brain may also suggest a role in central or executive functions (Engelhardt et al., 2009; Liu, 2014).

2.3 INHALANTS, SOLVENTS, AND ANAESTHETIC GASES

slang: *general:* air blast, bolt, boppers, climax, huff, kick, paint, rush, oz, spray
amyl nitrate: aimes, Amsterdam special, boppers, poppers, rush
gammahydroxybutyrate (GHB) and/or gamma butyrolactone (GBL): cherry meth, easy lay, fantasy, G, Gamma-O, grievous bodily harm, goop, growth hormone booster, jib, liquid ecstasy, liquid E, oxy-sleep, salty water, scoop, Vita G
isobutyl nitrate: poppers, quicksiliver, rush snappers, whiteout
nitrous oxide: balloons, buzz bomb, laughing gas, moon gas, nangs, nitro, nos, nox, whippets, whip-its
rubber cement ball that is burned and inhaled: snotball

Another distinct CNS depressant subgroup is inhalants, which include volatile gases—substances that exist in a gaseous form at body temperature—refrigerants, solvents, general anaesthetics, and propellants (table 2.4). Except for nitrous oxide, more commonly known as laughing gas, and related aliphatic nitrates, all inhalants are hydrocarbons. The misuse of these substances has been labelled volatile substance abuse (VSA). As these are typically one of the first kinds of drugs misused by youth, VSA is a significant public health concern. In addition, long-term exposure to solvents in the workplace has also been linked to a range of health issues in older adults, particularly dementia. It is generally believed that solvents alter CNS functioning through one of three means: altering the structure of lipid membranes by impairing ion channels; altering enzymes that bind to the brain's membrane; or producing toxic metabolites. While primarily affecting GABA, volatile substances also exert their complex effects on dopamine, glutamate, and serotonin receptor systems, as well as on cell membranes and ion channels (Brennan & Van Hout, 2014; Ciechanowski, 2012; Howard & Garland, 2012).

These substances not only have depressant effects but can also produce minor hallucinogenic effects upon the CNS. As solvents are inhaled, entry into the brain is extremely quick and the onset of effects virtually immediate, producing feelings of relaxation and warmth within 8 to 15 seconds and with effects generally lasting several hours. This class of psychoactive drugs has a significant abuse liability. The initial mood-enhancement effect is typically characterized by light-headedness, exhilaration, fantasy images, and excitation. Negative effects include nausea, increased salivation, sneezing and coughing, loss of coordination, depressed reflexes, and sensitivity to light, along with skin irritation and burns around the mouth and nose. In some users, feelings of invincibility may lead to reckless, dangerous, violent, or erratic behaviour. Other physical effects include pallor, thirst, weight loss, nosebleeds, bloodshot eyes, and sores on the nose and mouth (Hancock & McKim, 2018). Chronic use creates a range of medical problems, including damage to the cardiovascular, pulmonary, renal, and hepatic systems. VSA occurs primarily during early adolescence, a critical period of brain maturation during which the brain undergoes dramatic changes that improve its efficiency. This entire process can be negatively affected by solvent abuse, as can loss of boundaries between grey and white matter (Takagi, Lubman, & Yu, 2011).

Some solvents, such as benzene, can cause a reduction in the formation of blood cells in the bone marrow, while others may impair the functioning of the liver, and still others may impair the functioning of the liver and kidneys. Contrarily, amyl nitrate and butyl nitrate dilate blood vessels. Deep inhalation or sniffing repeatedly over a short period of time may result in disorientation and loss of self-control, unconsciousness, seizures, or hallucinations, both auditory and visual. Amyl and butyl nitrate have gained popularity among gay men to enhance sex as, along with producing euphoria, they open blood vessels, increasing blood flow, which relaxes smooth muscle. Smooth muscles are found in the bladder, digestive tract, vagina, and anal sphincter. Inhaling amyl or butyl nitrate also leads to a temporary reduction in blood pressure, which causes an increase in heart rate and a sense of light-headedness (Brennan & Van Hout, 2014). There have been some links made between the use of these two nitrogen-based inhalants and Kaposi's sarcoma, a rare form of cancer affecting the immune system (Canadian Centre on Substance Abuse, 2006). Long-term exposure to solvents in industrial settings has also been linked to the development of cancer (de Vocht et al., 2009).

The most commonly used nitrogen-based volatile substance is nitrous oxide, referred to as laughing gas. At room temperature, it is a non-flammable, colourless gas, with a slightly sweet taste and odour. Nitrous oxide is one of the oldest anaesthetic drugs, in use since the mid-1800s, with a high lethal dose level (table 1.4). Its therapeutic use has historically been limited to dentistry and obstetrics, where it is used to mask the pain women experience during labour and delivery because of its lower anaesthetic potency and anxiolytic properties. More recently, research has examined its therapeutic utility with individuals who suffer from treatment-resistant depression, as its mechanism of action is similar to that of ketamine (chapter 4.4) (Zarate & Machado-Vieira, 2015). Nitrous oxide also acts as a partial mu, kappa, and delta opioid receptor agonist, which is how it affects dopamine activity within the nucleus accumbens, producing feelings of euphoria. This has contributed to a long history of recreational use of nitrous oxide; however, as with all inhalants, chronic use can produce physical and psychological dependency. Chronic recreational use of nitrous oxide has also been associated with vitamin B_{12} deficiency, incontinence, limb spasms, a weakened immune system, memory loss, depression, and accidental overdose leading to death (Kaar et al., 2016).

Toluene has been found to depress neuronal activity by enhancing GABA and inhibiting glutamate neurotransmission, which in turn affects dopamine transmission, producing both sedation and euphoria. Toluene is typical of many carbon-based inhalants in that its administration can cause brain, liver, and kidney damage, hearing loss, memory impairment, and attention deficits. Once inhaled, the extensive capillary surface of the lungs allows for the rapid absorption of inhalants, and blood levels peak rapidly. Death can result from chronic solvent use, and from acute use due to heart failure, asphyxiation, or aspiration. SSD, sudden sniffing death, occurs when the cardiac muscle of a user becomes sensitive to the adrenal hormone epinephrine. If a user is suddenly startled and seeks to flee, suffers a panic attack, or engages in some other form of vigorous activity, epinephrine is secreted, and a dramatic and catastrophic cardiac arrhythmia can occur. The user can die of a heart attack, regardless of age or physical condition. Case studies of SSD have also been reported with butane and propane. As solvents are frequently sniffed from a plastic bag, it is also possible for a user to be rendered unconscious by the drug and accidentally suffocate if the bag is not removed from the face (Chenier, 2001; Ciechanowski, 2012; Office of National Statistics, 2018). Solvents are also among the most problematic psychoactivce agents with respect to issues related to pregnancy (appendix B).

Though first synthesized in the 1960s as an experimental GABA supplement, GHB (gammahydroxybutyrate) and GBL (gamma butyrolactone) are two inhalants that have gained increased attention in recent years. GHB is distinct because, although it is a CNS depressant, it also directly alters dopamine activity (Tunnicliff, 1997). GHB was originally marketed as a surgical anaesthetic but was never approved for sale in North America due to its unpredictable side effects, while GBL is a chemical used in a range of industrial cleaners. GHB can be made from GBL by simply adding a base, such as lye (sodium hydroxide [NaOH]), heating the mixture, and adding vinegar. Acetone is then added and the mixture dried, resulting in GHB powder. Both GBL and GHB can produce unconsciousness when as little as a teaspoon is slipped into an alcoholic drink, producing an enhanced pharmacodynamic effect greater than when either is consumed alone. GHB intoxication can result in a sedative state similar to catalepsy or seizure, and within 5 to 20 minutes the person who has consumed GHB can experience amnesia, nausea, vomiting, confusion, and seizure-like activity. Ingesting too much GHB can lead to respiratory difficulties and a coma-like state, or even death (Brennan & Van Hout, 2014).

In Europe, GHB remains in use as an anaesthetic, a hypnotic agent, a treatment for narcolepsy, and, interestingly, a pharmacological method of suppressing symptoms of alcohol dependence and opioid withdrawal syndrome. GHB serves as a precursor to the body's production of GABA, and there appears to be a distinct GHB receptor site in the brain. In sufficient quantities, GHB can also alter dopamine activity, thus explaining the associated euphoria. At dose levels that do not produce anaesthesia, there is an initial excitation of dopamine neurons, producing elevated levels of synaptic dopamine; at anaesthetic dose levels, GHB blocks impulse flow from dopamine neurons, resulting in a buildup of dopamine in the nerve terminals. GHB mimics natural physiological sleep, enhances REM sleep, and increases Stages 3 and 4 of slow-wave sleep. GHB has significant cardiovascular pharmacology, causing the dysregulation of blood pressure and leading to either hyper- or hypotension. Other side effects include nausea, vomiting, profuse sweating, drowsiness, visual disturbances, nystagmus (involuntary eye movement), loss of peripheral vision, short-term amnesia, uncontrolled shaking or seizures, bradycardia (slowed heartbeat), hypothermia, suppression of gag reflex, respiratory depression, and transient or unarousable unconsciousness, as well as negative impacts on working and long-term memory (EMCDDA, 2008a). Withdrawal from GHB is a severe and potentially dangerous condition, with more severe complicatons than most other CNS depressants (Neu, 2018).

Regular use of inhalants induces tolerance, making increased doses necessary to produce the same effects. After one year, a glue sniffer may be using several tubes of plastic cement to maintain the effect that was originally achieved with a single tube for the same length of time. Long-term effects of solvent abuse include the development of both physical and psychological dependency on inhalants. Peripheral nerve, liver, and kidney damage and infertility among male sniffers have all been documented. Neurological damage also occurs, affecting balance, gait, reasoning, and sensory perceptions such as taste and smell, with toluene destroying brain tissue of chronic abusers, leading to permanent, irreversible brain damage. Brain damage from solvent abuse does not happen immediately and is avoidable but will transpire with regular use (Al-Hairi & Del Bigio, 2010; Cruz, 2011). In a comparison study of 29 solvent abusers inhaling gasoline compared to 33 non-using controls, solvent abusers showed cognitive deficits in visual motor skills, learning and memory, paired associate learning, and executive functions. Paired associate learning performance did improve within six weeks of abstinence; however, impairments in visual motor speed, learning and memory, and executive function did not. Some of the impairments caused by solvent use can be resolved by simple abstinence; however, it can take memory and executive function months to improve after abstinence, and in some cases these functions may never fully recover (Dingwall et al., 2011).

Table 2.4: Inhalant Classification

Class	Examples	Found in
aliphatic/aromatic	benzene	lacquer thinner
hydrocarbons	butane	fuel
	gasoline	fuel
	hexane	cleaning fluids
	propane	fuel
	toluene	model cement, paint stripper, ink
	xylene	lighter fluid, ink
halogenated	chloroform	anaesthetics
	freons	aerosol propellant
hydrocarbons	halothane	cleaning fluids
	perchlorethylene	aerosol propellants
	trichlorethylene	industrial solvent, anaesthetic
aliphatic nitrates	amyl nitrate	room odorants
	butyl nitrate	industrial solvents
ketones	acetone	nail polish remover
	methylethyl ketones	model cement
	methylisobutyl ketone	household cements
esters	amyl acetate	plastic cements
	ethyl acetate	lacquer thinners
ether	diethylether	anaesthetic, GHB
gas	nitrous oxide	anaesthetic, propellant in canned whipping cream

QUIZ

1. What are the common effects produced by all CNS depressants?
2. Synthesized in the 1950s, these legal wonder drugs can produce a physical dependency in as little as four weeks of regular use. What subgroup of CNS depressants are they?
3. Predecessors of benzodiazepines, what potent CNS depressants produce a much more substantial physical dependency that can be life threatening if not treated medically?
4. These are common, over-the-counter remedies for allergies, and they are often also found in compound cold medications, where they serve a very different function. Many do not realize these drugs are psychoactive. What are they?
5. Members of this most common CNS depressant family of drugs will be found in virtually everyone's home in Canada. What are they?

2.4 ALCOHOL

slang: 2-4, 26-er, 26 ouncer, booze, brewski, browns, brown pop, fire water, 40 pounder, grog, hooch, kegger, mickey, shots, snort, suds, vino

Alcohol use is a leading risk factor for death and disability. "Alcohol is a colossal global health issue and small reductions in health-related harms at low levels of alcohol intake are outweighed by the increased risk of other health-related harms, including cancer" (Burton & Sheron, 2018, p. 987). There are three distinct forms of alcohol: methanol, also known as methyl alcohol or wood alcohol; isopropanol, isopropyl alcohol, or rubbing alcohol; and finally, the least toxic of the three, ethyl alcohol, or beverage alcohol (figure 2.7). Methanol has a range of industrial uses, from fuel to an industrial solvent to a denaturant for ethyl alcohol. Methanol itself is not toxic to humans; however, when metabolized by the liver, it is broken down into formic acid and formaldehyde, both of which are. While consumption of 80 millilitres is typically lethal for a

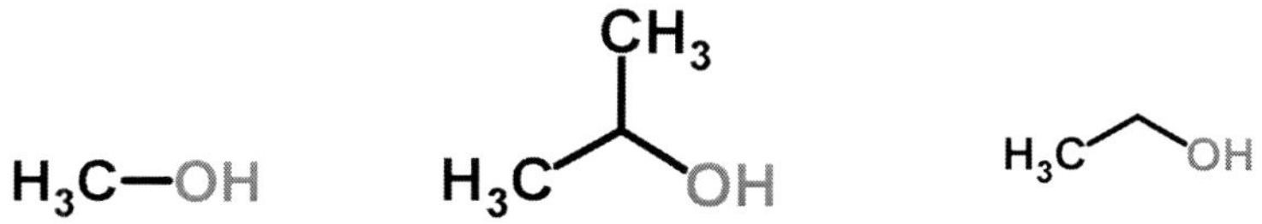

$H_3C{-}OH$

(a) Methanol CH_4O

CH_3

H_3C OH

(b) Isopropanol C_3H_8O

H_3C OH

(c) Ethanol C_2H_6O

Figure 2.7: Chemical Structure of the Three Types of Alcohol

healthy, 180-pound (82-kilogram) male, doses as little as 30 millilitres can be fatal. Isopropyl alcohol is found not only in rubbing alcohol, but also in aftershave, hand lotions, and antifreeze, and is abused by some in lieu of ethyl alcohol when ethyl alcohol cannot be readily obtained. Fatal doses range from 120 to 240 millilitres. However, it is beverage alcohol that is the most commonly misused psychoactive drug worldwide. It is the waste product formed when yeast utilizes sugar as an energy source during the process of fermentation. Ethyl alcohol is a water-soluble molecule that is rapidly absorbed into the bloodstream from the stomach, small intestine, and colon, and metabolized primarily in the liver by the actions of alcohol dehydrogenase (ADH). ADH converts alcohol to acetaldehyde, which is subsequently converted to acetate by the actions of acetaldehyde dehydrogenase (ALDH) (Carr, 2011).

Alcohol is pharmacologically distinct from other central nervous system depressants in a variety of ways, beginning with the fact that it affects more neurotransmitters than any other psychoactive drug (appendix A). Alcohol depresses the CNS in two ways: by increasing the presence of the inhibitory neurotransmitter GABA, and by decreasing the presence of the excitatory neurotransmitter glutamate. However, it also directly binds to receptors for acetylcholine and serotonin, as well as indirectly stimulating dopamine release in the ventral tegmental area of the brain, a key component of the CNS's reward system. It also has secondary effects upon adenosine, leading to a lowering of wakefulness while increasing endorphin release in the nucleus accumbens and orbitofrontal cortex. Another key pharmacological attribute is the small size of its molecule and the lack of binding to plasma in the blood. This allows it to flow freely in and out of any tissue where blood flows throughout the entire body, and as alcohol is a natural irritant to the body, this provides one explanation as to why it causes such widespread damage when misused (Paul, 2006).

Alcohol content varies from product to product, with 1 to 1.5 ounces of liquor, a 12-ounce bottle of beer (5% alcohol), a five-ounce glass of table wine (12% alcohol), and a four-ounce glass of fortified wine all containing the same amount of ethanol and considered a standard drink (figure 2.8). As alcohol has an anaesthetic effect upon the brain, short-term effects include relaxation, loss of inhibitions, impaired coordination, slowing down of reflexes and mental processes, attitude changes, and increased risk-taking to the point of bad judgment, including driving a car or working with machinery while under the influence. Drinking heavily over a short period of time may produce a poisoning effect commonly referred to as a hangover, witnessed by a headache, nausea, shakiness, and possibly vomiting, beginning eight to twelve hours after excessive alcohol consumption has ceased. A hangover is simply the body's reaction to administering too much alcohol. It is partly related to poisoning by alcohol and other components of the drink, and partly the body's response to dehydration and withdrawal from alcohol.

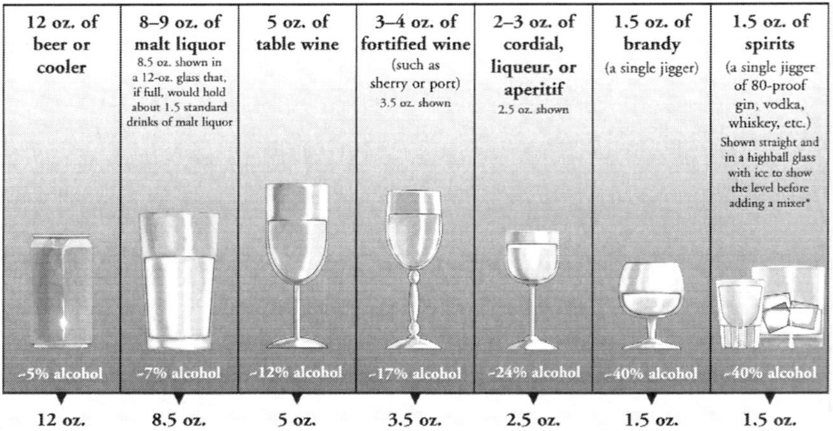

Figure 2.8: A Standard Drink

Source: National Institute on Alcohol Abuse and Alcoholism, *Helping Patients Who Drink Too Much: A Clinician's Guide*, NIH Publication No. 07-3769 (Washington: US Department of Health and Human Services, http://pubs.niaaa.nih.gov/publications/Practitioner/CliniciansGuide2005/guide.pdf, 2005, p. 24)

Table 2.5: Blood Alcohol Concentration Effects

BAC (mg%)	Behavioural Effect
.02	body warmth, decreased inhibition, euphoria, beginning of impairment of driving skills
.05	lowered alertness, relaxation of mood, inhibitions relaxed, driving noticeably affected
.08	legal limit of impairment in Canada muscle coordination weakened
.10	user becomes talkative, noisier, behaviour becomes more erratic, reaction time noticeably slower
.15	intoxication noticeable in body movement and speech, balance and movement is impaired, driving ability substantially impaired
.20	severely impaired coordination, motor processing, and perception; emotional and cognitive responses significantly impacted
.30	alcohol poisoning, stupor, or unconsciousness
.50	lethal dose level (LD 50)

Source: Alberta Gaming and Liquor Commission, 2018

While the effect upon human physiology as measured in blood alcohol concentration (BAC) is consistent (table 2.5), the amount of alcohol that must be consumed to reach a certain BAC level varies primarily by weight and sex, and to lesser degrees, to tolerance and age (table 2.6). Differences in the effects produced by beverage alcohol from person to person do not generally result from the type of drink consumed, but rather from the person's size, previous drinking experiences, and rate of consumption. A person's feelings and activities, as well as the presence of other people, also play a role in the way the alcohol affects behaviour. Alcohol has no half-life, but rather has linear elimination at the rate of approximately 15 milligrams per hour (0.015 g/hour).

Regular, long-term use of alcohol has been associated with damage to every human organ system (see also figure 2.9):

- Blood: anemia, easy bleeding or bruising
- Bones: interference with the formation of bones, reduced bone mass (thickness and volume), interference with the absorption of calcium, contributing to osteoporosis

Table 2.6: Blood Alcohol Content

Lean Body Weight		Number of Drinks									
						Female					
LB.	**KG**	**1**	**2**	**3**	**4**	**5**	**6**	**7**	**8**	**9**	**10**
100	45.4	.05	.09	.14	.18	.23	.27	.32	.36	.41	.45
120	54.4	.04	.08	.11	.15	.19	.23	.27	.30	.34	.38
140	63.5	.03	.07	.10	.13	.16	.19	.23	.26	.29	.32
160	72.6	.03	.06	.09	.11	.14	.17	.20	.23	.26	.28
180	81.6	.03	.05	.08	.10	.13	.15	.18	.20	.23	.25
200	90.7	.02	.05	.07	.09	.11	.14	.16	.18	.20	.23
220	99.8	.02	.04	.06	.08	.10	.12	.14	.17	.19	.21
240	108.8	.02	.04	.06	.08	.09	.11	.13	.15	.17	.19
						Male					
LB.	**KG**	**1**	**2**	**3**	**4**	**5**	**6**	**7**	**8**	**9**	**10**
100	45.4	.04	.08	.11	.15	.19	.23	.26	.30	.34	.38
120	54.4	.03	.06	.09	.12	.16	.19	.22	.25	.28	.31
140	63.5	.03	.05	.08	.11	.13	.16	.19	.21	.24	.27
160	72.6	.02	.05	.07	.09	.12	.14	.16	.19	.21	.23
180	81.6	.02	.04	.06	.08	.11	.13	.15	.17	.19	.21
200	90.7	.02	.04	.06	.08	.09	.11	.13	.15	.17	.19
220	99.8	.02	.03	.05	.07	.09	.10	.12	.14	.15	.17
240	108.8	.02	.03	.05	.06	.08	.09	.11	.13	.14	.16

Note: Rate of elimination male and female: 0.015 g/hour
Source: Alberta Gaming and Liquor Commission, 2018

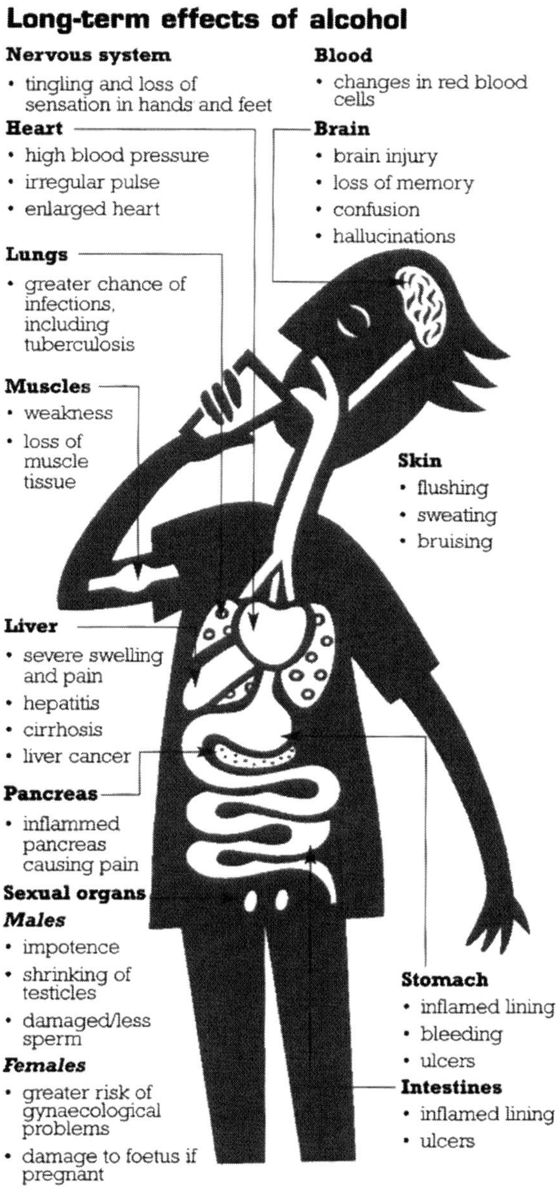

Long-term effects of alcohol

Nervous system
- tingling and loss of sensation in hands and feet

Blood
- changes in red blood cells

Heart
- high blood pressure
- irregular pulse
- enlarged heart

Brain
- brain injury
- loss of memory
- confusion
- hallucinations

Lungs
- greater chance of infections, including tuberculosis

Muscles
- weakness
- loss of muscle tissue

Skin
- flushing
- sweating
- bruising

Liver
- severe swelling and pain
- hepatitis
- cirrhosis
- liver cancer

Pancreas
- inflammed pancreas causing pain

Sexual organs

Males
- impotence
- shrinking of testicles
- damaged/less sperm

Females
- greater risk of gynaecological problems
- damage to foetus if pregnant

Stomach
- inflamed lining
- bleeding
- ulcers

Intestines
- inflamed lining
- ulcers

Figure 2.9: Long-Term Effects of Alcohol

Source: www.youngnungashealth.com

- Cardiovascular System: increased risk of arrhythmias, cardiac arrest, coronary death, heart failure, hypertension, peripheral arterial disease, and stroke
- Endocrine System: decrease in male testosterone level, impotence, decreased sperm production, infertility
- Liver: fatty liver, alcoholic hepatitis, fibrosis, cirrhosis (scarring of the liver due to the death of liver cells)
- Lungs: interference with immune system, leading to higher incidence of pneumonia and tuberculosis
- Muscles: disruption of the body's mineral balance, producing inflammation of the muscles, swelling, tenderness, and weakness, plus degeneration of muscle fibres
- Nervous System: loss of balance, seizures or convulsions, damage to peripheral nerves, dementia, Alzheimer's disease, Wernicke-Korsakoff syndrome, and loss of grey matter and supportive tissue in the brain, resulting in the deterioration of attention span, concentration, decision making, problem solving, planning, muscle control, sensory perception, and short-term memory, diminished activity in the prefrontal cortex of the brain, leading to increased expression of aggression
- Pancreas: pancreatitis, diabetes
- Stomach: gastritis, ulcer irritation (corrosion of the stomach wall), esophagitis (chronic heartburn) (Babor et al., 2001; Bell et al., 2017; Chang et al., 2018; Cservenka & Brumback, 2017; Heikkinen et al., 2017; Kalinin et al., 2018; Malik et al., 2008; O'Neill et al., 2017; Simou, Britton, & Leonardi-Bee, 2018; White, Altmann, & Nanchahal, 2002; WHO, 2018)

Along with these issues come enhanced risks of breast, bowel, colon, gastric, head and neck, larynx, liver, mouth and upper throat, esophageal, pancreatic, pharynx, prostate, and rectal cancers, regardless of the type of alcohol consumed (Angus et al., 2016; Connor, 2017; Heinen et al., 2009; Jayasekara et al., 2015; Lachenmeier, Kanteres, & Rehm, 2009; Zhang et al., 2007; Zhao et al., 2016), as well as injuries, assaults, and trauma that occur as a result of the consumption of alcohol. There is also the irreversible damage that occurs as a result of a woman's drinking during the course of her pregnancy. Collectively referred to as fetal alcohol spectrum disorders (FASD), FASD consists of three distinct conditions: fetal alcohol syndrome (FAS), fetal alcohol effects (FAE), and alcohol-related neurodevelopmental disorder (ARND) (appendix B). These conditions are considered the most preventable neurological disorders in Canada, with eight cases of FASD per 1,000 children (Lange et al., 2017). As alcohol moves freely across the placenta from mother to child, the risks for the unborn child increase the more a pregnant woman drinks, though at this time no safe amount of drinking has been established. Drinking alcohol during pregnancy may lead to brain injury; cognitive impairment; growth deficiencies; heart, face, joint, and limb abnormalities; lower birth weight; and hyperactivity with shorter attention spans in the child (Astley, 2010; Brown & Trickey, 2018; May & Gossage, 2011).

Alcohol is a risk factor for several mental illnesses, and likewise mental illness is a risk for alcohol misuse and abuse. There is a causal link between alcohol use and death by suicide, with over a quarter of suicides directly linked to alcohol use. It is unsurprising, then, that alcohol and depression are also linked, with rates of alcohol use higher among those with depression than in the general population. Similarly, there is a positive association between alcohol use disorders and post-traumatic stress disorder (PTSD). Many with PTSD turn to alcohol as a coping option even though alcohol use can intensify the severity of PTSD-related symptoms. Anxiety is also linked to alcohol use. Acute alcohol use can temporarily reduce anxiety and panic, but withdrawal from alcohol leads to increased feelings of anxiety, with women more likely than men to drink to cope with social anxiety. Alcohol misuse and abuse is also associated with a range of personality disorders, including antisocial and narcissistic personality disorders (Chief Public Health Officer of Canada, 2016).

When an alcohol-dependent person stops drinking, they will experience withdrawal symptoms ranging from mild to severe. These symptoms may consist of shakes or tremulousness (nearly always evident immediately to within 48 hours after the cessation of drinking), anxiety and agitation, flushing of the skin, sweating, sleeplessness, and restlessness, along with seizures that may occur during the first 48 hours, with a peak frequency between 13 and 18 hours, but with the potential to continue for up to five days after alcohol consumption ends. These initial symptoms may be followed by hallucinations, intense psychomotor agitation, and acute anxiety. Delirium tremens can start suddenly and usually peaks three days after the last alchoholic drink. Paranoia and disorientation to time, place, and person are also common. The phases of an alcohol overdose consist of confused thinking, poor judgment, mood swings, poor concentration, marked muscle coordination problems, slurred speech, nausea and vomiting, anaesthesia (sleepiness), memory lapses, and finally respiratory failure, coma, and possibly death (Dziegielewski, 2005).

Alcohol use disturbs the natural sleep cycle of users. There is a bidirectional association between alcohol use and sleep, as alcohol creates sleep disturbances, but likewise sleep disturbances lead to a greater use of alcohol—difficulty sleeping is cited as a risk factor for relapse to substance use. Alcohol use promotes production of adenosine, which allows for a fast sleep onset but may cause the individual to awaken before they are fully rested. Alcohol also affects sleep by disrupting the rhythm of both alpha and delta waves, leading to inadequate Stage 3 sleep that can persist for upwards of two years for those who had been physically dependent (Hasler et al., 2012).

Pharmacological Interventions

A range of pharmacological interventions have been attempted over the years to aid with cessation of excessive alcohol use. Two of the earliest drugs employed for this purpose were Antabuse (disulfiram [tetraethylthiuram disulfide]) and Temposil (citrated calcium carbimide). These substances, known as antidipsotropics, work by disrupting the body's ability to metabolize alcohol by inhibiting the enzyme aldehyde dehydrogenase, which is required by the body to break down the acetalydehyde, a metabolite of alcohol. This produces an extremely unpleasant reaction when alcohol is consumed. The initial reaction is a flushing of the face and neck, followed by dizziness, a pounding heart, headache, and finally nausea and vomiting. If the reaction is adequately intense, the user can even lose consciousness. The severity of the reaction varies from person to person, but the more one consumes ethyl alcohol, the worse the reaction will become. It may take several days to two weeks after the last dose of disulfiram before the body will be able to metabolize alcohol without a negative reaction. The effects of calcium carbimide are not as prolonged, typically lasting up to two days after the last dose of the drug (American Psychiatric Association, 2018). Roth and Fonagy (2005) reported that when used alone without counselling, antidipsotropics produced abstinence at no greater levels than a placebo. However, in a systemic review of the literature, Krampe and Hannelore (2010) found that disulfiram was consistently reported to be an effective therapeutic adjunct to alcohol cessation counselling and to be equal and even superior to the newer options, naltrexone and acamprosate.

Naltrexone (discussed further later in this chapter), an opioid antagonist, was developed to reverse the overdose effects produced by opioids, particularly heroin. Subsequent clinical trials found that it also had the capacity to lessen alcohol-induced positive reinforcement, decreasing cravings and leading to a lessened risk for lapse or relapse (Ragia & Manolopoulos, 2014). When naltrexone, marketed under the name Revia, is administered before consuming alcohol, the pleasurable effects some people experience when they drink are diminished or do not occur. Additionally, there is no experience of nausea, as occurs with the use of antidipsotropics. However, unlike its interaction with heroin, naltrexone does not prevent one from becoming impaired or intoxicated with the use of alcohol, as alcohol, unlike opioids, does not attach itself to only one type of receptor site in the brain (Berg, Pettinati, & Volpicelli, 1996; Garbutt, 2010; O'Malley et al., 1992; Volpicelli et al., 1992). In a review of 29 studies where naltrexone was provided in conjunction with psychosocial treatments, it was found that relapse rates were on average 36% less than when individuals received only counselling (Srisurapanont & Jarusuraisin, 2005). The main issue with naltrexone, however, is that it blocks not only the positive reinforcement from consuming alcohol but also that from other activities as well (Daniel, Martin, & Carter, 1992; Tarr et al., 2017).

Acamprosate was approved for use in Canada in 2007 to aid in diminishing alcohol cravings. While antidipsotropics work by making the user physically ill, and naltrexone by blocking the euphoria produced when alcohol reaches the brain, acamprosate works by balancing GABA levels through reducing the glutamate surge brought on by alcohol consumption, reducing the physical and emotional distress those dependent upon alcohol feel when they stop drinking. Acamprosate, marketed under the trade name Campral, is a synthetic delayed-release tablet with a structure similar to GABA. As with many substances, the actual mechanism of action remains somewhat unknown, though the hypothesis is that acamprosate decreases alcohol intake by affecting calcium channels and modifying transmission along GABA and glutamate pathways in the brain, which may result in decreased positive reinforcement of alcohol intake and decreased withdrawal cravings (Hunter & Ochoa, 2006; Ragia & Manolopolos, 2014). Campral is taken three times a day and reduces withdrawal effects such as sweating, anxiety, and sleep disturbances that occur as an individual withdraws from alcohol. Campral has no psychoactive properties and will not produce dependency (Hunter & Ochoa, 2006). The harms associated with using acamprosate are small, primarily issues with increased levels of diarrhea and vomiting (American Psychiatric Association, 2018).

In double-blind, placebo-controlled trials lasting up to one year, more individuals using acamprosate were able to remain abstinent compared to a placebo group, with minimal side effects arising (Scott et al., 2005). Clinical trials also demonstrated acamprosate to have a significantly larger effect size than naltrexone on the maintenance of abstinence, though naltrexone had a larger effect size than acamprosate on the reduction of heavy drinking and craving. For naltrexone, requiring abstinence before the trial was associated with larger effect sizes for abstinence maintenance and reduced heavy drinking compared with individuals receiving a placebo. In comparison, for acamprosate, detoxification before medication administration was associated with better abstinence outcomes compared with the placebo group (Maisel et al., 2012).

Baclofen is an orally administered muscle relaxant primarily used to prevent muscle spasms resulting from neurological conditions. It was also found to aid alcohol-dependent persons in maintaining abstinence and is well tolerated, even when users lapse. Effectiveness in producing abstinence appears to be dose dependent; an American study of 30 milligrams a day did not produce significant abstinence, whereas a German study administering three doses of 90 milligrams per day did. However, even in the German study, one-quarter of participants dropped out due to lapses and only half maintained abstinence through the entire study. Also, in higher doses baclofen can enhance alcohol's sedative effects, bringing its clinical utility into question (Müller et al., 2015). Bacolfen's use does produce higher rates of abstinence compared to those not receiving any type of pharmacological assistance. However, there is no superior effect of baclofen on increasing the number of abstinent days, or on decreasing heavy drinking, craving, anxiety, or depression (Rose & Jones, 2018).

Topiramate is a non-benzodiazepine anticonvulsant medication. Preliminary clinical trials have demonstrated that its use decreases alcohol's reinforcement of the CNS, leading to a decrease in alcohol consumption (Johnson et al., 2007). Topiramate appears to antagonize alcohol-rewarding effects by inhibiting dopamine release in the mesocorticolimbic system. It may also enhance the inhibitory function of GABA, which in turn antagonizes glutamate receptors, futher inhibiting dopamine release. Side effects of topiramate include an increased likelihood of cognitive dysfunction and numbness, tingling, dizziness, taste abnormalities, and decreased appetite or weight loss compared to those in a control group. However, the major limit of topiramate is that it appears that tolerance builds rapidly to its effects (American Psychiatric Association, 2018; Ragia & Manolopoulos, 2014).

Currently there is no definitive empirical evidence for pharmacological treatment alone to control drinking with persons who are alcohol dependent. Acamprosate and naltrexone show low to medium efficacy in reducing drinking across a range of studies, but with distinct limits and side effects. Also, none of the drugs currently in use have any secondary health benefits for users (Palpacuer et al., 2018).

QUIZ

1. What is the common ingredient of beer, rye, rum, red wine, and cherry brandy?
2. Which organ is responsible for metabolizing alcohol and attempting to minimize the damage this natural poison to the human body produces?
3. What pharmacological properties distinguish alcohol from other psychoactive drugs?
4. What is the condition that occurs among children whose mothers consume alcohol during their pregnancy?
5. What are the physical harms produced by alcohol?

2.5 OPIOIDS

The body's endogenous (internal) opioid system is part of not only the central and peripheral nervous systems but also the gastrointestinal tract and immune system. This is why, when an opioid is administered, not only does pain masking occur, but the user also experiences changes in mood, stress response, eating, digestion, and overall health (Toubia & Khalife, 2018). Opioids are classified as CNS depressants because their action slows down the brain's activity. However, they work on an entirely different neurotransmitter, endorphin, than the previously discussed CNS depressants, which leads some to place them in a unique category rather than as a subgroup within the depressant family. Opioids, acting primarily, but not exclusively, at the mu receptor site, are a key aspect of the brain's midbrain (meslomibic) reward pathway, stimulating both the nucleus accumbens (NAc) and the ventral tegmental area (VTA). Along with their primary effect, they also alter dopamine levels and the brain's reward system indirectly by inhibiting GABA neurons in the VTA, which in turn inhibits dopamine neurons in the VTA (figure 2.10) While opioids mask pain, they also inhibit GABA neurons, allowing dopamine neurons to fire more often and enhancing the sense of euphoria experienced by the user (Kosten & George, 2002; Lowinson et al., 2011).

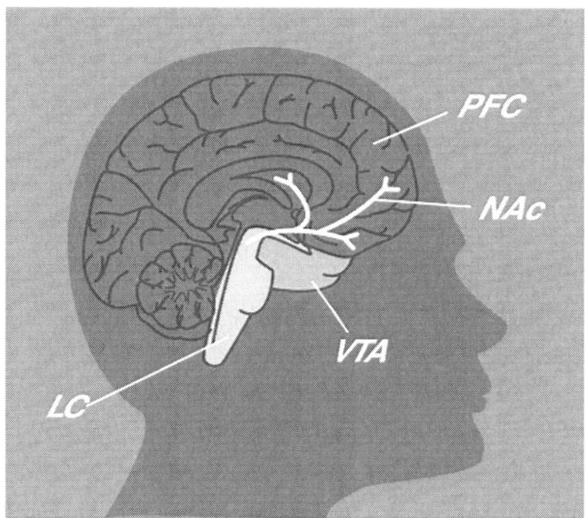

Figure 2.10: The Mesolimbic Reward System

Note: When opioids stimulate mu receptor sites in the brain, cells in the VTA produce dopamine, which is released into the NAc. This produces positive reinforcement and leads to further drug-seeking behaviour when the drug is fully metabolized. Feedback from the prefrontal cortex (PFC) to the VTA diminishes the drive to seek pleasure through high-risk behaviours. However, this process appears to be diminished when a person becomes drug dependent. Also, when opioid molecules link to mu receptors on brain cells in the locus ceruleus (LC), located at the base of the brain, noradrenaline is suppressed, resulting in drowsiness, slowed respiration, and lowered blood pressure. *Source:* T. Kosten and T. George, The neurobiology of opioid dependence: Implications for treatment (*Science & Practice Perspectives, 1*[1], 13–20, 2002)

A complicated relationship exists between the opioid receptor system and the dopamine system, with blockage of one or the other interfering with but not completely removing the reinforcing effects of opioids upon the brain. This explains, in part, some of the odd and high-risk physiological effects observed in opioid users, such as when tolerance to euphoria develops but there is no equivalent tolerance to respiratory depression. Along with respiratory depression, altering endorphin levels in the brain creates euphoria, sedation, decreased gastrointestinal motility, spinal analgesia, sedation, dyspnea (shortness of breath), dysphoria (a state of unease or anxiety), tolerance, withdrawal, and ultimately dependency. Changes in brain biochemistry resulting

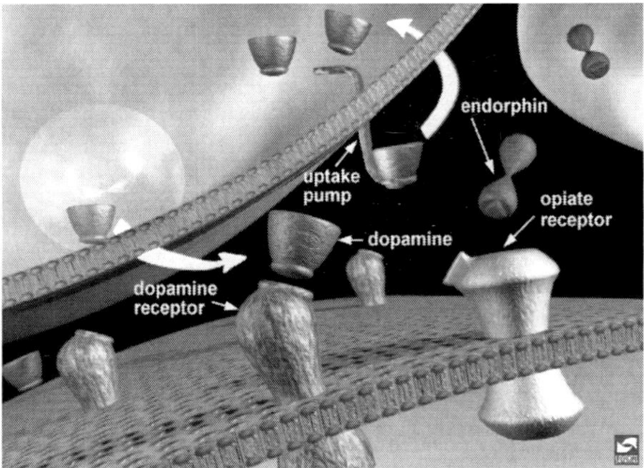

Figure 2.11: Neurotransmitter Response to an Opioid

Source: National Institute on Drug Abuse. Brain pathways are affected by drugs of abuse (http://www.drugabuse.gov/publications/addiction-science/why-do-people-abuse-drugs/brain-pathways-are-affected-by-drugs-abuse, 2008)

from the use of opioids are not temporary. Both chronic and, in some cases, limited use of drugs can produce long-lasting changes in brain neurochemistry, as well as in cell development and structure (Trescot et al., 2008).

Opioids are also called narcotics, from the Greek root meaning to deaden or numb; this is where the idea of opioids being painkillers rather than pain maskers is derived from. However, in Canada the legal definition of *narcotic* has been expanded to include many illicit substances, making it a less precise pharmacological term. *Opiates* is another commonly used word, and while accurate as it pertains to any opium derivative, it is less inclusive than opioid, which refers to any substance with morphine-like actions regardless of whether it is structurally related to morphine. Opioids occur naturally as well as in semi-synthetic and synthetic forms, all of which bind to the same locations in the brain as endogenous endomorphins.

While the impression is that opioids are primarily administered via intravenous injection, opioids are quite versatile when it comes to the pharmacokinetic principle of administration and can be administered orally, through all three forms of injection, across the mucous membrane, and transdermally. In decreasing CNS functioning, opioids also mask both the physical and psychological perception of pain, while also producing euphoria (Zhao et al., 2007). Opioids alter autonomic nervous system functioning, slowing down the gastrointestinal tract and acting as cough suppressants; one of their primary effects is depression of the medulla oblongata, which is responsible for controlling cardiac, respiratory, and vasomotor centres. Opioids, like all psychoactive agents, are metabolized primarily in the liver. Excretion occurs largely via the kidneys, although some metabolites are excreted in the feces. Elimination is usually a matter of a few hours, although a few members of this family of drugs, notably methadone, are metabolized and excreted much more slowly.

Opioids are used in medicine to relieve acute pain suffered as a result of disease, surgery, or injury, in the treatment of some forms of acute heart failure, and in the control of moderate to severe cough or diarrhea. They are of great value for pain control in the later stages of terminal illnesses, such as cancer, when dependence is no longer an issue. Opium customarily produces an exaggerated feeling of well-being and a temporary release from anxiety. Despite their media portrayal, in comparison to other psychoactive agents, opioids are relatively benign upon the body if properly used. The most harmful long-term implication of illicit opioid use is often the lifestyle users maintain, which is primarily a result of the global prohibition against heroin. However, abscesses, cellulitis, liver disease, HIV, hepatitis, and even brain damage may also result from infections associated with unsterile injection techniques. Pulmonary complications, including various types of pneumonia, may also arise from the unhealthy lifestyle of many opioid users, as well as the depressant effect of opioids upon respiration. Emboli, composed of small, undissolved particles or air bubbles, may block small blood vessels in the lungs, brain, heart, or other organs. With chronic use, weight loss, reduction in sex hormone levels, and suppression of the immune system are common (Hancock & McKim, 2018).

Within days of continuous use, tolerance begins to develop to many of the effects of opioids, including respiratory depression, analgesia, sedation, nausea, and enhancement of mood. If administration is intermittent, however, little change in drug sensitivity is observed. Nevertheless, regular users do become both psychologically and physically dependent upon opioids. With their powerful mood-enhancing and anxiety-relieving effects, opioids have a high psychological dependence liability. Other common effects arising from chronic use include constipation, nausea, drowsiness, dizziness and confusion, itching and sweating, tooth decay, and decreased energy, strength, and libido (Dziegielewski, 2005).

Opioids, despite producing sedation among users, actually interrupt sleep. Many opioid receptors are located in the same part of the brain that is responsible for sleep regulation. Natural endorphins are also believed to be involved in the induction and maintenance of one's sleep state. Opioid use increases the number of shifts in sleep-waking states while decreasing total sleep time, sleep efficiency, delta sleep, and time spent dreaming. Even a single dose of a potent opioid can reduce Stages 3 and 4 sleep (slow-wave sleep), contributing to opioid-produced fatigue. Opioids also decrease acetylcholine in some brain regions, which leads to a reduction in REM sleep (Dimsdale et al., 2007; Wang & Teichtahl, 2007). Another contributing factor is that while opioids activate mu receptor sites, which are involved in creating wakefulness, they have minimal impact upon kappa receptor sites, which promote sleep (Moore & Kelz, 2009).

The patterns of purposeful drug-seeking behaviour associated with opioids are difficult to break, and the relapse rate is substantial. Withdrawal from opioids, which may begin as early as a few hours after the last administration, produces uneasiness, yawning, tears, diarrhea, abdominal cramps, protracted goosebumps, and a runny nose. Additionally, the pain associated with withdrawal, particularly in long-term users, has been equated with being as severe as bone cancer. Not surprisingly, these symptoms are accompanied by a sizable craving for the drug. The most marked withdrawal indications peak between 48 and 72 hours after the last dose and subside over a week to 10 days, though some bodily functions may not return to normal levels for as long as six months depending on how long the drug was administered. Sudden withdrawal has occasionally been fatal in heavily dependent users who are in poor health. However, withdrawal is much less dangerous to life than are alcohol-, barbiturate-, and non-barbiturate sedative-hypnotic–induced withdrawal syndromes. Overall, the withdrawal symptoms from opioids are similar to an extremely severe and exceedingly painful case of the flu, with overdose being a much greater concern than withdrawal (table 1.4). An overdose of opioids is indicated by the combination of coma, depressed respiration, and pinpoint pupils. Respiratory depression from opioid administration almost always results in death within a few hours, although complications from pneumonia, pulmonary edema, or shock can also be fatal (Brick & Erickson, 2013).

Following are discussions of the properties of individual opioids and opioid antagonists, drugs that reverse the effects of opioids. Table 2.7, at the conclusion of the section, illustrates the comparative potency of the various opioids described below. The table should also be viewed in consideration of current opioid-prescribing standards in Canada, which recommend that doctors should keep the daily dose of opioids below the equivalent of 50 milligrams of morphine and avoid going above the equivalent of 90 milligrams per day, except in specific circumstances, which include severe physical trauma, lifelong chronic pain, and palliative care (Busse, 2017). In support of this best-practice recommendation are the findings of an American study that found the average equivalent of morphine reported in 221 overdose deaths was 98.1 milligrams (Bohnert et al., 2016).

Opioid Drugs

Buprenorphine

slang: bupe, orange guys, subbies, subs, tems

Semi-synthetic opioid, *(5β,6β,14β,18R)-17-(Cyclopropylmethyl)-18-(2-hydroxy-3,3-dimethyl-2-*[2]

Buprenorphine, derived from the morphine alkaloid thebaine, is a very complex drug in terms of its molecular structure. It is a partial mu receptor agonist as well as a kappa opioid receptor antagonist. Like all opioids, buprenorphine can be used to mask the perception of moderate

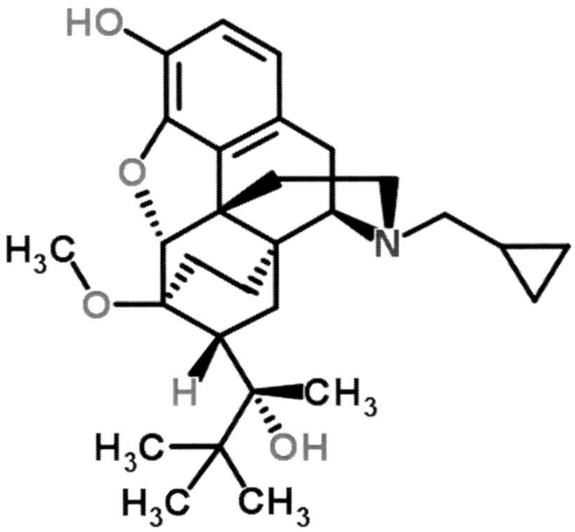

Figure 2.12: Buprenorphine

acute pain in non-opioid-tolerant individuals in lower dosages (approximately 200 micrograms), and to control moderate chronic pain. It has also been used effectively with terminally ill cancer patients, as it is upwards of 25 times more potent than morphine and can be used in conjunction with fentanyl (separate listing) for anaesthesia, counterbalancing the respiratory depression that can occur from fentanyl use alone. Versions of buprenorphine can be administered sublingually (Temgesic) and transdermally (Butrans and Norspan), as well as through injection (Buprenex). Buprenorphine is very lipid soluble, reaching the brain rapidly and exerting its effect quickly once it enters the bloodstream. While buprenorphine activates the mu opioid receptors, producing the same results—analgesia, euphoria, constipation, and respiratory depression—it does so to a certain limit. This is called the ceiling effect, for even if the dose of buprenorphine is increased, the effects of this opioid do not go above the ceiling limit. The ceiling effect of buprenorphine means that there is a limit on the respiratory depression it produces. This is one of the reasons this medication can be more safely prescribed than other opioids (Lutfy & Cowan, 2004).

Buprenorphine binds tightly to the mu opioid receptor because of its high receptor affinity. This prevents other opioids with lower affinity, such as heroin, from binding, resulting in a blunting or blocking of the euphoria, respiratory depression, and other effects of these opioids. If heroin is already on the receptor and then buprenorphine is introduced, because buprenorphine has a high affinity for the receptor, buprenorphine will displace the heroin. This can lead to a heroin user experiencing some withdrawal effects. Buprenorphine's high lipid solubility also allows for more of the drug to remain in the body, extending its effects for much longer periods of time than many other opioids. Buprenorphine produces less respiratory depression than most other opioids and has a long elimination half-life of 24 to 69 hours. However, it has poor oral bioavailability due to extensive first-pass metabolism. Approximately 70% of buprenorphine is eliminated in the feces, with the remainder eliminated via urine. Nausea, vomiting, sweating, headache, abdominal pain, and constipation are the most prominent side effects, and are likely to be the first noticeable effects of buprenorphine. Respiratory depression and respiratory arrest, and to a lesser degree circulatory depression, shock, and cardiac arrest, are the most serious side effects of buprenorphine use (Milne, Crouch, & Carabati, 2009).

Buprenorphine has been available as a pain-masking agent since the 1980s. However, when it was discovered that it had the ability to block other opioids from adhering to opioid receptors, making them ineffective, it gained greater prominence. In 2002, the United States Food and Drug Administration permitted buprenorphine to be used in combination with the opioid antagonist naloxone (see separate listing) under the name Suboxone (see separate listing) as an alternative to methadone for the maintenance and treatment of heroin and related opioid dependencies, as well as for opioid detoxification (Milne et al., 2009). It was approved for the same purpose in the European Union in 2006, and finally in Canada in 2007 (Handford et al., 2011).

Carfentanil

slang: drop dead, grey death, serial killer

Synthetic opioid, *4-Piperidinecarboxylic acid, 4-[(1-oxopropyl)phenylamino]-1-(2-phenylethyl)-, methyl ester* ($C_{24}H_{30}N_2O_3$)

The most well-known, licit analogue of fentanyl is carfentanil. Carfentanil has a potency 100 times greater than fentanyl, which makes it 10,000 times as potent as morphine for an equivalent dose. Like fentanyl, carfentanil was first synthesized by a team of chemists at Janssen Pharmaceutica, but 15 years later. It is intended to anaesthetize large animals and to be used in veterinary medicine rather than for human consumption. When mixed into heroin or other street drugs the risk of overdose is heightened even more than when fentanyl is added due to carfentanil's far greater potency (EMCDDA, 2017a).

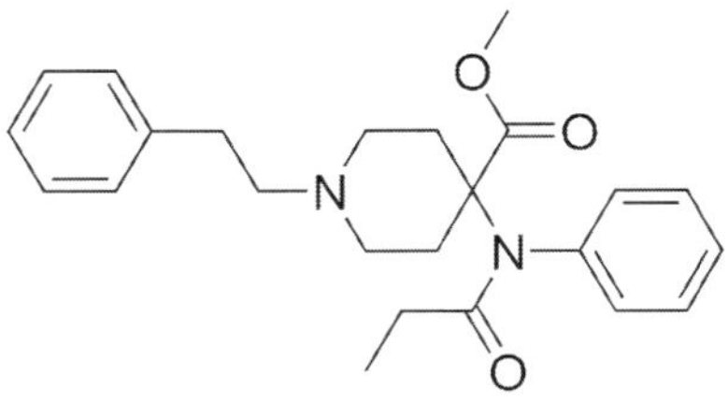

Figure 2.13: Carfentanil

Source: Wikimedia Commons

Codeine (Methylmorphine)

slang: AC/DC, Captain Cody, cody, coties, dreamer, fours, nods, school boy, sizzurp, syrup (codeine, antihistamine, Sprite, and dissolved Jolly Rancher candy)

Natural opioid, *(5α,6α)-3-Methoxy-17-methyl-7,8-didehydro-4,5-epoxymorphinan-6-ol* ($C_{18}H_{21}NO_3$)

Codeine is a natural derivative of the opium poppy with a relatively low potency (table 2.7). Therapeutically, it is used in cough syrups and in preparations containing non-opioid, non-psychoactive pain suppressants to create compound substances such as Tylenol (T-3). It is subject to non-medical use and abuse primarily due to its ready availability, as it is second in use among opioids in Canada, behind only morphine. Discovered in 1832, codeine is often

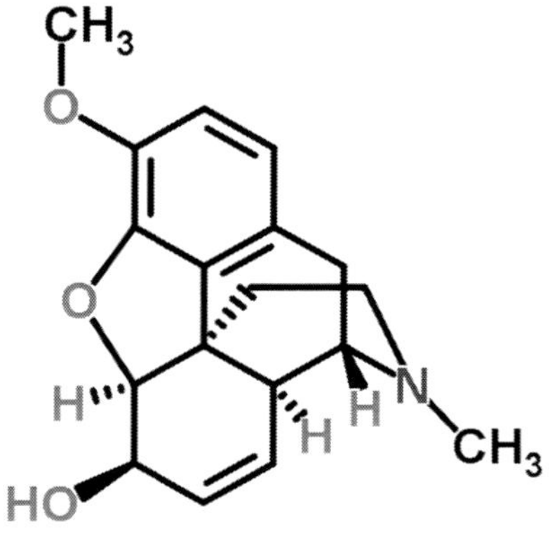

Figure 2.14: Codeine

used by opioid-dependent persons when more potent opioids are unavailable. Dependence, tolerance, and withdrawal are like that experienced by a morphine abuser, though far less intense. Seizures are possible with high doses of codeine, as is overdose (Madadi & Koren, 2008).

Desomorphine (Krokodil)

slang: croc, crocodile, krok, Russian magic, zombie drug

Synthetic opioid, *4-5-alpha-epoxy-17-methylmorphinan-3-ol* ($C_{17}H_{21}NO_2$)

Desomorphine, a synthetic, morphine-like substance that is upwards of 10 times more potent than morphine and thus closer to the potency of Dilaudid (see hydromorphone), was first synthesized in the 1930s in the United States. Desomorphine has a morphine-like chemical structure, though the structural modifications yield a more rapid onset and shorter duration of action. There is also less nausea and respiratory depression produced, and a reduced sedative effect. The pharmacology of desomorphine is not completely understood, although, given its structural similarity to morphine, it is most likely a mu opioid agonist. There is presently no accepted medical use for desomorphine in North America, though it is used medically in Switzerland under the brand name Permonid. In studies using both rats and monkeys, tolerance developed more slowly to desomorphine than to morphine, and it was far more effective as a general depressant and analgesic, but three times as toxic. Desomorphine produces relatively brief but powerful narcotic and analgesic effects. It also has a relatively powerful respiratory depressant effect, to which tolerance does not develop. Repeated administration of desomorphine at short intervals in persons with severe cancer pain indicated that the drug did produce a substantial degree of addiction liability (Drug Enforcement Administration, 2013).

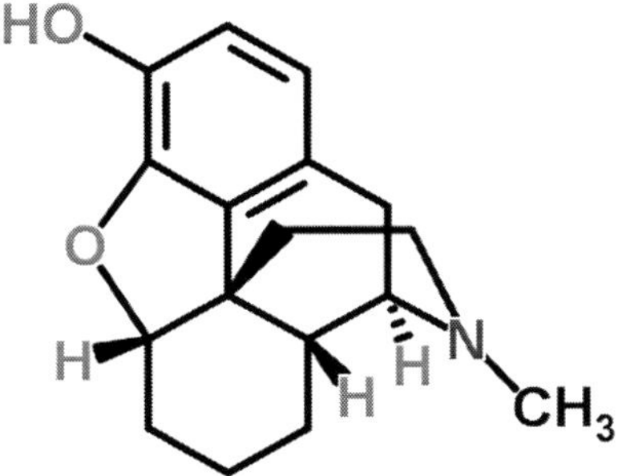

Figure 2.15: Desomorphine

Desomorphine is abused for its opioid-like effects and, as with all opioids, tolerance, dependence, and addiction arise with regular use. The effects of desomorphine are like those of other opioids and include euphoria, sedation, and analgesia. Likewise, common negative effects include constipation, nausea and vomiting, itching, urinary retention, decreased libido, and respiratory depression. Serious medical complications can include respiratory failure, allergic reactions, and seizures. Desomorphine is illicitly synthesized from codeine using iodine, gasoline, paint thinner, hydrochloric acid, lighter fluid, and red phosphorus in a process similar to that used for street methamphetamine, with the final street product equally contaminated with corrosive, toxic chemicals. The drug is typically administered intravenously (Leone & Ferrari, 2018).

Discussion of the illicit use of desomorphine as a cheaper alternative to heroin began appearing at the beginning of the century. It has since become most commonly used among Russian and Eastern European young adults, though unsubstantiated reports of use in both the United States and Canada occurred in 2013. Its street names, Krokodil or Crocodil, reflect the fact that in long-term abusers of illicitly produced desormorphine, the skin may present as greenish and scaly due to damaged blood vessels, thrombosis, and damaged soft tissues surrounding the injection sites. This can eventually develop into severe tissue damage, leading to thrombophlebitis (vein inflammation related to a blood clot) and gangrene. These conditions usually result in limb amputation and even death if the condition is untreated and have led to media reports calling Krokodil "the flesh-eating drug." As with most opioids, death can occur at high doses because of respiratory depression. Street desomorphine carries additional, potentially fatal risks associated with injecting impure chemicals into the body (Drug Enforcement Administration, 2013; Gahr et al., 2012).

Fentanyl

slang: Apache, blue dragon, China girl, Chinatown, Chinese food, crazy, dance fever, dragon's breath, fent, fire, friend, goodfella, great bear, jackpot, king ivory, murder 8, serial killer, shine, Tango and Cash, TNT, toe tag dope, white girl

Synthetic opioid, *N-Phenyl-N-[1-(2-phenylethyl)-4-piperidinyl]propanamide* ($C_{22}H_{28}N_2O$)

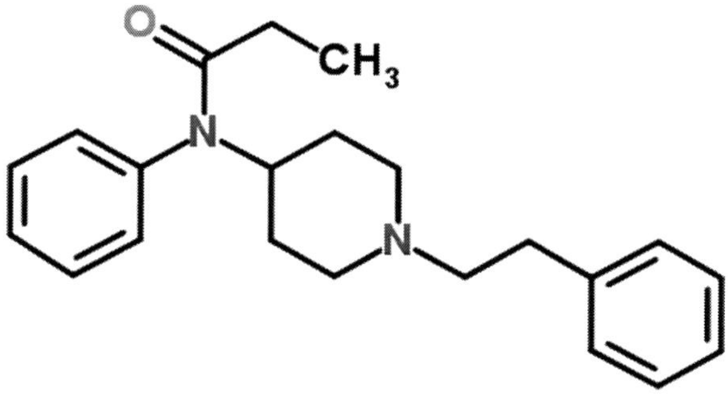

Figure 2.16: Fentanyl

Fentanyl citrate, a synthetic opioid synthesized by Paul Janssen in 1959, is the strongest opioid available for medical use intended for humans. It was produced to replace morphine and other opioids for use in cardiac surgery due to its higher potency—100 times greater than that of morphine (table 2.7). This means that less is required during surgery. As an additional benefit, fentanyl produces fewer adverse cardiovascular effects than does morphine and triggers substantially less histamine release (Nelson & Schwaner, 2009). Fentanyl and its licit derivatives, Alfentanil, Sufentanil, and Remifentanil, are used as analgesics and for anaesthesia before, during, and after surgery because of their potency but also their short onset and duration of action. Fentanyl also has a slow-release form that is used for continuous pain management for those with terminal illnesses or breakthrough pain as an outcome of extended opioid use due to chronic pain. Fentanyl is licitly administered in a variety of forms, including transdermal patches, injection, lozenges and lollipops, sublingual tablets, and even a nasal spray. Fentanyl readily moves through skin, muscle, mucous membrane, and fatty tissue, dispersing in the bloodstream and across cell membranes. When administered intramuscularly or transdermally, it may accumulate in tissue at the source of administration (National Institute on Drug Abuse, 2012a). Fentanyl is quickly metabolized through the liver and has no active metabolites. Within 72 hours approximately 75% of fentanyl is excreted, primarily through the urine as metabolites, with less than 10% unchanged drug (Grape, Schug, & Schug, 2010).

Fentanyl is fairly water soluble, quite soluble in alcohol, and extremely lipid soluble, with a protein-binding ability greater than either morphine or heroin, thus creating its greater potency than either, which has in turn led to issues of fentanyl misuse. As with most opioids, fentanyl works by binding primarily to the mu receptor site; however, it also increases the amount of serotonin found in the synapse, which means it can also contribute to serotonin syndrome when combined with other serotonin-enhancing psychoactive agents (Ailawadhi et al., 2007). Use of fentanyl leads not only to the masking of pain and depression of the CNS, but also to the depression of respiratory, cardiovascular, and gastrointestinal functioning. There is a substantial risk of tolerance with prolonged use of fentanyl, and if misused, intense euphoria occurs along with the freedom-from-pain perception. Serious medical consequences, including death, have occurred when people were accidently exposed to the fentanyl transdermal system. Fentanyl use has several other types of negative side effects, including neurological (fainting, dizziness, confusion, headache), cardiovascular (hypotension, bradycardia, arrhythmias), gastrointestinal (nausea, vomiting, constipation), respiratory (respiratory depression and coughing), genitourinary (urinary retention), dermatologic (pruritus, systemic rashes), and hematologic (hemolysis [destruction of blood vessels]). Withdrawal, besides being excruciatingly painful, is accompanied by agitation, anxiety, abdominal cramps, blurred vision, and vomiting (Smith, 2009).

When OxyContin prescribing was curtailed across North America, and no treatment was provided for those who had become addicted to this heavily marketed and prescribed drug, a surge in heroin use arose, as predicted by many experts in the field. However, along with this uptake in heroin came a new phenomenon: the mixing of fentanyl into heroin. Fentanyl was added for a few reasons, namely that, as it was legal to produce, it was cheaper than heroin, and being three to four times more potent meant that less heroin needed to be added to the mix for a greater profit. Fentanyl, both mixed with heroin and used on its own, is the leading cause of opioid overdose deaths across Canada and the United States. The impact has been so dramatic that it has led to a decrease in average life expectancy across North America, and in 2018 it was used by the state of Nebraska as a lethal injection to execute Carey Dean Moore, who had been convicted of capital crime (Smith, 2018).

In addition to fentanyl citrate, a series of distinct novel synthetic opioids have been documented. These are often called fentanyl analogues, designer fentanyls, or non-pharmaceutical fentanyls (NFPs) as they are based upon the core fentanyl molecule but are modified either intentionally or unintentionally during their illicit manufacture. Among these are: acetylfentanyl, alpha-methylfentanyl, butyrfentanyl cyclopropylfentanyl, 4-fluoroisobutyrylfentanyl, furanylfentanyl, 3-methylfentanyl, methoxyacetylfentanyl, ocfentanil, parafluorofentanyl, tetrahydrofuranylfentanyl, valerylfentanyl 4F-iBF, AH-7921, NT-45, and U-47700. Along with being illicit substances, each of these has been associated with overdose deaths either in North America or in Europe (Canadian Centre on Substance Abuse, 2016; EMCDDA, 2017b; 2018a; 2018c; 2018d).

Heroin (Diacetyl-Morphine or Diamorphine)

slang: aunt Hazel, Bart Simpson, big H, big Harry, black tar, blue velvet, bobby brown, boy, brown crystal, dragon, dust, H, hardball (mixed with cocaine), harry, horse, junk, Mexican Mud, nickel deck, scag, smack, speedball (mixed with cocaine), red chicken, spider, white lady, white stuff

Semi-synthetic opioid, *(5α,6α)-17-Methyl-7,8-didehydro-4,5-epoxymorphinan-3,6-diyl diacetate* ($C_{21}H_{23}NO_5$)

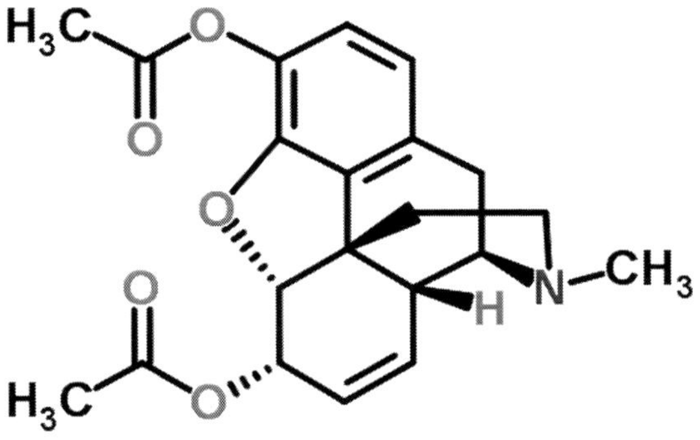

Figure 2.17: Heroin

Heroin, synthesized in 1898, is a semi-synthetic opioid that is a modified version of morphine. Its chemical structure produces an extremely potent euphoric response, which has led to its being nearly universally prohibited, which has in turn led to its having become a major contributor to opioid overdose deaths globally. Heroin modifies the action of dopamine in the nucleus accumbens and the ventral tegmental area of the brain. Once crossing the blood-brain barrier, heroin is converted to morphine, which acts as a powerful agonist at the mu opioid receptors subtype. This binding inhibits the release of GABA from the nerve terminal, reducing the inhibitory effect of GABA on producing more action potentials and thus increasing the amount of dopamine released into the synapse. Continued activation of the dopamine reward pathway leads to the exaggerated feelings of euphoria (National Institute on Drug Abuse, 2007). The physical effects of heroin use may include restlessness, vomiting, nausea, fatigue, dry mouth, and a warm, heavy feeling throughout the body, as well as constipation, increased urination, contraction of the pupils, itchy skin, and slowed breathing. In larger doses, the pupils of users contract to pinpoints, the skin becomes cold, moist, and bluish, and breathing becomes slowed or even stopped, causing death. Additional effects experienced by long-term users can include pulmonary complications, menstrual irregularities and decreased libido in women, and a reduction in reproductive hormone levels for both men and women while negatively affecting sperm morphology and motility. Ongoing heroin use has also been shown to impair attentional processing and cortical plasticity, which diminishes the brain's ability to reorganize itself and form new neural connections (Dusunen, 2018; EMCDDA, 2013; Shen et al., 2017).

Heroin is referred to as diamorphine or diacetyl-morphine when used medicinally to treat severe pain resulting from heart attacks or injuries, as occurs in the United Kingdom. The more common term, *heroin*, is usually only used when illicit use of the substance is being discussed. Tolerance to heroin develops rapidly with regular use, and both physical and psychological dependency occur quickly. Overdose generally occurs due to users injecting pure or minimally cut heroin instead of the typical dose, which tends to be diluted with substances such as

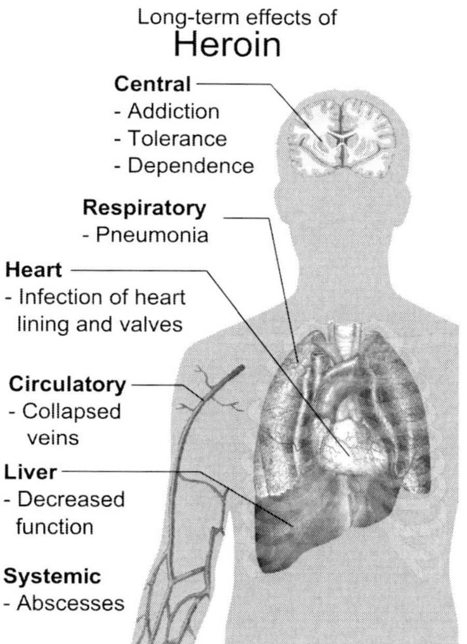

Figure 2.18: Long-Term Effects of Heroin

Source: Wikimedia Commons

sugar, baking soda, or baby powder. Withdrawal symptoms for individuals dependent upon heroin usually appear four to five hours after the last dose and can be quite severe. These symptoms often last seven to ten days and include severe anxiety, insomnia, increased perspiration, chills, shivering, and tremors. However, while extremely painful and unpleasant, heroin withdrawal is much less life-threatening than withdrawal from the heavy use of alcohol, barbiturates, or non-barbiturate sedative-hypnotics. Heroin is used primarily by intravenous injection, though it can also be smoked, inhaled, swallowed, and administered by skin popping (EMCDDA, 2013).

Although hypersomnia is a trait associated with heroin use, the drug diminishes the benefits of sleep in several ways. Heroin use increases Stage 1 sleep while diminishing Stages 2, 3, and 4 along with decreasing time spent in REM sleep. This impacts both sleep efficiency and quality, leading to enhanced drowsiness while awake, despite extended sleep time. Heroin users also report an increase in night terrors and strange dreams once they begin using this opioid. Treatment-seeking heroin-dependent subjects frequently report sleep-related problems that contribute to high relapse rates (Liao et al., 2011).

Hydrocodone (Novahistex DH)

slang: hydro, vickies, vike, vikings

Synthetic opioid, *(5α)-3-Methoxy-17-methyl-4,5-epoxymorphinan-6-one ($C_{18}H_{21}NO_3$)*

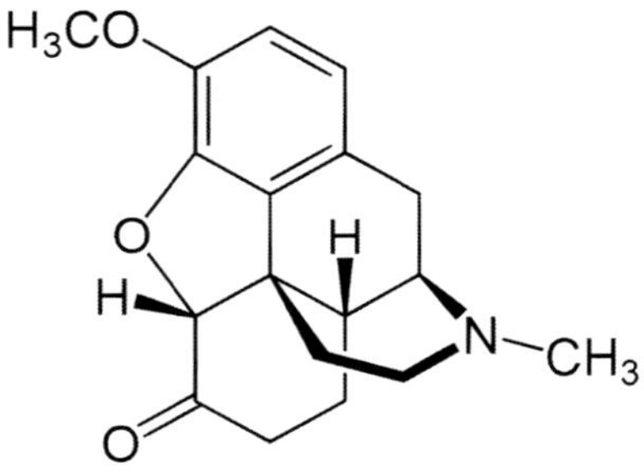

Hydrocodone, also referred to as dihydrocodeine, is a semi-synthetic mu agonist first synthesized in 1955 that is more potent than codeine. It is used for both cough suppression and pain management, and when combined with acetaminophen is sold as Vicodin. The half-life of the drug is approximately four hours, with high doses producing substantive euphoria and sedation. Dependence is greater on hydrocodone than on codeine, with tolerance also occurring much more rapidly. The severity of the withdrawal reaction ranges between those produced by codeine and by morphine. Prior to the emergence of OxyContin, hydrocodone was the most prescribed opioid in North America, which led to its becoming a common cause of emergency room admissions (Walsh et al., 2008).

Figure 2.19: Hydrocodone
Source: Wikimedia Commons

Hydromorphone (Dilaudid)

slang: D's, delats, dillies, hospital heroin, hydro, juice, M2's

Semi-synthetic opioid, *(5α)-3-Hydroxy-17-methyl-4,5-epoxymorphinan-6-one ($C_{17}H_{19}NO_3$)*

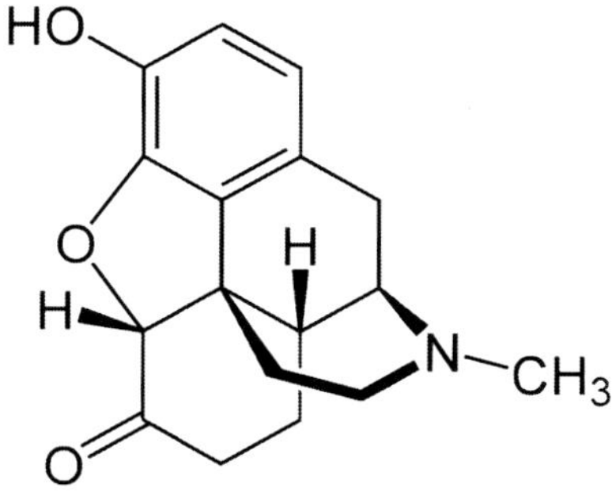

Hydromorphone, first synthesized in 1936, is a potent morphine derivative. It is used to mask severe pain, particularly for those with a terminal illness, though it can also be used to suppress the cough reflex. Dilaudid, as it is known commercially, produces less nausea, vomiting, and drowsiness, but greater respiratory depression, than does morphine. This drug has a pain-masking potential seven to eight times that of morphine, which means that it has a higher potency and efficiency (table 2.7). The reason for this increase in effectiveness is due to the increased lipid solubility of Dilaudid compared to morphine. Increased lipid solubility allows Dilaudid to cross the blood-brain barrier more readily than morphine, exerting greater effects on the CNS. Tolerance and physical dependence develop, with withdrawal symptoms similar to that of a very severe and prolonged bout of flu. The psychological features of withdrawal from hydromorphone are depression, anxiety, insomnia, and loss of appetite, combined with periods of agitation. As well, a smaller amount of hydromorphone is required to produce an overdose than other opioids. In double-blind experiments (where neither the user nor the researcher is aware of what substance is being administered), the effects of hydromorphone could not be distinguished from heroin (Hong, Flood, & Diaz, 2008).

Figure 2.20: Hydromorphone

Source: Wikimedia Commons

An extended-release form of hydromorphone manufactured by Purdue Pharma (2004) is also available. Marketed as Palladone, it too is a controlled substance and is available in 12-, 16-, 24-, and 32-milligram capsules. It is intended only for adults with long-term, constant chronic pain. However, as with any extended-use substance, the drug is released much faster into the central and peripheral nervous systems than intended if it is chewed or crushed, and a significant euphoric reaction and risk of overdose can occur.

Kratom

slang: 4 × 100, herbal heroin, kapow

natural opioid: mitragynine and 7-hydroxymitragynine (7-HMG)

Mitragynine, *9-methoxy-corynantheidine* ($C_{23}H_{30}N_2O_4$)

7-Hydroxymitragynine, *Methyl (7α,16E,20β)-7-hydroxy-9-methoxy-16-(methoxymethylene)-1,2-didehydro-2,7-dihydrocorynan-17-oate* ($C_{23}H_{30}N_2O_5$)

Kratom is obtained from the leaves of *Mitragyna speciosa*, a tropical deciduous tree within the coffee family that is native to Southeast Asia. The two psychoactive components of the plant are mitragynine and 7-hydroxymitragynine (7-HMG), which are partial opioid agonists of both mu and delta. These chemicals operate on opioid receptors and produce similar effects to morphine; however, the chemical structures are quite different. Kratom has stimulant properties at low doses (2–15 grams) and opioid properties, including the ability to produce euphoria, at higher doses (15 grams or more) (Bergen-Cico & Macclurg, 2016).

There has been great controversy surrounding this drug. The United States Drug Enforcement Agency proposed to prohibit it in 2018 after the Food and Drug Administration (2018) indicated that there were no adequate or well-controlled scientific studies involving the use of kratom as a treatment for opioid use withdrawal or any other disease conditions. The substance is currently prohibited in Australia, Denmark,

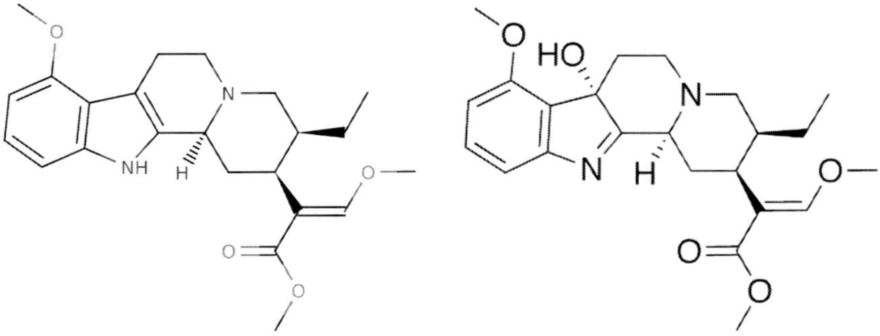

Figure 2.21: Kratom—Mitragynine and 7-Hydroxymitragynine

Source: Wikimedia Commons

Germany, Malaysia, and Thailand. Traditionally kratom has been used by labourers not only to relieve minor pain and act as a sedative but also to provide energy, and it has been used to treat malaria, infections, diarrhea, coughs, and mood disorders (Rosenbaum, Carreiro, & Babu, 2012). While kratom is not allowed to be marketed as a consumable product in Canada, it can still be obtained through a physician's prescription.

Kratom can be consumed in both fresh and dried (leaf or powder) forms, or as a concentrated liquid extract. Its minor side effects may include sleep disruption, itchiness, vomiting, and constipation. More significant side effects include insomnia, weight loss, cardiovascular issues, liver toxicity, respiratory depression, seizures, and physical dependency and painful withdrawal from the substance (Bergen-Cico & Macclurg, 2016; Galbis-Reig, 2016). Hemby et al. (2018) reported that mitragynine does not appear to have abuse potential and in studies with rats led to a reduction in morphine intake when administered. In contrast, 7-HMG did indicate substantive abuse potential that could also lead to increased craving not only for kratom but also for other, more potent opioids.

Meperidine (Demerol)

slang: demmies, peth

Synthetic opioid, *Ethyl 1-methyl-4-phenyl-4-piperidinecarboxylate* $(C_{15}H_{22}ClNO_2)$

One of the earliest synthesized opioids, meperidine was first made available in Germany in 1939. It is effective as a short-acting analgesic and can be used for the relief of most types of moderate to severe pain, including post-operative pain and the pain of labour. It can be administered via intramuscular, subcutaneous, or intravenous injection, or orally in liquid or tablet form. Because of the anticholinergic effects, eperidine was believed to

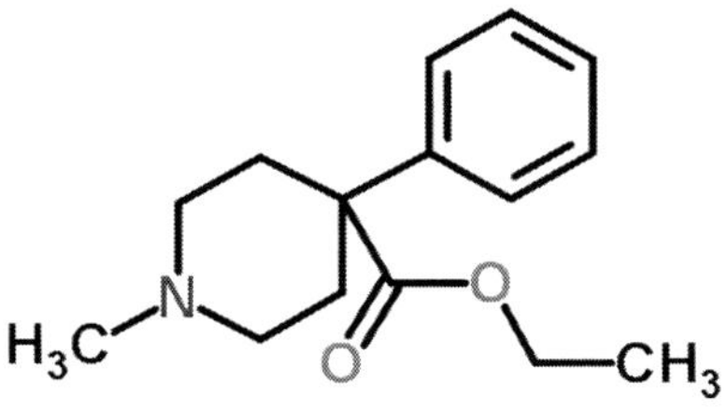

Figure 2.22: Meperidine

be less likely to produce physical dependency when compared to other opioids. However, prolonged use does certainly lead to dependence, and withdrawal symptoms arise more rapidly than they do with morphine withdrawal. Demerol can also produce CNS excitement at high doses, manifested by muscle twitches, tremors, and agitation. Meperidine, like morphine, acts primarily as an agonist to the mu opioid receptor and on kappa, which may explain its anti-shivering effects. One of meperidine's metabolites, normeperidine, has serotonin properties, making meperidine a greater risk for contributing to seizures associated with serotonin syndrome. Withdrawal for those physically dependent upon the drug begins in three hours, peaks in eight to twelve hours, and ends in four to five days. There is little nausea, vomiting, and diarrhea, but muscle twitching, restlessness, and anxiety are much worse than with morphine (Yasaei & Saadabadi, 2017).

Methadone

slang: dollies, done, fizzies, juice, meth, my drink, the drink

Synthetic opioid, *6-(Dimethylamino)-4,4-diphenyl-3-heptanone* ($C_{21}H_{27}NO$)

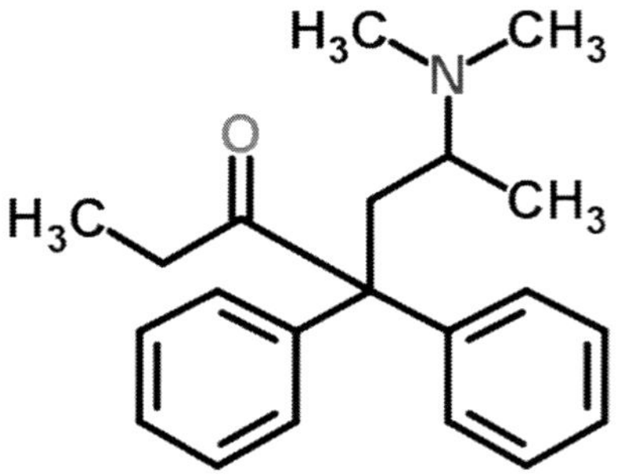

Figure 2.23: Methadone

Methadone is a long-acting mu opioid receptor agonist with morphine-like properties. It was first synthesized by the Germans for use during World War II as an alternative to opium-based analgesics. The drug's rights were bought by an American pharmaceutical company as part of wartime reparations; however, it never became a popular pain-masking agent because, unlike the vast majority of opioids, it does not produce a sense of euphoria. Methadone did take on a new fundamental function as a harm-reduction agent during the 1960s when it began to be used as a pharmacological treatment option for heroin dependency. Unlike morphine, methadone is highly effective when administered orally, and as it is excreted slowly, a single dose effectively staves off the withdrawal effects of other opioids for up to 24 hours. When methadone binds to the mu opioid receptor in the CNS, it causes an effect like endogenous endomorphins. This activates the opioid receptor, which provides analgesia with minimal euphoria (Alford, Barry, & Fiellin, 2013). When methadone binds to the NMDA receptor, it blocks glutamate neurotransmission. It is believed that these two neuropharmacological actions contribute to the efficacy of methadone as an analgesic because selective mu opioid agonists and NMDA antagonists produce pain relief in both acute and chronic pain conditions (Bart & Walsh, 2013). As methadone is highly lipid soluble, it easily passes through the blood-brain barrier, but because it binds very tightly to the plasma proteins in the blood, it does not rush to the brain as quickly as other opioids. Methadone inhibits ascending pain pathways and alters the perception of and response to pain, but, as noted above, while it has morphine-like actions and cross-tolerance, it does not produce euphoria for opioid users when taken orally. This has led it to its current primary use in substitution therapy for opioid-dependent individuals. However, tolerance and withdrawal do readily occur in methadone users, though their development is much slower than with other opioids. Without other forms of intervention, chronic users eventually become both psychologically and physically dependent upon methadone. However, if a physically dependent individual is switched from any opioid to methadone, as part of a harm-reduction, drug-substitution initiative, the person's physical dependency would be transferred to methadone. Along with being an addicting drug in all three meanings of the term, methadone's other side effects include weight gain, constipation, numbness in the extremities, and for some, hallucinations when they first begin to use the substance (Trafton & Ramani, 2009; Weschules, Bain, & Richeimer, 2008).

When administered orally, methadone is rapidly absorbed from the gastrointestinal tract and can be detected in the blood within 30 minutes. After repeated administration, there is gradual accumulation in the tissues. The half-life of methadone is 15 to 60 hours, and it undergoes extensive biotransformation in the liver, primarily to two inactive metabolites that are eliminated by the kidneys and excreted through the bile. In total, nine methadone metabolites have been identified, including two that are active: methadol and normethadol. Drowsiness, sedation, dizziness, light-headedness, mood swings from euphoria to dysphoria, depressed reflexes, altered sensory perception, stupor, and coma have all been found in those using methadone chronically. This psychoactive drug has the ability to produce strong analgesia, headache, dry mouth, facial flushing, nausea, constipation, respiratory depression, muscle flaccidity, pupil constriction, and decreased heart rate. Other possible side effects include sedation, alteration in cognitive and sensory efficiency, vomiting, urinary retention, sweating, sleep disorders, and concentration disorders. Overdose is certainly possible, particularly when first administered, and its symptoms can include slow, shallow breathing, respiratory depression, clammy skin, convulsions, extreme somnolence, apnea, circulatory collapse, cardiac arrest, coma, and possibly death (Srivastava & Kahan, 2006; Wolff, 2002).

Numerous European studies of individuals in long-term methadone maintenance programs have demonstrated that methadone does not cause significant psychomotor or cognitive impairment when administered regularly and appropriately, and when the subject abstains from administering other psychoactive drugs. A meta-analysis illustrated that methadone is superior to a placebo in terms of retaining people in treatment and decreasing use of other opioids. Comparative studies have shown methadone to lead to both a reduction in mortality and reduced HIV rates for individuals on a methadone maintenance regimen compared to those who were not (Mattick et al., 2014; Risser et al., 2001; Russolillo, Moniruzzaman, & Somers, 2018). Methadone maintenance use has also been demonstrated to improve mental health upon commencement (Fingleton, Matheson, & Jaffray, 2015).

Nonetheless, methadone remains a mu agonist, and thus its administration impacts sleep and dreaming similarly to all other opioids. In its early use, methadone reduces the length and amount of REM sleep cycles and delays the initial REM episode, each of which detrimentally affects the ability to dream. Additionally, by increasing awakenings throughout sleep, methadone causes more light sleep, disrupting a person's ability to achieve slow-wave, restorative Stages 3 and 4 sleep. With sustained use and steady dosing, methadone users develop a tolerance to these sleep patterns. If a person is involved in a methadone treatment protocol rather than methadone maintenance and methadone use is safely ended, REM and sleep-quality abilities are restored to normal after an extended period (Hsu et al., 2012).

Morphine

slang: dreamer, first line, God's drug, M, Miss Emma, monkey, morph, Mr. Blue, mud, Murphy, white stuff

Natural opioid, *(5α,6α)-17-Methyl-7,8-didehydro-4,5-epoxymorphinan-3,6-diol* ($C_{17}H_{19}NO_3$)

Morphine was named after the Greek god of dreams, Morpheus, by German pharmacist Friedrich Serturner. Morphine is a natural substance derived directly from the opium poppy. It is used clinically for pain management, especially with continuous dull pain, and is considered the prototypical opioid analgesic. Discovered in 1803, it has the second-greatest dependency liability after heroin. It is the standard against which the potency of all other opioids is assessed (table 2.7). While it is most commonly injected, it can also be smoked, inhaled, or swallowed. As morphine is not as lipid soluble as heroin, codeine, or methadone, the onset of action is not as prompt. Drowsiness and mental clouding occur at doses higher than those required for pain relief. Lethargy and impaired concentration and cognition are also common with use of this psychoactive agent (Adovkat et al., 2018).

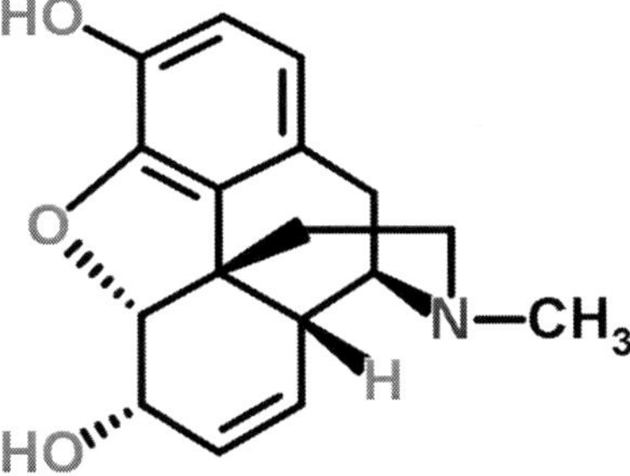

Figure 2.24: Morphine

Morphine inhibits GABA neurons, producing its major effects on the CNS primarily through mu receptors, though it also has some impact on kappa and delta receptors. Mu_1 receptors are involved in pain modulation, analgesia, respiratory depression, the creation of euphoria, and decreased gastrointestinal activity, while mu_2 receptors are involved in producing respiratory depression, drowsiness, nausea, and mental clouding (table 1.2). The effect produced by binding at the kappa receptor sites includes sedation, dysphoria, and mild respiratory depression, along with analgesia, while binding at the delta receptor sites also produces analgesia, as well as dysphoria, delusions, and hallucinations.

Morphine has a short half-life of two to seven hours. Withdrawal can begin within six to twleve hours after the last dose and may last five to ten days. Early withdrawal symptoms include watery eyes, runny nose, yawning, and sweating. Major withdrawal symptoms peak between two and three days after the last dose and include drug craving, restlessness, irritability, dysphoria, loss of appetite, tremors, severe sneezing, diarrhea, nausea and vomiting, elevated heart rate and blood pressure, chills alternating with flushing and excessive sweating, goosebumps, abdominal cramps, body aches, muscle and bone pain, muscle spasms, insomnia, and severe depression. Morphine also increases light sleep (Stage 2) but decreases deep sleep (Stages 3 and 4) and dreaming (REM sleep) (National Highway Traffic Safety Administration, 2014; Wang et al., 2013).

Opium: The Natural Opioid

slang: A-bomb (when mixed with cannabis), aunti, Aunti Emma, big O, black pill, Chinese molasses, Chinese tobacco, dream stick, dreams, God's medicine, hop tar, joy plant, midnight oil, mud, O

Opium is a black or brown tarry substance that comes from the opium poppy and is the source of natural opioids. Opium is not a single drug and thus does not have a systemic name or molecular formula; rather, it contains several active opioid components that naturally occur in the plant's resin. Within opium, you will find both morphine, which can compose over 10% of opium, and codeine, as well as the less-used thebaine. Each one of these has its own unique chemical structure and properties and acts independently upon the CNS when opium is administered, though the effects are complementary. Opium is a crude, resinous preparation obtained from the unripe seed pods of the opium poppy. It has an unpleasant odour and bitter taste that frequently produces nausea when initially consumed. Opium is smoked because of its euphoric properties, while therapeutically it can be used to treat diarrhea and dysentery. However, it has been largely replaced as an analgesic by other naturally occurring, semi-synthetic, and wholly synthetic substitutes, such as morphine, hydromorphone, and meperidine. Nonetheless, a highly purified form of opium marketed as Pantopan is still occasionally used in situations where a person cannot tolerate morphine. Dependence and tolerance are much lower and less marked with opium than with morphine (Dziegielewski, 2005).

Oxycodone (Percodan)/OxyContin/OxyNEO (oxycodone HCl controlled-release)

slang: blue, blueberries, cotton, hillybilly heroin, kicker, killers, O's, OC, Ox, Oxy, Oxycoffin, Oxycotton, percs

Semi-synthetic opioid, *(5α)-14-Hydroxy-3-methoxy-17-methyl-4,5-epoxymorphinan-6-one* ($C_{18}H_{21}NO_4$)

For years the leading drug used to treat chronic pain was the short-acting semi-synthetic opioid oxycodone. Oxycodone has been in use clinically since 1917, produced by modifying codeine. It is a white, odourless, crystalline powder with powerful mood-enhancing, analgesic, and sedative effects. It is available alone or in combination with non-opioid analgesics such as ASA (Percodan) or acetaminophen (Percocet). Administration is exclusively oral. Oxycodone has the potential to produce powerful physical dependence in users because of its potent effects (Kalso, 2005). In 1995, a time-release version of oxycodone, OxyContin, was introduced and was inaccurately and actively marketed as being a non-addicting opioid. Consequently, it became the preferred prescribed medication across North America for individuals

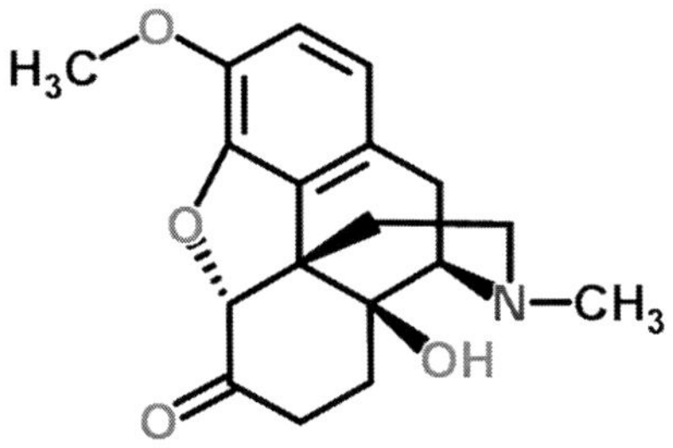

Figure 2.25: Oxycodone

suffering with chronic back pain as well as pain due to cancer and osteoarthritis. OxyContin was also prescribed for those with chronic pain who had developed a level of opioid dependency. It quickly became first the most prominently prescribed drug for the management of moderate to severe pain when a continuous, around-the-clock analgesic was needed for an extended period of time, and then the go-to opioid for anyone with any type of pain (Smith, 2009).

As OxyContin is the same drug as oxycodone, only with a longer duration of action, it has the same systemic name and molecular formula. The solubility of oxycodone and OxyContin is similar to morphine, which has the lowest solubility of the opioids, as opposed to that of fentanyl, which has the highest solubility among therapeutic opioids, which also explains why effects last longer (Biancofiore, 2006). OxyContin controlled-release, when orally administered, begins to enter the bloodstream within 15 minutes. It can begin masking pain within 35 to 40 minutes, producing peak relief within a few hours. After the initial rapid first phase, with an average half-life of 37 minutes accounting for 38% of the dose, a slower, more controlled phase with a half-life of 6.5 hours begins (Smith, 2009). OxyContin is to be taken every 12 hours; however, issues arose with this opioid because, rather than being administered as intended, it was crushed and injected or administered via the mucous membrane of the nose or simply chewed and swallowed. This leads to a rapid release of the opioid properties that were intended to be gradually discharged, producing a much more immediate, potent, and shorter-acting psychoactive effect. These altered methods of administration led to issues with drug diversion and increased reports of overdose and death. Between 2000 and 2005, of the people received by the medical withdrawal service of the Centre for Addiction and Mental Health in Toronto, Ontario, for the treatment of opioid dependence, those who had a problem with OxyContin increased steadily from fewer than 4% to 55% (Sproule et al., 2009). OxyContin is sufficiently potent to lead to death by respiratory depression among naive or non-tolerant users, even if used properly.

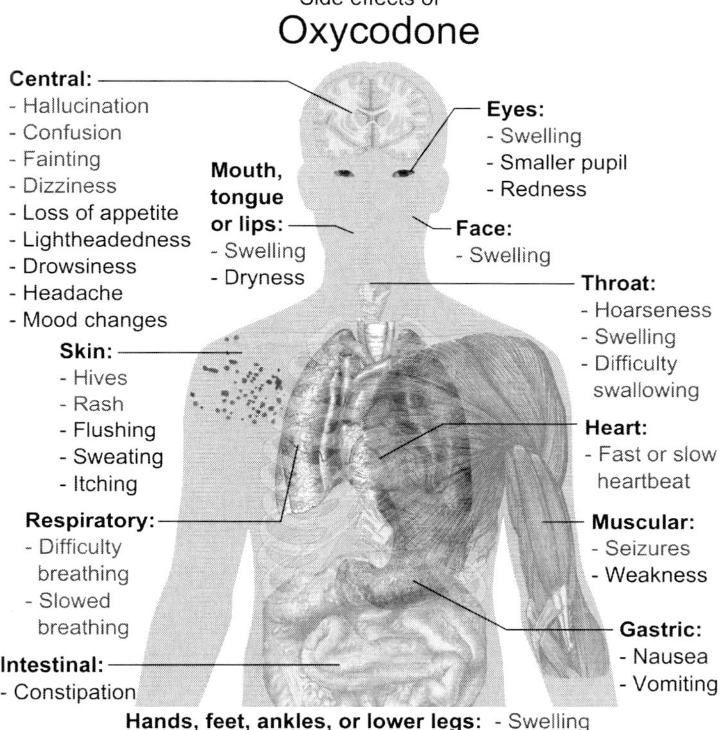

Figure 2.26: Side Effects of Oxycodone

Source: Wikimedia Commons

Propoxyphene (Darvon)

slang: 65's, footballs, N's, pink footballs, pinks, yellow footballs

Synthetic opioid, *4-(Dimethylamino)-3-methyl-1,2-diphenyl-2-butanyl propionate ($C_{22}H_{29}NO_2$)*

Propoxyphene is a mild analgesic used to relieve mild to moderate pain as an alternative to codeine. It was synthesized in 1955 and dependency, tolerance, and withdrawal are similar to those produced by codeine. Darvon, its market name, has one-half to two-thirds the potency of codeine when administered orally. Propoxyphene was marketed as being stronger than aspirin, but not as potent or allergy producing as morphine or even codeine. However, by 1977, propoxyphene was among the most misused opioids and the second-leading agent in prescription drug–induced deaths in the United States, as it has a narrow margin of therapeutic to toxic levels. At four times the standard dose, Darvon can slow the heart and breathing to dangerous levels, while at six times the standard dose it can be lethal (Barkin, Barkin, & Barkin, 2006).

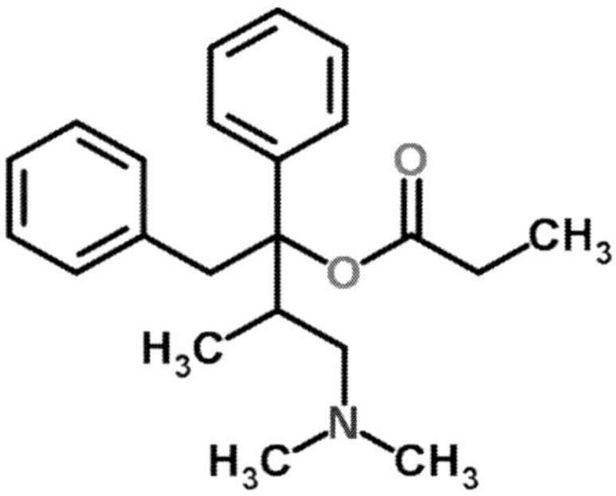

Figure 2.27: Propoxyphene

Darvon's side effects include drowsiness, dizziness, nausea, sedation, constipation, light-headedness, headache, and euphoria or, interestingly, mood depression. More serious side effects include abdominal pain, hallucinations, skin rashes, yellow skin and eyes, and visual disturbances. Both Canada and the United States withdrew the drug in 2010 as research studies found that even at doses normally taken to manage pain, propoxyphene significantly increased the risk of serious abnormal heart rhythms. Ironically, the drug that most often replaced Darvon prescriptions was OxyContin (Government of Canada, 2013; Larochelle et al., 2015).

Suboxone (buprenorphine and naloxone)

slang: box, oranges, sobos, stop signs, stops, sub, subs

Synthetic opioid agonist-antagonist

Suboxone is an opioid agonist-antagonist. It is composed of the partial µ-opioid receptor agonist buprenorphine (separate listing) in combination with the opioid antagonist naloxone (separate listing) in a 4:1 ratio. When this combination drug is taken sublingually, it takes from two to ten minutes to dissolve. Used in this manner, the naloxone exerts no clinically significant effect, leaving only the opioid agonist effects of buprenorphine. However, when buprenorphine is administered in combination with naloxone through any form of injection, the opioid antagonism of naloxone causes the user to go into withdrawal immediately. This overwhelmingly negative physical response greatly reduces the abuse potential of the compound drug (Orman & Keating, 2009). Suboxone has been found to be an effective maintenance therapy for opioid dependence when administered orally and has generally similar efficacy to methadone, even when it is administered less often (Handford et al., 2011). Additionally, Suboxone users reported more clarity of thinking, greater confidence, and lower stigma compared to those using methadone (Tanner et al., 2011). A recent study in the United Kingdom found that Suboxone users suffered fewer poisonings and had a lower risk of mortality than did methadone users, though on average the period of usage was shorter for Suboxone than for methadone (Hickman et al., 2018). However, Suboxone is approximately three times more expensive than methadone.

Suboxone, like methadone, can produce a physical dependency, and as with all opioid substances can slow and even stop respiration, though it is less likely than methadone to produce an overdose (Orman & Keating, 2009). Typical starting dose is four milligrams of Suboxone once daily up to a maximum recommended daily dose of 24 milligrams, with the ultimate goal being to gradually decrease dose levels to zero over a minimum period of months. The drug is a white to creamy hexagonal tablet and has two dose levels: a 2-milligram buprenorphine/0.5-milligram naloxone version, and a more potent 8-milligram/2-milligram version (Milne et al., 2009).

Pentazocine (Talwin)

slang: *general:* tall

Talwin and antihistamines: T's and blues

Talwin and Ritalin: kibbles and bits, one and ones, poor man's heroin, ritz & T's, T's & R's

(1R,9R,13R)-1,13-Dimethyl-10-(3-methyl-2-buten-1-yl)-10-azatricyclo[7.3.1.0^{2,7}] trideca-2,4,6-trien-4-ol ($C_{19}H_{27}NO$)

Like Suboxone, Talwin is an opioid agonist-antagonist with moderate analgesic properties. Pentazocine was created with the goal of relieving pain without producing dependency or leading to misuse, as do other opioids. However, tolerance can develop to Talwin, though it is slower than with most opioids. What makes Talwin distinct is that it has no cross-tolerance with other opioids. Withdrawal effects include abdominal cramps, chills, hypothermia, vomiting, and both a physical and psychological craving for the drug. Unfortunately, when combined with a tripelennamine hydrochloride type of antihistamine, such as Benzoxal, and injected, a heroin-like effect is produced. This combination is referred to as "T's and blues." Combining Talwin with Ritalin produces a similar effect (Fudala, 2006).

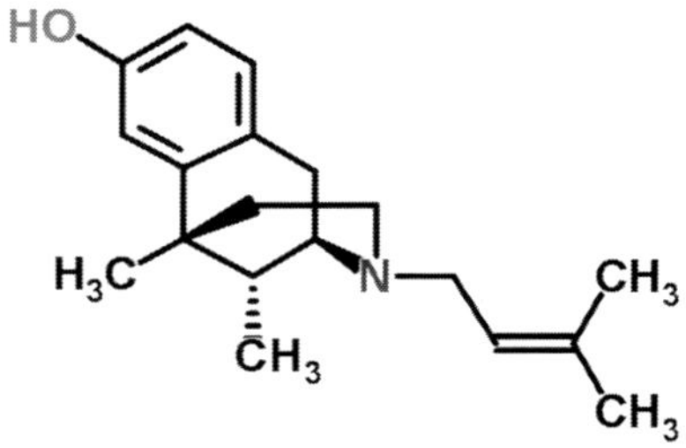

Figure 2.28: Pentazocine

Tramadol

slang: chill pills, trammies, ultras

Synthetic opioid, *(1R,2R)-2-[(Dimethylamino)methyl]-1-(3-methoxyphenyl)cyclohexanol* ($C_{16}H_{25}NO_2$)

Tramadol is a synthetic codeine analogue prescribed for the management of moderate to moderately severe pain in adults who require treatment for only a few days. It has only half the potency of morphine, and yet there are many potential side effects with its use. Seizures have been reported in patients receiving tramadol even when it is prescribed within the recommended dosage range. Tramadol, along with altering mu opioid receptor sites, also produces increased serotonin and norepinephrine levels similar to those produced by antidepressant drugs

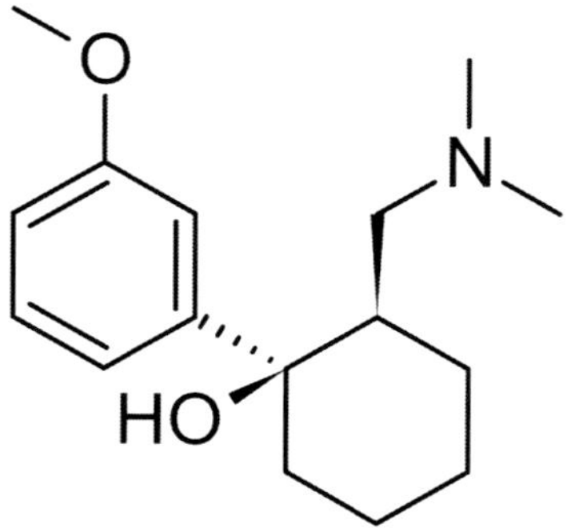

Figure 2.29: Tramadol
Source: Wikimedia Commons

(chapter 5.1) such as venlafaxine (Effexor). Thus, the risk of seizures is further increased for individuals who are also using selective serotonin reuptake inhibitors, tricyclic antidepressants, or other opioids (Grond & Sablotzki, 2004).

When taken orally in pill form, the liver metabolizes tramadol into several chemicals, including *O*-desmethyltramadol, which produces much more potent effects than tramadol itself. There is an extended-release version of this drug (Tridural) as there are with several opioids, and as is the case with all these versions, if the drug is not swallowed whole but rather chewed or crushed, it can be released far too quickly, leading to a more intense physical reaction but also to a potentially fatal dose in naive opioid users (Grond & Sablotzki, 2004).

Tramadol, like all opioids, has the potential to cause physical and psychological dependence. Withdrawal symptoms may include: anxiety, sweating, insomnia, rigors (a sudden feeling of cold with shivering accompanied by a rise in temperature), pain, nausea, tremors, diarrhea, upper respiratory symptoms, piloerection (involuntary bristling of body hair), and rarely, even panic attacks, severe anxiety, and hallucinations. During withdrawal, individuals can also exhibit periods of anger, hostility, and aggression, while post-withdrawal periods can lead to increased levels of anxiety, depression, and obsessive-compulsive symptoms (El-Hadidy & Helaly, 2015).

QUIZ

1. What is the main therapeutic function of opioids?
2. With which group of psychoactive drugs are opioids associated?
3. Synthesized in Germany in the 1930s, this has become the most prominent opioid substitution drug on the planet. What is it?
4. What are the effects of withdrawal from opioids?
5. With opioids, why is the risk of overdose greater than the risk of withdrawal?

Table 2.7: Opioid Potency Comparison

Potency	Drug	Trade Names
100	Fentanyl	
40	Buprenorphine	Suboxone
10*	Heroin	
10	Methadone	
8	Levorphanol	
7	Oxymorphone	Numorphan
5	Hydromorphone	Dilaudid
3	Desomorphine	Permonid
1.5	Oxycodone	Percocet, OxyContin
1.2	Hydrocodone	Vicodin
1	Morphine	
0.5	Tramadol	Ultram, Conzip
0.5	Tapentadol	Tapal, Nucynta, Palexia
0.4	Meperidine	Demerol
0.2	Dihydrocodeine	Panlor
0.1	Codeine	Tylenol 3
0.07	Propoxyphene	Darvon

*depending upon purity
Sources: Pereira et al., 2001; Vieweg, Lipps, & Fernandez, 2005

Opioid Antagonists

Opioid (narcotic) antagonists are not psychoactive agents, but rather drugs that bind to the opioid receptors with higher affinity than do opioid agonists without activating mu, delta, or kappa receptor sites and without producing tolerance. Through this blocking action they prevent the body from responding to both externally administered opioids and natural endorphins. The two most prominent are naloxone (Narcan, Nalone) and naltrexone (Revia, Depade, Vivitrol). Narcan's primary use is to reverse the negative effects of an opioid overdose, counteracting the effects of respiratory depression, sedation, and hypotension (low blood pressure). Naltrexone is an orally administered, long-acting, competitive antagonist at opioid receptor sites that blocks both the subjective and objective effects of opioids. Initially used as a treatment adjunct for those with a heroin dependency, it is now also used clinically with individuals who have a dependency not only to opioids but also to alcohol.

Naloxone (Narcan)

slang: none

(5α)-17-Allyl-3,14-dihydroxy-4,5-epoxymorphinan-6-one ($C_{19}H_{21}NO_4$)

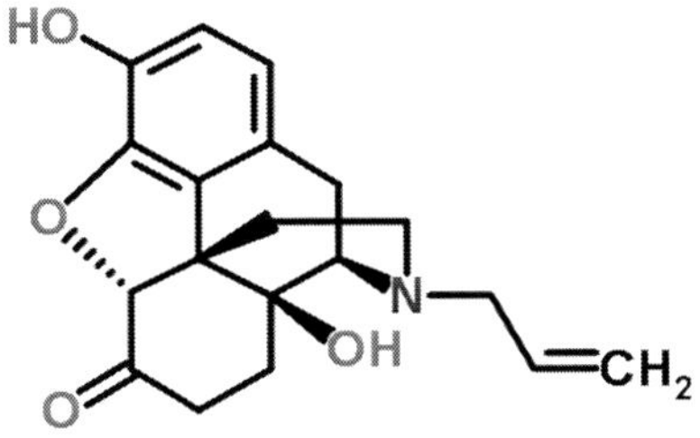

Naloxone, developed in the 1960s as a true antagonist, has a chemical structure similar to oxymorphone but offers neither pain relief nor any type of psychoactive properties. It is a partial inverse mu opioid antagonist that has poor oral and sublingual bioavailability, so it has negligible effects when administered orally. However, if the tablet is crushed, dissolved, and injected, it almost immediately brings on opioid withdrawal (Milne et al., 2009). As a result, naloxone has several therapeutic uses not only in combination with buprenorphine in Suboxone (see above) but also as a means of reversing the opioid-induced respiratory depression, sedation, and hypotension that is commonly observed in cases of opioid

Figure 2.30: Naloxone

overdose. It can also reverse the psychotomimetic and dysphoric effects of agonist-antagonists such as pentazocine, but it does not have the ability to antagonize the respiratory depression caused by high doses of other CNS depressants. Naloxone begins working within 30 seconds of administration and can also be used in the control of seizures induced by meperidine or propoxyphene. However, due to its short half-life of 30 to 90 minutes, which is far shorter than the average half-life of most opioids, repeat dosing is often necessary (Barker & Hunjadi, 2008).

When Naloxone is administered to an opioid-free individual, even in high doses there is typically no discernible effect other than occasional mild dysphoria. However, an opioid-dependent individual who administers naloxone will quickly enter acute withdrawal, exhibiting a range of symptoms that can include body aches, diarrhea, tachycardia (excessive beating of the heart), fever, runny nose, sneezing, goose pimples, sweating, yawning, nausea or vomiting, nervousness, restlessness or irritability, shivering or trembling, abdominal cramps, weakness, increased blood pressure, and in some cases, seizures. Naloxone crosses the placenta and may precipitate withdrawal in the fetus as well as in the mother. In a neonate, opioid withdrawal may also include convulsions, excessive crying, and hyperactive reflexes. Side effects of naloxone in non-dependent individuals tend to be limited to gastrointestinal symptoms. It is on the World Health Organization's list of essential medicines, which summarizes the most important medications needed in a basic health care system, and has become part of emergency overdose kits distributed through harm-reduction programs (Sirohi et al., 2009). Naloxone's ability to save lives has been documented repeatedly globally (Bird et al., 2016; Kerensky & Walley, 2017; McDonald, Campbell, & Strang, 2017).

Naltrexone (Revia)

slang: none

(5α)-17-(Cyclopropylmethyl)-3,14-dihydroxy-4,5-epoxymorphinan-6-one ($C_{20}H_{23}NO_4$)

Naltrexone is an antagonist at both mu and kappa receptor sites, with properties like naloxone but with a much longer duration of action, having a half-life of four to ten hours. It blocks or attenuates the effects of any opioid. It is rapidly and completely absorbed after oral administration, undergoing substantial first-pass extraction and metabolism by the liver. As with naloxone, even after prolonged use naltrexone's discontinuation does not produce any withdrawal effects, respiratory depression, gross behavioural effects, or euphoria. Naltrexone is particularly efficient at suppressing the effects of heroin. As previously discussed, Naltrexone has also been used in pharmacotherapy as an anti-alcohol craving drug, for if it is taken prior to consuming alcohol it blocks the reinforicing endorphin effect alcohol produces. In non-opioid-dependent persons, side effects tend to be limited to gastrointestinal irritation and, in some individuals, small increases in blood pressure (Minozzi et al., 2011; Pullen et al., 2018).

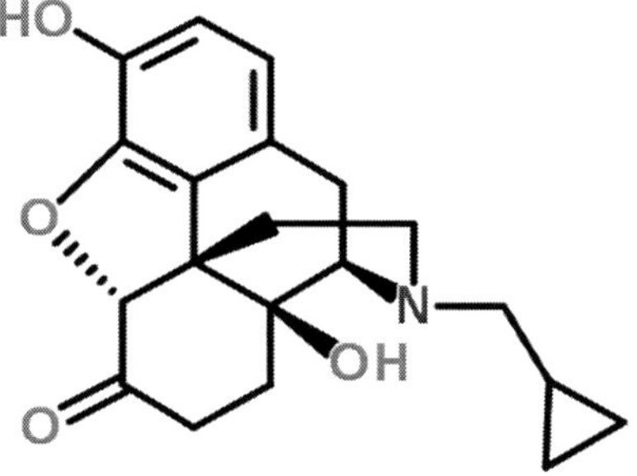

Figure 2.31: Naltrexone

CASE STUDIES

Ruth and Simon

Ruth and Simon are a couple who just completed their post-secondary studies and found out Thursday morning that they were both successful in obtaining employment with the same organization and begin work on Monday. They went out to celebrate at lunch, when they both received calls on their cell phones that they would be drug tested, including an alcohol screen, as the final step in their application process and would need to be at the lab at 5 p.m. Ruth is female, five-foot-six, and weighs 120 pounds. Simon is male, six-foot-one, and weighs 180 pounds. Ruth is a runner, while Simon lifts weights, so both are in good physical shape, and with no history of alcohol or drug abuse. Ruth has consumed two glasses of Prosecco, while Simon had three bottles of Guinness between 11:30 a.m. and 12:30 p.m. In order to pass the drug test, they must have a blood alcohol reading of 0.0. Is either Ruth or Simon at risk of failing their drug test and thus losing their new job?

Joshua

Joshua is a 45-year-old labourer who has used ethyl alcohol increasingly over the past decade. His consumption has reached the point where it is regularly interfering with his work, and he is on the verge of losing his job. With his union's intervention, Joshua has agreed to participate in a psychopharmacology treatment initiative but must agree to begin each session by blowing into a breathalyzer. Between his first and second sessions, Joshua had a lapse, and is now fearful of being dismissed from the program due to this one-time drug use. To improve the breathalyzer reading, Joshua tried to speed up the elimination of alcohol from his body by drinking coffee and having a cold shower. Based on what you know about the metabolism of alcohol, what impact will this have on his reading?

If you were the scientist behind the initiative Josh is participating in, what pharmacological properties would you want the new medication you are developing to help reduce alcohol consumption to have?

Noella

Noella is a 52-year-old heroin user who has been on a methadone maintenance program for 12 years. In general, she has done well; however, she occasionally chips (occasional integrated use with no physical or psychological dependency), and when she is feeling anxious and cannot access heroin, she will take benzodiazepines to provide her with a feeling of euphoria. Thus, on occasion, her urine drug screenings do show positive for benzodiazepines. Noella is using when she is involved in a traffic collision that results in a broken pelvis that is serious but not life-threatening. When the ambulance arrives at the hospital, the emergency room physician, not having time to do a proper assessment, prescribes an opioid to treat her extreme pain. What will the result of the injection be?

If the physician had had time to learn of Noella's methadone use, what action should she have taken in terms of treating Noella's pain?

Assuming Noella had been using diazepam regularly for the last few months, if the assessment had included a drug test and the urine drug screen came back positive, would that indicate that Noella is addicted to benzodiazepines?

What impact might the regular use of diazepam over the past few months have had with regards to the collision?

As benzodiazepines are the safest sedative-hypnotic and rarely produce an overdose, is Noella at risk for serious consequences when she combines high doses of diazepam with her methadone? What if she mixes diazepam with heroin?

After the surgery, Noella is admitted to hospital to recover. Like the emergency room doctor, the surgeon was unaware of her diazepam use. After several days without diazepam, what withdrawal symptoms is Noella at risk of experiencing?

Rick

Rick is in his late 30s. He is involved in teaching, training, and community education. He is bright, highly educated, creative, and motivated. He married after many years of school and now has a young family. He has had many jobs, regularly moving up in responsibility by changing employers. This past year, he took on a new course at a major urban university to supplement his private practice just as major economic cutbacks were affecting his students. Rick has had relatively good health with a few minor maladies, which he typically resolved by visiting his family physician and receiving prescription medicine. One exception to this has been ongoing chronic headaches, a constant complaint for the past several years, though Tylenol 3 typically decreased the pain. While in university, Rick often displayed inappropriate use of alcohol, including binge drinking, showing up for exams hungover, and two 12-hour driving suspensions in his final term of graduate school.

After finishing university and marrying, Rick undertook a controlled drinking regimen and did not experience many serious problems, except with the occasional post–baseball tournament party. However, in preparing a course this past year and feeling frustrated by university- and government-induced cutbacks, his headaches increased in severity, frequency, and intensity. This time, his physician prescribed Fiorinal (1/4), of which Rick was told to take a maximum of four tablets per day but never for more than three days in a row. Rick maintained this schedule for the first month, but as he entered the winter semester, the increased commuting and marking caused him to exceed the recommendations and use more medication more often. He continued to use the drug regularly and then found out he could approach the university medical services clinic for additional medication, including Fiorinal (1/2), when he ran out between visits to his regular physician.

Recently, Rick has been away from home more often, has been argumentative with his family, colleagues, and students, and is no longer able to lecture for three hours at a time, let alone attempt to conduct all-day workshops, nor does he tolerate students skipping class or coming in late.

What are the possible outcomes if Rick does not receive any assistance?

What action would you take in assisting Rick?

Consider the following:

- the pharmacology of the drug
- the pharmacological difference between Fiorinal (1/4) and Fiorinal (1/2)
- the three components of addiction

NOTES

1. Unless otherwise noted, the source of every chemical structure in this chapter is ChemSpider (www.chemspider.com).
2. The source for systemic names and molecular formulas for all opioids is www.chemspider.com. The systemic name describes the chemical structure of a substance, providing basic information about its chemical properties, while the molecular formula represents the number and type(s) of atoms that are present in a single molecule of the substance.

CHAPTER 3

Stimulants

OVERVIEW

Central nervous system (CNS) stimulants are drugs that increase not only the activity of the CNS but also that of the peripheral nervous system (PNS) and, as a result, the autonomic nervous system (ANS), creating both euphoria and mood enhancement. In increased doses, the euphoria is followed by excitement and then agitation. Even greater doses produce irritability, violent behaviour, spasms, convulsions, and, in extreme cases, death. More common and frequent short-term effects include enhanced concentration, increased vigilance, increased blood pressure, increased strength, reduced fatigue, reduced appetite, and feelings of power. While all stimulants increase alertness, as a family, they exhibit considerable differences in their effects and relative potencies.

3.1 COCAINE

slang: angie, base (crack), baseball (crack), bazooka (mixed with cannabis), beam me up Scotty (mixed with PCP), Bernie's Flakes, big C, blow, bonecrusher (crack), C, coke, crack, flake, hardball (mixed with heroin), hunter, jelly, king's habit, line, nose candy, nose powder, Peruvian lady, snow, snowflake, speedball (mixed with heroin), stardust, white horse, Yale

Methyl (1R,2R,3S,5S)-3-(benzoyloxy)-8-methyl-8-azabicyclo[3.2.1]octane-2-carboxylate ($C_{17}H_{21}NO_4$)[1]

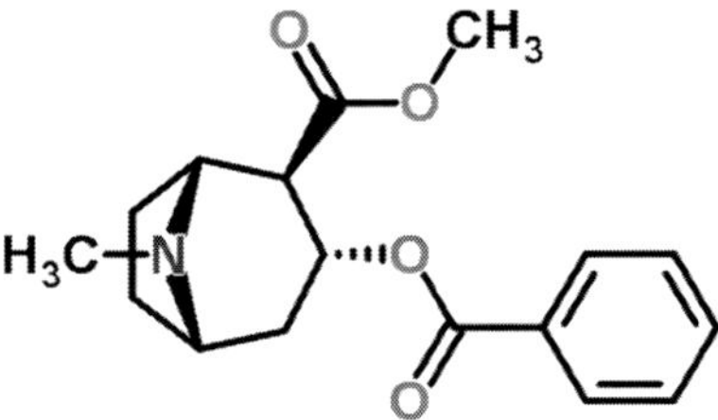

Figure 3.1: Cocaine

Cocaine is a potent stimulant that interferes with the reabsorption process of catecholamines, particularly dopamine, a chemical messenger associated with pleasure and movement. Cocaine prevents the reuptake of dopamine by blocking the dopamine transporter, which leads to increased extracellular dopamine, resulting in the chronic stimulation of post-synaptic dopamine receptors (figure 3.2). This produces a pronounced euphoria; however, when dopamine levels fall, users experience a crash that is just as pronounced. Cocaine also interferes with the uptake of norepinephrine and serotonin (5-HT), leading to the accumulation of these neurotransmitters at post-synaptic receptors. Cocaine is also a local anaesthetic, acting by blocking the initiation and conduction of nerve impulses, making it the only CNS stimulant that has depressant properties. Cocaine concentrates its effects upon the reward areas of the brain, rich in dopamine synapses. As the duration of stimulation of dopamine in the synapse is far greater than normally

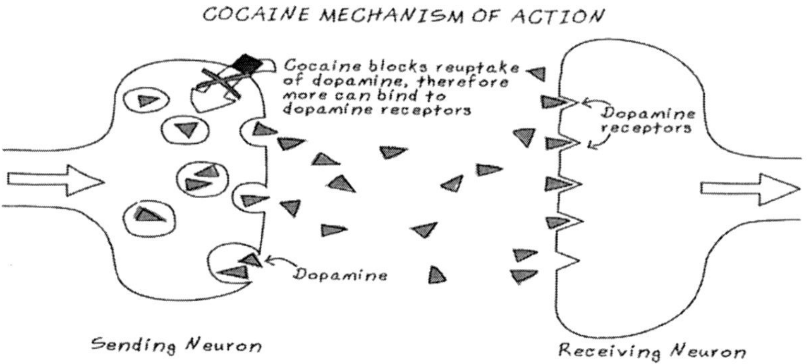

Figure 3.2: Cocaine Mechanism of Action

Source: B. Sproule, *Pharmacology and Drug Abuse*, 2nd edition (Toronto: Centre for Addiction and Mental Health, 2004)

occurs when a person engages in any enjoyable activity, such as eating or sex, the reinforcement potential is likewise far greater, increasing the potential for abuse. Cocaine is rapidly metabolized, having among the shortest half-lives of any psychoactive agent, approximately one hour. Cocaine is broken down by the liver into two major metabolites, benzoylecgonine (BE) and ecgonine methyl ester (EME), and four minor ones, norcocaine, p-hydroxycocaine, m-hydroxycocaine, p-hydroxybenzoylecgonine (pOHBE), and rn-hydroxybenzoylecgonine (Cadet et al., 2014).

Cocaine hydrochloride is derived from the leaves of the erythroxylon coca bush, which is native to the Andes, primarily Peru and Bolivia, although two other varieties are also used for cocaine production: one from the Amazon Basin, and the other from Colombia. Traditionally, inhabitants of the Andes used the leaves of the coca bush to make coca tea or mixed it with ash or lime and placed it in the mouth, like chewing tobacco. The juice trickles into the stomach and serves as a mild stimulant to facilitate heavy labour at high altitudes. Coca's cultivation for medicinal purposes, such as stomach upset, colic, nausea, diarrhea, headache, dizziness, toothache, ulcers, asthma, and fatigue, dates to the beginnings of recorded history in South America. Coca leaves are also a source of vitamins B and C. Cocaine was used medicinally throughout North America and Europe during the late 1800s and early 1900s as a component of many patent medicines. It was also used extensively as an anaesthetic for eye operations and in dentistry and facial surgery, remaining in use as a preferred local anaesthetic in a few circumstances in Canada until the beginning of the 21st century. Presently, coca is still grown legally in Peru and Bolivia, with one of its applications being a decocainized flavouring agent that is used by international soft drink manufacturers (EMCDDA, 2008b; Weil, 1978).

In contrast, the extraction process to produce illicit cocaine powder is toxic. It entails mixing coca with a range of noxious chemicals, such as kerosene, gasoline, acetone, potassium hydroxide, and/or toluene, and then placing the mixture into a press and crushing it until a thick paste is produced. The mixture is then treated with hydrochloride or sulphuric acid to further remove impurities, resulting in crystalline cocaine powder: cocaine hydrochloride. The few legal importers of cocaine, particularly those using it for medical purposes, do not use such a harsh refinement process.

Cocaine may be smoked, sniffed (snorted), injected directly into the veins, or rubbed along the gums. To obtain crack from cocaine hydrochloride, all one needs to do is add a weak base, such as a combination of baking soda and water. Crack and cocaine are the same substance, only in different forms, which means that their pharmacodynamics are identical. Crack is cocaine that can be smoked, while cocaine hydrochloride is not heat soluble, except with significant modification. The absorption of crack is so rapid a user can experience the drug effect within eight seconds. This rapid delivery to the brain and its equally efficient elimination is a major cause of cocaine abuse (Cadet et al., 2014).

The short-term effects of cocaine are akin to those produced by the body's own adrenaline. A naive or infrequent cocaine user will feel and exhibit various behaviours, such as enhanced mood, self-confidence, and self-esteem; increased energy, sex drive, concentration, alertness, and motor activity; decreased appetite; garrulousness (talkativeness); anxiety; and rapid respiration. Cocaine also increases body temperature and heart rate and is a vasoconstrictor, leading to headaches, a rise in blood pressure, and consequently an increased risk of stroke. High doses can cause cardiac arrhythmia, hypothermia, seizures, and, unlike any other stimulant, respiratory depression. Vomiting also brings its own risk of death by aspiration. With larger doses, the person will experience stronger, more frequent highs and exhibit bizarre, erratic, sometimes violent behaviour and even cocaine-induced psychosis during periods of sustained administration. Symptoms subside when administration is discontinued, but periods of severe depression may persist. The risk of convulsions increases with larger doses, and sometimes a sensation of something crawling under the skin is perceived. With long-term use, cocaine, when snorted, can cause tissue damage in the nasal passages and midfacial bones due to its irritating properties as it is highly acidic. When smoked over the long term, cocaine can also cause damage to the lungs and to the pleasure-perceiving portions of the brain. Chronic cocaine use has also been linked to such diverse problems as thiamine deficiency, renal failure, and memory loss. Death from overdose can occur from cocaine alone or in combination with other substances that affect the respiratory control centre in the brain. As cocaine has anaesthetic properties, it is very dangerous when combined with CNS depressants such as alcohol, barbiturates, or any opioid, having the increased potential to produce death through respiratory arrest. Anorexia and weight loss, gastrointestinal disturbances, and impotence have also been observed in chronic users, as well as increased risk of aneurysms, strokes, seizures, and hemorrhaging in tissues surrounding the brain (Centre for Addiction and Mental Health, 2006).

Cocaine users also have widespread loss of grey matter that is directly related to the duration of their cocaine abuse, meaning that the longer they use cocaine, the greater the loss of grey matter, and that this reduction in volume is, in turn, associated with greater compulsivity to use cocaine (Ersche et al., 2011). Chronic cocaine users can experience an alteration of the functional and structural balance between the ventral striatum and the prefrontal cortex of the brain compared to non-users. This alteration can contribute to having difficulties in setting priorities and making decisions, and in inhibiting inappropriate behaviours (Vaquero et al., 2016). However, neural recovery is possible. Parvaz and colleagues (2017) found that with abstinence, even if there is an occasional lapse, there can be an increase in lost grey matter. In their study, as grey matter increased, so did the cognitive skills of former cocaine users. This has implications for harm reduction as well, for if cocaine use can be lessened, the risk of grey matter loss is also lessened (figure 3.3).

Over the course of a single binge, cocaine users become less sensitive to the mood-enhancing effects of the drug and consequently tend to increase the dose in attempting to compensate for the decreased effect. This acute tolerance has been demonstrated in laboratory situations as well. Sensitivity to the drug can, however, be restored with a period of abstinence. The powerfully reinforcing effects of cocaine, both as a euphoriant and as a treatment of post-drug craving, are overwhelming for many users. Experiments with laboratory animals suggest that cocaine has among the strongest behaviourally reinforcing

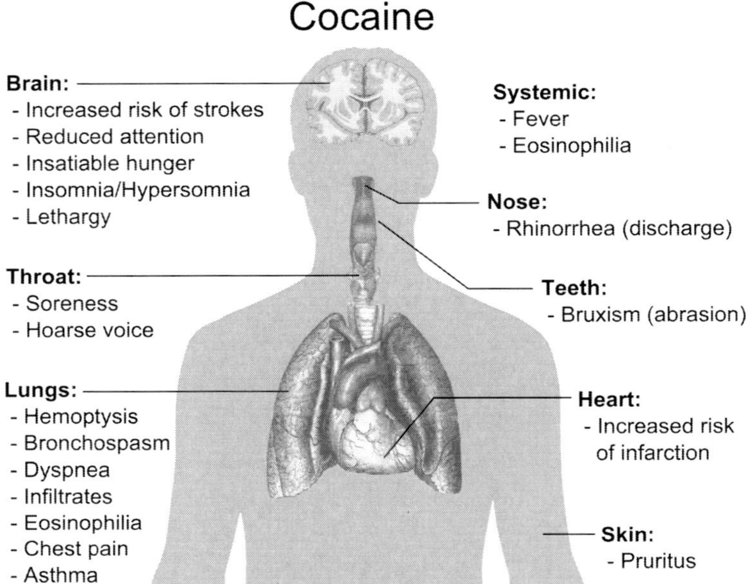

Figure 3.3: Side Effects of Chronic Use of Cocaine
Source: Wikimedia Commons

qualities of all psychoactive drugs. Given the choice, experimental animals have selected cocaine over food, water, and access to a sexual partner (Bozarth & Wise, 1985; Carelli, 2002; Carelli & Deadwyler, 1994; Carelli, Ijames, & Crumling, 2000). Cocaine has also been shown to trigger rapid growth in new brain structures linked to memory and learning in a manner that encourages drug-seeking behaviour (Muñoz-Cuevas et al., 2013).

Cocaine use and withdrawal both affect sleep and the human circadian clock (Stowie, Prosser, & Glass, 2015). A single administration of cocaine will suppress REM sleep, though rebound with increased REM occurs if the use is acute rather than chronic. Similarly, time spent sleeping is lessened with cocaine use but increases after use to compensate for sleep deprivation while using the drug. However, for those who had become dependent upon cocaine a different pattern has been observed. As REM sleep increases in the first few days of abstinence, slow-wave sleep (Stages 3 and 4) decreases. In Stages 3 and 4 sleep the body works to recover physically as compared to the psychological balancing that occurs during REM sleep. Individuals who are cocaine-dependent show a substantive decrease in short-wave sleep such that Stages 3 and 4 are almost completely absent. Amounts of Stage 3 sleep in young adult cocaine-dependent persons is equivalent to persons who are on average 30 years older. Regular cocaine users' behaviour has been equated to individuals with chronic insomnia, with both groups having difficulty falling asleep, both at night and during the day. Loss of sleep depth produces poor cognitive and motor performance and further increases risk of cardiovascular disease, hypertension, and infectious disease, as sleep depth contributes to homeostatic regulation of the autonomic, neuroendocrine, and immune systems (Irwin, Bjurstrom, & Olmstead, 2016; Morgan & Malison, 2007; Schierenbeck et al., 2008).

Cocaine dependence can have devastating effects on the lives of individuals, not only because of the pharmacological effects of the drug, but also because of its cost. Upon abrupt discontinuation of drug administration, abstinence symptoms like those associated with amphetamine withdrawal (chapter 3.2) are observed. Symptoms of this crash include fatigue, severe mood depression, lethargy, and irritability, and can also include abdominal and muscle cramps, nausea, vomiting, dehydration, and a general apathy. Restlessness, anxiety, sweating, shaking, and irregular heartbeat are also common symptoms of cocaine withdrawal (Ciccarone, 2011).

The risks associated with cocaine use and pregnancy have been widely documented (appendix B). Cocaine, like most psychoactive drugs, is transferred across the placenta, and its use may cause placental abruption, the premature detachment of the placenta from the uterus. This can cause bleeding, preterm birth, and, in severe cases, fetal and maternal death. Cocaine-using women have a significantly higher chance of giving birth prematurely, with the fetus suffering withdrawal symptoms. Babies born to mothers using cocaine have been reported to grow slower, have smaller heads, suffer brain injury, and be more irritable and fussier, although the long-term effects have not been observed to be as severe as with fetal alcohol syndrome (Ross et al., 2015).

3.2 AMPHETAMINE AND METHAMPHETAMINE

Amphetamine

slang: amp, beans, bennies, black & white, black beauty, black Cadillacs, black mollies, brain pills, bumblebees, crank, dexies, lid poppers, pep pills, splash, truckers, uppers, wake-ups

1-Phenyl-2-propanamine ($C_9H_{13}N$)

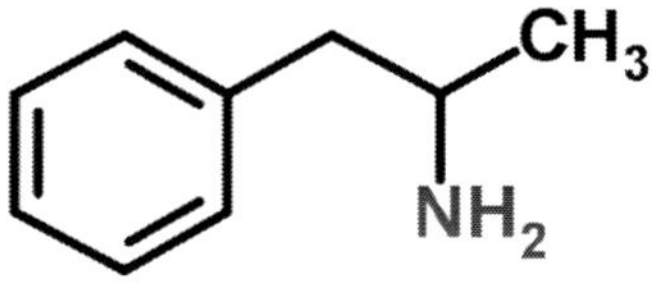

CH_3

NH_2

Figure 3.4: Amphetamine

Globally, amphetamines are the second-most-used illicit drug after cannabis. This includes fenethylline (Captagon), an amphetamine variant that gained notoriety due to its popularity in the Middle East because its manufacture and distribution was a major source of income for ISIS (EMCDDA, 2018b). Amphetamines are a group of synthetic drugs whose action upon the body resembles that of adrenaline. Chemically related to the naturally occurring catecholamine neurotransmitter substances norepinephrine, serotonin, and dopamine, amphetamines are used to raise energy levels and reduce appetite and the need for sleep while providing feelings of clear-headedness, power, and significant euphoria. Amphetamines work by increasing synaptic levels of primarily dopamine, but also serotonin (5-HT) and norepinephrine, as well as partially blocking reuptake like the pharmacodynamic action of cocaine (figure 3.5). Norepinephrine is responsible for methamphetamine's alerting, anorectic (appetite-suppessing), locomotor, and sympathomimetic effects; dopamine also stimulates locomotor effects, but in excess is responsible for producing psychosis and perception disturbances, while changes to serotonin (5-HT) contribute to delusions and psychosis experienced by amphetamine users. Amphetamine's effects are similar to cocaine's, but its onset is slower, and the duration longer (table 3.1). The more amphetamine or methamphetamine a person uses, the more neurotransmitter is released into the synaptic cleft (Pérez-Mañá et al., 2013).

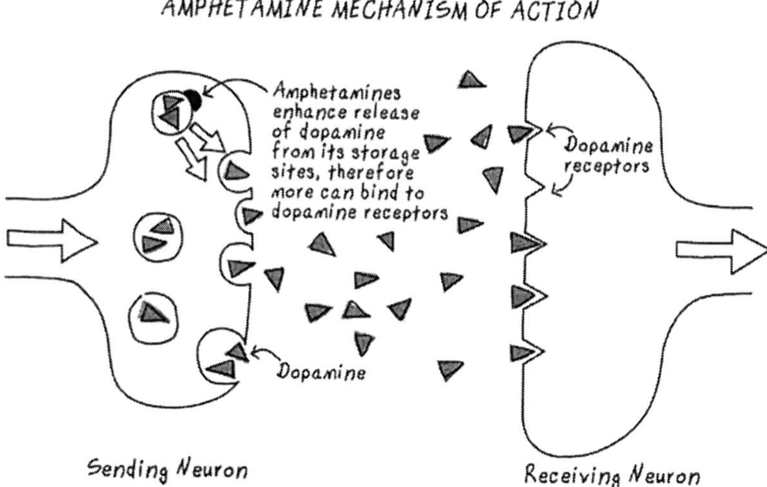

Figure 3.5: Amphetamine and Methamphetamine Mechanism of Action

Note: The same process illustrated for dopamine is what occurs with norepinephrine and serotonin when amphetamine or methamphetamine is administered. The action for all three neurotransmitters occurs simultaneously.
Source: B. Sproule, *Pharmacology and Drug Abuse*, 2nd edition (Toronto: Centre for Addiction and Mental Health, 2004)

Although the first synthesis of amphetamines occurred in 1887, the physiological effects of these compounds were not fully appreciated until the late 1920s. At that time, it was reported that these compounds could constrict blood vessels, increase blood pressure, and dilate the bronchial tubes. Between 1935 and 1945, the mood-altering and stimulant properties of amphetamines were recognized, and they were subsequently used to treat overeating, depression, narcolepsy, Parkinson's disease, and hyperactivity in children, and for the relief of sedation caused by some anti-epileptic drugs. Amphetamines also attracted positive clinical attention because of their reported ability to elevate the mood of depressed individuals. The effects of amphetamines upon non-mental state and mood are in many respects akin to those of cocaine: first, relief from fatigue, increased ability to concentrate, and improved

Table 3.1: Cocaine-Methamphetamine Comparison

Action	Amphetamine	Cocaine
Length of action: 20–30 minutes		✓
Length of action: 4–6 hours	✓	
Produces self-esteem	✓	✓
Increases alertness	✓	✓
Postpones sleep	✓	✓
Decreases appetite	✓	✓
Increases blood pressure	✓	✓
Produces seizures	✓	✓
Acts as a local anaesthetic		✓
Increases body temperature	✓	✓
Causes cardiac arrhythmias	✓	✓
Elicits paranoid psychosis	✓	✓
Causes depression during withdrawal	✓	✓
Has a high dependency liability	✓	✓

physical performance; then euphoria, followed later by depression and fatigue during the withdrawal phase. It was previously believed that the dependence liability of amphetamines was low, leading some to have historically been sold widely without prescription to aid with decongestion and, in the United States, as appetite suppressants and legal stimulants. However, the fact that these were addicting agents, in all three meanings of the term, was eventually noted and restrictions began being placed on over-the-counter sales of amphetamines (Hancock & McKim, 2018).

Amphetamines as a group can be consumed orally, inhaled, or injected for a faster onset of effects. Following oral administration, peak amphetamine concentrations occur in 2.5 to 3.5 hours, with a mean elimination half-life of 10.1 hours. Following intravenous injection, the mean elimination half-life is slightly longer, averaging 12 hours. Drug testing for amphetamine shows positive results for one to four days, but metabolites can be found for up to a week following heavy use. Overall effects typically last four to eight hours, and residual effects up to half a day (National Highway Traffic Safety Administration, 2014).

Like adrenaline, the effects of amphetamines are exerted not only on the brain, but also on the heart and lungs. At low doses, the physical effects include reduction of appetite, increased breathing and heart rate, a rise in blood pressure, and dilation of the pupils. If larger doses are taken, dry mouth, fever, sweating, headache, blurred vision, and dizziness may occur. Even greater dose levels produce flushing, pallor, rapid or irregular heartbeat, tremors, loss of coordination, and physical collapse. Deaths from burst blood vessels in the brain, heart failure, and high fever have been reported as a direct result of excessive amphetamine use. The long-term effects of amphetamine use include malnutrition, physical exhaustion, memory and learning impairments, a tendency to engage in irrational, violent acts, hallucinations, confusion, and an increased susceptibility to infection. Infections may also arise due to the use of unsterile needles from intravenous injection, or from repeated injections at the same location. Some infectious diseases are passed from user to user via shared needles. Impure amphetamines often contain materials not readily soluble in water. The particles can pass into the body and block small blood vessels or weaken their walls, resulting in kidney damage, lung problems, stroke, or other tissue injuries (Büttner, 2011).

This drug group also produces amphetamine psychosis, a transient state that resembles paranoid schizophrenia, including auditory hallucinations and paranoid thinking. This is primarily due to the massive amount of dopamine this drug's action releases into the synaptic cleft. In predisposed individuals, amphetamine use may make them susceptible to an increased risk of repeated episodes of psychosis even if abstinent (Lappin, Sara, & Farrell, 2017). Regular use of amphetamines induces tolerance to some of their effects, making increased doses necessary to produce the same effects. Tolerance does not develop to all effects at the same rate; however, it does develop rapidly to the mood-enhancing effects, necessitating an increase in dosage. While a therapeutic dose averages 30 milligrams, doses of up to 1 gram have been given to tolerant users without them demonstrating any exaggerated effects. Cross-tolerance between amphetamines and other amphetamine-like CNS stimulants has been clinically observed, though there does not appear to be cross-tolerance with cocaine due to their disparate pharmacodynamics. Physical and psychological dependence both occur with chronic amphetamine use. Animals made dependent upon amphetamines and then withdrawn will work extremely hard to obtain more of the drug and will keep trying approximately twice as long as similar animals made dependent upon heroin and then withdrawn. Long-term use of amphetamines lowers dopamine levels in the brain (Sproule, 2004).

Methamphetamine

slang: blade, chalk, chrissy, crank, crystal, crystal meth, dust, glass, go, ice, ice cream, quartz, Scooby Snax, tina, weak, whiz, yaba, yellow barn

N-Methyl-1-phenyl-2-propanamine ($C_{10}H_{15}N$)

Methamphetamine is an analogue of amphetamine, which means that it alters neurotransmitters in the same manner as amphetamine. However, methamphetamine also activates histamine H_3-receptors, inducing additional dopamine release in the nucleus accumbens (Munzar et al., 2004). Methamphetamine first enjoyed recreational popularity in Canada in the 1970s, but the harsh toll it took upon the body led it to be a relatively short-lived phenomenon. It re-emerged during the rave era of the 1990s, becoming known as "poor man's cocaine" and a drug that was more readily accessible in that it could be produced locally. The majority of street methamphetamine is produced in clandestine laboratories by breaking down *l*-ephedrine or *d*-pseudoephedrine (PPA, a decongestant) with hydriodic acid, or with

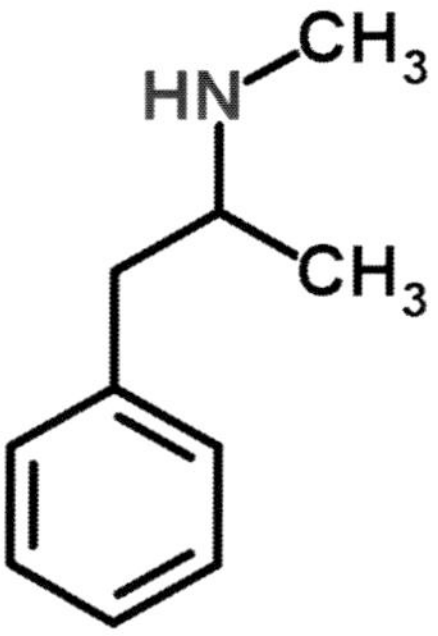

Figure 3.6: Methamphetamine

sodium or lithium in condensed form using liquid ammonia or red iodine. Methamphetamine, like all amphetamines, is a white, odourless, bitter-tasting crystalline powder whose use can lead to memory loss, aggressive behaviour, violence, and paranoid and psychotic behaviour if abused. Part of this behaviour is due to the fact that its use allows an individual to remain awake for extended periods of time (Pérez-Mañá et al., 2013).

Crystal meth is a further synthesized form of methamphetamine that can be smoked, creating a fast, intense stimulant response somewhat like that of crack cocaine, only lasting much longer—from six to twelve hours. Due to the addition of a methyl group, methamphetamine is more lipid soluble than amphetamine, allowing more rapid transport of the drug across the blood-brain barrier (Barr et al., 2006). Among the reasons for its popularity is that initially, users experience an increased and intensified sex drive along with feelings of enhanced sexual pleasure, though this dissipates with as little as six months of regular use. This feeling is produced because methamphetamine can release up to 12 times as much dopamine in the CNS as eating one's favourite food or engaging in non-drug-enhanced sex. There is no known behaviour humans engage in that can release that much dopamine (Ciccarone, 2011).

Early-stage effects of methamphetamine include euphoria, excitation, exhilaration, rapid flight of ideas, increased libido, rapid speech, motor restlessness, hallucinations, delusions, psychosis, insomnia, reduced fatigue or drowsiness, increased alertness, heightened sense of well-being, feelings of increased physical strength, and poor impulse control. Physically, a user will experience increased heart rate, blood pressure, and respiration rate, as well as elevated temperature, palpitations, irregular heartbeat, dry mouth, abdominal cramps, suppressed appetite, twitching, pallor, dilated pupils, faster reaction time, increased strength, and more efficient glucose utilization. As the drug is metabolized, euphoria is replaced with dysphoria, restlessness, agitation, nervousness, paranoia, violence, aggression, lack of coordination, pseudo-hallucinations, delusions, psychosis, and drug craving, while physically, as fatigue brings sleepiness with sudden starts, itching, picking, and/or scratching can occur. Binge use of methamphetamine begins with a rush lasting upwards of five minutes, highlighted by an intense euphoria, rapid flight of ideas, sexual stimulation, high energy, obsessive-compulsive activity, thought blending, and dilated pupils. This is followed by a less intense phase, which can last upwards of one hour; during this phase, a user will experience less intense euphoria, hyperactivity, continued rapid flight of ideas, obsessive-compulsive activity, and thought blending. The crash phase after a binge can last one to three days, during which the user will experience intense fatigue, uncontrollable sleepiness and catnapping, continuing stimulation, and drug craving. Withdrawal is highlighted by anhedonia (an inability to feel pleasure), waves of intense craving, depression, hypersomnia (excessive sleeping), exhaustion, and extreme fatigue. Light sensitivity, irritability, nervousness, headache, tremors, anxiety, suspiciousness, paranoia, aggressiveness, delusions, hallucinations, irrational behaviour, and violence are also all possible during withdrawal. In overdose, symptoms may include hyperthermia, tachycardia, severe hypertension, convulsions, chest pains, cardiovascular collapse, and possibly death (Cruickshank & Dyer, 2009). A disproportionate occurrence of hemorrhagic stroke has been documented among young methamphetamine users. This is even more problematic in that methamphetamine-related stroke is associated with poor clinical outcomes (Lappin, Darke, & Farrell, 2017).

The toxic ingredients used to synthesize illicit forms of the drug lead to severe tooth decay, which has been labelled "meth mouth." Teeth become stained black and rot to the point where they fall out or need to be pulled because of the damage to the gums and roots. Ongoing methamphetamine administration also appears to cause reduced levels of dopamine, which can result in symptoms like those of Parkinson's disease. Also, like amphetamines, chronic methamphetamine abuse can produce symptoms of psychosis that resemble schizophrenia and are characterized by suspiciousness, paranoia, picking at the skin, preoccupation with one's own thoughts, and auditory and visual hallucinations. Violent and erratic behaviour is frequently seen among chronic abusers, as are panic attacks. Use of methamphetamine also produces substantive sleep disruptions. Even a single morning oral administration of methamphetamine can produce robust disruptions in nighttime sleep, with larger amounts creating greater issues. The lack of REM sleep, and thus the lack of dreaming, is another contributing factor in creating paranoid and psychotic behaviour among methamphetamine users (Herrmann et al., 2017; National Highway Safety Traffic Administration, 2014).

3.3 METHYLPHENIDATE (RITALIN AND CONCERTA)

slang: *general:* Diet Coke, kibble and bits, kiddie cocaine, kiddie speed, r-ball, silver bullet, smarties, vitamin R, west coast

mixed with Talwin: ritz & T's, T's & R's

Methyl phenyl(2-piperidinyl)acetate ($C_{14}H_{19}NO_2$)

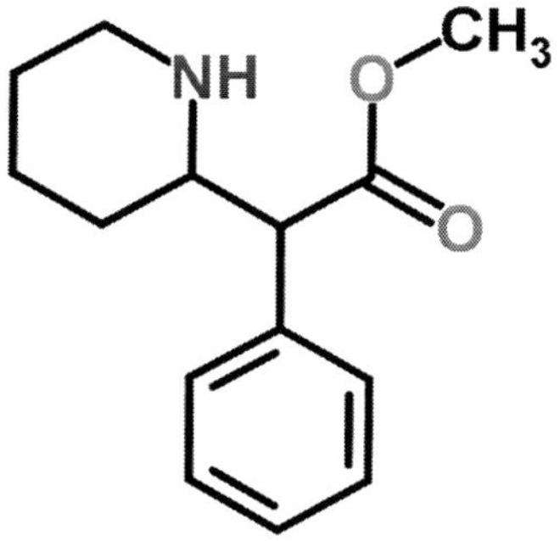

Figure 3.7: 3-4 Methylphenidate

The pharmaceutical company Ciba-Geigy synthesized methylphenidate (Ritalin) in the 1940s to break a patent by a rival pharmaceutical company. Ritalin was initially marketed to treat chronic fatigue, depression, psychosis associated with depression, and narcolepsy, and to offset the sedative effects of other medications, including barbiturate overdose (Alexander & Stockton, 2000). Presently, Ritalin, pemoline (Cylert), and the extended-release version, Concerta, along with Adderall, which is a minor amphetamine (dextroamphetamine) and not methylphenidate, are all used to treat attention-deficit/hyperactivity disorder (ADHD) in both children and adults. ADHD is a condition that children are born with but that is often confused with, and misdiagnosed in children with, a behavioural or conduct disorder. Methylphenidate is able to relieve the symptoms of ADHD, which include short attention span, impulsivity, hyperactivity, and generally poor behavioural adjustment (Brands et al., 1998).

It is hypothesized that ADHD is caused by decreased dopamine, norepinephrine, and glutamate activity in the CNS, especially the prefrontal cortex and peripheral cortex, which are responsible for self-regulation functions. This leads to self-regulation disorders compromising the sufferer's attention, self-control, and behaviour. Methylphenidate works primarily to inhibit the reuptake of dopamine and norepinephrine, which improves the levels and utility of these neurotransmitters in the brain as well as increasing serotonin levels. This is an action more similar to cocaine than to amphetamines, and methylphenidate does possess some structural and pharmacological similarities to cocaine, though methylphenidate is far less potent and has a far longer duration (Calipari et al., 2012; Daniali et al., 2013; Devilbiss & Berridge, 2008). These stimulants will increase the attention span of not only children or adults suffering from ADHD, but of anyone, including indivduals with fetal alcohol syndrome or fetal alcohol effects.

Children with ADHD who used methylphenidate, compared to those with ADHD who did not, have less severe lifetime negative health outcomes. Those properly prescribed this drug as medication had less risk of being seriously injured, contracting a sexually transmitted infection, becoming pregnant, or suffering from a substance use and abuse disorder (Chorniy & Kitahima, 2016; Quinn et al., 2017). Recently, methylphenidate has been prescribed to some individuals with Alzheimer's disease. One study reported that methylphenidate improved the apathy in a group of community-dwelling veterans with mild Alzheimer's disease, along with improving their cognition, functional status, and depression while lessening caregiver burden (Padala et al., 2018). Another study found combining methylphenidate with the antidepressant Celexa, a selective serotonin reuptake inhibitor (chapter 5.1), demonstrated an enhanced response in the mood and well-being of the study's participants at a rate superior to either drug alone (Lavretsky et al., 2015).

Unfortunately, the use of Ritalin and Concerta, like all psychoactive agents, produces unwanted side effects. Methylphenidate has been demonstrated to delay and reduce REM sleep periods (Sangal et al., 2006). It also produces a loss of appetite, nervousness, tics, Tourette's syndrome, cardiac arrhythmia, increased blood pressure, rash, dry mouth, and abdominal pain (Sumnall et al., 2008). The use of methylphenidate has also been shown to delay physical growth and development in children, in either height or weight or both (Faraone et al., 2008). Further, a small but significant number of heart attacks, strokes, and sudden deaths have been linked to the use of this drug in children and young adults (Breeding & Baughman, 2003; Cooper et al., 2011), as well as suicidal ideation and self-harming action (Health Canada, 2016).

3.4 ANOREXIANTS

slang: fen-phen, preludes, slims

Diethylpropion, *2-(Diethylamino)-1-phenyl-1-propanone N-Ethyl* ($C_{13}H_{19}NO$)

Fenfluramine, *N-ethyl-1-[3-(trifluoromethyl)phenyl]propan-2-amine* ($C_{12}H_{16}F_3N$)

Diethylpropion and fenfluramine are examples of lesser amphetamines that have been regularly prescribed over short periods of time to assist with weight reduction and the treatment of clinical obesity, replacing the more potent amphetamines that were used as anorexiants prior to the early 1970s. In the 1950s research was published supporting the use of anorexiants among overweight pregnant women (Birnberg & Abitbol, 1958). Fenfluramine, in particular, does not produce nearly as much CNS stimulation as other amphetamines, and in fact causes drowsiness in some users. However, its excessive use has become

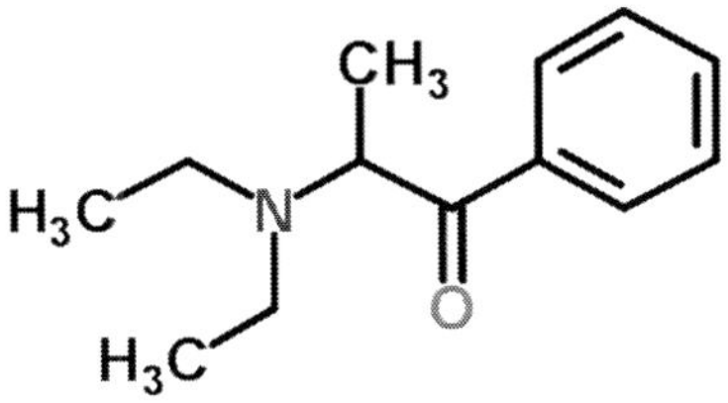

Figure 3.8: Diethylpropion

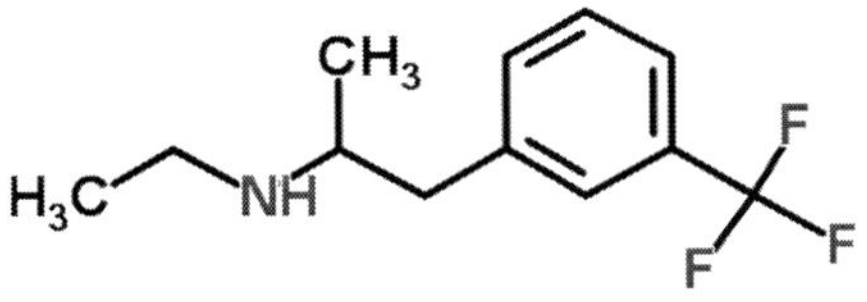

Figure 3.9: Fenfluramine

associated with cardiovascular problems, especially when used in combination with phentermine. In general, though, anorexiants are not drugs of choice among illicit users, but large doses may be consumed as a last resort if more potent stimulants are unavailable. Examples of anorexiants include phentermine (Ionamin), diethylpropion (Tenuate), fenfluramine (Ponderal), phenmetrazine (Preludin), and phentermine (Duromine, Metermine, Suprenza) (Brands et al., 1998).

3.5 DECONGESTANTS

slang: pseudococaine, robo-tripping

Phenylpropanolamine (PPA), *2-Amino-1-phenyl-1-propanol* ($C_9H_{13}NO$)

Propylhexdrine (PDE), *1-Cyclohexyl-N-methyl-2-propanamine* ($C_{10}H_{21}N$)

Pseudoephedrine (PSE), *(1S,2S)-2-(methylamino)-1-phenylpropan-1-ol* ($C_{10}H_{15}NO$)

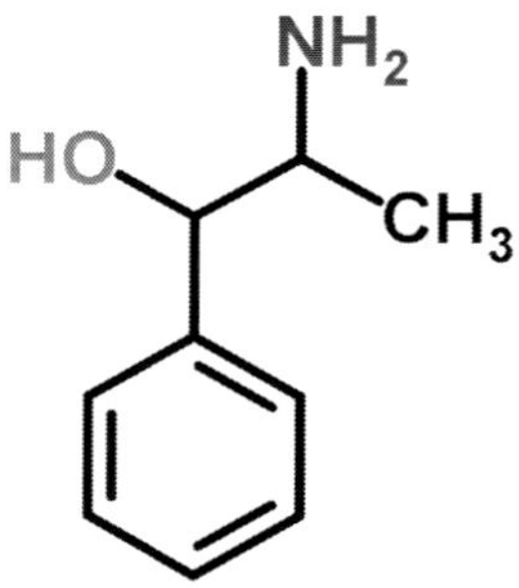

Phenylpropanolamine (PPA), propylhexedrine PDE), and pseudoephedrine (PSE) are the most prominent decongestants. They all have chemical structures similar to that of amphetamine, though with a much lower dependency liability. Each has been available as an over-the-counter (OTC) medication, though as a group they have come under increasing legal scrutiny since 2000 due to direct health risks, athletic-performance-enhancing capabilities, and their use as a precursor in the production of methamphetamine (chapter 3.2), which has led to a dramatic modification in their OTC status. Like other CNS stimulants, decongestants constrict blood vessels, and through this process relieve nasal and sinus congestion. They also became widely used as anorexiants due to their greater accessiblity. Decongestants have

NH_2 HO CH_3

Figure 3.10: Phenylpropanolamine

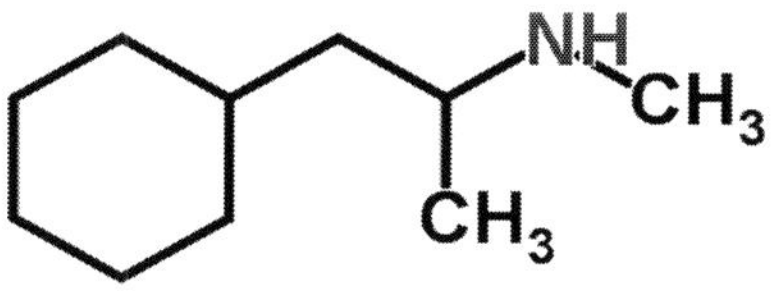

Figure 3.11: Propylhexedrine

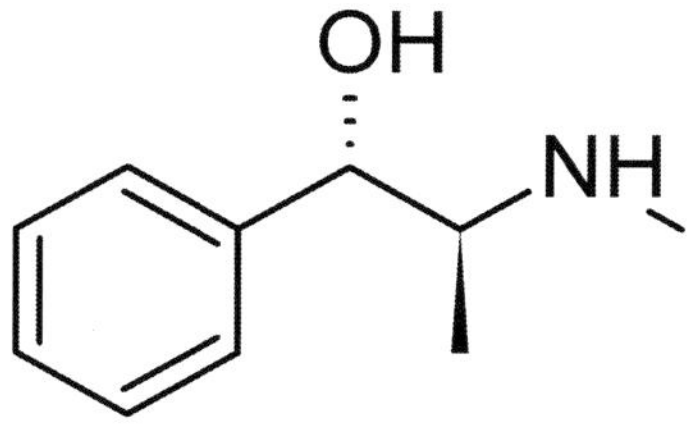

Figure 3.12: Pseudoephedrine

historically been found in many cold and allergy medications, often in combination with an antihistamine (chapter 2.2), though the two belong to distinct pharmacological categories, as antihistamines, which block the binding of histamines in the CNS, are depressants.

Decongestants mimic the effects of transmitter substances of the sympathetic nervous system, including epinephrine (adrenaline), norepinephrine (noradrenaline), and most importantly, dopamine, working as norepinephrine-releasing agents and to a lesser extent dopamine-releasing agents. Decongestants primarily produce their therapeutic action by activating receptors found on blood vessels of the mucous membrane that lines the nasal passage (nasal mucosa). This occurs through either direct binding at the receptor site or through the enhanced release of norepinephrine, which produces vasoconstriction. As vasoconstriction increases, blood flow through the nasal mucosa decreases, resulting in shrinkage of the inflamed tissue. Decongestants can be administered topically, directly onto the nasal mucosa, or orally. Both PPA and PDE are readily and completely absorbed, undergoing minimal first-pass metabolization, while PSE undergoes extensive biotransformation in both the gut wall and liver. As a result, prolonged topical administration of PPA and PDE produces tachyphylaxis, and in turn rebound congestion. Peak concentration is reached between 30 minutes and two hours and depends in part upon the amount of food in the stomach, which impedes absorption. Elimination is predominately renal (via the kidney), with half-lives being relatively short—approximately 2.5 hours for PSE, 4 hours for PPA, and 6 hours for

PDE (De Sutter et al., 2012; Hendeles, 1993; Johnson & Hricik, 1993; Kanfer, Dowse, & Vuma, 1993).

Common side effects of decongestants include sleeplessness, anxiety, dizziness, excitability, and nervousness. Given that decongestants are CNS stimulants, the discovery that, when used beyond recommended limits for extended periods of time, they produced health risks associated with all stimulants—increased blood pressure and the associated cardiovascular issues, including heart attacks, strokes, and seizures, as well as kidney failure—was unsurprising. Anxiety, restlessness, and insomnia can also occur. However, when decongestants are administered at recommended therapeutic doses for the management of nasal or sinus congestion, hypertension is unlikely to be a problem except in the most sensitive of individuals. Unfortunately, when they are self-administered as stimulants, high doses are often taken because of their relatively weak central nervous system effects (Cantu et al., 2003).

Phenylpropanolamine was synthesized in the early 20th century and used initially to induce mydriasis (pupil dilation). By the 1930s it was discovered that PPA could increase blood pressure when administered either intravenously or orally. Soon afterwards, PPA's appetite-suppression ability was discovered; however, PPA is not simply a lesser variant of amphetamines but is an anorexiant of its own class without the substantive side effects that compromise the anorectic capacity of amphetamine. It also has the capacity to produce insomnia and anxiety to a far lesser extent than amphetamine. By the latter half of the 20th century, PPA became the most frequently used OTC drug in the United States (De Sutter et al., 2012; Erickson et al., 2001; Johnson, 1991; Wellman, 1990).

Despite concerns raised as early as 1982 (Bernstein & Diskant, 1982), it was not until this century that restrictions on PPA were imposed. The work of Kernan and colleagues (2000) at Yale demonstrated that the use of PPA as an appetite suppressant by women aged 18 to 49 had led to hemorrhagic (bleeding into the brain or into tissue surrounding the brain) stroke not only after prolonged use—longer than recommended for use to counteract the symptoms of a cold—but also, for a small number of women, after only a few doses. In November 2000 the United States Food and Drug Administration (2016) issued a public health warning regarding the use of PPA that eventually led to its discontinuation not only in the United States but globally, including in Canada, the United Kingdom, and India.

Propylhexedrine is structurally similar to and has pharmacological properties like amphetamines, though it too is not an amphetamine but rather a cycloalkylamine, meaning it is less potent. PDE works by reversing the transporters for dopamine, norepinephrine, and serotonin, leading to a release of monoamines into the synaptic cleft as well as antagonizing transporters in the CNS, which leads to a further increase in the affected neurotransmitters. It has the lowest abuse potential of the prominent decongestants and is the key component of the OTC Benzedrex inhaler. It is also found in the anorexiant Eventin and in anticonvulsants, where its function is to offset the sedative effects of the barbiturate component (Sulzer et al., 2005).

When administered by inhalation, PDE produces a local vasoconstrictor effect, prompting its therapeutic use as a decongestant. If converted to a crystalline version, it can be crushed into a fine white powder and administered intranasally or dissolved in water for intravenous use. PDE is also quickly and well absorbed from the gastrointestinal tract after oral ingestion. When PDE is administered by oral, intranasal, or intravenous routes, amphetamine-like intoxication symptoms, including euphoria, have been observed, as well as signs of tolerance typical of other CNS stimulants. Because PDE stimulates sympathetic nerves, when taken above recommended medical dosage levels, side effects include sweating, talkativeness, euphoria, pupil dilation, emotional lability, anorexia, tachycardia, palpitations, dry mouth, anxiety, and dysphoria. Withdrawal effects include fatigue, depression, suicidal ideation, hunger, and extreme desire for sleep. Ongoing excessive use of PDE can produce hypertension, heart attack symptoms and arrhythmia, psychotic reactions, shock, and in a handful of cases, death. As with similar drugs, using PDE to keep oneself awake for extended times can lead to a temporary state of sleep deprivation, during which an individual may experience hallucinations, including auditory, visual, and tactile sensations (formication), paranoia, irritability, and impaired memory (Fernandez & Francis, 2012; Holler et al., 2011). PDE use has been empirically demonstrated to enhance performance beyond an athlete's typical abilities in sports ranging from track to weight lifting to hockey. As a result, this substance has been placed on the list of banned substances by both the International Olympic Committee and the World Anti-Doping Agency at levels beyond therapeutic dose levels (240 milligrams/day) and is among the drugs urine screens search for among competing athletes (Bents, Tokish, & Goldberg, 2004; Gill et al., 2000).

Pseudoephedrine is an antagonist that enhances the release of norepinephrine. It is a naturally occurring alkaloid in plants such as gymnosperm shrubs, which grow throughout the northern hemisphere, though the majority of PSE is commercially produced from the yeast fermentation of dextrose. PSE has been used therapeutically for not only the common cold but also much more substantive health issues including asthma, heart failure, narcolepsy, and, at one time, depression. Like all decongestants, it has a chemical structure similar to ephedrine; however, PSE, while having the same potency as PPA, causes less CNS stimulation. As fears regarding the health incidences caused by PPA grew, it was replaced in OTC products by PSE (Yakoot, 2012). Unfortunately, the similarity in chemical structure to amphetamines has made PSE a sought-after chemical precursor in the illicit manufacture of not only methamphetamine but also methcathinone (chapter 3.6). The use of PSE for this purpose became so problematic that, under the Combat Methamphetamine Epidemic Act (CMEA) of 2005, the United States included how much of the drug could be sold at one time, how it should be displayed and sold, and how employees were to be trained to sell it. Peak onset of PSE is 30 to 60 minutes, as is the case with most orally administered substances, with a duration of three to four hours, although extended-release versions can last eight to twelve hours (Erickson et al., 2001; Hodges et al., 2006).

3.6 KHAT (QAT)

slang: Abyssinian tea, African salad, African tea, Arabian tea, Bushman's tea, cat, Catha, chat, Flower of Paradise, jimma, oat, Somalia tea

Cathinone, *(2S)-2-Amino-1-phenyl-1-propanone* ($C_9H_{13}NO$)

Methcathinone, *2-(Methylamino)-1-phenyl-1-propanone* ($C_{10}H_{13}NO$)

Globally, the most popular stimulant from the monoamine group is a plant native to East Africa: khat, or qat. This small shrub, whose scientific name is *Catha edulis*, is widely cultivated in the countries of Yemen, Somalia, and Ethiopia and is widely used throughout East Africa and the Arabian peninsula. Khat leaves contain cathinone and methcathinones, which are chemically related to synthetic amphetamine. Among many Islamic nations, its use is considered much more acceptable than that of other psychoactive drugs, including alcohol, with estimates of use indicating that there were as many as five million daily users throughout the Horn of Africa at the turn of the century (Spinella, 2001).

Khat has crimson-brown leaves that turn yellow-green and leathery with age. Its use in Canada increased with the influx of Somali refugees and immigrants that occurred as an outcome of the civil war that began in 1991. In East Africa and South Arabia, where it is most commonly

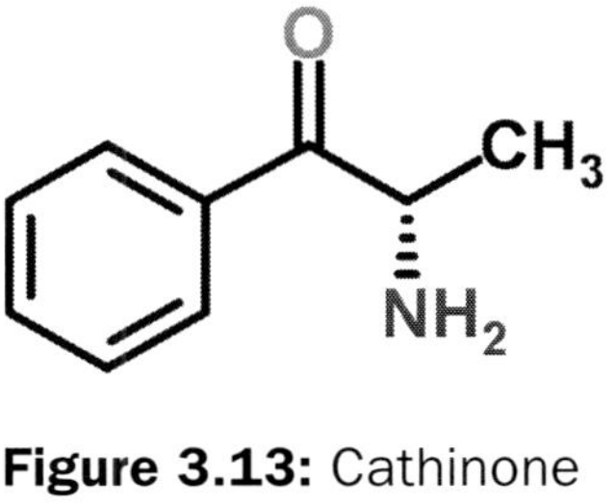

O CH3 NH2

Figure 3.13: Cathinone

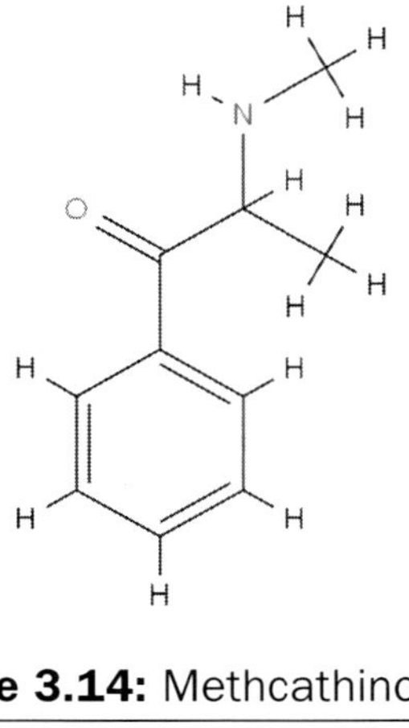

H H N H H O H H H H H H H H H

Figure 3.14: Methcathinone

used, it is a social drug, ingested by chewing the leaves or brewing them in tea, though it can also be smoked. The literal translation of the Arabic word used to refer to khat consumption, *takhzeen*, is "storage." Khat leaves are rolled into a ball and stored in the chewer's cheeks, giving them a characteristic bulging appearance. The active constituents of khat are slowly released from the leaves and mix with the user's saliva, which is then swallowed. Several categories of khat exist, with concentrations of cathinone and methcathinone varying from 75 to 350 milligrams per 100 grams. Cathinone, the main active ingredient, is sometimes described as a natural amphetamine because its structure is similar, though khat also contains tannins and alkaloids at lower concentrations (Khatib et al., 2013).

As it takes between two and three hours of chewing khat to reach maximum plasma concentrations of cathinone, this CNS stimulant produces lower levels of physical dependency than does either cocaine or amphetamines. Research has shown that cathinone exerts its psychostimulant effects not only by increasing the levels of dopamine transmission, but also by increasing serotonin levels, like MDMA (chapter 4.3). Increasing serotonin levels adds to the stimulant effects of dopamine. It is also believed that cathinone inhibits the reuptake of noradrenaline from the synaptic cleft, which is similar to cocaine's pharmacodynamics. Users report that khat provides stimulant effects like that of several cups of coffee or low doses of amphetamines (Carvalho, 2003; Dhaifalaha & Šantavýb, 2004).

Like all stimulants, khat temporarily dispels perceptions of hunger, fatigue, and depression while enhancing concentration and motor activity. Khat users typically experience increased alertness, hyperactivity, and euphoria, though overstimulation of dopamine pathways can lead to aggressive behaviour, anxiety, irritability, and insomnia. There have been a variety of health concerns raised with chronic khat use. Along with its ability to suppress appetite, khat can produce acid reflux and anorexia, prevent sleep, increase respiration, produce hypertension and hyperthermia, and lead to hyperactive behaviour, followed by withdrawal effects highlighted by a general malaise. The effects of khat on the autonomic nervous system can lead to a variety of cardiovascular issues, such as tachycardia, hypertension, and extreme pupil dilation, as well as lesser issues such as dry mouth and constipation. Sperm motility, sperm count, and semen volume were lower among khat users. Its use has also been directly associated with the development of cancer of the mouth and esophagus. Chronic khat use can also produce mania, as well as psychosis in predisposed users. Depression has been found to be particularly associated with khat cessation, and sudden abstinence can lead to lethargy and craving. Nightmares for two to three nights before normal sleeping patterns return have been frequently reported. Some chronic khat users have been reported to suffer permanent brain damage, including symptoms like those associated with Parkinson's disease, and in severe cases, paranoid psychosis. Khat use can also impair both cognitive flexibility and the updating of information in working memory. While recreational use is not associated with significant impairment, physical and psychological dependency to this substance is possible (Caulfield, 2015; Colzato et al., 2011; Hassan, Gunaid, & Murray-Lyon, 2007; Khatib et al., 2013).

3.7 METHYLENEDIOXYPYROVALERONE (BATH SALTS)

slang/brand names: arctic blast, blue silk, charge, cloud 10, flakka, gold rush, gravel, hurricane Charlie, ivory snow, ivory wave, kamikaze, lunar wave, meow meow, monkey dust, mystic, ocean burst, plant fertilizer, pure ivory, purple wave, red dove, scarface, snow leopard, stardust, vanilla sky, white knight, white lightning, wicked X, zombie drug, zoom

1-(1,3-Benzodioxol-5-yl)-2-(1-pyrrolidinyl)-1-pentanone ($C_{16}H_{21}NO_3$)

MDPV (3,4-methylenedioxypyrovalerone), often in combination with related substances mephedrone (2-(Methylamino)-1-(4-methylphenyl)-1-propanone) and/or methylone (1-Propanone, 1-(1,3-benzodioxol-5-yl)-2-(methylamino)), was given the innocuous name "bath salts" primarily to

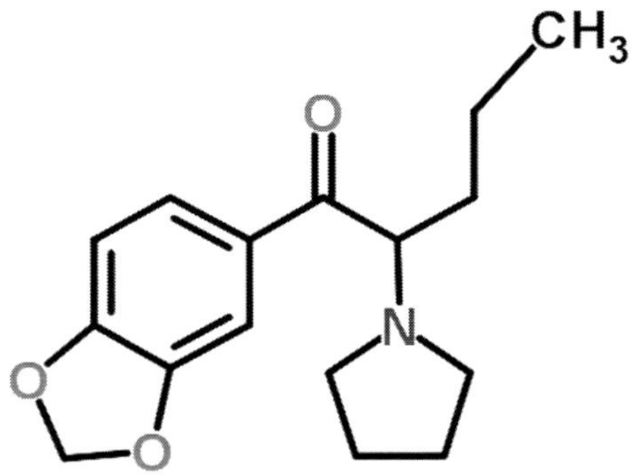

Figure 3.15: Methylenedioxypyrovalerone (MDPV)

avoid its prohibition, which was a successful outcome for some time. These substances are formally classified as norepinephrine dopamine reuptake inhibitors and are chemically related to the stimulant leaf khat in that they are derived from cathinone and methcathinone, but are synthetic substances of greater potency. Bath salts also have some structural similarity to methylenedioxymethamphetamine (MDMA/ecstasy) (chapter 4.3) and have also been reported to produce a false-positive drug test for phencyclidine (PCP) (chapter 4.4), both of which are hallucinogens (Kyle et al., 2011; Macher & Penders, 2012).

While cathinone was synthesized by pharmaceutical companies in the late 20th century, its derivatives, including methcathinone, did not become broadly used within the drug trade until the beginning of the 21st century. The tenuous legal status of bath salts, arising in part from the base chemical composition, but also a result of the shifting of the molecular structure to stay one step ahead of legal restrictions on the various synthetic versions, has contributed to this drug's proliferation. This has contributed to over 200 variations having been identified since this drug became a broader public health issue (Canadian Centre on Substance Abuse, 2012), and has also found cathinones discussed under the banner of Novel Psychoactive Substances (chapter 4.6) by the United Nations Office on Drugs and Crime (UNODC).

Cathinone and methcathinone both release dopamine, in a similar manner to the action of amphetamine and methamphetamine, upon the human dopamine (DA) transporter (hDAT). This inhibits the normal removal of dopamine, noradrenaline, and serotonin from the synapses, disrupting cognition, enhancing the perception of pleasure, and increasing muscle movements. MDPV also behaves as a cocaine-like reuptake inhibitor of dopamine. In addition, MDPV use appears to reduce the connectivity between the frontal cortical and striatal areas of the brain, including connectivity between the prelimbic prefrontal cortex and other areas of the frontal cortex, including the hypothalamus, ventral, and dorsal striatal areas. This type of reduced brain functional connectivity has been found in persons suffering from psychosis and has been linked to cognitive dysfunction, audiovisual hallucinations, and negative affective states (Cameron et al., 2013; Colon-Perez et al., 2016).

In animal studies, MDPV was found to have physical reinforcement effects equivalent to methamphetamine, with similar patterns of escalation over time, though at lower dose levels. This indicates that MDPV has reinforcing properties and activates brain reward circuitry, implying that it produces physical and psychological dependency in humans similar to other CNS stimulants (Watterson et al., 2012). The potency of bath salts has been compared more to that of cocaine than khat, although MDPV is much more potent than cocaine and its effect is longer lasting (Baumann et al., 2012); in laboratory studies rats will self-administer MDPV at even greater rates than methamphetamine (Aarde et al., 2013). Fatalities have been reported with this drug, which is not surprising given the lack of any type of quality control in its production or guidelines regarding its administration (Prosser & Nelson, 2012).

Bath salts are versatile in that they may be administered via oral ingestion, nasal insufflation, smoking, intravenous or intramuscular methods, or via the rectum. Intoxication effects last six to eight hours. The use of these drugs produces effects similar to those of other stimulants: initial intense euphoria, increased physical activity, an inability to sleep, disrupted REM cycles, and a lack of desire for food or water, along with an increased craving for more of the drug as the initial dose is metabolized. However, use can also lead to cardiovascular and neurological toxicity, including tachycardia (a resting heart rate over 100 beats per minute), hypertension, the constriction of blood vessels (affecting blood flow throughout the body), chest pain, arrhythmias, hyperthermia, seizures as severe as stroke, cardiorespiratory collapse, myocardial infarction (heart attack), and cerebral edema (swelling of the brain due to a buildup of fluid) (Wieland, Halter, & Levine, 2012). Behavioural effects include erratic behaviour, inattention, impaired working memory, a lack of recall of how much of the substance has been consumed, panic attacks, anxiety, agitation, severe paranoia, hallucinations, psychosis, self-mutilation, and behaviour that can be aggressive and violent. In extreme cases, the user moves beyond suicidal ideation to suicidal actions. Overdoses are characterized by profound toxicities, but because of the shifting pharmacology composition of various forms of bath salts, there is an increased level of unpredictable effects from person to person and variant to variant. The most common withdrawal-related symptoms are fatigue, insomnia, nasal congestion, and impaired concentration, along with depression, anxiety, increased appetite, irritability, extensive sweating, and craving for continued use. The treatment of bath salt overdose should be primarily supportive. However, if pharmacological intervention is required, it should include sedation with intravenous benzodiazepines, as well as seizure-prevention measures, intravenous fluids, close intensive care unit monitoring, and restraints to prevent harm to self or others if seizure or violent activity commences (Antnowicz, Metzger, & Ramanujam, 2011; McClean, Anspikian, & Tsuang, 2012; Ross et al., 2012).

Confirmed deaths caused by the use of bath salts have begun to appear in the peer-reviewed literature (Zaami et al., 2018). The first reported case was published in 2012 and involved a 40-year-old male who had both injected and snorted bath salts. He had become agitated and aggressive, and experienced a cardiac arrest. He was successfully resuscitated, but he subsequently developed hyperthermia, rhabdomyolysis (the breakdown of muscle fibres and release of their contents into the bloodstream), coagulopathy (a condition in which the blood's ability to clot is impaired, producing prolonged and/or excessive bleeding), acidosis (an abnormal increase in the acidity of the body's fluids, caused either by accumulation of acids or by depletion of bicarbonates), and a lack of oxygen to the brain, which in combination led to his death.

This manner of death is consistent with excited delirium syndrome (Murray, Murphy, & Beuhler, 2012).

3.8 BETEL/ARECA NUT

slang: juicey, panns (combination of betel, lime, and areca)

Methyl 1-methyl-1,2,5,6-tetrahydro-3-pyridinecarboxylate hydrobromide (1:1) ($C_8H_{14}BrNO_2$)

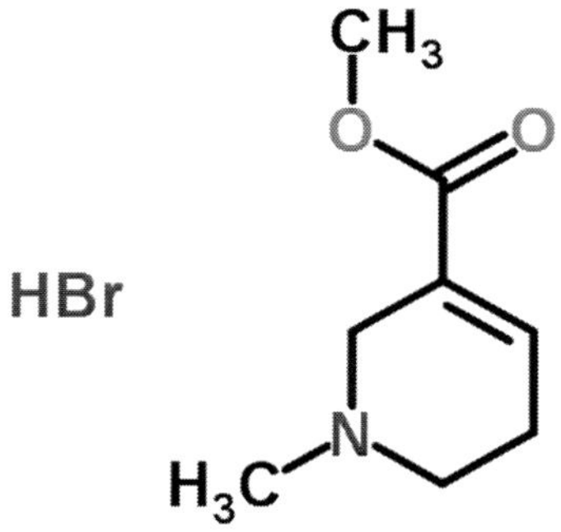

Betel (*Piper betle*) is the leaf of a vine belonging to the Piperaceae family, which also includes pepper and kava. The betel plant is an evergreen and perennial creeper with glossy, heart-shaped leaves and white catkin. The betel plant is found throughout South and Southeast Asia, particularly India, Nepal, Bangladesh, and Sri Lanka. Its fruit is the areca nut, which has historically been used in those cultures as a mild stimulant and for its medicinal properties. Areca nut is the fourth most commonly used psychoactive substance in the world, after caffeine, nicotine, and alcohol, with approximately 600 million daily users. Its dependency liability among users is equivalent to that of another stimulant: nicotine (Herzog et al., 2014). Betel quid is a combination of betel leaf, areca nut, and slaked lime. In many countries, tobacco is also added, and the product is known as gutka, ghutka, or gutkha. Other ingredients and flavourings can also be added, such as cardamom, saffron, cloves, anise seeds, turmeric, or mustard. Betel quid products are not necessarily chewed; instead, they are placed in the mouth or applied to the oral cavity and remain in contact with the oral mucosa, like chewing tobacco (Floraa, Mascie-Taylorb, & Rahmanc, 2012; Gupta & Ray, 2004).

Figure 3.16: Betel/Areca Nut

Long-term use has been associated with a broad range of illnesses as well as premature death compared to non-users. Areca nut use is known to cause esophageal and oral precancerous lesions, including erythroplasia, a reddened patch in the mouth, and leukoplakia, a white patch on the mucous membranes in the mouth that cannot be wiped off, as well as carcinomas of the lip, mouth, tongue, esophagus, and pharynx. Betel use has also been linked to hypertension, diabetes, and the development of cardiovascular disease (Wu et al., 2015).

3.9 NICOTINE

slang: butts, cigs, coffin sticks, darts, smokes, stogies
chewing tobacco: chaw, chew, dips, snuff, throw a lip

3-(1-Methyl-2-pyrrolidinyl)pyridine ($C_{10}H_{14}N_2$)

Compared with all other psychoactive agents, nicotine, in combination with its agent of delivery, tobacco, is the leading cause of premature death in Canada and the world. There are more than 2,000 additional deaths per 100,000 persons per year of heavy smokers (>20 cigarettes/day) compared with those who have never smoked (Vallance et al., 2018). Nicotine is an alkaloid and a member of the nightshade family of plants, which also includes common, useful vegetables such as the tomato, eggplant, red bell peppers, and hot peppers, but also poisonous plants such as mandrake, belladonna, and morning glory, which has hallucinogenic properties (chapter 4.2). Nicotine is a pale-yellow colour with an oily consistency that turns brown upon contact with air, and is a highly toxic substance. Tobacco smoke comprises some 500 compounds, including tar, ammonia, acetaldehyde, acetone, benzene, toluene, benzo(a)pyrene, dimethylnitros-amine, methylethylnitrosamine, naphthalene, carbon monoxide, and carbon dioxide (Brands et al., 1998).

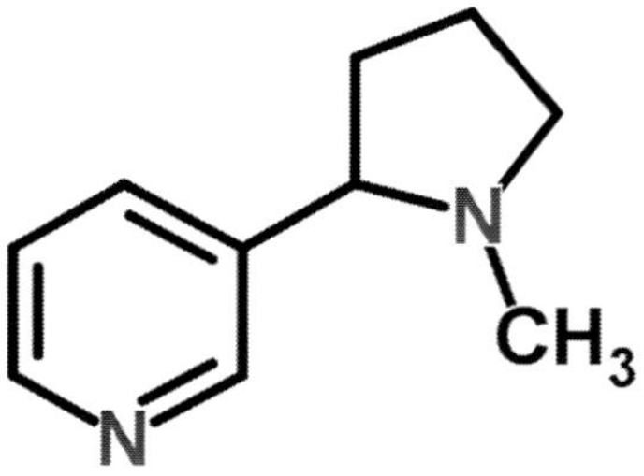

N N CH_3

Figure 3.17: Nicotine

Nicotine is the psychoactive agent found in tobacco that makes its use a compulsive behaviour. It occurs naturally in only three species of tobacco plants: *Nicotiana tabacum*, *Nicotiana rustica*, and *Nicotiana persica*. These plants produce nicotine so that insects do not eat their leaves, thus acting as a natural insecticide. All three species contain between 0.6% and 0.9% nicotine. An average cigarette contains 12 milligrams of nicotine, with light cigarettes averaging 6 milligrams, heavy 18 milligrams, and strong 24 milligrams of nicotine per cigarette.

The brain has specific receptor sites for nicotine called *nicotinic acetylcholine receptors* (nAChRs). When these are activated, they exert their major reinforcing effects on dopamine, GABA, and glutamate receptors in the brain's ventral tegmental area (VTA). This mimics the body's natural acetylcholine neurotransmission process, increasing dopamine flux in the reward pathway by mimicking acetylcholine at presynaptic nicotine receptor sites and exciting dopamine neurons. Nicotine also prevents the breakdown of dopamine, leaving more of the neurotransmitter to be active in the synaptic cleft. Nicotine receptors are located throughout the brain; however, nicotine exerts its greatest effects on brain reward systems in the nucleus accumbens (NAc). Regular smokers continually stimulate the NAc, causing the complex activation of the core and shell of the nucleus and thereby dependence. Research indicates that opioid, GABA, cannabinoid, and dopamine receptors are all involved in the creation of nicotine dependence (Balfour, 2004; Berrettini & Lerman, 2005; Pandey et al., 2018; Yan et al., 2018).

Nicotine is delivered in cigarette smoke, along with tar in the form of tiny particles suspended in the gaseous phase. The drug is absorbed rapidly from the lungs and can reach the brain within eight seconds. As cigarette smoke acidifies the saliva, the drug is not efficiently absorbed orally. Smokers do not absorb much nicotine unless they inhale the smoke, though nicotine can be effectively absorbed across the oral or nasal mucosa if the drug is administered in the form of chewing tobacco or snuff. The elimination half-life of nicotine is extremely short, approximately 30 to 60 minutes. Frequent smokers often light their next cigarette before all the nicotine from the previous one is eliminated from the body. When they do, the drug can accumulate in the tissues over the course of a day's regular use (Hancock & McKim, 2018).

Nicotine, as it is a central nervous system stimulant, increases heart rate, pulse rate, and blood pressure, depresses the spinal reflex, reduces muscle tone, decreases skin temperature, increases acid in the stomach, reduces urine formation, precipitates a loss of appetite, increases adrenaline production, and stimulates, then reduces, brain and nervous system activity. In non-smokers, small doses, even less than one cigarette, may produce an unpleasant reaction that includes coughing, nausea, vomiting, dizziness, abdominal discomfort, weakness, and flushing. Regular smoking has been empirically demonstrated to shorten lives by five to ten years (Woloshin, Schwartz, & Wlech, 2008). Long-term effects of smoking and nicotine ingestion include five forms of cancer—lung, liver, colorectal, prostate, and breast; chronic obstructive pulmonary disease (OPD); asthma; tuberculosis; cardiovascular disease, including the narrowing or hardening of blood vessels in the heart and brain, leading to an increased risk of atrial fibrillation, heart attack, or stroke in all age groups; shortness of breath; more respiratory infections, such as colds and pneumonia; chronic bronchitis; and oxygen deprivation of all body tissues (figure 3.18). Ingestion of nicotine is also linked to eye disease, dental disease, stomach ulcers, impotence, cognitive decline, memory loss, and increased risk of both dementia and schizophrenia (Aune et al., 2018; Bassett et al., 2014; Catino et al., 2017; Choi, Choi, & Park, 2018; Gage et al., 2017; Karma et al., 2015).

Nicotine readily crosses the placenta, creating many primary and secondary issues (appendix B). For example, women who smoke during pregnancy tend to have smaller babies and are more likely to give birth prematurely. They also have a greater number of stillbirths and deaths among their newborn babies. Sudden infant death syndrome (SIDS) is also more common in the infants of smokers than those of non-smokers, as is the risk of having a child who develops ADHD (Lee et al., 2018; Reece et al., 2018; Thapar et al., 2003).

Tolerance to nicotine does develop and is most clearly reflected in the many short-term symptoms, which are either not present or are greatly reduced while the chronic user is smoking. Regular smokers quickly become less sensitive to the effects of nicotine, as well as to those of carbon monoxide and the constituents of tar. Tolerance to the

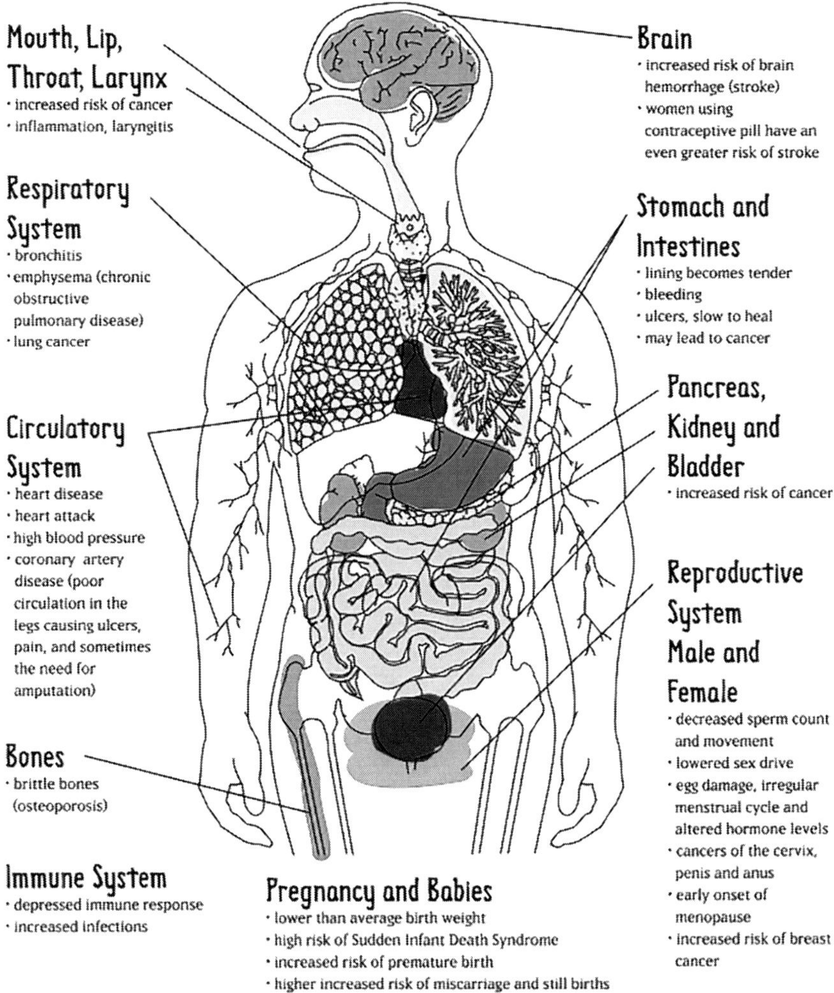

Figure 3.18: The Long-Term Health Effects of Smoking Tobacco

Source: Northern Territory Department of Health, *The Public Health Bush Book*, volume 2 (https://digitallibrary.health.nt.gov.au/prodjspui/handle/10137/7207, 2005)

nausea and dizziness experienced by the novice smoker develops particularly rapidly. A significant long-term effect of smoking is physical and psychological dependence upon tobacco. Both types of dependence are commonly observed when daily use exceeds 10 cigarettes. Particular emotional states and environmental events, even after some months or years of abstinence, can precipitate a craving for a cigarette. Nicotine, in the new smoker, produces primarily aversive effects. The initiation of a smoking habit, therefore, is highly dependent upon psychosocial factors, although biological factors may also play a role. Signs of tobacco dependence include a history of several unsuccessful attempts to reduce consumption even though a serious tobacco-related physical disorder is present, and the appearance of withdrawal symptoms while abstaining. The feeling of relaxation that regular smokers often report when smoking is due to the body's dependence upon nicotine and staving off withdrawal effects (Hancock & McKim, 2018).

Physical dependence on nicotine leads to multiple withdrawal symptoms when a smoker attempts to quit. A person in the early stages of withdrawal may experience anxiety, irritability, increased appetite, mild confusion, emotional depression, difficulty concentrating, anger, sleeping problems, and changes in blood pressure and pulse rate. A key reason why tobacco smokers often gain weight after quitting smoking is nicotine suppresses leptin, a hormone in the brain that controls appetite, just as cocaine and amphetamines do. Once nicotine ingestion has ended, leptin is more readily released and triggers appetite, resulting in increased eating and thus weight gain if activity level does not correspondingly increase (Suhaimi et al., 2016).

Those who use smokeless tobacco may avoid the problems associated with inhalation but are far from risk free, as there is an enhanced risk of mouth cancer. Even in casual users, there is a loss of taste to salty, sweet, and bitter foods. Along with discolouration of the teeth comes the risk of damage to both the teeth and gums, leading to gum disease and loss of teeth. Also, the nicotine in either chewing tobacco or snuff leads to an increased risk of heart attacks and stroke. In a study of people using multiple psychoactive drugs, it was discovered that a majority found cigarettes more difficult to quit than their primary drug of choice (Kozlowski et al., 1989).

All CNS stimulants negatively affect sleep, but nicotine is particularly deleterious to sleep quality. Given nicotine's short half-life, smokers wake earlier on average than non-smokers to address withdrawal. This may be in part responsible for the association between nicotine addiction severity and poor sleep outcomes, shorter sleep duration, and excessive daytime sleepiness among tobacco smokers. Both tobacco smokers and smokeless tobacco users have twice the odds of insufficient sleep compared to non-smokers, while individuals exposed to second-hand smoke also obtain less sleep on average and have greater sleep disruption than do non-smokers not exposed to second-hand smoke (Branstetter et al., 2016; Caviness & Anderson, 2018; Sabanaygam & Shankar, 2011).

Hirayama's (1981) ground-breaking research examined the effects of second-hand smoke upon non-smokers. He studied 265,000 Japanese persons over 14 years and found a statistically significant relationship between the mortality rates of non-smoking wives of heavy-smoking husbands and those of non-smoking wives of non-smoking husbands: non-smoking women married to heavy-smoking husbands were twice as likely to die from lung cancer as those married to non-smoking spouses. This relationship has since been observed in multiple studies with different populations. The worldwide burden of disease study conducted by Oberg and colleagues (2011) found that globally, 40% of children, 33% of male non-smokers, and 35% of female non-smokers were exposed to second-hand smoke. This exposure was estimated to have caused 379,000 deaths from heart disease, 165,000 from lower respiratory infections, 36,900 from asthma, and 21,400 from lung cancer. This totals over 600,000 people across the world who died prematurely due to nicotine and tobacco use who were not smokers themselves, representing approximately 1.0% of worldwide mortality per year. This is not that surprising when one learns that environmental tobacco smoke contains more contaminants than mainstream smoke (the smoke exhaled after taking a puff), including up to 3 times more tar, 31 times more 4-aminobiphenyl, 40 times more ammonia, 10 times more benzene,

5 times more carbon monoxide, 3 times more cadmium, twice as much phenol, and up to 6 times more nicotine. Second-hand smoke has also been linked to far-ranging health issues including increased risk of dementia, breast cancer, hearing loss, coronary heart disease, heart attacks, and Alzheimer's disease. In children it has been correlated with depression, respiratory infections, asthma, ear infections, and childhood cancer (Diver, Jacobs, & Gapstur, 2018; Fabry et al., 2010; Institute of Medicine, 2009; Llewellyn et al., 2009; Wellman et al., 2018).

There is positive news, however, for those who stop ingesting nicotine. After one day, as the pain of withdrawal is occurring, toxins are being flushed from the body. Within three months, formerly nicotine-dependent individuals find it becomes easier to breathe. After one year of abstinence, the risk of heart disease is lowered by half. At a former smoker's fifth anniversary of cessation, the risks of mouth, esophageal, and bladder cancer have dropped by half as well. The risk of dying from lung cancer is 70% lower after 12 years without smoking. Finally, after 15 years of not smoking, a typical pack-a-day, decade-long smoker has the same risk of dying as anyone else their age (Canadian Cancer Society, 1987).

Despite nicotine being the most lethal of all psychoactive drugs, it does have some potential uses other than killing insects. Research that began at Duke University in Durham, North Carolina—the heart of the American tobacco belt—as well as subsequent work at the University of Vermont Medical College of Medicine has found that nicotine may be beneficial in combatting Alzheimer's disease and other memory-degrading diseases including schizophrenia, and cognition and memory in general. Nicotine has also been shown to alleviate some symptoms of Tourette's syndrome, Parkinson's disease, and arthritis, calm hyperactive children, and relieve some anxiety disorders (Finckh et al., 2007; Koukouli et al., 2017; Ritz et al., 2007; Singer et al., 2004).

3.10 CAFFEINE

slang: *coffee:* bean juice, brew, cup of joe, cup of tar, dirt, java, joe, morning jolt, mud, rocket fuel, worm dirt

1,3,7-Trimethyl-3,7-dihydro-1H-purine-2,6-dione ($C_8H_{10}N_4O_2$)

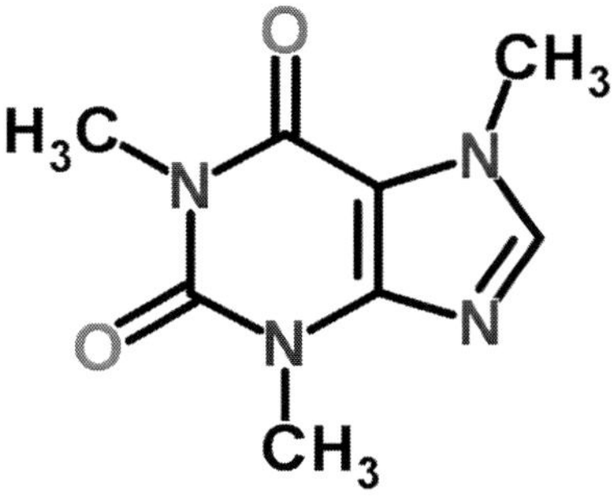

While alcohol is the most commonly misused psychoactive drug in the world, caffeine is the world's most-used psychoactive drug, with estimates of 120,000 tons consumed globally each year. This is in part due to its low dependency liability (Fagerstrom, 2018). Over 80% of Canadians consume caffeine on a regular basis; an estimated 15 billion cups of coffee alone are sold annually in Canada. Caffeine, a xanthine alkaloid, blocks the actions of adenosine, an inhibitory neurotransmitter, by binding to its receptor and preventing post-binding changes from taking place. Caffeine is a competitive antagonist and, through blocking the effects of adenosine, leads to increased firing of dopamine neurons, particularly in the NAc. It also readily crosses the blood-brain barrier (National Institute on Drug Abuse, 2008).

Figure 3.19: Caffeine

When consumed orally, caffeine begins to reach all tissues of the body within five minutes. Peak blood levels are reached in about 30 minutes. Half of a given dose of caffeine is metabolized in about four hours, more rapidly in smokers and less rapidly in newborn infants, women in late pregnancy, and sufferers of liver disease. Normally, almost all ingested caffeine is metabolized. Less than 3% appears unchanged in urine, and there is no day-to-day accumulation of the drug in the body. Due to its tendency to constrict cerebral blood vessels, caffeine is used in combination with other drugs to combat migraine and other cerebrovascular headaches associated with high blood pressure. However, contrary to popular belief, caffeine is not effective in ameliorating headaches due to other causes, and in some instances may even exacerbate pain. In other medical uses, caffeine is employed to counteract certain symptoms, such as respiratory depression, associated with CNS-depressant poisoning. It is also used

- as a respiratory stimulant in babies who have had apnea episodes (periods when spontaneous breathing ceases);

- as an emergency bronchodilator in asthmatic children;
- as a substitute for methylphenidate for children with attention deficit disorder;
- as an anti-fungal agent in the treatment of skin disorders;
- as an aid in fertility, because of its ability to enhance sperm mobility; and
- as a mild stimulant for an assortment of medical problems (Hancock & McKim, 2018).

When taken even in moderate amounts, such as one or two cups of brewed or percolated coffee, caffeine can produce stimulant effects upon the central nervous system similar to those of small doses of amphetamines. These can include mild mood elevation, feelings of enhanced energy, reduced performance deficit due to boredom or fatigue, postponement of feelings of fatigue and the need for sleep, and a decrease in hand steadiness, suggesting impaired fine motor performance. Moderate caffeine consumption has been associated with enhanced alertness, reasoning, verbal fluency, concentration, and decision making. It can also improve speed, endurance, energy output, strength, and reaction time, while increasing the body's metabolic rate and the rate at which it burns fat (Ruxton, 2008). Caffeine has also been associated with enhancing consolidation of long-term memories (Borota et al., 2014).

As caffeine is a stimulant psychoactive drug, consuming it prior to going to bed will alter a person's sleep patterns, including delaying the onset of sleep, diminishing the total amount of sleep, and reducing the amount of REM sleep the user experiences. A study conducted by Drake et al. (2013) on the effect of caffeine being consumed at bedtime and three and six hours prior to sleep found that even consuming coffee six hours in advance of sleep produced disruptive sleep. Thus, given caffeine's half-life, anyone experiencing any type of sleep disturbance should not consume caffeine within 10 hours of going to bed.

Caffeine, like steroids, is stored in intracellular sites in the body. While low to moderate daily doses of caffeine do not appear to produce harmful effects in healthy adults, higher daily consumption, approximately 1,000 milligrams (one gram) of caffeine for a healthy,

180-pound male 20 to 40 years of age—and less for women, older persons, lighter persons, and especially children—can result in caffeinism. Coffee and espresso will put you in the 77 to 135 milligram range, while tea will typically have between 15 and 70 milligrams of caffeine per cup. Excessive caffeine consumption mimics anxiety, worsening existing symptoms. Caffeine stimulates production of both cortisol and adrenaline, which enhance the flight response while also depleting magnesium, which aids in controlling anxiety. Excessive caffeine consumption is characterized by irritability, restlessness and agitation, headache, light-headedness, rapid breathing, tremors, muscle twitches, increased sensitivity to sensory stimuli, light flashes, tinnitus, gastrointestinal upset, and abnormally rapid and irregular heartbeat, while also increasing respiration, blood pressure, and metabolism even in young and casual users. Chronic, long-term caffeine misuse has been linked to ulcers, persistent anxiety, increased cholesterol levels, bone loss in older women, and depression. Caffeine also crosses the placenta, and high levels of consumption have been linked with fetal arrhythmia, as the fetus does not yet possess the enzymes necessary to metabolize caffeine (appendix B). Caffeine effects appear with decreasing doses as a person becomes older; thus, intake should decrease with age (Gupta & Gupta, 1999; Ruxton, 2008; Svatikova et al., 2015).

Tolerance develops to most of caffeine's effects, with clinical experiments demonstrating that tolerance to the cardiovascular effects of caffeine can develop within four days. Consumption of 350 to 600 milligrams of caffeine on a regular basis causes physical dependence. There is also evidence that users may develop a mild psychological dependence upon caffeine, such as is manifested by the well-recognized morning coffee habit. Clearly, factors such as taste and aroma are important as reinforcers, since coffee drinkers cannot always be persuaded to switch to tea and vice versa (Hancock & McKim, 2018).

Interruption of the regular use of caffeine produces a characteristic withdrawal syndrome, the most conspicuous feature of which is an often severe headache that can be temporarily relieved by ingesting caffeine. The absence of caffeine also makes regular users feel irritable, lethargic, anxious, and fatigued. Withdrawal can begin between 3 and

48 hours after the last administration of caffeine. Relief from these withdrawal effects is often given as a reason for reusing the drug. Caffeine, however, is not a totally harmless psychoactive agent. Overdose is possible and has been recorded in the literature, especially with the introduction of energy drinks (Center for Behavioral Health Statistics and Quality, 2014), though the lowest known dose fatal to an adult was 3,200 milligrams and was deemed accidental (Kerrigan & Lindsey, 2005). The typical fatal oral dose is in the range of 5,000

Table 3.2: Short- and Long-Term Effects of Caffeine Use

Amount	Short-Term Effects	Long-Term Effects
250 mg/day (2–3 cups of coffee)	increased alertness postpones fatigue mild stimulation of heart smooth muscle relaxation increase in blood sugar levels increased rate of respiration increased urine flow insomnia or disturbed sleep mild mood elevation increased neural activity stimulation of gastric acids	no noted physical effects no noted psychological effects
500–750 mg/day (5–7 cups of coffee)	irritability restlessness rapid and/or irregular heartbeat increased blood pressure insomnia mild physical dependency mild psychological dependency	anxiety restlessness rapid and/or irregular heartbeat gastrointestinal irritation sleep disturbance or insomnia physical dependency psychological dependency
1,000+ mg/day (9+ cups of coffee)	extreme restlessness extreme agitation rapid and/or irregular heartbeat increased acid in stomach & urine high blood sugar levels headaches enhanced reflex time physical dependency psychological dependency	extreme restlessness extreme agitation high blood pressure ulcers & gastric irritation high blood sugar levels headaches tremors & muscle twitches physical dependency psychological dependency excessive sensitivity to pain, touch, and other stimuli

to 10,000 milligrams, the equivalent of over 50 to 100 cups of coffee taken in a very short space of time, though biological factors, including sugar content and liquid capacity, historically made caffeine overdose through oral means very difficult. Increasing numbers of hospitalizations have been reported among those consuming large quantities of energy drinks and caffeine pills, particularly in younger, urban males (McCarthy, Mycyk, & DesLauriers, 2006). Substantially lower doses can prove problematic to children, for, like nicotine, caffeine can also be used as an insecticide. Table 3.2 illustrates the short- and long-term effects of caffeine consumption.

QUIZ

1. Which neurotransmitter do stimulants primarily alter to produce their psychoactive effects?
2. Which stimulant has both anaesthetic and stimulant properties?
3. What two natural stimulants have insecticide capability?
4. What stimulant is useful in fighting cold symptoms?
5. What is the most efficient way to administer coca and methamphetamine?
6. True or false: Tobacco smoking relaxes you.
7. True or false: Tobacco smoking only affects the person smoking.
8. True or false: Tobacco smoking leads to more relapses than any other psychoactive drug.
9. True or false: Drinking five cups of coffee a day can lead to a physical dependency on caffeine.
10. What are the therapeutic uses for caffeine?

CASE STUDIES

Chuck

Chuck is a 27-year-old unemployed man. He is currently using cocaine or crack whenever he has enough money to buy some. He has also used methamphetamine. He has tried to quit, or at least cut down on his use of these drugs, but he has not been successful.

What are the differences and similarities between cocaine and crack?

How are cocaine and methamphetamine similar? Explain your answer in terms of the pharmacodynamics and pharmacokinetics of the two drugs.

Alex, Ben, and Violet

Alex, Ben, and Violet are all celebrating one year of sobriety from the drugs that they were physically dependent upon, all of which were CNS stimulants. Alex states that his withdrawal was the most difficult, because he had been using crack cocaine for six months. Ben counters that he had been dependent upon amphetamines for over a year, and thus his withdrawal was far more difficult. Violet tells them they didn't have nearly the withdrawal problems she experienced after she stopped smoking after 10 years. Based only upon pharmacological principles, which of the three had the most difficult withdrawal? Explain why.

Salman and Bijay

Salman and Bijay are new graduate students attending university in Canada. Salman is Somali, while Bijay grew up in Nepal. During orientation week, they are exposed to some of the exploits of Canadian first-year students and are fascinated by the focus on alcohol and its importance in bonding and joining rituals. Salman asks Bijay if he uses any psychoactive substances, and he replies, "No, not really, I just chew betel quid." In response, Salman says that he grew up chewing khat. Both agree that they will not have any issues with psychoactive drugs compared to their Canadian counterparts. Do you agree or disagree with Salman and Bijay's beliefs? Use pharmacological points to either support or contradict the two graduate students, comparing their drugs of choice to the second-most popular campus drug. Conclude by examining the risks associated with the most popular campus drug, and one that Bijay, Salman, and most other university students will end up using, particularly when essays are due.

Anthony

Anthony is nine years old and is demonstrating the following characteristics:

- difficulty concentrating or paying attention for long
- jumping from one activity to another
- difficulty playing quietly
- talking excessively
- interrupting others when they are speaking
- difficulty listening to others
- losing things

He is the youngest of four siblings, with older brothers aged 13, 11, and 10. Born on December 7, he is in a class of 32 students with a second-year teacher, and is struggling as he enters the second month of school. Discuss the pros and cons of giving Anthony Ritalin at this juncture in his life. What other options exist besides a pharmacological intervention?

NOTE

1. The source for systemic names and molecular formulas of all stimulants is ChemSpider (www.chemspider.com). The systemic name describes the chemical structure of a substance, providing basic information about its chemical properties, while the molecular formula represents the number and type(s) of atoms that are present in a single molecule of the substance. Unless otherwise noted, the source for figures depicting chemical structures is also ChemSpider.

CHAPTER 4

Hallucinogens

OVERVIEW

Hallucinogens are distinct from other psychoactive drugs in that they do not primarily affect the central nervous system (CNS) by creating euphoria; rather, they disrupt the messages being perceived. These psychoactive substances produce radical changes in a person's mental state by creating a disconnect between the physical world and the user's perception of the physical world, leading to sensory hallucinations.

4.1 HALLUCINOGENS

Drugs in this family produce sensations of separation from self and reality, as well as unusual changes in thoughts, feelings, and perceptions, including delusions and illusions but not typically delirium. Illusions and delusions may include a loss or confusion of body image, altered perceptions of colours, distance, and shape, and an apparent distortion, blending, or synthesis of senses whereby one sees sounds and smells colours. These agents can also produce severe anxiety, panic, and uncertainty that can persist long after the drug has been metabolized. This experience has been called having a "bad trip" and is an ongoing and overwhelming feeling of distress due to the interaction of the drug on the CNS (Hancock & McKim, 2018).

Hallucinogens may be administered orally, inhaled, injected, or, in the case of lysergic acid diethylamide (LSD), absorbed transdermally. In low doses, hallucinogens produce a range of effects, though users may experience dissimilar reactions to the same drug on different occasions, finding the effects sometimes pleasant and at other times disturbing and threatening. Flashbacks, formally known as hallucinogen post-perceptual disorder (HPPD), are usually visual in nature and have been reported to occur months or even years after even a single experience with a hallucinogen. HPPDs are typically quite alarming and can be dangerous, depending upon what the person is doing when they reoccur. However, there appears to be more discussion of flashbacks than there are actual documented instances (Halpern & Pope, 2003). When flashbacks do occur, they may precipitate or intensify already-existing psychoses or anxieties in some users. The long-term effects for the majority of hallucinogens, with the exception of cannabis, are purely psychological, as tolerance to the physical effects occurs within days of regular use. This total state of tolerance, such that no psychoactive effect is perceived, is called tachyphylaxis.

There are both natural and synthetic hallucinogens, with most synthetic hallucinogens being prohibited. Hallucinogens are banned based on their chemical structure. This in turn has led chemists to alter the chemical formulas, turning an illicit drug into a licit one in terms of possession and distribution. As a result, an ongoing series of new hallucinogens, placed within the Novel Psychoactive Substances category (chapter 4.6), have been synthesized in formal and makeshift laboratories, with a range of negative outcomes.

The War on Drugs that has been running in some capacity since 1971 contributed to a virtual shutdown on research involving hallucinogens in North America. Prior to then, hallucinogens including psilocybin, LSD, and mescaline were being used in psychiatric clinical trials, many of which were conducted in Canada. However, these drugs did not appear to be of great value in treating psychosis, and in fact research findings reported that the use of these substances made many individuals' condition worse. However, contemporary research using hallucinogens, which is just beginning to re-emerge, has found that this family of drugs may have value in treating other mental health issues, such as depressive disorders; anxiety disorders, including post-traumatic stress disorder (PTSD); trauma; physical dependency to other categories of psychoactive drugs; and the psychological challenges associated with death and dying. This will be an area of pharmacological practice to closely monitor in the coming years (Rucker, Iliff, & Nutt, 2018).

Microdosing is the term used to describe the practice of administering small doses of hallucinogens, approximately one-tenth the typical recreational dose level. While the goal of microdosing is to alter a person's perception, it is not intended to produce hallucinations, which is why much smaller doses are used than those consumed by recreational substance users. The goals of microdosing include producing positive affect, addressing mental health issues, boosting creativity, enhancing problem-solving ability, productivity, and, of course, as applies to much drug consumption, curiosity. This is a new practice, and as most hallucinogens are illicit, the observed outcomes are anecdotal, with no solid evidence-informed research in this area yet. For the most part LSD-like hallucinogens are used by those microdosing, as these enhance serotonin in the CNS while having no secondary side effects. In microdosing, drug administration is typically every third day, as even at small doses tachyphylaxis develops to hallucinogens other than cannabis (Fadiman, 2011; Johnstad, 2018; Prochazkova et al., 2018).

Hallucinogens can be placed into one of four groups according to their chemical structure:

1. Indolealkylamines (LSD-like): hallucinogens that have no secondary psychoactive effects and are similar to and primarily affect serotonin (5-hydroxytryptamine). Members of this subgroup of hallucinogens include LSD, morning glory seeds (LSA), and psilocybin (magic mushrooms).
2. Phenylethylamines (mescaline-like): substances that affect serotonin, producing hallucinations, but also with structural

similarities to amphetamines (catecholamines), leading to secondary stimulant effects that include enhanced energy, endurance, sociability, and sexual arousal, along with rapid pulse, dilated pupils, impaired motor coordination, and muscle weakness. Phenylethylamines are also closely related to the neurotransmitter norepinephrine. At high doses, phenylethylamines can produce agitation and marked stimulation of the peripheral nervous system, manifested in both an abnormally accelerated heart rate and high blood pressure. Of all hallucinogens, this group has the smallest gap between effective and lethal dose (table 1.4). Members of this family include mescaline, ecstasy (3,4-Methylenedioxymethamphetamine), and scopolamine, which is better known by its slang term, devil's breath.

3. Dissociative anaesthetics (arylcycloalkylamines): hallucinogens such as phencyclidine (PCP), ketamine (Special K), and *Salvia divinorum* that possess CNS-depressant properties along with their hallucinatory effects. Again, the hallucinogenic effects are primarily a result of the drug's effect on serotonin.
4. Cannabis: including hashish and hash oil. Cannabis affects the CNS quite differently from other hallucinogens, altering cannabinoids rather than serotonin, and there have been arguments made, with merit, that this psychoactive substance belongs in its own unique category. Along with creating hallucinations and memory loss at high doses, cannabis products also produce CNS-depressant effects and are the only hallucinogens that produce physical dependency and thus are fully addicting agents.

To these four categories has been added a separate grouping: Novel Psychoactive Substances (NPS). These are all synthetic substances, some of which were initially synthesized by pharmaceutical companies. NPS are placed together in that in most jurisdictions they have been sold legally, despite their risks, because they have not yet been made illegal through the judicial process.

4.2 LSD-LIKE HALLUCINOGENS: INDOLEALKYLAMINE

d-Lysergic Acid Diethylamide (LSD)

slang: acid, aeon flux, barrels, Beavis & Butthead, big D, black star, black sunshine, black tabs, blotter, blue vials, California sunshine, chocolate chips, fields, golden dragon, heavenly blue, instant zen, lens, Lucy in the Sky, microdots, Mighty Quinn, pink panther, purple hearts, royal blues, sunshine, Syd, tabs, twenty-five, wedding bells, windowpane, yellow sunshine, zen

(8β)-N,N-Diethyl-6-methyl-9,10-didehydroergoline-8-carboxamide ($C_{20}H_{25}N_3O$)[1]

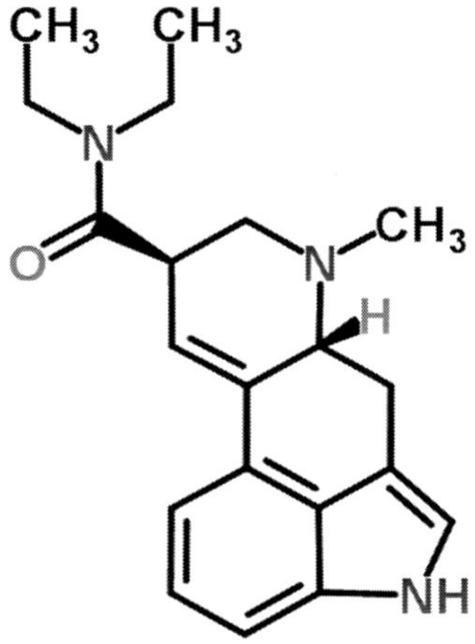

LSD, a colourless, tasteless, odourless, semi-synthetic drug derived from a fungus that grows on rye and other grains, is primarily a non-selective 5-HT (serotonin) agonist, though it also has direct secondary agonist effects on dopamine. LSD is the most potent of all known hallucinogens; a dose as small as 0.05 milligrams (50 micrograms) may produce changes in perception, mood, and thought. The initial effects of LSD are felt in less than an hour when consumed orally, and generally last from eight to twleve hours before gradually tapering off. Interestingly, the half-life of LSD is approximately three hours, which is often when peak sensations are felt. Shortly after ingestion, LSD can produce various physical symptoms, including increased heart rate and blood pressure, elevated body temperature, reduced appetite, nausea, vomiting, abdominal discomfort, rapid reflexes, motor incoordination, relaxed bronchial muscles, and pupillary dilation (Doblin, 2002; Muller et al., 2017).

Figure 4.1: d-Lysergic Acid Diethylamide (LSD)

LSD produces a marked slowing of the firing rate of serotonin neurons, particularly in regions of the brain that mediate emotional processing, self-processing, and social cognition, while also inducing hyper-connectivity in sensory and somatomotor areas of the brain. LSD use also increases visual cortex cerebral blood flow while greatly expanding primary visual cortex connectivity. This effect is what is believed to produce visual hallucinations. Hearing may be intensified or merged with other senses due to LSD use, and one's sense of time may also be affected. A distinct function of LSD is its ability to decrease connectivity in the brain, which can also diminish a user's capacity to differentiate the boundaries of one object from another and of oneself from the environment. For some, this is a pleasant sensation, but for others, the feeling of loss of control may result in a panic reaction. Additionally, LSD use has been shown to decrease amygdala reactivity to fearful stimuli among individuals with no mental health issues along with the production of psychedelic effects. LSD interrupts rational cognitive processes, affects perception, and can result in feelings of fear and panic. A user may experience several different emotions at the same time, or swing rapidly from one mood to another. In individuals who are vulnerable, LSD use can be a trigger for psychosis, and it can exacerbate and intensify existing symptoms (Carhart-Harris, Kaelen, et al., 2016; Preller et al., 2018).

Historically, LSD users have indicated more positive than negative reactions to using the drug. A controlled empirical study conducted in the United Kingdom found that LSD use produced positive psychological effects including heightened mood and increased optimism, with no changes in delusional thinking, though there were increased scores on a psychosis symptom scale post–drug use (Carhart-Harris, Kaelen, et al., 2016). Chronic LSD use has been linked to amotivational syndrome, apathy, and disinterest in the environment and with social contacts, as well as a general passive attitude toward life, though chromosomal damage does not occur, as was once feared. While, as noted above, they are discussed more than experienced, LSD can produce flashbacks (HPPD) days and even months after its last use. It is still unknown how, when, or why flashbacks occur. It has been theorized that LSD causes HPPD through the destruction of inhibitory serotonin interneurons at the neurons' nucleus and GABA neurons at axon terminals (figure 1.7). Another possible explanation is that exposure to LSD combined with other psychoactive drugs, especially those that also enhance serotonin, dysregulates visual and cue processing in individuals with a genetic vulnerability for HPPD (Goldman, Galarneau, & Friedman, 2007). However, in neither acute nor chronic use is LSD toxic (table 1.4). While there are no documented deaths directly attributable to the pharmacological effects of LSD in humans, there have been many reports of deaths due to LSD-associated accidents and suicides, including one that was the antecedent event for the creation of the short-lived Ontario Substance Abuse Bureau in the 1990s. Effects are unpredictable and will depend on the dose ingested as well as the user's personality and mood, and their expectations and surroundings. Low doses of LSD administered one hour prior to going to sleep increase initial REM periods but then lead to shortened subsequent periods, the opposite pattern to normal REM sleep. Test subjects also had less eye movements during REM sleep when using LSD compared to non-drug-using sleep periods, though overall time spent in REM sleep was longer when given LSD (Passie et al., 2008).

LSD is among the hallucinogens for which there is ongoing research to determine its therapeutic potential, though there was also a time the CIA attempted to weaponize it as a truth serum (Lee & Shlain, 2001). During the middle of the 20th century more benign studies were conducted to determine if taking LSD, under the trade name Delysid, could aid as a pharmacological treatment for alcohol dependency or as a way to minimize the negative emotions of being diagnosed with a terminal illness (Smart & Storm, 1964). Contemporary studies have again found that controlled, therapeutic dose levels of LSD, as part of a broader treatment regimen, could contribute to a decrease in alcohol misuse (Krebs & Johansen, 2012; Winkelman, 2014) as well as in reducing anxiety and thus improving the quality of life among individuals diagnosed with a life-threatening illness (Gasser, Kirchner, & Passie, 2015).

Psilocybin

slang: Alice, boomers, buttons, caps, fungus, magic mushrooms, Mexican mushrooms, mushies, pizza topping, shrooms, Simple Simon, tweezes

3-[2-(Dimethylamino)ethyl]-1H-indol-4-yl dihydrogen phosphate ($C_{12}H_{17}N_2O_4P$)

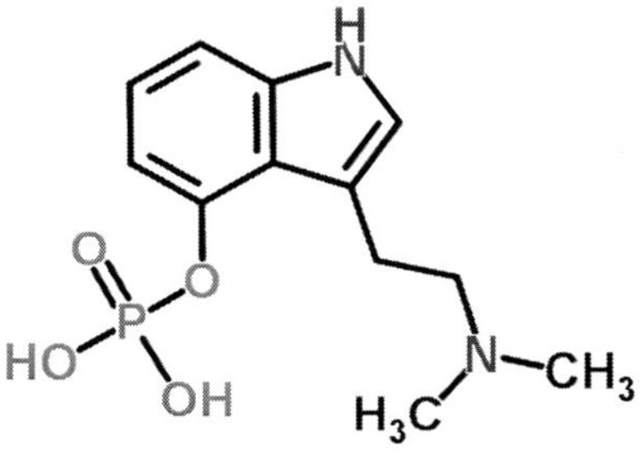

Figure 4.2: Psilocybin

Psilocybin is the active ingredient in the *Psilocybe mexicana* mushroom and some of the other Psilocybe and Conocybe species. Indigenous groups in southern Mexico, including the Hopi, historically used this psychoactive agent in religious ceremonies, and it continues to be used by the Yaqui tribe as part of their seeing ceremony, as it has the capacity to alter states of consciousness. Psilocybin is a water-soluble psychoactive that when metabolized is biotransformed into psilocin, which is highly lipid soluble. Psilocybin is a trytamine derivative that is chemically related to both LSD and dimethyltryptamine (DMT) but is approximately 100 times less potent and has a shorter duration of effect. In its pure form, psilocybin is a white crystalline material, but it may also be distributed in crude mushroom preparations, intact dried brown mushrooms, or as a capsule containing a powdered material of any colour. It is usually taken orally but may also be injected if properly prepared. Doses of the pure compound generally vary from 4 to 10 milligrams, although amounts up to 60 milligrams are not unusual. Psilocybin induces psychedelic effects by reducing the reuptake of serotonin by neurons in the CNS, allowing this neurotransmitter more time to act in the synapse. Through activating 5-HT_{2A} serotonin receptors, psilocybin diminishes brain activity and connectivity, particularly in the prefrontal cortex between the amygdala and the brain's primary visual cortex. This produces disjointed and uncoordinated activity in the brain network that is linked to high-level thinking, including self-consciousness. Much of this occurs in the default mode network, which plays a key role in integrating sensory information and allowing us to perceive images in a precise and constrained manner. However, unlike LSD, psilocybin does not bind to dopamine receptors (Kraehenmann et al., 2015; Lee & Roth, 2012).

The initial effects of psilocybin are felt approximately half an hour after oral ingestion and usually last several hours. The short-term effects include an increase in blood pressure, heart rate, and body temperature. Initially, nausea, vomiting, and intestinal cramping are experienced by the user. Later, distortions of visual stimuli and pseudo-hallucinations are likely to occur. These are accompanied by distortions of time, space, and body image, heightened sensory awareness, synaesthesia (the perception of the melding of the senses), and a loss of boundaries between oneself and the environment. Concentration, attention, cognition, and memory are impaired. Psilocybin places a person into a similar state as during REM sleep that has been called a waking dream state. As with other indolealkylamines, recreational psilocybin use can exacerbate mental illness symptoms in persons with or predisposed to psychotic conditions. Psilocybin does not produce physical dependency and thus is not an addicting agent. It also has low physiological toxicity but in upwards of one-third of users can still produce an acute negative psychological state, "a bad trip" that sometimes, though rarely, persists (Carbonaro et al., 2016). Psilocybin remains considered among the least problematic psychoactive drugs in terms of physical harm produced, with the most significant risk being high-risk behaviours users engage in as a result of being disconnected from their physical environment (Carhart-Harris et al., 2012; Passie et al., 2008).

As with LSD, study into the therapeutic utility of this drug was virtually eliminated due to the repercussions of the ongoing War on Drugs. However, this has slowly changed, with many potential uses for controlled doses of psilocybin having been reported. As with the more potent LSD, research with psilocybin has indicated it has utility in treating the physical dependency component of alcohol (Bogenschutz et al., 2015), and nicotine addiction (Johnson et al., 2014), decreasing anxiety among those who are terminally ill (Grob et al., 2011), and treating depression that standard antidepressant medication has not had an impact upon (Carhart-Harris, Bolstridge, et al., 2016; Roseman et al., 2017). Also, in a controlled study with 18 volunteers, 17 of whom had never used any type of hallucinogen, psilocybin produced short-term perceptual subjective effects, including, at dose levels of both 20 and 30 milligrams per 70 kilograms of weight, extreme anxiety and fear in 7 of the volunteers and reported mystical-type experiences in 13. One month after sessions at the greatest dose levels, volunteers rated the psilocybin experience as having substantial personal and spiritual significance and attributed to the experience sustained positive changes in attitude, mood, and behaviour, with lower doses having a less pronounced positive effect. A follow-up 14 months later found that their drug-induced perceptions were undiminished and consistent with changes reported by community observers of their behaviour (Griffiths et al., 2011).

Dimethyltryptamine (DMT)

slang: 45-minute psychosis, businessman's special, businessman's trip, Dimitri, fantasia, snakes

2-(1H-indol-3-yl)-N,N-dimethylethanamine ($C_{12}H_{16}N_2$)

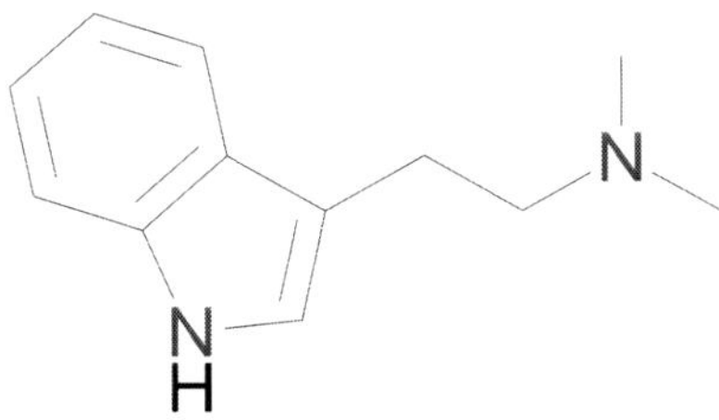

Figure 4.3: Dimethyltryptamine (DMT)

Source: Wikimedia Commons

DMT is a tryptamine hallucinogen, similar to psilocybin in its effects. DMT occurs naturally in the human brain, excreted by the human pineal gland, and is believed to play a role in dreaming, and possibly the perception of near-death experiences and related mystical states. Historically DMT was primarily only available in a synthetic form in the Western world until ayahuasca became recognized as a natural source of the psychoactive substance. Ayahuasca was used by shamans in Bolivia, Brazil, Colombia, Ecuador, and Peru for physical healing and spiritual purposes for centuries before the arrival of European conquistadors and colonists. Ayahuasca translates from the Quechua language of the North Andes as "soul vine" or "vine of the dead" (dos Santos, 2013). In North America DMT is often consumed in combination with cannabis; the cannabis is soaked in a solution of DMT and then dried and smoked in a pipe or cigarette. DMT can also be made into a tea and consumed orally. DMT targets serotonin receptors in exerting its psychedelic effects (Fontanill et al., 2009).

Acute administration of DMT has limited physical risk associated with it, nausea and vomiting being the most common response in both naive and experienced users. However, even in low doses DMT can produce significant perceptual, cognitive, and affective modifications, highlighted by hallucinations, and the greater the dose, the greater the reaction. The experience of using ayahuasca is typically pleasant, although not physically easy, highlighted by changes in visual perception, synaesthesia between the auditory and visual senses, feelings of deep introspection, and enhanced mood that can last four to six hours. DMT affects the frontal and paralimbic brain regions as well as the amygdala and parahippocampal, which affect emotional arousal. Naive ayahuasca users have described their first use of ayahuasca as producing a significant reduction in the intensity of minor psychiatric symptoms (dos Santos, 2013). DMT does not induce any deterioration of sleep quality, initiation, or maintenance, though it does inhibit REM sleep, decreasing its duration both in absolute values and as a percentage of total sleep time (Barbanoj et al., 2008). There has been no documentation of individuals becoming physically dependent to ayahuasca or any other source of DMT (Gable, 2006).

With DMT, the sensory and perceptual effects tend to be more immediate and intense than those of other hallucinogens, which speaks to the lipid solubility of the substance. As a result, anxiety reactions and panic states are more frequently associated with DMT than with other hallucinogens, partially because of the unexpectedly rapid onset of its effects. These symptoms can be substantively exacerbated if a person has a serious mental health issue such as schizophrenia or bipolar disorder (dos Santos, Bouso, & Hallak, 2017). Likewise, the effects of DMT also disappear much more rapidly than those of other members of this family, typically within 30 to 60 minutes after administration. DMT also acts as a monoamine oxidase inhibitor (MAOI) (chapter 5.1). MAOIs are antidepressants that can interact with a variety of drugs and foods, such as red wine and old cheese, and these combinations can produce hazardous and potentially fatal results (dos Santos, 2013).

Some exploration of therapeutic uses for ayahuasca/DMT has been initiatied, with the belief that it may be useful in treating anxiety and depression, as the substance's primary effects are upon serotonin (Osorio et al., 2015; Sanches et al., 2016). However, most of the treatment potential of this drug up to now has focused on ayahuasca's ability to assist with resolving issues of withdrawal and physical dependency to other psychoactive drugs, including alcohol and opioids, especially as use of DMT does not produce physical dependency itself (Loizaga-Velder & Verres, 2014; Winkelman, 2014).

Lysergic Acid Amide (LSA)

slang: flying saucers, heavenly blues, morning glory, pearly gates

(8β)-6-Methyl-9,10-didehydroergoline-8-carboxamide ($C_{16}H_{17}N_3O$)

The predominant psychoactive ingredient in the Convolvulaceae family of plants, which includes Hawaiian baby woodrose and morning glory, is an ergot alkaloid called lysergic acid amide (LSA). LSA is a natural alkaloid that is chemically related to LSD, but approximately one-tenth as potent. However, an increasing body of evidence indicates that this alkaloid is in fact produced by Clavicipitaceous fungi that have infected the plants. The seeds, if eaten whole,

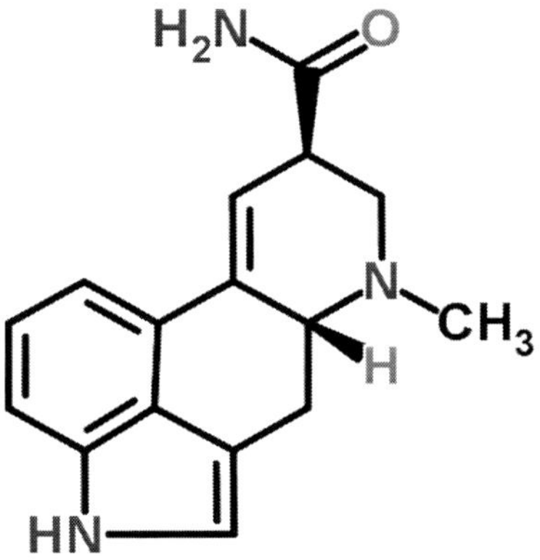

Figure 4.4: Lysergic Acid Amide (LSA)

usually pass through the digestive tract with little effect upon the user. When the seeds are chewed, effects begin after approximately 30 to 90 minutes and are those of LSD. To produce hallucinations, usually 5 to 10 seeds of Hawaiian baby woodrose or 150 to 200 seeds of morning glory, equivalent to a 0.02- to 0.03-milligram dose of LSD, need to be consumed. LSA-induced effects typically last four to eight hours and include vivid visual, tactile, and auditory hallucinations as well as perceptual changes, depersonalization, tachycardia, hypertension, flushing, and synaesthesia. As with other members of this family, as well as positive experience, negative psychedelic responses have been reported. With LSA this can entail memory loss, anxiety, fear attacks, acute psychosis, and suicidal thoughts and attempts (Zawilska, 2011).

Morning glory seed (MGS) has long been used as a traditional Chinese medicine for the treatment of edema (swelling), ascites (fluid retention in the abdomen), obesity, and intense fever. In recent years, long-term exposure to MGS has been shown to pose progressive renal damage in clinical practice, which could translate to those using it regularly for recreational purposes (Chao et al., 2010). LSA has also been added to the list of causes of posterior reversible encephalopathy syndrome, a medical condition characterized by headache, confusion, seizures, and visual loss (Legriel et al., 2008).

4.3 MESCALINE-LIKE HALLUCINOGENS: PHENYLETHYLAMINES

2,5 Dimethoxy-4-methyl amphetamine (DOM)

slang: STP: serenity, tranquility, and peace, or super terrific psychedelic

2,5 Dimethoxy-4-methyl amphetamine, 2-(1H-indol-3-yl)-N,N-dimethylethanamine ($C_{12}H_{19}NO_2$)

DOM, commonly referred to as "STP," is chemically related to mescaline and amphetamines. It was originally synthesized in 1964 during attempts to find a treatment for schizophrenia. Typically administered orally, it is considerably more potent than mescaline, but less potent than LSD. Physical effects at higher dose levels include sleeplessness, dry mouth, nausea, blurred vision, sweating, flushed skin, and shaking, while at low doses it produces amphetamine-like symptoms. Exhaustion, confusion, excitement, delirium, and convulsions may also occur in large doses. Severe adverse reactions are frequent, and the effects of the drug may last from 16 to 24 hours. Although there have been no official reports of deaths directly attributable to STP, users who have already experienced psychological disturbances may suffer a prolonged psychotic reaction. Tolerance to DOM develops within three days, and thus there have been no reports of physical dependence upon this hallucinogen. There are no current therapeutic uses for this psychoactive agent (Brands et al., 1998).

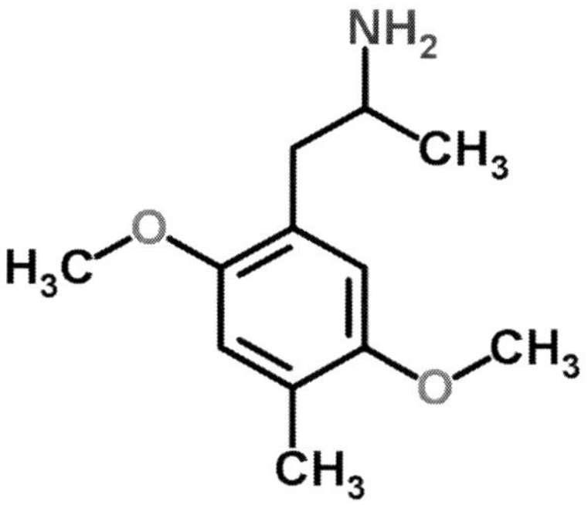

Figure 4.5: 2,5 Dimethoxy-4-methyl amphetamine (DOM)

Ibogaine

slang: Evoker, Ibo, Iboga, Indra

12-Methoxyibogamine ($C_{20}H_{26}N_2O$)

Ibogaine derives from the root bark of *Tabernanthe Iboga*, a shrub that grows in west central African rainforests where it is used medicinally to stave off fatigue, hunger, and thirst, and as part of local spiritual practices. The salt form, ibogaine hydrochloride, is a white bitter powder (as are most hallucinogens) that is administered orally. Oral administration results in effects not being perceived

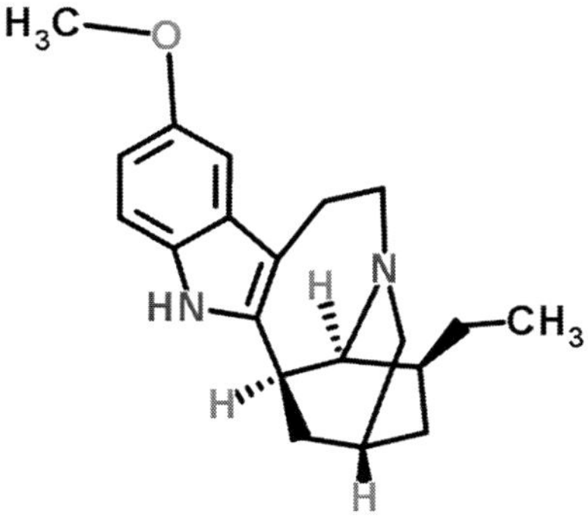

Figure 4.6: Ibogaine

until 40 to 60 minutes after ingestion. Peak effects last up to 2 hours, with total duration of action approximately 8 hours and another 48 hours required for full recovery from the effects. During its peak, ibogaine produces intense visions and a trance- or dream-like state, though users are typically aware of who and where they are, followed by what is described as a period of introspection. Ibogaine also produces nausea and vomiting, causes severe dizziness, and affects coordination and movement; its use has been described as a physically taxing experience. Due to its secondary stimulant effects, the cardiovascular system is stressed by ibogaine. The drug can produce irregular heartbeat, seizures, related symptoms of metabolic dysfunction, and in severe instances, respiratory arrest (Koenig & Hilber, 2015; Rubi et al., 2016).

The mechanism of action of ibogaine is novel among hallucinogens. It works as a potent serotonin reuptake inhibitor while also affecting nicotine acetylcholine, mu, and kappa opioid receptors. It also affects glutamate receptors that are involved in learning, memory, and the creation of new neural pathways. What has made ibogaine of interest in the West are claims, now backed by research studies, that a single treatment can reduce opioid withdrawal symptoms and craving, and lead to abstinence or sustained reduced use (Brown & Alper, 2018; Koenig & Hilber, 2015; Noller, Frampton, & Yazar-Klosinski, 2018). Ibogaine has also been proposed to have value in treating physical dependency and withdrawal from psychoactive drugs in general, including alcohol, methamphetamine, and nicotine (Maillet & Friedhoff, 2015; Maillet et al., 2015). Ibogaine clinics exist in countries globally, yet the drug is banned in many others, including the United States and United Kingdom, as its consumption, even in regulated doses, has led to sudden death for some users, including during clinical trials (Rubi et al., 2016). In 2017 it was moved onto Health Canada's prescription drug list and can now be legally obtained only with the consent of a physician. Interestingly, it was among the hallucinogens tested by the CIA in the 1950s to assess if it had military value (Smith, Raswyck, & Davidson, 2014).

Jimson Weed

slang: angel's trumpet, devil's apple, devil's weed, gypsy weed, loco weed, stink weed, thornapple

Atropine, *(3-endo)-8-Methyl-8-azabicyclo[3.2.1]oct-3-yl tropate,* ($C_{17}H_{23}NO_3$)

Hyoscyamine, *(3-endo)-8-Methyl-8-azabicyclo[3.2.1]oct-3-yl (2S)-3-hydroxy-2-phenylpropanoate,* $C_{17}H_{23}NO_3$

Jimson weed (*Datura stramonium*), a member of the nightshade family, has oak-like, poisonous leaves and tubular white or lavender flowers. Jimson weed is native to South America and was introduced to North America sometime during the 1800s. It now grows wild throughout the continent and is referred to by various names (see list of slang terms). The psychoactive components of jimson weed are two related members of the alkaloid family, atropine and hyoscyamine, which are also active ingredients in belladonna, another poisonous plant. The large, jagged, bitter-tasting leaves produce vivid hallucinations if dried and smoked. Non-psychoactive effects include dilated pupils, flushed skin, confusion, blurred vision, increased heartbeat, and anxiety. In the fall, thorny fruit pods are produced by the plant, and if eaten, these can lead to bizarre and violent behaviour that may necessitate hospitalization until the effects subside. As little as a teaspoon of seeds can produce an overdose that results in circulatory collapse, coma, and, in severe cases, even death due to its secondary stimulant effects on the ANS (Hancock & McKim, 2018).

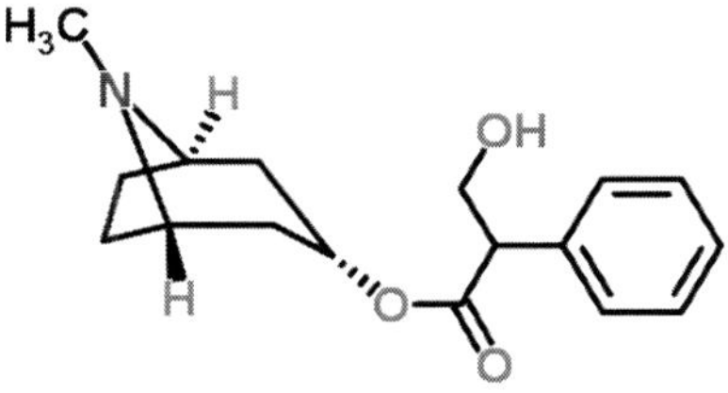

Figure 4.7: Atropine

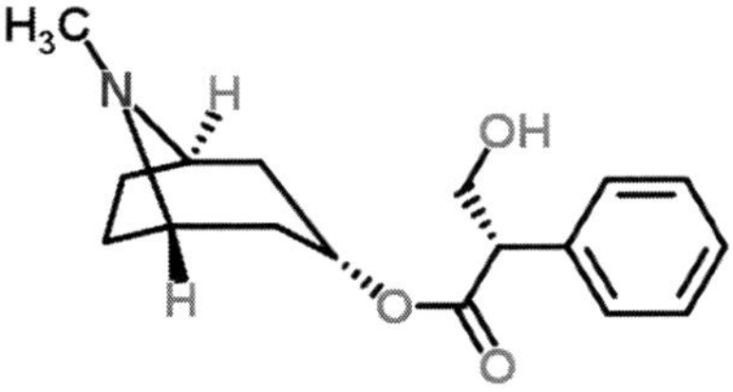

Figure 4.8: Hyoscyamine

Mescaline

slang: big chick, big chief, blue caps, britton, buttons, cactus, cactus head, half moon, mesc, mescal, moon, San Pedro, topi

2-(3,4,5-Trimethoxyphenyl)ethanamine ($C_{11}H_{17}NO_3$)

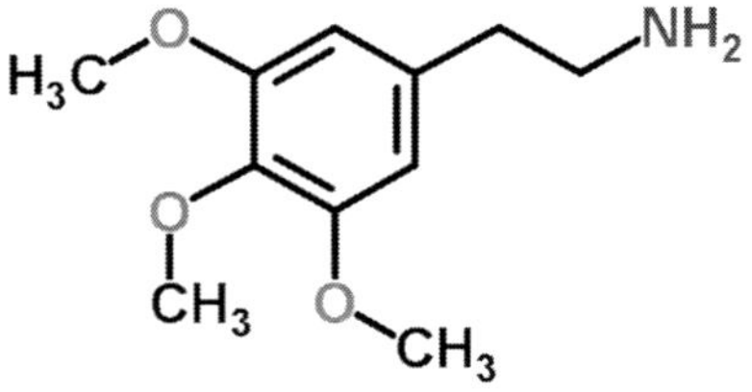

Mescaline is the only entirely natural alkaloid in this drug family, though it can be synthesized. It is prepared from the Mexican peyote cactus and the San Pedro cactus, found in Ecuador and Peru. It has historically been used in the religious ceremonies of Indigenous peoples in Mexico, such as the Aztecs, and remains in use as a sacrament within the Native American church, where is it also used as part of a holistic method for treating alcohol dependency among members of that faith group (Winkelman, 2014).

Figure 4.9: Mescaline

The heads or buttons of the cactus are dried and then sliced, chopped, or ground, and sometimes placed into capsules. Peyote can also be smoked, and occasionally users inject it. It is considerably less potent than LSD but its effects can be much more powerful than those of cannabis. Mescaline has stimulant properties akin to ephedrine and amphetamines, while also altering the brain's serotonin system (Winkelman, 2014). At low doses, from three to six peyote buttons or 300 to 500 milligrams of mescaline, effects appear slowly and last from 10 to 18 hours. Physical effects include dilation of pupils, an increase in body temperature, some muscular relaxation, nausea, and vomiting. The common psychological effects include euphoria, heightened sensory perception, visual hallucinations that users generally realize are imaginary, perceived alterations of body image, and difficulty in thinking. Accounts of mystical or religious experiences have been regularly reported with the use of this psychoactive substance and have been highlighted in both television programs and movies. High doses can cause headache, dry skin, hypotension (low blood pressure), cardiac depression, and slowing of the respiratory rate. Hallucinations typically begin one to two hours after administration. There have not yet been any reports of harmful dependence or withdrawal reactions among those who use peyote on a regular basis as part of their religious beliefs (Hancock & McKim, 2018). Nazi scientists at the Dachau concentration camp experimented unsuccessfully with mescaline as a truth serum preparation, prior to the CIA's similar experiments with LSD (Lee & Shlain, 2001).

3,4-Methylenedioxyamphetamine (MDA)

slang: love drug, love trip, Sally

1-(1,3-Benzodioxol-5-yl)-2-propanamine ($C_{10}H_{13}NO_2$)

3,4-Methylenedioxyamphetamine is a totally synthetic chemical related to both mescaline and amphetamines, and thus producing a combination of both LSD- and stimulant-like effects. MDA was patented as a cough suppressant in 1956, as a tranquilizer in 1960, and as an appetite inhibitor in 1961, but it was never marketed for any of these uses due to its negative side effects (Kalant, 2001). MDA is typically administered orally, and when consumed in this manner, effects are perceived after approximately half an hour and may last up to 8 hours. Its half-life is 16 to 38 hours. For many users, low doses of MDA, from 60 to 150 milligrams, are reported to artificially produce a sense of peacefulness and emotional closeness to others. For this reason, it has been labelled the "love drug." Users generally report a sense of well-being, along with heightened tactile sensations, intensification of feelings, a heightened level of consciousness, and increased self-insight, but without hallucinations or sensory distortions. Physical effects, which become more

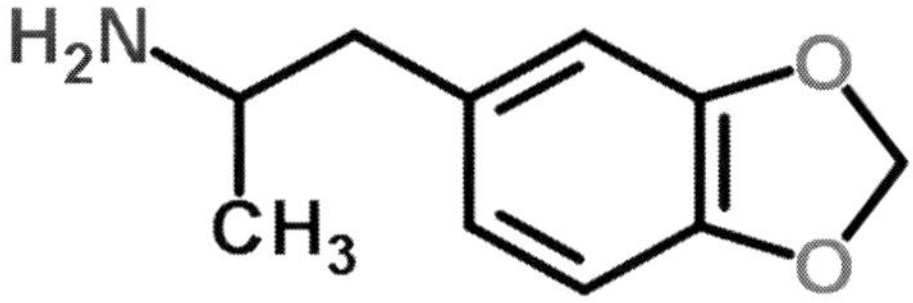

Figure 4.10: 3,4-Methylenedioxyamphetamine (MDA)

pronounced as dosage increases, include dilation of pupils, increased blood pressure, increased body temperature, profuse sweating, and dryness of the nose and throat. Doses of 300 to 500 milligrams all produce significant amphetamine-like effects, including hyperactive reflexes, hyper-responsiveness to sensory stimuli, hypothermia, and agitation. Hallucinations, seizures, and respiratory insufficiency due to the spasm of chest muscles can also occur. These serious physical reactions require immediate medical treatment, as MDA-associated deaths and near-deaths have been regularly reported (Hancock & McKim, 2018).

3,4-Methylenedioxymethamphetamine (MDMA)

slang: Adam, b-bombs, Bermuda triangle, bickie, blue kisses, blue lips, blue nile, California sunrise, clarity, E, ecstasy, elephants, euphoria, Eve, love pill, M&M's, Molly, rolling, running, Scooby snacks, snowball, speed for lovers, swans, thizz, X, XTC, yuppie psychedelic

(1,3-Benzodioxol-5-yl)-N-methyl-2-propanamine ($C_{11}H_{15}NO_2$)

3,4-Methylenedioxymethamphetamine, more commonly referred to as ecstasy, was first manufactured in 1912 by the German pharmaceutical company Merck. It is a derivative of oil of sassafras and oil of nutmeg and was created by chemists looking for amphetamine-like drugs to help suppress appetite. However, ecstasy differs from amphetamine and methamphetamine in that it has an additional molecule ring that gives it similar properties to mescaline. This molecular formation makes it highly lipid soluble, which allows the transference of MDMA from the bloodstream to the inside of a neuron in the brain much quicker, in turn allowing for a shorter onset of psychoactive effect, but also a shorter

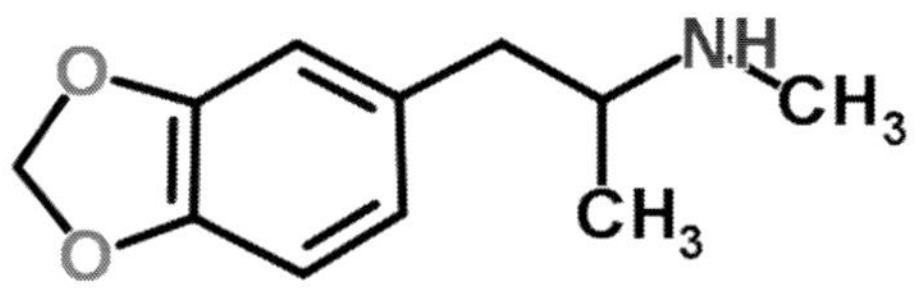

Figure 4.11: 3,4-Methylenedioxymethamphetamine (MDMA)

period of activity. MDMA is metabolized into MDA, but because of the enhanced lipid solubility, MDMA's effects are shorter acting, lasting approximately four hours, with gradual return to metabolic baseline over the course of another two to three hours (Piper, 2006).

MDMA acts upon several neurotransmitters, increasing the amount of serotonin released into the synapse while having secondary effects on dopamine and norepinephrine, producing increased neurotransmitter activity as amphetamines do. It is the release of dopamine that contributes to both the drug's psychological action and its neurotoxicity. Despite having hallucinogenic properties, the most important desired effect among users is typically the euphoric feeling that the drug produces. MDMA generally does not directly interfere with cognitive functioning and is reported to produce a warm, emotionally grounded feeling with a sense of self-acceptance, and a reduction of fear and defensiveness along with an altered perception of reality. Users also report that it provides a sense of pleasure, emotional insight, and enhanced self-esteem (Dorland, 2012; Rigg & Sharp, 2018).

During the 1970s, psychiatrists conducted some preliminary clinical trials in efforts to facilitate psychotherapy using MDMA, which led to its being labelled "the penicillin of the soul." MDMA was touted as having the ability to assist in overcoming neuroses, increase self-confidence, and induce feelings of euphoria through the release of serotonin, which reduces the fear response to a perceived emotional threat. Inconsistent outcomes with the drug, and the subsequent emergence of MDMA as a street drug, particularly in association with raves, contributed to a restriction of its clinical use and a fading in interest of MDMA's therapeutic potential (Rigg & Sharp, 2018). However, the Multidisciplinary Association for Psychedelic Studies group (https://maps.org/) has actively advocated for ongoing investigation of the therapeutic usefulness of MDMA and other hallucinogens since 1986. This advocacy has borne fruit, with multiple studies now indicating that MDMA-assisted psychotherapy is an effective treatment for some individuals suffering from post-traumatic stress disorder (Feduccia & Mithoefer, 2018; Mithoefer et al., 2018; Ot'alora et al., 2018). Related research has found that MDMA, used in conjunction with counselling, can produce positive outcomes for autistic adults with social anxiety (Danforth et al., 2015; 2018). However, individuals in psychotherapy clinical trials also reported many distinct physical side effects, including sweating, blurred vision, fluctuations in blood pressure, loss of appetite, and stiffness of the bones.

Issues arising from the unregulated use of MDMA have included lethargy, kidney damage, hypertension, weight loss, anorexia, anxiety and panic attacks, depression, aggression, the altering of brain chemistry after cessation, increases in body temperature, dehydration, memory loss, and a few documented cases of seizures, along with long-term problems with emotion, memory, and pain. Lesser issues, such as exhaustion, have also been reported, as have flashbacks (den Hollander et al., 2012; Martins & Alexandre, 2009; Zimmermann & Becker, 2016). Non-therapeutic MDMA dose levels can cause the acute depletion of presynaptic serotonin (5-HT), the depression of 5-HT synthesis, and the destruction of serotonin neurons following ongoing administration of high doses. Acute use of MDMA and other serotonin-depleting hallucinogens on weekends has led to what has become known as Blue Mondays and Suicide Tuesdays. Users regularly experience temporary feelings of depression while the brain works to build back up to homeostatic levels of serotonin that were depleted during weekend drug use.

One MDMA metabolite is a potent neurotoxin that can also destroy serotonin-producing neurons, which play a direct role in regulating aggression, mood, sexual activity, sleep, and sensitivity to pain, though it is unusual for people to reach toxicity levels when taking MDMA recreationally. Ongoing MDMA use has been found to produce long-lasting damage to brain areas critical for thought and memory, harming nerve cells that use the neurochemical serotonin to communicate in areas of the brain where conscious thought occurs and contributing to the development or exacerbation of clinical depression. Though there is evidence of the recovery of serotonin levels over time, some regions never return to their original levels, while others recover to levels higher than baseline (Kish et al., 2010; Verheyden, Maidment, & Curran, 2003; Vollenweider et al., 1999). MDMA users typically experience restless, disturbed sleep for up to 48 hours following drug use. Total sleep time has been found to be reduced, with increased time spent in transition, Stage 1 sleep and less time in Stage 2. While there was no reported change in REM sleep, there was an increased risk of sleep apnea with continued use of MDMA (McCann et al., 2009; Schierenbeck et al., 2008).

MDMA has a lethal dose level of 16 compared to ketamine's (chapter 4.4) rate of 38, while psilocybin (chapter 4.2) and cannabis (chapter 4.5) score 1,000. Reported fatalities from MDMA use have been attributed to the pressure the drug can exert on the heart and respiratory system, as well as through causing swelling of the lining of the brain; hyperpyrexia (when the body's temperature rises above 106.7°F); creation of blood clots and excessive bleeding; toxic damage to the liver; dehydration; or hypermetabolic reactions on hot, crowded dance floors, though absolute numbers remain low (Kalant, 2001). Another concern is when other drugs that have more problematic side effects, such as PMA (paramethoxyamphetamine) and PMMA (paramethoxymethamphetamine), are sold as MDMA, and the user is unaware which drug they are taking. Persons most vulnerable to the negative effects of MDMA are those with pre-existing heart disease, epilepsy, diabetes, or mental health issues. Media reports and contemporary music have given a new slang term to MDMA, Molly, which is often touted as "pure" MDMA. Interestingly, in most adverse reactions that led to hospitalization, it was found that the "pure" Molly was actually adulterated MDMA that included the core bath salt chemical synthetic cathinone, PMA, or PMMA (Rigg & Sharp, 2018; Rogers et al., 2009; Zakzanis & Young, 2001).

Nutmeg

slang: flubsauce (nutmeg and yogurt), hell spice

6-Allyl-4-methoxy-1,3-benzodioxole ($C_{11}H_{12}O_3$)

The known active ingredient in nutmeg, myristicin, is chemically related to trimethoxyamphetamine (TMA). While it is best known as the Christmas spice, nutmeg has been used for a variety of other reasons, including as an antidiarrheal agent, appetite enhancer, tonic, and aphrodisiac. It has also been demonstrated to have analgesic, antifungal, antimicrobial, and anti-inflammatory properties. To obtain a psychoactive effect, nutmeg kernels may be eaten, ground, or powdered, with the powder form typically snorted. Large doses of nutmeg may produce feelings of depersonalization, delusions, and unreality. Low doses may also produce mild, brief euphoria, lightheadedness, and CNS stimulation, as nutmeg appears to affect the brain's norepinephrine, dopamine, and serotonin systems. At higher doses, users may experience rapid heartbeat, excessive thirst, agitation, anxiety, acute panic, vomiting, and hallucinations. The effects begin slowly, last several hours, and are most often followed by excessive drowsiness. Recovery from nutmeg intoxication is slow and involves an extremely physically unpleasant hangover effect (El-Alfy et al., 2009).

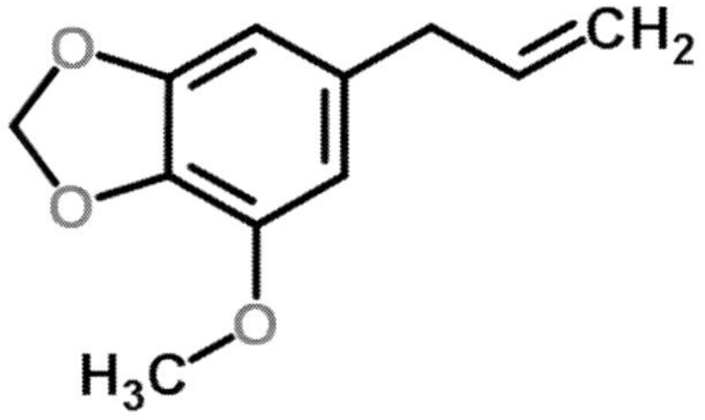

Figure 4.12: Nutmeg

Paramethoxyamphetamine (PMA)

slang: chicken powder, chicken yellow, death, Dr. Death

1-(4-methoxyphenyl)propan-2-amine ($C_{10}H_{15}NO$)

Paramethoxyamphetamine is referred to as the "death drug" due to the unusually high incidence of fatalities its use produces among users. PMA is a more toxic derivative of amphetamine, having both more pronounced hallucinogenic and stimulant effects than MDMA. In low

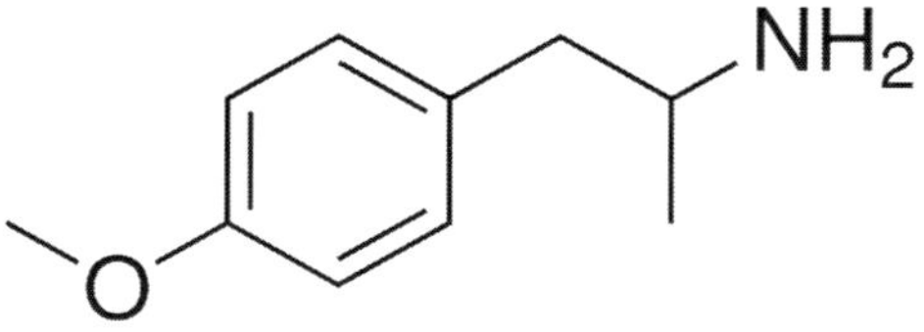

Figure 4.13: Paramethoxyamphetamine (PMA)

doses, PMA can have a superficially similar effect to MDMA, as they both alter the same neurotransmitters; however, it is significantly more toxic than MDMA, as a user needs to administer less of it to have an adverse reaction. The physical effects of PMA usually include greatly increased pulse rate and blood pressure, increased and laboured respiration, highly elevated body temperature, erratic eye movements, muscle spasms, nausea, and vomiting. PMA typically does not produce the positive feelings of warmth and comfort that are associated with ecstasy. The chemical modification that changes MDA to PMA makes PMA highly toxic. At the same dose as MDA, PMA can produce seizures that can lead to coma and death because of the way it interferes with the body's cardiovascular system and temperature regulation, and because it can produce hypoglycemia (inadequate glucose in the bloodstream), and hyperkalaemia (high levels of potassium in the blood). PMA is not typically sold overtly. Rather, it is represented to buyers as MDMA, leading people to unwittingly take it believing that it is ecstasy. Given the illicit nature of MDMA, in many instances chemists were in fact attempting to manufacture ecstasy but ended up producing PMA (or PMMA) instead. Another contributing factor may be that PMA takes longer than ecstasy to take effect, which may lead individuals to take another dose and end up with double the stimulant effect (Caldicott et al., 2003; Holden, 2013; Hancock & McKim, 2018).

Paramethoxymethamphetamine (PMMA)

slang: death, double-stacked, Dr. Death, killer, mitsubishi, mitsubishi double-stack, red death, red mitsubishi, white mitsubishi

4-methylmethamphetamine ($C_{11}H_{17}N$)

Paramethoxymethamphetamine is a highly toxic hallucinogenic analogue of methamphetamine. Like methamphetamine, it is a synthetic drug possessing both hallucinogenic and stimulant properties, as PMMA both releases serotonin into the synapse and blocks its reuptake as well as releasing dopamine and norepinephrine. PMMA is metabolized by the liver into the toxic amphetamine analogue, which means that its pharmacodynamics are similar to PMA. PMMA mimics the hallucinogenic

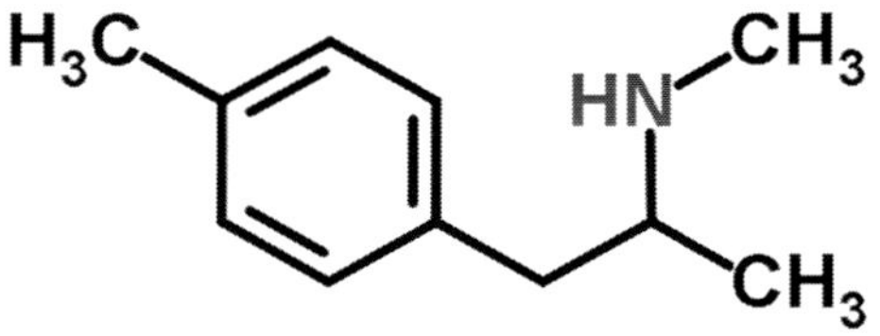

Figure 4.14: Paramethoxymethamphetamine (PMMA)

effects of MDMA, though the physical side effects are more pronounced and more severe. Like MDMA, PMMA's side effects are tachycardia, hypertension, rapid and involuntary eye movement, hallucinations, and severe hyperthermia, leading to kidney failure and death among a minority of users. As with PMA, PMMA hallucinogenic effects take longer to be perceived than either MDA or MDMA, which often leads users to take more of the drug, which, when metabolized, overwhelms the user's biological systems as PMMA is even more toxic than PMA (Lurie et al., 2012). There have been documented deaths due to PMMA ingestion globally, including in nations as far flung as Australia, Belgium, Ireland, Israel, Norway, Taiwan, and Canada (Johansen et al., 2003; Lin, Liu, & Yin, 2007; Ling et al., 2001; Lurie et al., 2012; Simpson, 2015; Vevelstad et al., 2012; Voorspoels et al., 2002).

Scopolamine (Devil's Breath)

slang: burundanga, devil's breath, homicide (scopolamine and heroin)

(−)-(S)-3-Hydroxy-2-phenylpropionic acid (1R,2R,4S,7S,9S)-9-methyl-3-oxa-9-azatricyclo[3.3.1.0^{2,4}]non-7-yl ester ($C_{17}H_{21}NO_4$)

Scopolamine, or devil's breath, is an extremely potent hallucinogenic drug that blocks the neurotransmitter acetylcholine in the central and peripheral nervous systems. One of the earliest alkaloids isolated from plant sources, scopolamine has been in use in its purified form since the late 1800s, though its history of use dates to pre-contact with European colonizers. Scopolamine inhibits parasympathetic nerve impulses by selectively blocking the binding of acetylcholine to its receptor site in nerve cells. The nerve fibres of the parasympathetic system are responsible for the involuntary movement of smooth muscles in the gastrointestinal tract, urinary tract, and lungs. Along with being a neuromuscular blocker, scopolamine's major effect is its ability to block the retention of new information and the ability of users to be able to fix their attention onto a task, while also producing auditory and visual hallucinations, disorientation, euphoria, a feeling of fatigue, and motor incoordination. Sedation occurs following low or moderate doses, with restlessness occurring in higher doses (Safer & Allen, 1971). Scopolamine impairs memory functions, with the deficit appearing to be in the storage process, leaving retrieval processes unaffected. This means that users can engage in activities but will have no memory of doing so. Subjectively, scopolamine produces a larger sedative effect than does the benzodiazepine diazepam (Ghoneim & Mewaldt, 1975). In the laboratory, scopolamine is used as a standard reference for inducing cognitive deficits in healthy humans, and in animal studies, it has been demonstrated to disrupt senses and attention (Klinkenberg & Blokland, 2010).

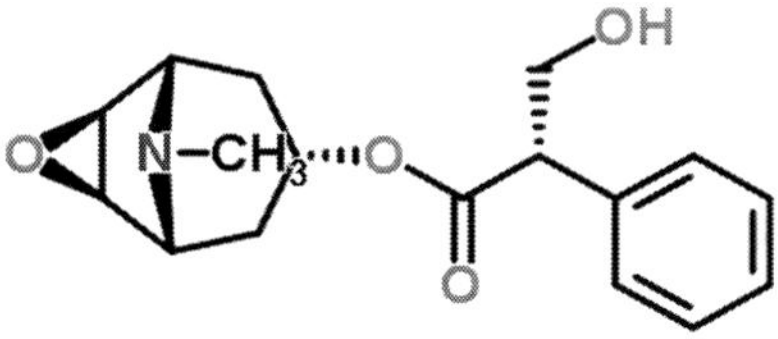

Figure 4.15: Scopolamine

Interestingly, low doses of this drug are used therapeutically for those with overactive bladders (Andersson, 2004) and as an aid in counteracting the effects of motion sickness, as well as for preventing the nausea and vomiting associated with recovery from anaesthesia and surgery (Spinks & Wasiak, 2011). Scopolamine was previously used for treating symptoms of Parkinson's disease and can be safely prescribed to children as young as six months of age. However, even in therapeutic use there is a risk of distinct CNS effects, including CNS depression, dreamless sleep, disorientation, confusion, memory disturbances, and dizziness. Excitement, restlessness, hallucinations, or delirium may paradoxically occur, especially when scopolamine is used in the presence of severe pain, and its use may result in the impairment of performance of activities requiring mental alertness, physical coordination, or visual acuity. Additionally, toxic symptoms may occur even at therapeutic dose levels. More serious reactions are possible at higher doses, including confusion, agitation, rambling speech, hallucinations, paranoid behaviour, and delusions, as well as complete disorientation, active delirium, and accelerated pulse rate. Withdrawal from the drug can cause nausea, vomiting, headache, dizziness, and disturbances of equilibrium. Mental confusion and dizziness may be observed with both withdrawal and acute toxicity. Scopolamine also has the capacity to aggravate seizures or psychosis in users predisposed to those conditions (Canadian Pharmacists Association, 2017).

While scopolamine has been used recreationally for its hallucinogenic properties, recreational use has historically been minimal in North America, as the psychedelic experiences produced are often unpredictable and unpleasant, and frequently result in not only negative but also dangerous physical effects. What has brought this drug to greater notoriety, however, is its illicit use in Colombia (particularly associated with criminal organizations), where the drug can be obtained from the native-growing borrachero tree, which in local parlance is called the "get you drunk tree." When scopolamine is extracted from the trees, which grow naturally not only in the countryside but also in urban areas, a colourless, odourless, and tasteless powder is obtained. The powder can be readily dissolved in liquids or even sprinkled into a person's food, with results akin to what occurs when the benzodiazepine Rohypnol is added to alcohol, producing a state of near-amnesia. Media reports have claimed that those drugged with scopolamine can become so compliant and docile that they have been known to assist thieves in robbing their homes and emptying their bank accounts. The drug is reported to produce a state similar to sleepwalking, where the individual has no free will. There are also reports of the CIA having experimented with the drug as a truth serum, but that the hallucinogenic nature of the drug made the results too inconsistent to be of use (Stebner, 2012).

Trimethoxyamphetamine (TMA)

slang: Christmas trees, true mon amis, tutor marked assessment

1-(2,3,4-Trimethoxyphenyl)-2-propanamine ($C_{12}H_{19}NO_3$)

Trimethoxyamphetamine is an infrequently encountered hallucinogen that also has stimulant effects. TMA is more potent than mescaline

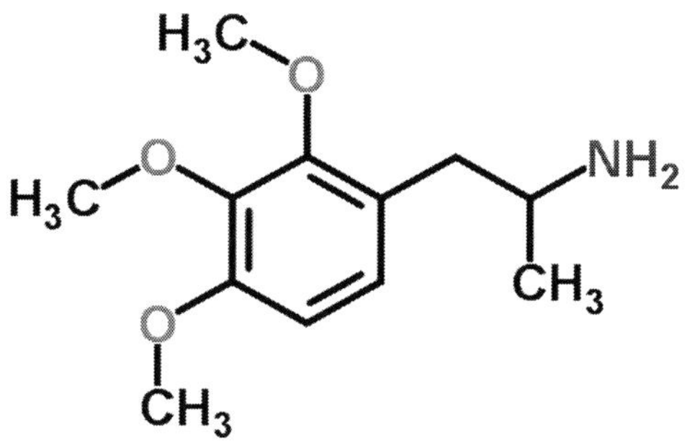

Figure 4.16: Trimethoxyamphetamine (TMA)

and may be taken orally or injected. After approximately two hours, the user experiences intensified auditory and tactile sensations and mescaline-like hallucinations. TMA also produces some unusual effects as the size of the dose is increased. However, the amount required to produce an effect is very close to the toxic level. The mescaline-like effects observed at lower doses of TMA tend to be replaced at higher doses by such behaviour as unprovoked anger and aggression (Brands et al., 1998).

4.4 DISSOCIATIVE ANAESTHETICS: ARYLCYCLOALKYLAMINES

Ketamine

slang: big K, blind, breakfast, breakfast cereal, cat killer, cat tranquilizer, cat valium, clean acid, donkey, horsey, jet fuel, K, K-rod, ket, kitkat, kitty, special K, squid, super acid, super K, vitamin K, wonky

2-(2-Chlorophenyl)-2-(methylamino)cyclohexanone ($C_{13}H_{16}ClNO$)

Ketamine, an *N*-methyl-D-aspartate (NMDA) glutamate receptor antagonist, is a white, powdery, synthetic dissociative anaesthetic. Its administration blocks glutamate from binding at receptor sites, decreasing excitation in the brain, which is why it eases depression symptoms. It also binds to mu opioid receptor sites, which is why it can produce pain relief at lower doses and unconsciousness at higher dose levels. As it is also a

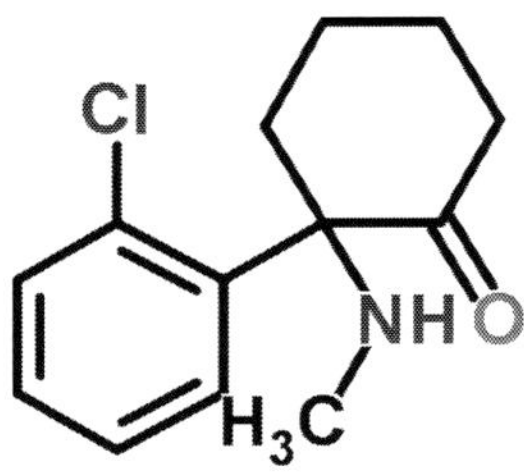

Figure 4.17: Ketamine

hallucinogen, even small doses of ketamine produce increased binding of serotonin in the nucleus accumbens. It also has a weak effect on dopamine. Despite its hallucinogenic properties, also produced in part by blocking NMDA, ketamine is considered an essential medicine used for anaesthesia and analgesia (pain relief) in adults and children, especially for short surgical procedures when an individual only needs to be unconscious for 10 to 15 minutes (Schwenk et al., 2018). It has been listed on the World Health Organization (WHO) Essential Medicines List for over 30 years, with the WHO Expert Committee on Drug Dependence continually fighting against attempts to place ketamine onto the international drug control conventions list, due to its essential role in surgery in low-to-middle-resource countries where ketamine is the primary or only general anaesthetic option for emergency surgery. Ketamine is inexpensive and can be administered orally or via injection without requiring expensive anaesthetic inhalation techniques or technology (WHO, 2014a). However, at large doses ketamine can significantly suppress the respiratory system as well as produce substantive disassociation from reality. Ketamine is more commonly used in North America as a small animal tranquilizer. While it produces anaesthesia quickly, even low doses have the potential to produce delusions and mental confusion that can progress to hallucinations and degrees of dissociation bordering on a schizophrenic-like state and even psychosis. Ketamine has also been used as a date-rape drug, for a small dose, when mixed with alcohol, produces a greater effect than either drug alone (Iadarola et al., 2015).

While ketamine is structurally similar to PCP, it is 10 times less potent. When ketamine is used in surgery, recovery tends to be slower than when other anaesthetics are employed. Violent dreams and flashbacks have been associated with both clinical and non-medical use of the drug. In larger doses, the "K-hole" effect occurs, a distinct feeling of mind and body separation that in severe circumstances can lead to stupor or unconsciousness, with a resulting feeling of confusion and loss of short-term memory. Some have equated this to an out-of-body or near-death experience. Short-term physical effects can include a loss of motor control, leading to difficulties in walking, standing, and talking, temporary memory loss, numbness, nausea, decreased awareness of the environment, sedation, increased distractibility, disorientation, and out-of-body experiences. Chronic use can lead to urinary tract infections and the development of ulcers in the bladder, neurocognitive impairment, and deficits in both working and episodic memory. It is possible to overdose on ketamine, and deaths have been reported from its misuse, especially when it is combined with ethyl alcohol (Morgan & Curran, 2012). Ketamine use increases non-rapid eye movement sleep (NREM) intensity and duration, and while it does not increase or decrease REM sleep, ketamine use does tend to produce more vivid and violent dreaming (Feinberg & Campbell, 1993; Hejja & Galloon, 1975).

As ketamine affects both glutamate and endorphins, it has also been found to produce antidepressant responses in those who are resistant to typical antidepressants in a matter of hours, versus days and weeks for other antidepressants (chapter 5.1). It does so by rapidly promoting the formation of synapses between neurons in the CNS, including increased density and function in the prefrontal cortex, and through reversing synaptic deficits produced by chronic stress reactions in the brain (Duman & Aghajanian, 2012).

Treatment-resistant depression (TRD) is defined by the inability of at least two mainstream antidepressants to reverse a depressive mood episode. Ketamine has been found to produce positive affective responses in indivduals with a diagnosis of TRD, including major depressive disorder, bipolar depression, pain disorders, and comorbid depression and pain disorders. Ketamine has also been demonstrated to have anti-anxiety and anti-suicidal ideation properties (Allen & Ivester, 2017; Canuso et al., 2018; Iadarola et al., 2015; Singh et al., 2016). Preliminary studies have demonstrated that ketamine can be of value as a pharmacological component for treating substance use disorders (Ettensohn, Markey, & Levine, 2018). Ketamine has been shown to effectively prolong abstinence among participants in small studies who had been dependent on both alcohol and heroin. Providing ketamine in therapeutic dose levels also reduced craving for and self-administration of cocaine in non-treatment-seeking cocaine users. However, results remain preliminary and more research is required to determine if ketamine works by enhancing the brain's neuroplasticity and recovery, by disrupting functional neural networks, by blocking reconsolidation of drug-related memories, or by some combination of these factors (Ezquerra-Romano et al., 2018).

However, ketamine is a psychoactive drug and even in controlled clinical use, side effects occur among users. In the various clinical trials demonstrating the utility of this drug, test subjects reported a broader range of side effects than did those in placebo groups. This included, not surprisingly, drug-induced hallucinations, dissociation, perceptual disturbance, odd body sensations, and depersonalization. Individuals who received ketamine in these trials, and benefited from it, also reported increased anxiety, followed by agitation or irritability, euphoria, panic, and/or apathy. Physical changes included increased blood pressure and heart rate; palpitations or arrhythmia; chest pain, tightness, or pressure; dizziness; decreased blood pressure and heart rate; headaches; and memory loss, confusion, and cognitive impairment. Thus, while ketamine has great therapeutic potential, that does not diminish the fact that, like other therapeutic psychoactive agents, it also has the potential to produce a broad range of negative and potentially harmful side effects (Allen & Ivester, 2017; Short et al., 2017).

Phencyclidine (PCP)

slang: amoeba, angel dust, animal tranquilizer, beam me up Scotty (mixed with cocaine), black dust, busy bee, crystal, DOA (dead on arrival), hog, elephant tranquilizer, embalming fluid, mint leaf, mint weed, monkey tranquilizer, orange crystal, rocket fuel, soma, snorts, tic tac, wack

1-(1-Phenylcyclohexyl)piperidine ($C_{17}H_{25}N$)

The pharmaceutical company Parke-Davis originally developed PCP in the 1950s as an experimental general intravenous anaesthetic called

Sernyl to reflect the idea of the serenity it was hoped the drug would create. PCP was withdrawn after just over a decade of use due to the undesirable side effects it produced, which included convulsions during surgical procedures, delirium, confusion, visual disorientation, dysphoria, delirium, and dramatic hallucinations as the person awoke. Not to be a total economic loss, PCP was relabelled Sernylan and marketed as an anaesthetic for non-human primates. A decade later, PCP was available to street drug users and abuse became widespread throughout North America in the 1970s, primarily because PCP was extremely inexpensive and relatively easy to produce (Carroll, 1990; UNODC, 2013).

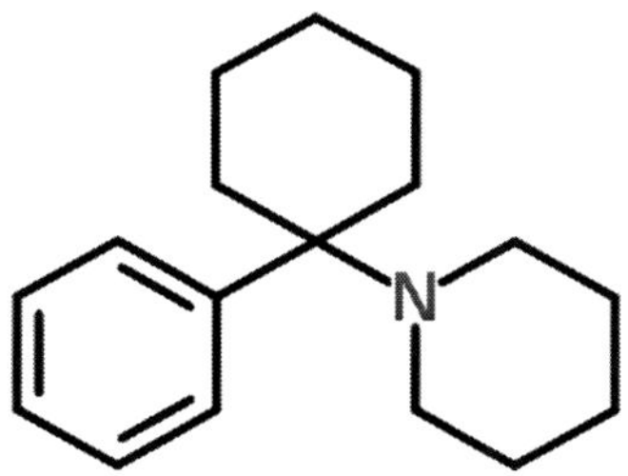

Figure 4.18: Phencyclidine (PCP)

PCP is a difficult drug to classify accurately; different doses produce different effects as it interacts with most neurotransmitter systems and has the ability to temporarily disrupt communication between neurotransmitters throughout the entire CNS. PCP is not chemically related to either LSD or mescaline, as it produces its hallucinogenic effects by blocking a specific neurochemical receptor site: the NDMA subtype of glutamate. However, it also exhibits anticholinergic and opioid-like activities while blocking dopamine reuptake and thus elevating the amount of dopamine available in the synaptic cleft to bind to neurotransmitters. This gives it not only hallucinogenic and CNS-depressant effects, but also weak stimulant properties. Less than two milligrams of PCP can produce a psychoactive reaction. In some instances, effects have lasted from 10 to 14 days, though a much more typical range is 3 to 18 hours (Hancock & McKim, 2018).

PCP is highly lipid soluble and is stored in fat and brain tissue. At low doses, it can produce feelings of euphoria, relaxation, and sedation. Perceptual distortions of time, space, and body image as well as visual or auditory stimuli are common. There is often a feeling of dissociation from the environment such that the user feels totally isolated.

Impairment of higher cortical functions such as attention, concentration, judgment, motor coordination, and speech can also occur. Physiological effects include constriction of the pupils, blurred vision, an increase in body temperature, and mild stimulation of the cardiovascular system. Higher doses of PCP, which can be as little as 10 milligrams in a non-tolerant user, can induce an acute toxic psychosis, including paranoia, confusion, disorientation, restlessness, hallucinations, anxiety, agitation, personal alienation, delusions, and bizarre and sometimes violent behaviour. Muscular rigidity and spasms, twitching, or absent reflexes may appear at high doses. When administered in large amounts, PCP has an analgesic effect that prevents users from experiencing pain resulting from injuries. This factor tends to increase the severity of injuries a person experiences while under the influence of the drug, as the user fails to take protective action when engaged in physical activities, including acts of aggression or violence. Other physiological effects experienced at high doses include irregularities in heartbeat, fluctuations in blood pressure, abnormally high body temperature, respiratory depression, and severe nausea, vomiting, and hypersalivation. At very high doses, 150 to 200 milligrams, seizures, coma, and respiratory arrest may result in death. Hypertensive crises, stroke, and renal failure have also been reported, as have stupor, catatonic rigidity, and accidental and/or violent death (Hancock & McKim, 2018).

The long-term effects of PCP include the possibility of flashbacks, prolonged anxiety, social withdrawal and isolation, severe depression, memory impairment, and the inability to think abstractly. Impairment of thought, along with unpredictable and violent behaviour, has also been observed in chronic PCP users. These symptoms may take several months to abate once the user has stopped ingesting the substance. A toxic psychosis has also been observed in chronic users with no other history of psychiatric disorder, though the exact role of PCP in the etiology of these symptoms is unclear. Tolerance does appear to develop to PCP use. Withdrawal symptoms have been reported in animals, but the development of physical dependence has yet to be confirmed.

Psychological dependence appears to occur in some users, but the prevalence is unknown (Carroll, 1985; Pradham, 1984).

Salvia Divinorum

slang: diviner's sage, magic mint, Maria Pastora, Sage of seers, Sally-D, Salvia, Ska Maria Pastora

Methyl (2S,4aR,6aR,7R,9S,10aS,10bR)-9-acetoxy-2-(3-furyl)-6a,10b-dimethyl-4,10-dioxododecahydro-2H-benzo[f]isochromene-7-carboxylate ($C_{23}H_{28}O_8$)

The psychoactive plant *Salvia divinorum* is a member of the mint family and is related to sage. It grows naturally in the northeastern Sierra Mazateca mountain region of the Mexican state of Oaxaca, where historically the Mazatec people ingested it by chewing fresh leaves or by drinking the extracted juices of the leaf for divinatory rituals, healing ceremonies, and medical purposes. The plant grows to over a metre high and has hollow, square stems, large leaves, and occasional white flowers with violet pods. There have historically been no legal restrictions against its use, and with the growing drug trade out of Mexico, it has become increasingly accessible in other parts of North America. Salvia produces short-lived but intense hallucinations, typically lasting less than half an hour. This is because this psychoactive substance is incredibly lipid soluble, passing through the blood-brain barrier even more easily than cocaine or nicotine. This also accounts for why the drug's actions are limited, for the quicker a drug enters the CNS, the faster it is metabolized, and the effects begin to dissipate. The drug seems to affect neurotransmitters

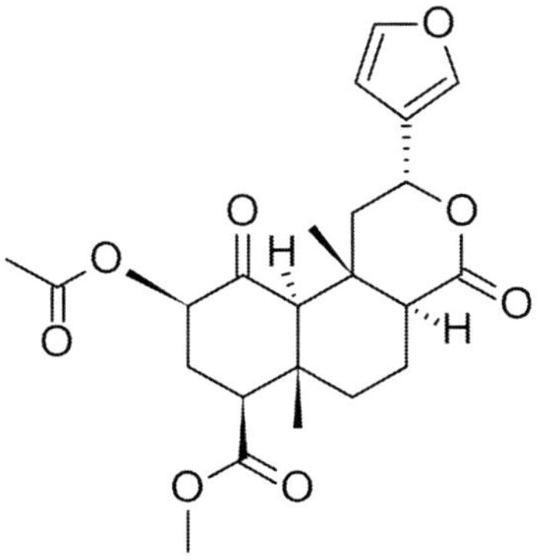

Figure 4.19: Salvia Divinorum

Source: Wikimedia Commons

in the cerebellum and visual cortex to the greatest extent, which are parts of the brain responsible for motor function (cerebellum) and vision (visual cortex). The active ingredient of the plant is comparable to that of the synthetic hallucinogen LSD, though the actual mechanisms of action are very different, and while some severe, psychotic-like reactions have been documented, the overall effects have more typically been characterized as positive rather than negative. While the long-term physical and psychological effects in humans have not been documented, limited studies with rats indicate long-term use has a negative impact upon learning and memory. However, there has been no indication that Salvia produces physical dependency, as is the case with most hallucinogens, though dissociative effects are common (Currie, 2013; EMCDDA, 2011).

The main active ingredient in the plant, Salvinorin A, has been posited to be the most potent naturally occurring hallucinogen, active at doses as low as 200 micrograms. Salvinorin A has no affinity for serotonin or other receptors commonly associated with hallucinogenic effects. Instead, it is unique among hallucinogens in that it is an activator of kappa receptors, which are typically triggered by opioids. These nerve cells are linked with the regulation of human perception and to perception-altering diseases, including schizophrenia and Alzheimer's disease (Roth et al., 2002). The subjective effects of Salvia include psychedelic-like changes in visual perception, mood, and body sensations, emotional swings, feelings of detachment, a highly modified perception of external reality and the self that leads to a decreased ability to interact with one's surroundings, loss of consciousness, short-term memory loss, lack of physical coordination, slurred speech, and awkward sentence patterns. Ataxia (a lack of muscle coordination affecting speech, eye movements, swallowing, walking, and other voluntary movements) as well as depersonalization and unconsciousness have also been associated with the use of this psychoactive agent. Physical effects include dizziness, nausea, decreased heart rate, and chills, contrasted by increased feelings of body warmth and sweating. After the peak effects, normal awareness of self and the immediate surroundings returns, but lingering effects may be felt. As in most cases of withdrawal, these effects have a completely different characteristic than the active drug use experience (Mahendran et al., 2016; Wolowich, Perkins, & Cienik, 2006). At present, physical dependency has not been reported, but that did not stop *Salvia divinorum* from being added to Canada's Controlled Drugs and Substances Act, which made it a prohibited substance as of July 2015 (Government of Canada, 2015).

4.5 CANNABIS

slang: A-bomb (mixed with heroin or opium), Acapulco Gold, Acapulco Red, ace, BT, bazooka (mixed with cocaine), BC bud, bhang, blunt, boom, chronic, Columbian, doobie, dope, gangster, ganja, grass, hemp, herb, home grown, jay, kiff, Mary Jane, Maui Wowie, Northern lights, pot, purple haze, ragweed, reefer, sinse, skunk, smoke, spliff, tea, Thai stick, weed

(6aR,10aR)-6,6,9-Trimethyl-3-pentyl-6a,7,8,10a-tetrahydro-6H-benzo[c]chromen-1-ol ($C_{21}H_{30}O_2$)

In 1923, Canada become one of the first nations to ban cannabis, adding it to the legislation entitled An Act to Prohibit the Improper Use of Opium and other Drugs that also prohibited codeine, heroin, morphine, opium, eucaine, and cocaine use. Restricting the use of these particular drugs was due in part to underlying racism and in part to the beginnings of an international movement to control the use of psychoactive drugs globally through the work of the League of Nations, the forerunner of the United Nations, that arose in the aftermath of World War I. Little behind the legislation related to pharmacological principles. Nearly a century later, Canada became the second nation after Uruguay to legalize cannabis, though again, it was not primarily driven by pharmacological factors.

Cannabis is a strain of hemp that is classified as a hallucinogen because of its ability to alter perception at low doses and produce hallucinations at high doses; however, it affects a totally different neurotransmitter than all other hallucinogens: endocannabinoids. While there are three distinct strains of cannabis, *Cannabis sativa*, *Cannabis*

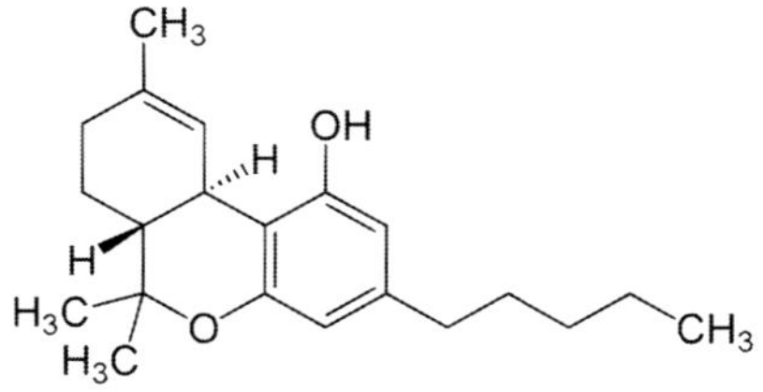

a) Δ9-Tetrahydrocannabinol

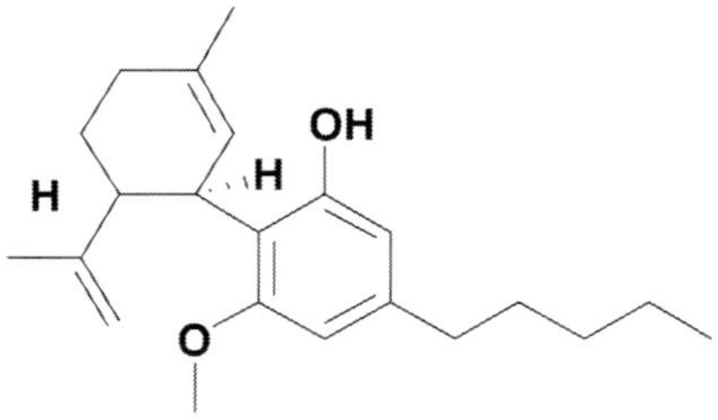

b) Cannabidiol

Figure 4.20: Cannabis

indica, and *Cannabis ruderalis*, it is *Cannabis sativa* that is primarily used recreationally and, now more than ever, therapeutically. *Cannabis sativa* contains over 421 different chemical compounds, including over 60 cannabinoids, and while smoking this drug more than 2,000 compounds may be produced. Cannabis is obtained primarily from the flowers of the plant, and to a lesser extent the leaves and shoots (Huestis, 2009).

There are two distinct components to cannabis: the psychoactive constituent, Δ9-tetrahydrocannabinol (THC), first isolated and synthesized in 1964; and then dozens of non-psychoactive cannabinoids, the most prominent being cannabidiol (CBD), which is primarily responsible for the therapeutic effects produced by cannabis (Barnes & Barnes, 2016). The pharmacological actions of THC result from its partial agonist activity at the cannabinoid receptor CB_1, located primarily in the CNS. THC also affects the CB_2 receptor found primarily in the immune system. The psychoactive effects of THC are mediated by its activation of CB_1 receptors. The presence of these specialized cannabinoid receptors in the brain led researchers to the discovery of the endocannabinoid neurotransmitter anandamide (Ashton, 2001). Cannabis use also increases dopamine release in the brain, producing a sense of euphoria while activating GABA, decreasing anxiety as well as altering endorphins to mask pain (appendix A). However, regular cannabis use leads to a decrease in dopamine levels, which contributes to a range of negative consequences (Bloomfield et al., 2016).

Cannabis contains natural cannabinoids called phyto-cannabinoids, the amount of which varies among different strains. Phyto-cannabinoid concentration is not uniform throughout the plant, being present in the leaves and stems but not the seeds or roots, and with the greatest concentration occurring in the non-fertilized female flower heads. The ratio of CBD to THC determines the degree of therapeutic to psychoactive impact of the drug. In contrast to THC, CBD does not bind to or directly affect either CB_1 or CB_2 (Barnes & Barnes, 2016).

There are a variety of forms of cannabis. The most common form consists of the dried, chopped-up flowering tops, stems, and leaves from the cannabis plant, ranging in colour from grey-green to greenish-brown. The potency of this form of cannabis can range from 1–20% THC and have a texture from a fine powder to a coarse mixture that looks similar to tea. This form is typically smoked or cooked into foods such as brownies or cookies. This constitutes the two primary mechanisms of administering cannabis: inhalation, which produces a fast alteration of the CNS; and oral, which takes much longer but also produces a longer, though less predicatable, effect. Other variations of cannabis are cannabis oil, hashish, hash or honey oil, and shatter. The use of shatter is also referred to as dabbing (Alberta Gaming and Liquor Commission, 2018b).

Cannabis oil is typically added to other oils, such as coconut, olive, canola, or vegetable oil, and contains both THC and CBD. The greater the CBD content of cannabis oil, the greater the therapeutic utility of this form of cannabis. The remaining forms of cannabis are primarily used for recreational purposes to obtain a sense of euphoria. Hashish is the dried, sticky resin of the cannabis plant. It comes in solid pieces ranging in colour from light brown to black, and in texture from dry and hard to soft and crumbly. Hashish now typically has a lower THC concentration than cannabis, ranging from 2–10%. It is usually smoked in a water pipe or added to a cigarette or even to a cannabis joint. Hash oil is made by purifying hashish with a solvent. It is typically a thick, greenish-brown or reddish-brown oil with a THC content ranging from 15–50%, though some samples with more than 60% THC levels have been found. Hash oil is usually added to tobacco and smoked. The most potent form of cannabis, in terms of THC content, is shatter, with some samples containing 90% THC. Shatter is hard, brittle, and amber-coloured, while wax is soft and feels like lip balm, and honeycomb, not surprisingly, resembles honeycomb or a dried sponge. In general, the greater the concentration of THC, the more expensive the product (Alberta Gaming and Liquor Commission, 2018b).

Approximately half of the THC in a cannabis joint is inhaled in the mainstream smoke; nearly all of this is absorbed through the lungs, rapidly entering the bloodstream, reaching the CNS, and interfering with the endogenous (natural) cannabinoid neurotransmitter system. Effects are perceptible within seconds, and fully apparent in a few minutes. Bioavailability after oral ingestion is much less; blood concentrations reached are 25–30% of those obtained by smoking the same dose, partly because of first-pass metabolism in the liver. The onset of effect is delayed, becoming apparent from 30 to 120 minutes after ingestion, depending on the amount of food in the stomach, but the duration is prolonged because of continued slow absorption from the gut (Ashton, 2001). THC binds to anandamines, which are concentrated in areas within the reward system of the brain, the limbic system. Other parts of the brain with large amounts of anandamide receptors include those that regulate the integration of sensory experiences with emotions, as well as those controlling functions of learning, motor coordination, and some autonomic nervous system functions, though not breathing (figure 4.21). The action of THC in the hippocampus explains its ability to interfere with memory, and the action of THC in the cerebellum is responsible for its ability to cause incoordination and loss of balance (EMCDDA, 2009).

Once absorbed, THC and cannabinoids are rapidly distributed to all tissues. Cannabis is metabolized in the liver into more than 20 distinct metabolites, some of which are psychoactive and all of which have long half-lives, lasting from hours to days. Metabolites are partly excreted in the urine (25%), though the majority move into the gut (65%), from which they are reabsorbed, further prolonging their actions. As cannabinoids are very lipid soluble, they accumulate in fatty tissues, reaching peak concentrations in four to five hours. With repeated dosage, high levels of cannabinoids can accumulate in the body and continue to reach the brain with greater concentrations, affecting the limbic, sensory, and motor areas. However, this does not create impairment for this entire time. Like THC, CBD is subjected to a significant first-pass metabolism, and while both are primarily excreted in the feces, unlike THC, a large proportion of CBD is excreted unchanged. Cannabis has one of the longest half-lives of any psychoactive agent—up to two weeks for a chronic user after the last use, and up to five or six days for a casual user, though once a chronic user stops consuming cannabis, they could still test positive up to 45 days after the last administration (Huestis, 2009).

Documentation of medical use of cannabis exists as far back as 4000 BCE in China. Cannabis is also known to have been used therapeutically in ancient Egypt and in India in at least the second millennium BCE. It is also clear that ancient Greek and Roman cultures used cannabis; the first detailed account of the medical use of cannabis appeared in the first century CE. Table 4.1 presents 27 areas for which there is empirical support for cannabis's therapeutic utility—if a potential benefit is not listed, as of 2018, insufficient scientific evidence had been gathered in support of that claim. The therapeutic utility of cannabis is due primarily to cannabinoids rather than THC. While not necessarily superior to other drugs in treating all these conditions, as with any drug, some individuals respond better than others when they self-administer medical cannabis. However, there are limits on the therapeutic potential of cannabinoids because of both their acute and chronic side effects, and because tolerance appears to develop rapidly to some of the beneficial effects, though the euphoric effects of the drug seem to mitigate some of these limits of its use. Also, cannabis is a psychoactive agent, and the greater the THC levels, the greater the risks that arise with using this drug, for it remains an intoxicating agent.

At low to moderate doses, the psychoactive effects of cannabis products are similar to those of alcohol: relaxation, disinhibition, a feeling of euphoria, and the tendency to talk and laugh more than usual. Cannabis can cause unpleasant effects in some users, but these seem to occur less frequently and generally with less intensity than

Table 4.1: Therapeutic Uses for Cannabis: The Effects of CBD

Antibiotic-resistant infections (Englund et al., 2013)	Pain relief (Elikkottil, Gupta, & Gupta, 2009; Vigil et al., 2017)
Antiemetic (prevention of vomiting) (Martin & Wiley, 2004)	Pain relief (neuropathic)* (Weizman et al., 2018)
Anti-inflammatory (Nagarkatti et al., 2009)	Palliative treatment for cancer patients (Bar-Lev Schleidera et al., 2018)
Antipsychotic (Morgan & Curran, 2008; Bhattacharyya et al., 2018)	Parkinson's disease (Fernandez-Ruis, Romero, & Ramos, 2015)
Anxiety reduction (acute) (Walsh et al., 2013)	Post-traumatic stress disorder symptom reduction (Greer, Grob, & Halberstadt, 2014; Hill et al., 2018; Mizrachi, Segev, & Akirav, 2016)
Appetite enhancement (Robson, 2014)	Rheumatoid arthritis (Englund et al., 2013)
Cachexia (wasting syndrome) (Martin & Wiley, 2004)	Sleep disturbance associated with obstructive sleep apnea syndrome, fibromyalgia, chronic pain, and multiple sclerosis are decreased (National Academies of Sciences, Engineering, and Medicine, 2017)
Depression relief (acute) (Cuttlera, Spradlina, & McLaughlin, 2018)	Sleep in Stage 4 is increased and falling asleep is easier (Lafaye et al., 2018; Schierenbeck et al., 2008)
Diabetes (Englund et al., 2013)	Social anxiety disorder symptom reduction (Nelemans et al., 2016)
Epilepsy (Lawson & Scheffer, 2018; Stockings et al., 2018)	Spasticity reduction (Barnes & Barnes, 2016)
Fibromyalgia (Fiz et al., 2011)	Spinal cord injuries: reduction in pain and muscle spasms (Graves, 2018)
Inflammatory bowel disease (Storr et al., 2014)	Stress relief (Cuttlera et al., 2018)
Multiple sclerosis (Lakhan & Rowland, 2009)	Tourette syndrome symptom reduction (Abi-Jaude et al., 2017)
Nausea relief (Robson, 2014)	

Note: As important as the list of documented findings regarding the therapeutic utility of using CBD is the finding that patient-managed medical cannabis use has been found to be associated with clinically significant improvements in self-reported symptom relief. This is due to both the euphoria produced when cannabis is used and the actual physical relief felt by individuals (Stith et al., 2018).
**attributed* to Δ9-tetrahydrocannabinol (THC)

with other hallucinogens. It is estimated that two to three milligrams of cannabis will produce a sense of euphoria; however, this is dependent on THC content. Using cannabis can increase the pulse and heart rate and heighten the appetite, while physically reddening the eyes and producing a quite reflective, sleepy state in the user. While cannabis affects memory, coordination, and cognition, cannabinoid receptors are not found in the brain stem areas that control breathing. This is a major contributing factor regarding why there is limited risk of cannabis producing an overdose, though dysphoria, dizziness, and anxiety can occur in conjunction with the euphoria. Lethal dose estimates, which also depend on sex, body weight, and genetic factors, range from 15 to 70 grams (Mechoulan & Parker, 2013). Second-hand exposure to cannabis smoke can lead to cannabinoid metabolites in bodily fluids sufficient for positive results on testing of oral fluids, blood, and urine, and can lead to psychoactive effects. The chemical composition of second-hand cannabis smoke is similar to that of second-hand tobacco smoke, although differences in the concentrations of the various toxic components exist (Holitzki et al., 2017).

At very large doses, the effects of cannabis with a greater THC concentration are like those of LSD and other hallucinogenic substances. The user may experience anxiety and mood disorders, confusion, restlessness, depersonalization, excitement, anxiety reactions, and even acute psychosis. Smaller doses occasionally produce panic reactions in inexperienced users. Flashbacks have also been reported to occur occasionally. These are defined as recurrences of cannabis-induced symptoms that appear spontaneously days to weeks after the acute drug effects have worn off. Flashbacks are most likely to occur in users who have also taken other hallucinogens. The underlying mechanism is not clear, but it is likely that the drug experience has triggered some change in thought patterns that can be evoked by environmental stimuli (Brick & Erickson, 2013; Cheung et al., 2010).

Also, cannabis can enhance or trigger a psychotic episode in persons with family history of this type of mental health problem;

cannabis-induced psychosis has been a recognized diagnosis for over a decade (González-Pinto et al., 2008). Cannabis use has been confirmed to have an adverse effect on mental health, with frequent current use having a larger effect than infrequent current use or past use. Factors that make individuals more susceptible to cannabis use also make them more susceptible to mental illness (Van Dam, Bed, & Earleywine, 2012; van Ours & Williams, 2009). Those who continued to use cannabis during a first psychotic episode experienced a higher severity of illness, lower psychosocial functioning, less insight, lower premorbid functioning (functioning prior to use of the drug), and longer duration of untreated psychosis. Compared to all other groups of people in treatment, persistent cannabis use was linked to the worst outcomes and the greatest degree of service disengagement (Schimmelmann et al., 2012). Cannabis use has not been shown to cause schizophrenia; however, for those who are genetically predisposed to schizophrenia, there seems to be a correlation between cannabis use and onset of psychotic symptoms. Children whose mothers have schizophrenia are at a 5 times greater risk of developing schizophrenia, and a 2.5 times greater risk of developing cannabis-induced psychosis. Thus, while it may not be psychologically dangerous for most people to use this drug, there is a distinct risk among a small proportion of the population (Arendt et al., 2008). Figure 4.21 illustrates THC's effects on the brain, while table 4.2 summarizes 21 issue areas that chronic cannabis use negatively impacts.

A single joint is equivalent to between two and five cigarettes in terms of damage to the lungs, largely due to differences in how the two drugs are inhaled and the smoke retained in the lungs (Aldington et al., 2007). Cannabis condensates have been found to be more toxic than those of tobacco, containing 50–70% more carcinogenic hydrocarbons than does tobacco smoke, though tobacco condensates appear to induce genetic damage in a concentration-dependent manner, whereas the matched cannabis condensates do not (Maertens et al., 2009). Other problems associated with tobacco smoking, such as constriction of airways, also appear to be more of an issue with cannabis smoke, as the intake of tar and other carcinogens is greater with cannabis than

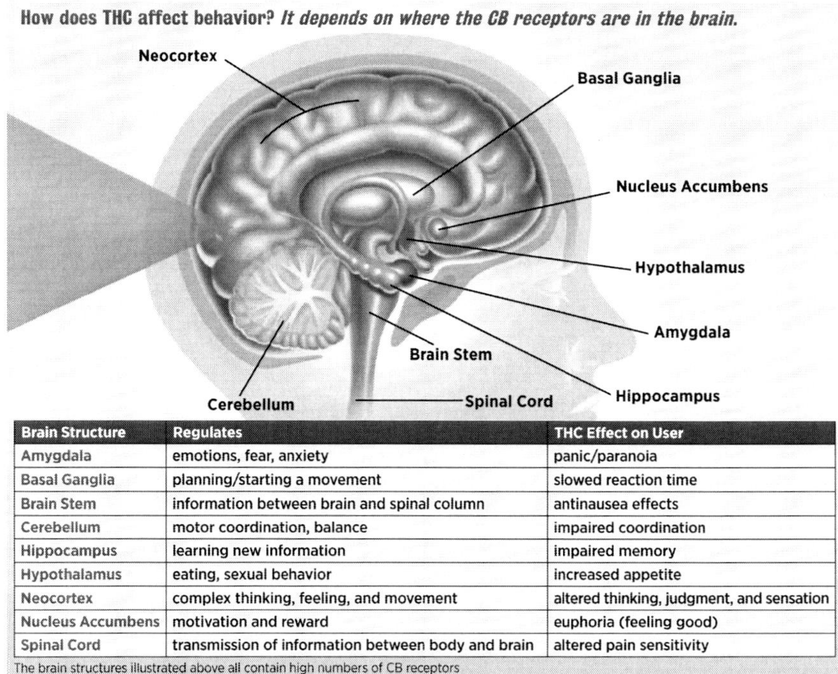

Brain Structure	Regulates	THC Effect on User
Amygdala	emotions, fear, anxiety	panic/paranoia
Basal Ganglia	planning/starting a movement	slowed reaction time
Brain Stem	information between brain and spinal column	antinausea effects
Cerebellum	motor coordination, balance	impaired coordination
Hippocampus	learning new information	impaired memory
Hypothalamus	eating, sexual behavior	increased appetite
Neocortex	complex thinking, feeling, and movement	altered thinking, judgment, and sensation
Nucleus Accumbens	motivation and reward	euphoria (feeling good)
Spinal Cord	transmission of information between body and brain	altered pain sensitivity

The brain structures illustrated above all contain high numbers of CB receptors

Figure 4.21: How THC Affects the Brain

Source: Scholastic, The Science of Marijuana: How THC Affects the Brain, *Heads Up: Real News About Drugs and Your Body* (http://headsup.scholastic.com/students/the-science-of-marijuana, 2011)

with tobacco smoke, as is the amount of carbon monoxide introduced in the blood. Studies that examined lung cancer risk factors or premalignant changes in the lungs found an association between cannabis smoking and increased tar exposure, decreased immune response, increased risk of tumours, increased oxidative stress, and bronchial abnormalities compared to tobacco smokers and to non-smokers (Mehra et al., 2006; Tzu-Chin et al., 1988).

Considerable tolerance to most of the acute effects of cannabis can develop within a week if the drug is administered several times per day. Less frequent smokers report a loss of sensitivity to the desired effects of the drug over the course of several months of regular administration.

Table 4.2: Risks Associated with Cannabis Use

Amotivational syndrome	• Chronic cannabis use has been associated with apathy and diminished ability to concentrate, follow routines, or successfully master new material, leading to educational underachievement and impaired vocational motivation (Silins et al., 2014).
Anxiety	• While short-term cannabis use can decrease anxiety, long-term use can enhance this state (Mammen et al., 2018). • There is an increased incidence of social anxiety disorder among regular cannabis users (National Academies of Sciences, Engineering, and Medicine, 2017).
Bone mineral density	• Heavy cannabis use is associated with low bone mineral density, high bone turnover, and an increased risk of fracture (Sophocleous et al., 2017).
Brain development	• Heavy cannabis users demonstrated smaller hippocampus and amygdala volumes, indicating that chronic cannabis use has a selective, detrimental impact on the morphology of the mediotemporal lobe of the brain as well as leading to lower grey matter density (Cadet, Bisagno, & Milroy, 2014; Gilman et al., 2014; Lorenzetti et al., 2015). • Repeated exposure to THC changes the structure of dendrites in at least two parts of the brain, the medial prefrontal cortex (mPFC) and the nucleus accumbens (NAc) (Gilman et al., 2014; Kolb et al., 2018). • Abnormalities in brain maturation have been found in the areas of the brain that facilitate mood and cognitive function, with greater cannabis use associated with greater impairment (deShazo et al., 2018).
Cannabinoid hyperemesis syndrome (CHS)	• CHS is characterized by recurrent episodes of intractable nausea and vomiting along with abdominal pain among individuals who have been using cannabis regularly for years. There is also a risk of renal (kidney) failure due to dehydration. Compulsive bathing as a means of symptom relief is also a characteristic of CHS. Standard medication to resolve nausea and vomiting does not work and abstinence from cannabis is required. CHS is believed to occur as a result of accumulation of THC in fatty tissues, which leads to intestine stimulation that overrides the effects of the central nervous system (King & Holmes, 2015).
Cardiovascular system	• There is some evidence of cannabis use triggering acute myocardial infarction (heart attack), ischemic stroke (obstruction of blood vessel supplying blood to the brain), and subarachnoid hemorrhage (bleeding in the brain) (Hall & Degenhardt, 2009; National Academies of Sciences, Engineering, and Medicine, 2017). • Cannabis use is associated with an acceleration of cardiovascular age (Reece, Norman, & Hulse, 2016). • Increased duration of marijuana use is associated with increased risk of death from hypertension (Yankey et al., 2017).

Cognitive deficits	• Individuals with more persistent cannabis dependence generally show greater neuropsychological impairment (Meier et al., 2012). • THC alters short-term object-recognition memory through hippocampal/neurogranin signalling (Busquets-Garcia et al., 2017). • Cannabis acutely impairs episodic and working memory, planning and decision-making, response speed, latency (time to process information), and accuracy (Ranganathan & D'Souza, 2006; Volkow et al., 2016). • Acute cannabinoid intoxication induces amnesia (Etienne et al., 2016).
Crohn's disease	• The use of cannabis for more than six months at any time for individuals with inflammatory bowel disease symptoms was a strong predictor of surgery in patients with Crohn's disease (Storr et al., 2014).
Dental	• Chronic cannabis use is associated with periodontal disease (tooth decay) (Meier et al., 2016).

Dependency	• Cannabis produces both physical and psychological dependency including withdrawal, which consists of behavioural, mood, and physical symptoms highlighted by physical weakness, sweating, restlessness, dysphoria, sleeping problems, anxiety, and craving for continued use. Approximately 10% of users will become addicted (Bonnet & Preuss, 2017; Curran et al., 2016; Hall, 2015; Zehra et al., 2018).
	• Cannabis use disorder (CUD) is a problematic pattern of cannabis use leading to clinically significant impairment or distress, as manifested by at least two of the following, occurring within a 12-month period:
	  · cannabis used in larger amounts or over a longer period than was intended
	  · a persistent desire or unsuccessful efforts to cut down or control use
	  · a great deal of time spent in activities necessary to obtain cannabis, use cannabis, or recover from its effects
	  · craving, or a strong desire or urge to use cannabis
	  · recurrent use resulting in a failure to fulfill major role obligations at work, school, or home
	  · continued use despite having persistent or recurrent social or interpersonal problems caused or exacerbated by the effects of cannabis
	  · important social, occupational, or recreational activities given up or reduced because of cannabis use
	  · recurrent use in situations in which it is physically hazardous
	  · continued use despite knowledge of having a persistent or recurrent physical or psychological problem that is likely to have been caused or exacerbated by cannabis
	  · tolerance, as defined by either a (1) need for markedly increased cannabis to achieve intoxication or desired effect, or (2) markedly diminished effect with continued use of the same amount of the substance
	  · withdrawal (American Psychiatric Association, 2013).

(continued)

Depression	• Self-report research indicates that while cannabis can reduce perceived symptoms of depression in the short term, particularly negative affect, its continued use may exacerbate baseline symptoms of depression over time (Cuttlera et al., 2018).
Education	• Cannabis use causes acute impairment of attention and learning (Volkow et al., 2016). • Regular cannabis use in adolescence approximately doubles the risks of early school-leaving (Hall, 2015). • Persistent cannabis dependence has been associated with a decline in IQ score. In a prospective study of a birth cohort of 1,037 individuals followed until age 38, IQ decline was most pronounced among the most persistent cannabis users (Meier et al., 2012).
Mental health	• Cannabis products that are high in THC but low in CBD are particularly hazardous for mental health (Englund et al., 2013). • Chronic cannabis use can increase the severity of post-traumatic stress disorder symptoms (National Academies of Sciences, Engineering, and Medicine, 2017). • Regular cannabis use increases the risk of developing bipolar disorder as well as enhancing symptoms of mania and hypomania in individuals diagnosed with bipolar disorder (Marwaha et al., 2017). • Increased incidence of suicidal ideation, suicide attempts, and death by suicide occurs among heavier cannabis users compared with non-users (National Academies of Sciences, Engineering, and Medicine, 2017).
Motor vehicle collisions	• Cannabis use is a contributing factor to an increased risk of motor vehicle collisions and fatalities (Bonar et al., 2019; Hall, 2015; Santamarina-Rubio et al., 2009).
Pancreatitis	• Acute pancreatitis is a serious disease with a mortality rate as high as 20%. Cannabis use has been documented as a minor contributor to this condition (Herrero et al., 2016).
Poisoning	• There is a risk of children accidentally consuming cannabis products intended for adults and being poisoned, with a range of outcomes including a reduced level of consciousness, drowsiness, impaired coordination, slurred speech, headaches, apnea, hypotonia (low muscle tone), and seizures. No fatalities have been recorded from poisonings due to cannabis consumption among children to this time (Croche, Alonso, & Loscertales, 2011; Le Garrec, Dauger, & Sachs, 2014; Spadari et al., 2009).
Pregnancy	• Birth weights for babies of women using cannabis at least once per week before and throughout pregnancy were lighter than those of the offspring of non-users (Crume et al., 2018; Fergusson, Horwood, & Northstone, 2002; Hayatbakhsh et al., 2012). • Newborns exposed to marijuana exhibit sleep disturbances, an issue that can last for a few months up to three years (Ross et al., 2015).

Psychosis/ Schizophrenia	• Cannabis use can produce psychosis-like effects including delusions and delirium (Morgan & Curran, 2008). • Both epidemiological and clinical studies have implicated regular cannabis use as a risk factor for the development of psychosis and for poor clinical outcomes after its onset among adolescents. Cannabis use is considered a preventable risk factor for psychosis, with ongoing cannabis use worsening symptoms (Bhattacharyya et al., 2018; Bourque, Afzali, & Conrod, 2018; Schizophrenia Commission, 2012). • Chronic cannabis use is associated with changes in resting-state brain function, particularly in dopamine nuclei associated with psychosis (Manza, Tomsi, & Volkow, 2018). • A meta-analysis found that the age at onset of psychosis for cannabis users was 2.7 years younger than for non-users (Large et al., 2011). • Continued cannabis use after onset of psychosis predicts adverse outcome, including higher relapse rates, longer hospital admissions, and more severe positive symptoms than for individuals who discontinue cannabis use and those who are non-users. Reduction in cannabis use is a crucial interventional target to improve outcome in individuals with psychosis (Schoeler et al., 2016).
Respiratory disease	• There is a greater occurrence of minor respiratory issues such as ongoing coughing, wheezing, shortness of breath after exercise, nocturnal chest tightness, chest sounds without a cold, early-morning phlegm, and mucus among regular cannabis users compared to non-users (Ghasemiesfe et al., 2018). • Cannabis smoking aggravates both asthma (McInnis & Plecas, 2016) and bronchitis symptoms (National Academies of Sciences, Engineering, and Medicine, 2017). • There is increased respiratory illness among children of chronic cannabis users (National Academies of Sciences, Engineering, and Medicine, 2017).
Sleep	• Regular cannabis use increases slow-wave sleep, which leads to a decrease in REM sleep and in turn dreaming, while difficulty sleeping and strange dreams are among the most consistently reported symptoms of cannabis withdrawal (Schierenbeck et al., 2008). • Daily marijuana users reported more sleep disturbance than non-daily users (Conroy et al., 2016).
Sperm mobility	• While there is limited data on the clinical effects of cannabis use and the impact on male factor infertility, the information available suggests that cannabis has a negative impact on male reproductive health (Rogers et al., 2017).

Despite earlier beliefs to the contrary, both psychological and physical dependence to cannabis do occur. Physical dependence can occur with as little as two joints per day. Withdrawal symptoms occur 4 to 8 hours after the abrupt termination of drug administration and consist of irritability, insomnia, anxiety, depressed mood, restlessness, anger, sleep disturbances, weight loss, sweating, intestinal cramps, and extended amotivational syndrome symptoms. Symptoms can begin to fade within 48 hours of abstinence as receptors rebound to normal functioning, returning within one month of abstinence. Likewise, sleep disturbances can last three to four weeks after cessation of drug use (Bonnet & Preuss, 2017; Zehra et al., 2018). THC appears to deepen sleep and allows the user to fall asleep faster, increasing slow-wave sleep. However, as cannabis dose amounts increase, REM sleep goes down, and

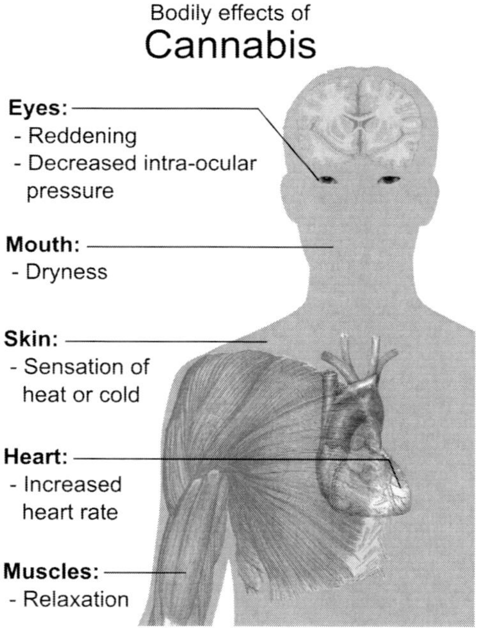

Figure 4.22: Bodily Effects of Cannabis

Source: Wikimedia Commons

once nightly cannabis use stops, sleep worsens during the withdrawal period (Angarita et al., 2016). Circadian rhythm is deregulated by CBD but not by THC, which is consistent with clinical observations of the use of therapeutic cannabis to treat insomnia (Lafaye et al., 2018).

Users have also been reported to "green out" after using cannabis, which describes what happens when a person feels particularly unwell after using the drug. This unpleasant experience can make the user go pale or green and feel sweaty, dizzy, and nauseous. It is equivalent to an overdose state, with some people even reporting passing out after using cannabis. Combining cannabis with alcohol appears to increase the likelihood of a user "greening out" (Vandrey et al., 2008). Increasing cannabis use in late adolescence and early adulthood is also associated with a range of adverse outcomes later in life, including poorer education outcome, lower income, greater dependency on social assistance, greater unemployment, and lower relationship and life satisfaction (Ferguson & Boden, 2008).

4.6 NOVEL PSYCHOACTIVE SUBSTANCES (NPS)

Synthetic psychoactive drugs are typically deemed licit or illicit based upon their chemical structure, which is one reason why this book has included the chemical formula and structure of each drug discussed. A response to circumvent this system that has become prominent in this century is the ongoing creation of new designer drugs, or "legal highs," that have been more formally called novel psychoactive substances or new psychoactive substances. Novel psychoactive substances (NPS) are defined by the United Nations Office on Drugs and Crime as drugs, either in a pure form or part of a preparation, that are not controlled by the 1961 Single Convention on Narcotic Drugs or the 1971 Convention on Psychotropic Substances, but that pose a threat to public health. While some are new chemical creations, others were synthesized in the 20th century but did not emerge as psychoactive substances of misuse or abuse until recently. The United Nations Office on Drugs and Crime (2017) has documented over 700 of these substances, which speaks to both the ingenuity of chemists and the ongoing interests, by humans, to alter their central nervous system functioning. While the majority of these substances fall within the hallucinogen family (52%), a large minority (36%) belong to the stimulant family, with many of these being synthetic cathinones such as mephedrone (4-MMC), methylone (bk-MDMA), 4,4′-DMAR (4-methyl-5-[4-methylphenyl]-4,5-dihydrooxazol-2-amine), flakka and pyrovalerone (3,4-methylenedioxypyrovalerone). The remaining 12% were split between opioids (4%), sedative hypnotics (3%), and drugs whose pharmacology was still undefined (5%) (UNODC, 2017). Following is a summary of the characteristics of five hallucinogenic NPS groups, three of which also have stimulant properties.

Phenethylamines

Examples: 4-bromo-2,5-dimethoxyphenethylamine, (2C-B) Bromo-Dragonfly, 2C-B-Fly4-Methylampheamine (4-MA), Methiopropamine (MPA)

Novel phenethylamines are based upon a simple variation on the natural phenylethylamine mescaline molecule that was discussed in chapter 4.3. These synthetic variations tend to be more potent and produce more arousal, as they have stronger amphetamine-like characteristics than does mescaline. Typical effects are sensory-enhanced hallucinations, particularly visual hallucinations, stimulant-like euphoria, and heightened erotic sensations. The side effects are also quite potent, highlighted by insomnia but also including sweating while experiencing cold in the extremities, followed by fluctuations in body temperature, agitation, vascoconstriction, chest pain, painful urination, headache, nausea, tachycardia, anorexia, anxiety, negative affect, and in extreme cases, paranoia. 4-bromo-2,5-dimethoxyphenethylamine, (2C-B), known as nexus, bees, or venus, will begin to produce effects with as little as a two-milligram dose level, though typical consumption is 15 to 25 milligrams. Onset, when orally administered, is 45 to 75 minutes, with an overall effect time of up to eight hours and with after-effects lasting another two to four hours (Society for the Study of Addiction, 2016; UNODC, 2013).

Piperazines

Examples: 1-Benzylpiperazine (BZP), 1-(3-chlorophenyl) piperazine (*m*CPP), 2-Methoxphenidine, Ethylphenidate

Despite claims by some suppliers that piperazines are herbal products, they are totally synthetic drugs with a chemical structure similar to MDMA, having both hallucinogenic and stimulant properties. The most prominent novel piperazine, BZP, was created by chemists at the pharmaceutical company Burroughs Wellcome as an antidepressant drug. However, the drug was never released commercially, as its primary effect was amphetamine-like. Doses as small as 50 to 100 milligrams lead to increased pulse rate, blood pressure, and pupillary dilation.

Piperazines also have stimulant properties, as they both release and inhibit the reuptake of dopamine, serotonin, and noradrenaline (norepinephrine). They also produce euphoria, intensify sensory experience, and enhance mood, though they remain less potent than amphetamines and produce fewer hallucinogenic effects than does either MDA or MDMA. The negative side effects of novel synthetic piperazines are similar to those produced by more powerful CNS stimulants. These include agitation, excessive sweating, hypertension, tachycardia, seizures and vomiting, and cardiotoxicity (damage to the heart muscle) (Society for the Study of Addiction, 2016; UNODC, 2013).

Substituted Tryptamines

Examples: Alpha-Methyltyptamine (AMT), 5-methoxy-N,N-dimethyltryptamine (5-MeO-DMT), 5-methoxy-N,N-diisopropyltryptamine (5-MeO-DIPT)

This third group of NPS is chemically most similar to LSD (chapter 4.2). While they produce primarily hallucinogenic effects, unlike LSD-like hallucinogens, they also produce minor secondary stimulant effects, even at low doses. Substituted tryptamines also produce far more negative side effects than the LSD-like hallucinogens, including agitation, restlessness, confusion, lethargy, vomiting, pupil dilation, jaw clenching, and increased blood pressure, temperature, and respiration (Society for the Study of Addiction, 2016; UNODC, 2013).

Phencyclidine-Type Substances

Examples: 3-methoxy-PCP, 4-methoxy-PCP, 3-methoxy-PCE, methoxetamine (MXE; Mexxy)

This is the smallest subgroup of NPS, all of which are derivatives of either the phencyclidine (PCP) or ketamine core molecule. Little research has been conducted on these substances, though it is believed that their primary action is on glutamate. In general, intoxication from these derivatives can produce effects from mild neurologic and physiological reactions, euphoria, and dissociation from the physical body, to stupor or a light coma state. Their use has also been linked to cognitive impairment and physical agitation, which is sometimes expressed as violent behaviour. Overdose is also possible (Roth et al., 2013).

Synthetic Cannabis (Synthetic Cannabinoid Receptor Agonists: SCRAs)

brand names: 24 Karat Gold, AK-47, Annihilation, Aroma, Black Mamba, Bliss, Blue Cheese, Blue Lotus, Boom Kron, ChillX, Cowboy Kush, Crazy Clown, Genie, Gin N' Juice, Gorillaz, Grape Drank, Happy Joker, Kronic, Moon Rocks, Scooby Snax, Sence, Smoke, Space Cadets, Spice Arctic, Spice Diamond, Spice Egypt, Spice Gold, Spice Silver, Yucatan Fire

chemical names: AB-CHMINACA, AM 251, AM 694, CP 47-497, CP 59-540, HU 210, 5F-MDMB-CHMICA, MDMB-PINACA, NCP-47,497-C8, JWH-015, JWH-018, JWH-073, JWH-081, JWH-122, JWH-210, JWH-250, JWH 398

Synthetic cannabinoid receptor agonists (SCRA), often referred to as synthetic cannabinoids, are a large family of chemically unrelated structures functionally similar to Δ9-tetrahydrocannabinol (THC), the psychoactive component of cannabis. Like THC, they bind to the same cannabinoid receptors in the brain and other organs as anandamide—CB_1 and CB_2—though their binding capability is far greater than that of any form of natural cannabis. As with natural cannabis, CB_1 produces psychoactive effects, whereas CB_2 primarily affects the immune system and produces senations of hunger. Unlike cannabis, there is no cannabidiol (CBD) in synthetic cannabis. Artificial versions of natural cannabis, also called designer cannabis or herbal cannabis, were among the first novel psychoactive agents to be marketed. They have nothing in common with the natural cannabis plant but are purely synthetic analogues, despite being actively marketed as being legal cannabis. The original pharmacological intent of many of these drugs were as analgesics. The first such analogue was HU-210, created in Israel in 1988 with a potency in the same range as the shatter (crystal) version of cannabis. In looking for alternatives to opioid analgesics, pharmaceutical companies have created a variety of synthetic drugs that were never brought to market because of excessive potency or negative side effects, including cyclohexylphenols (CP-series), indazoles (AB-CHMINACA, 5F-MDMB-PINACA), naphthoylindoles (JWH-018, JWH-073, JWH-398), and phenylacetylindoles (Spice/JWH-250). Over time, these have formed the foundation of the global synthetic cannabinoid trade (UNODC, 2013).

As with the other more recent groups of NPS, these drugs became a popular means to obtain the same effects of cannabis in Canada without the negative legal ramifications when cannabis was still an illicit drug. These substances continue to be used, primarily by smoking, in nations were cannabis remains an illegal substance. The most common versions, Spice and K2, contain a mixture of plant material and chemical-grade synthetic cannabinoids, while in Canada, a distinct brand called Izms emerged during the early part of the 21st century. The effects of smoking these synthetic drugs are reported as cannabis-like; however, the drugs tend to be two to fifty times more potent than cannabis and have more toxic side effects. Along with producing a positive psychoactive effect, synthetic cannabinoids increase energy and decrease inhibitions. Similar to natural cannabis, synthetic cannabis can create a sense of hunger and drowsiness is users, impacting concentration and coordination. Negative side effects can include tachycardia, hypertension, muscle jerking, vomiting, seizures, and psychotic behaviour, including engaging in acts of violence. Chronic use has been linked to kidney damage and fatal heart attacks, with even acute use having been documented to produce severe agitation, anxiety, panic, irritability, confusion, memory loss, and temporary psychosis in a minority of instances. There have been regular reports of overdoses and deaths due to the use of synthetic cannabinoids (Hermanns-Clausen et al., 2013; Lauritsen & Rosenberg, 2016; Malyshevskaya et al., 2017; Rosenbaum et al., 2012).

Among the most prominent synthetic cannabinoids is Spice. Spice is an analgesic member of the naphthoylindole family that acts as a full agonist at both the CB_1 and CB_2 cannabinoid receptors, with some selectivity for CB_2 but with up to five times greater affinity for CB_1 than THC. It is a synthesized analogue of THC and has been shown to produce similar effects in animals (Uchiyama et al., 2009).

K2 is the name of the second-highest mountain on earth after Mount Everest. In this context, the term refers to a research chemical that acts as a potent but non-selective full agonist for the cannabinoid receptor. While not as potent as Spice, there have been anecdotal reports of individuals experiencing panic attacks and vomiting at doses as small as two milligrams, which is much less than with other synthetic cannabinoids. Convulsions, respiratory depression, and heart attacks have been reported with the use of K2, and caution needs to be taken when administering this substance, as it is active at doses as small as 500 micrograms, it has a very steep dose-response curve, and tolerance to the effects builds up very quickly (Jinwala & Gupta, 2012; Mir et al., 2011). Overall, users of both synthetic and organic cannabis report more negative effects with the use of the former than the latter. Both physical and psychological dependency to the full range of synthetic cannabinoids occurs (Winstock & Barratt, 2013).

QUIZ

1. In the 1960s, this drug was used experimentally as a way to aid with alcohol dependency, and with individuals who were terminally ill. At the same time, the CIA considered using it as a chemical agent. What is the drug?
2. Referred to as "magic mushrooms," what psychoactive agent is a naturally occurring hallucinogen?

3. Produced from the heads or buttons of the peyote cactus, this is the only entirely natural alkaloid in the hallucinogen family. What is it?
4. Why are hallucinogens other than cannabis not considered addicting agents?
5. More associated with Christmas than the drug culture, this common spice is a potent hallucinogen, although it has some quite nasty side effects. What is it?
6. Which family of plants does cannabis belong to?
7. What is the psychoactive ingredient that makes cannabis a psychoactive agent?
8. Which neurotransmitter does cannabis affect?
9. A typical joint has two to five more times of what than a cigarette has?
10. Although this phenomenon, a spontaneous reoccurrence of the sensation that occurred during a prior drug experience, is more commonly associated with other hallucinogens, with the increasing amount of THC in cannabis, there are now reports of cannabis users experiencing it. What is it?

CASE STUDIES

Debbie

Debbie, age 17, comes for an assessment. When you ask Debbie what brought her to see you today, she indicates that last week, after smoking a joint of cannabis she got from a new source, because she is underage and still buys on the black market, she had an experience similar to what she used to get after using LSD. She hasn't used LSD for over a year, so she was quite surprised by this experience and had become anxious. What do you think may have happened to Debbie?

Jackie and Barbara

Jackie and Barbara are two addiction-education students tasked with debating whether various hallucinogens should be legalized, legalized with controls, or totally prohibited, using only pharmacological principles. What arguments should they put forward for the following hallucinogens in order to win the debate?

- psilocybin
- ecstasy
- ketamine

How should Jackie and Barbara describe the differences between a hallucinogenic experience and the euphoric experience gained from the use of other drugs, such as alcohol?

Mikaeli

Mikaeli is 19 years old and living at home. Her mother has just brought her to their family physician due to concerns about her increased feelings of anxiety and of being watched by others. Mikaeli is also having trouble sleeping and concentrating, is irritable and restless, and feels tense. Before the doctor makes any sort of assessment, what drug use that can cause these types of symptoms must be considered? Remember to consider both psychoactive drug intoxication effects and psychoactive drug withdrawal effects.

NOTE

1. The source for the systemic names and molecular formulas for all hallucinogens is ChemSpider (www.chemspider.com). The systemic name describes the chemical structure of a substance, providing basic information about its chemical properties, while the molecular formula represents the number and type(s) of atoms that are present in a single molecule of the substance. Unless otherwise noted, the source for figures depicting chemical structures is also ChemSpider.

CHAPTER 5

Psychotherapeutic Agents

OVERVIEW[1]

Psychotherapeutic agents are psychoactive substances used to treat individuals with specific forms of mental health issues. They modify thought processes, mood, and emotional reactions to the environment. Many substances within this family of drugs, particularly those that have been in use for longer periods of time, produce unpleasant side effects, including involuntary movements and tremors, a shuffling gait, nausea, dry mouth, insomnia, constipation, weight gain, and sexual dysfunction, including diminished libido, anorgasmia, impotence, and delayed ejaculation (Gafoor, Booth, & Gulliford, 2018; Healy, Le Noury, & Derelie, 2017). As these psychoactive agents also tend to change mood slowly, over a period of days and in many cases weeks, they are not generally subject to non-medical use, and thus issues of abuse or addiction are limited. However, tolerance and both physical and psychological dependency do develop to most of these substances, though they tend to be minimal (Procyshyn, Bezchlibnyk-Butler, & Jeffries, 2017). Sleep promotion occurs with antidepressants and antipsychotics that block receptors that mediate the wake-promoting effects of a number of neurotransmitters, including serotonin, histamine, acetylcholine, norepinephrine, and dopamine. These effects can potentially improve sleep at night, but they also have the potential to cause daytime sedation depending on when the drug is administered and the dose level. Psychotherapeutic agents can both enhance and disrupt the sleep cycle depending on how and when they are administered (Krystal, 2010).

The major distinction between psychotherapeutic agents and the other psychoactive substances discussed in previous chapters is that when used appropriately with specific populations, the long-term consequence, in a normative sense, is positive mood and behavioural change. These psychoactive agents move a user back toward homeostasis rather than away from it. They are not a cure for mental health problems. Rather, their effects on the central nervous system, and thus upon behaviour, are intended to be balancing as opposed to destabilizing. A major critique has arisen, however, as to whether these drugs do in fact balance the CNS, or alter the CNS and make an acute problem a chronic one over time.

5.1 ANTIDEPRESSANTS

Depression

Major depressive disorder (MDD) is a chronic, recurring, and debilitating mental illness that is prevalent globally and which substantively impairs social functioning and can be life threatening. In Canada, upwards of 5% of the population annually experience a major depressive episode (MDE) (Sanyal et al., 2011). MDD has been found to have comorbidity with other *Diagnostic and Statistical Manual* (DSM) mental disorders such as anxiety disorders, substance abuse, and impulse control (Hillhouse & Porter, 2015). Depression is a disturbance of mood that can exist alone or, at times, in conjunction with corresponding excessive elevation of mood (mania). Depression may be caused by a chemical imbalance in the CNS that occurs biologically due to inadequate levels of monoamine transporters serotonin, norepinephrine, and dopamine, but also in response to environmental stress and trauma. Clinical studies have found that depression is also associated with the reduced size of brain regions that regulate mood and cognition, including the prefrontal cortex and the hippocampus, and decreased neuronal synapses in these areas (Duman & Aghajanian, 2012). A state of depression, as opposed to MDD, may arise in response to a single event or be a more chronic condition. Depression consists of various symptoms, including but not limited to:

- persistent sadness
- a lack of interest in previously enjoyed activities
- thoughts of death or suicide
- difficulty sleeping
- feelings of worthlessness
- feelings of guilt
- difficulty concentrating
- change in appetite
- agitation
- irritability
- feeling tired and worn out

There is also a mood disorder called dysthymia, which, unlike a major depressive episode, is a more chronic, low-grade, persistent state. It does not completely impair functioning, but it does impede an individual's ability to carry out necessary daily functions. Dysthymia is defined as a chronic sadness that lasts more than two years (Cuijpers et al., 2010). The greatest fear with depression overall, however, is that it may escalate to self-harming behaviour if not addressed. Ironically, there is also an increased risk of self-harm when a person first begins taking psychotherapeutic drugs and mood begins to improve but has not yet returned to a balanced, homeostatic level.

Overview of Antidepressants

All antidepressants work in a similar way, by increasing the brain's concentration of various neurotransmitters. Antidepressants can block or reverse neuronal deficits, although first-generation antidepressants, labelled typical antidepressants, have limited efficacy and delayed response times of weeks to months (Duman & Aghajanian, 2012). There are two distinct types of first-generation antidepressants: monoamine oxidase inhibitors (MAOIs) and tricyclic antidepressants (TCAs). A second generation of antidepressants emerged at the end of the 20th century. This group consists of SSRIs (selective serotonin reuptake inhibitors), NDRIs (norepinephrine-dopamine reuptake inhibitors), and SSNRIs (selective serotonin-norepinephrine reuptake inhibitors) (table 5.1). Second-generation antidepressants have become more prominent and dominant, as they act faster and have fewer negative side effects. They work much more specifically than their predecessors, and as their name indicates, they block the reuptake of different neurotransmitters and thus allow the chemical to remain in the synaptic space for a longer period, leading to more chemically balanced brain functioning (figure 5.2).

The primary effects of antidepressants, along with mood elevation, include improved appetite, increased physical activity, improved thinking and memory, and lessened feelings of guilt, helplessness, and inadequacy. However, the side effects of these substances remain problematic, as there are many and they can be quite severe. In general, antidepressants can initially cause restlessness and agitation before they begin to alleviate the symptoms of depression, and this agitation can be severe enough to lead to hostility, either expressed outwardly against others or inwardly toward the user. There is a distinct risk of suicide as these drugs begin to work but have not yet become fully functional, particularly among children and young adults who receive higher than-modal-therapeutic doses at the onset of treatment (Miller et al., 2014).

Overall, the second generation of antidepressants work about the same in alleviating depression, though some individuals respond better to some variants compared to others. Between 10% and 20% of second-generation antidepressant users will develop tachyphylaxis, which has been not so favourably labelled as "poop-out syndrome" (Procyshyn et al., 2017). These psychoactive drugs have also been found to increase the risk of type 2 diabetes among younger users (Burcu et al., 2017). Sexual dysfunction and weight gain are also unwanted side effects of antidepressant use in general (Gafoor et al., 2018; Healy et al., 2017; Serretti & Mandelli, 2010), as well as, ironically, a risk of inducing mania with individuals who have unipolar depression (Patel et al., 2015).

If a person abruptly stops taking antidepressants, discontinuation syndrome occurs, which is in essence withdrawal. Like opioid withdrawal, this has been likened to having the flu, though the pain is not nearly as intense or severe as that produced by opioid withdrawal. Withdrawal symptoms from antidepressants can be grouped into six categories: sensory (feelings of tingling and/or numbness), disequilibrium (dizziness, vertigo), somatic (lethargy, headaches, anorexia), affective (anxiety, sadness, irritability), gastrointestinal (nausea, vomiting, diarrhea) and sleep disturbances (Warner et al., 2006).

Finally, there is an ongoing debate regarding if antidepressants serve much use, beyond a placebo effect, for dysthymia as well as for MDD. Many users indicate that they feel better using antidepressants, especially second-generation ones, yet historically there was limited empirical support for these claims. It can take months for some of these drugs to make some people feel less depressed, yet during this time users still experience the negative side effects without the positive benefits. This is not a new concern; Whitaker (2005) argued that there is no evidence that those with depression do suffer from abnormally low levels of serotonin or norepinephrine. He further claimed that antidepressants create more depression than they mitigate. This is supported by empirical studies that have reported minimal difference between the effectiveness of antidepressant drugs and placebos, particularly in less severely depressed persons but also in the long term for those diagnosed with MDD.

A second argument against the ongoing use of antidepressants derives from evolutionary medicine. This field argues that any disruption of evolved adaptations degrades biological functioning. Thus, as serotonin regulates many adaptive processes, it is not surprising that antidepressants produce many adverse side effects when they alter serotonin levels. In this hypothesis, it is argued that in the short term, antidepressants do in fact increase serotonin levels; however, these modest effects destabilize the CNS over the long term, increasing the brain's susceptibility to future episodes of depression once administration is stopped while at the same time negatively affecting other organ systems requiring serotonin. This theory claims that antidepressants cause neuronal damage by reverting mature neurons to an immature state, thus producing more harm than good by disrupting adaptive processes regulated by serotonin not only in the CNS but throughout the entire body (Andrews et al., 2012). These views have recently been challenged by new studies that indicate there are clearly superior outcomes among individuals taking antidepressants compared to those given placebos (Cipriani et al., 2018; Hieronymus et al., 2018). One explanation for this dichotomy may be the imprecise prescribing practices of physicians and a lack of DSM criteria used in prescribing antidepressants (Thomas-MacLean et al., 2005). This then leaves us not with the question of if these drugs work or if they produce harm, for the answer to both questions is yes, but rather with the question, for whom do they best work and in what situations?

Monoamine Oxidase Inhibitors (MAOIs)

Monoamine oxidase is an enzyme that breaks down monoamine neurotransmitters, including serotonin, dopamine, epinephrine, and norepinephrine, as well as tryptamine (chapter 4.2) and phenethylamines

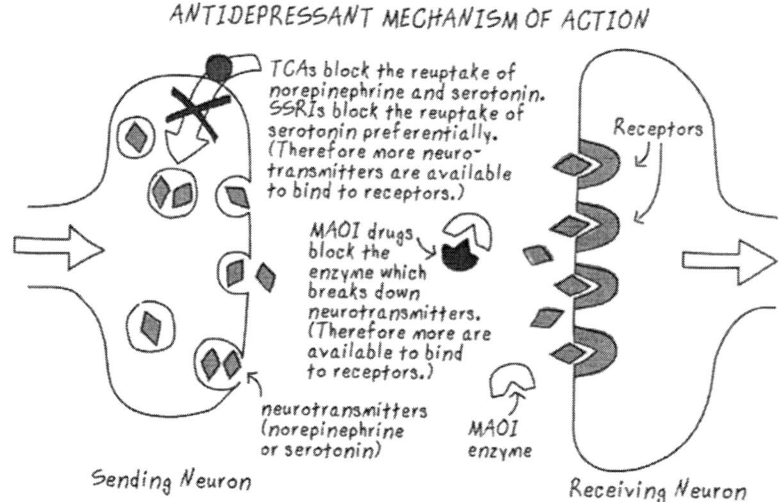

Figure 5.1: TCA and MAOI Mechanisms of Action

Source: B. Sproule, *Pharmacology and Drug Abuse*, 2nd edition (Toronto: Centre for Addiction and Mental Health, 2004)

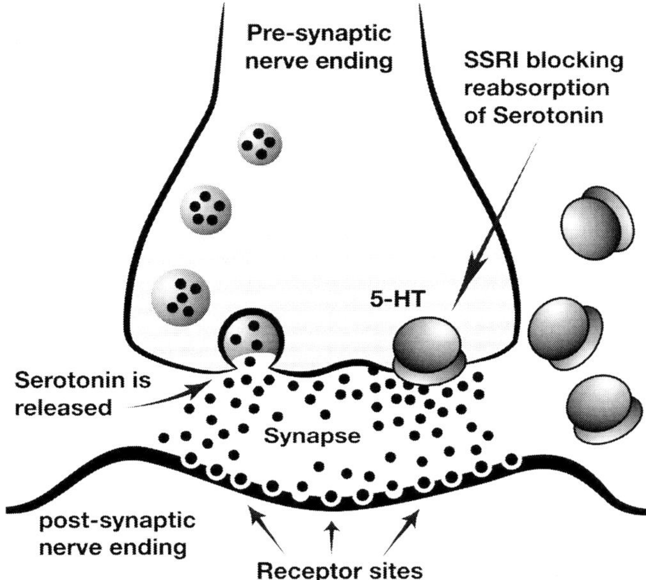

Figure 5.2: SSRI Mechanism of Action

Source: K. Lattimore et al., "Selective Serotonin Reuptake Inhibitor (SSRI) Use during Pregnancy and Effects on the Fetus and Newborn: A Meta-Analysis" (*Journal of Perinatology* 25, 2005), Figure 1

(chapter 4.3). MAOIs work by preventing the release of monoamine oxidase, leading to more monoamine transmitters in the synaptic cleft and thus a greater action throughout the brain (figure 5.1). Blocking monoamine oxidation also produces sedation and, along with this, lowered vigilance and significantly decreased reaction time, making operating machinery or motor vehicles more hazardous. Weight gain is also a common side effect of MOAI use (Hancock & McKim, 2018; Raman-Wilms, 2014). Another risk factor involves eating foods containing high amounts of tyramine, such as cheese or dairy products; when combined with MAOIs, cardiovascular problems including increased heart rate and hypertension arise (Hillhouse & Porter, 2015). Discontinuation syndrome from MAOIs is considered the most problematic of all antidepressant subgroups, as MAOI withdrawal can lead to worsening of depressive episodes, acute confusional state, anxiety symptoms, and even catatonia (Warner et al., 2006).

Tricyclic Antidepressants (TCAs)

Tricyclic antidepressants also work by preventing the reuptake of monoamines by nerve terminals, specifically serotonin and norepinephrine, but also antihistamine and dopamine, to a lesser extent, by competing for the binding site. Some TCAs will increase serotonin concentrations more than they increase norepinephrine (e.g., clomipramine), while others increase norepinephrine concentrations more than serotonin concentrations (e.g., nortriptyline and desipramine). This family of antidepressants brings the cell back to normal functioning by prolonging the exposure of the receptors to the neurotransmitters in the synaptic cleft over several weeks. TCAs do not produce adequate immediate stimulation to create a significant shift in mood, and in fact, initial effects can take 10 to 14 days, and it can be upwards of two months before the full effect is perceived. However, side effects such as dizziness, memory impairments, and drowsiness can begin immediately. TCAs produce a number of other side effects, mainly due to their interference with the autonomic nervous system, including decreased saliva production leading to poor dental health, blurred vision, low blood pressure, and suppressed REM sleep (Hancock & McKim, 2018; Raman-Wilms, 2014).

Selective Serotonin Reuptake Inhibitors (SSRIs)

In the late 1960s evidence began to emerge linking serotonin and MDD. Pharmaceutical company Eli Lilly (2016) began developing drugs that would selectively inhibit the reuptake of serotonin at serotonin transporters, leading to an increase in serotonin concentrations within the synaptic cleft to further activate serotonin receptors. It took nearly two decades from the beginning of this process for the Food and Drug Administration in the United States to approve for human consumption the first SSRI, fluoxetine, marketed under the trade name Prozac, and the revolution in modern antidepressant psychotherapeutics was officially launched (Hillhouse & Porter, 2015).

Prozac was quickly joined by other SSRIs, including Celexa, Lexapro, Paxil, and Zoloft. SSRIs range from 20- to 1,500-fold more selective for inhibiting serotonin over norepinephrine at their respective transporter proteins. SSRIs are now also commonly prescribed not only to individuals with depression but also to those with anxiety disorders, especially if the anxiety is related to feelings of depression. Long-term SSRI treatment is also being studied as a means to delay progression from mild cognitive impairment to Alzheimer's dementia (Bartels et al., 2018).

As their name indicates, SSRIs only inhibit reuptake and do not stimulate the release of serotonin or any other neurotransmitter. The most common side effects produced by SSRIs are nausea, headaches, insomnia, weight gain, and sexual dysfunction, with a slight risk of seizure if the user suddenly stops taking the drug (Turner et al., 2008). However, as use in the general population escalated, reports of SSRI-triggered mania and psychosis rose from 10–20% of users (Whitaker, 2005).

Selective Serotonin-Norepinephrine Reuptake Inhibitors (SSNRIs)

The second of the new-generation, or atypical, antidepressant drugs, venlafaxine (Effexor), was introduced in the 1990s. As suggested by their descriptive name, SSNRIs target not only serotonin but also norepinephrine transporters. SSNRIs are like TCAs in that they inhibit the reuptake of serotonin and norepinephrine at the serotonin and norepinephrine transporters, respectively. However, SSNRIs have minimal or no pharmacological action at histamine, dopamine, or post-synaptic serotonin receptors. Side effects of SSNRIs include both sedation and insomnia, sleep cycle disruption, decreased REM sleep, increased sleep awakenings, and production of vivid nightmares. Headaches are also a common side effect. As tolerance builds, upwards of one-third of users in some studies have experienced breakthrough depression after several months, and as with other antidepressants there is substantive reporting of tachyphylaxis, weight gain, and sexual dysfunction (Hillhouse & Porter, 2015).

Norepinephrine Dopamine Reuptake Inhibitors (NDRIs)

The primary NDRI is bupropion (Wellbutrin and Zyban), which binds in the CNS unlike any other antidepressant, as it has no affinity for serotonin at all. NDRIs bind well to norepinephrine but have an even greater affinity for dopamine. It is believed the bupropion also produces some additional release of norepinephrine and dopamine into the synaptic cleft. Despite this substantive difference in action, bupropion outcome efficacy for treating MDD is on the same level as both SSRIs

Table 5.1: Antidepressants by Pharmacological Category

Type	Drug	Brand Name
Monoamine Oxidase Inhibitors	isocarboxazid moclobemide phenelzine selegiline tranylcypromine	Marplan Manerix Nardil Emsam Parnate
Tricyclic Antidepressants	amitriptyline amoxapine clomipramine despramine doxepin imipramine nortriptyline	Elavil Asendin Anafranil Norpramin, Pertoframe Adapin, Sinequan Tofranil Allegron, Aventyl, Noritren, Nortrilen, and Pamelor
Selective Serotonin Reuptake Inhibitors (SSRIs)	citalopram fluoxetine fluvoxamine nefazodone paroxetine sertaline trazadone vortioxetine	Celexa Prozac Luvox Serzone Paxil Zoloft Deseryl Trintellix, Brintellix
Selective Serotonin-Norepinephrine Reuptake Inhibitors (SNRIs)	duloxetine milnacipran venlafaxine	Cymbalta Savella Effexor
Norepinephrine Dopamine Reuptake Inhibitors (NDRIs)	bupropion	Wellbutrin Zyban

Source: Adapted from Procyshyn et al., 2017

and SSNRIs; additionally, it has demonstrated some ability to alleviate seasonal affective disorder (SAD). Not surprisingly, NDRIs also produce negative side effects such as chronic dry mouth, nausea, restlessness, tremors, nausea, and insomnia, though less sexual dysfunction and seizure risk upon withdrawal is reported with bupropion use as compared to other atypical, second-generation antidepressants. However, there remains a similar rate of tachyphylaxis—one in five to one in ten regular users (Procyshyn et al., 2017). Bupropion also has a significant impact on an individual's overall quality of sleep, delaying REM and producing more insomnia than other antidepressants due to how it inhibits the reuptake of dopamine, noradrenaline, and norepinephrine (Alberti et al., 2015).

Zyban has developed an interesting off-label use. Off-label use refers to the prescribing of drugs for conditions for the which there was no formal clinical testing or for which there is no official sanction. Bupropion is prescribed to smokers trying to quit to assist in overcoming their nicotine cravings because it has been found to interact with nicotine by blocking the activation of specific nicotinic acetylcholine receptors (nAChRs). By doing so, bupropion decreases the effects of nicotine withdrawal, including cravings, hypothermia, seizures, and motor impairment (Slemmer, Martin, & Damaj, 2000). Due to the length of time antidepressants take to alter CNS functioning compared to other categories of psychoactive substances, the minimal euphoria they produce, and the multiple negative side effects, misuse is rare (Evans & Sullivan, 2014).

5.2 ANTIPSYCHOTICS

Psychosis

Psychosis is a condition where an individual is out of touch with reality, unable to determine what is tangible in the physical world and what is not. It is typically characterized by delusions and hallucinations, as well as behaviour that is inappropriate to the situation or environmental circumstances, ambivalence toward making even simple decisions, and an impaired ability to care for oneself, up to the point of catatonia. Psychosis is associated with several mental health issues; schizophrenia, a severe, chronic brain disorder that affects approximately 1% of the Canadian population, is the most prominent. Schizophrenia is a lifelong condition characterized by an onset in late adolescence or early adulthood that produces a deterioration in functional ability and diminished social acceptability, making it among the most disabling and economically devastating mental health conditions (Cruz, 2011).

Psychosis may occur in conjunction with mood disorders, including bipolar conditions, schizoaffective disorder, personality disorders, and autism spectrum disorder, as well as in response to the acute use of or withdrawal from psychoactive drugs and with seniors experiencing dementia (Guzman, 2012). However, not everyone who experiences first-episode psychosis (FEP) in late adolescence or early adulthood progresses to more severe symptoms. How to best treat, pharmacologically, FEP remains actively debated. Some psychiatrists argue for ongoing maintenance treatment with long-acting injectable antipsychotics. Others advocate a delay in diagnosing FEP as schizophrenia and treating the initial episode with low doses of orally administered medication, tapering it as quickly as possible based on each individual's response to the drug. While both camps agree that antipsychotics are essential, the debate is about how much of the drug should be administered and for how long, once the acute symptoms subside (Galletly, Suetani, & Dark, 2018).

There are several prominent competing theories regarding the cause of psychosis. The dopamine theory of schizophrenia proposes that positive symptoms are the result of overactivity in the mesolimbic dopamine pathway. This is, in part, based on the observation that CNS stimulants that increase dopamine availability in the CNS, such as cocaine and amphetamines, trigger psychotic-like effects in individuals who otherwise have no symptoms of schizophrenia. This theory believes psychosis is caused in part by an increase in communication between brain cells due to the overactivity of dopamine, which results when an individual produces too much dopamine, has too many dopamine receptors, or has an insufficient amount of monoamine oxidase, the enzyme that metabolizes dopamine. However, it has also been argued that serotonin is involved, as may be norepinephrine (Brick & Erickson, 2013; Grunder, Hippius, & Carlsson, 2009). A competing theory is that schizophrenia is caused by underactive glutamate neurotransmission, based on the observation that PCP, which is a glutamate antagonist, can elicit temporary psychosis symptoms (Seeman, 2013b). Also, it is widely recognized that the entire range of stresssors—emotional (relationship issues, bereavement), physical (irregular sleep, binge drinking, use of other psychoactive drugs), environmental (inadequate housing, lack of social support, unemployment), trauma (physical assault, sexual assault, bullying), and major life changes (starting a new school or job) can play a role in triggering a psychotic episode (Bromley, Choi, & Faruqui, 2015).

Psychosis has three phases, though not every person who experiences a psychotic episode will necessarily experience clear symptoms of all three phases. The first phase is called prodromal, typically lasting several months, though the duration varies. The prodromal phase involves symptoms that may not be obvious, including changes in feelings, thoughts, perceptions, and behaviours. This is followed by the acute, or active, phase, where individuals experience positive psychotic symptoms, though some negative symptoms may also emerge. During this phase is usually when a person is diagnosed, and drugs are prescribed. The third phase is called the recovery, or residual, phase. Here the acute symptoms lessen in intensity, though some do not always totally disappear. After recovery from FEP, some people never experience a second episode, while others progress in the illness. This is where the debate arises regarding how long drug use should be maintained and to what degree, for it is unknown if continued administration of antipsychotics minimizes future episodes of psychosis, or causes them (Bromley et al., 2015).

The symptoms of psychosis have been divided into four categories: positive symptoms, negative symptoms, cognitive deficits, and mood symptoms. Positive symptoms consist of delusions, hallucinations, and thought disorders. Delusions are fixed, false beliefs that a person comes to believe are true and that often become central organizing principles of their lives. They can be associated with feelings of persecution or of constantly being observed. Hallucinations and disorganized thinking are false sensory perceptions that have no basis in corresponding external sensory stimuli. Auditory hallucinations are the most common sensory disturbance, but hallucinations pertaining to sight, touch, smell, and taste also occur. Negative symptoms consist of a loss of affective responsiveness. This may be apathy, social withdrawal, impaired affect, or anhedonia, while cognitive deficits include issues with attention, memory, executive function, and behaviour, including the ability to initiate and stop actions, monitor and change behaviour as needed, and engage in future planning. Mood symptoms are highlighted by dysphoria, a state of anxiety and restlessness, and depression (Cruz, 2011; Sue et al., 2011).

Overview of Antipsychotics

Antipsychotics, or neuroleptics, are psychoactive drugs used to treat not the illness but rather the underlying symptoms of various psychoses, including schizophrenia, by reducing behavioural and physiological responses to stimuli and producing drowsiness and emotional quieting. They work on positive symptoms, but have minimal impact on negative symptoms or cognitive deficits. Antipsychotics are not effective in alleviating emotional flatness or social withdrawal, or increasing interpersonal communication. The term *neuroleptic* refers to the ability of a drug to cause a syndrome known as neurolepsis, which consists of psychomotor slowing, emotional quieting, and emotional indifference. Like antidepressants, antipsychotics do not create euphoria; rather, they are balancing agents, returning users to a more homeostatic state, and at this time no physical or psychological dependency to these drugs has been documented. Antipsychotics work by interfering with the transmission of dopamine (figure 5.3), with an emphasis on blocking D_2, one of the four dopamine receptor sites (Procyshyn et al., 2017). Unfortunately, upwards of one-third of individuals diagnosed with a psychotic episode do not respond to antipsychotics that target dopamine, which speaks to how complicated a condition psychosis is and how we still do not yet fully understand the condition's biological underpinnings (Rampino et al., 2019).

A major concern with the use of antipsychotics is the range of negative adverse effects they can cause by blocking D_2 throughout the entire CNS. This can range from insomnia, nightmares, disrupted sleep patterns, and vivid dreaming to confusion, disorientation, disruptions in concentration, headaches, spasms and shaking, and sedation and fatigue (Inaba & Cohen, 2011). Additionally, the action of many of these psychoactive drugs causes an imbalance of acetylcholine, leading to extrapyramidal side effects, which include impairment or loss of voluntary movement, involuntary movement of the face and jaw, tremors, feelings of restlessness leading to constant motion such as rocking, muscle rigidity, and Parkinson's-like symptoms (Raman-Wilms, 2014).

Psychosis is a serious mental health issue, and while antipsychotic drug trials indicate approximately twice as many individuals receiving the drugs improve compared to those receiving a placebo, still only a minority of those experience an overall positive response given the nature of the side effects (Leucht et al., 2017). Nevertheless, the overall clinical evidence indicates there are more negative outcomes experienced by those with a proper diagnosis of psychosis who do not receive treatment compared to those who receive antipsychotic drugs. This is especially true for the acute treatment of psychosis and prevention of relapse (Goff et al., 2017).

First-Generation Antipsychotics (FGAs)

Also referred to as typical antipsychotics, dopamine antagonists, neuroleptics, and classic antipsychotics, first-generation antipsychotics are drugs used primarily for the treatment of schizophrenia and related psychotic disorders. The use of FGAs has declined in the last few years, mainly because of an increase in prescriptions of second-generation agents. However, as FGAs are considerably less expensive than newer antipsychotics, they remain a cost-effective option in the treatment of psychotic disorders (Alessi-Severini et al., 2008).

However, as with antidepressants, the effectiveness of FGAs has been questioned. An early clinical experiment by Schooler and colleagues (1967) reported on a one-year outcome study that found individuals in the control group, who received a placebo, were less likely to

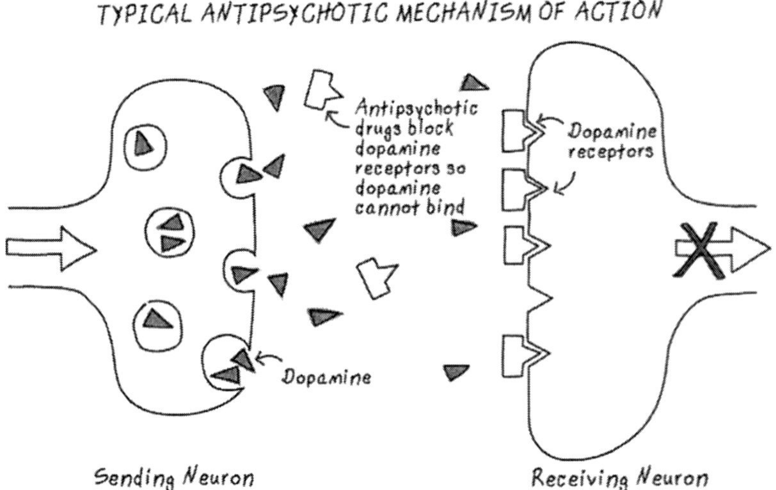

Figure 5.3: Typical Antipsychotic Mechanisms of Action

Source: B. Sproule, *Pharmacology and Drug Abuse*, 2nd edition (Toronto: Centre for Addiction and Mental Health, 2004)

be hospitalized than those diagnosed with schizophrenia who were prescribed chlorpromazine, thioridazine, or trifluoperazine. This raised the question of whether these drugs, while effective in the short term, made individuals more vulnerable to psychosis in the long term. FGAs work by blocking the majority of dopamine D_2 receptors in the brain. However, if this above-normal level of dopamine receptors is the person's homeostatic balance point, the brain will literally work to produce more dopamine receptor sites in order to reach the natural set point, regardless of the social consequences. This then makes the person even more sensitive to dopamine, which increases the the risk of relapse, which in turn requires increased amounts of the drug be administered, which increases the side effects (Whitaker, 2005). Amato and colleagues (2018) found that while initially both FGAs and SGAs blocked synaptic release of dopamine, over time they stopped doing so, and rather than blocking release began to enhance the release of dopamine. This offered another possible explanation as to why individuals in placebo groups relapsed less than those in treatment groups.

Second-Generation Antipsychotics (SGAs)

The designation of second-generation antipsychotics was made to differentiate FGAs, which are dopamine agonists, from SGAs, which are dopamine-serotonin antagonists. Along with their effects on dopamine, which can include both D_2 and D_3, SGAs also have affinity for the specific serotonin receptors, and in the case of cariprazine (Vraylar), histamine as well. SGAs also are less likely to produce extrapyramidal symptoms; however, they can affect metabolic rate, which contributes to weight gain among users of these drugs (table 5.2). Clozapine and olanzapine are associated with the greatest risk of significant weight gain. In comparison, risperidone, quetiapine, amisulpride, and zotepine generally show low to moderate levels of weight gain, while ziprasidone and aripiprazole treatment are generally associated with minimal mean weight gain (Newcomer, 2005).

SGAs became available on the Canadian market in the 1990s. Their introduction, and the fact that they were viewed as safer, if more expensive, options than FGAs, led to a marked increase in antipsychotic medication prescribing for children and youths. Two of the newer SGAs, aripiprazole (Abilify) and risperidone (Risperdal), have been demonstrated to ameliorate ADHD symptoms and to reduce irritability, aggression, self-injury, tantrums, and mood swings in children with autism spectrum disorder. However, they often lead not only to weight gain but also to an increased occurance of type 2 diabetes and the development of high cholesterol (Lamberti et al., 2016; Loy et al., 2012). SGAs have also become routinely prescribed for institutionalized seniors exhibiting dangerous agitation or psychosis where there is a risk of violence to themselves, other residents, or staff. While the effect size is small, use of SGAs has been reported to reduce distress, improve quality of life, and reduce caregiver burden, with aripiprazole and risperidone demonstrating the best results. However, use of SGAs, and FGAs as well, with this population comes with increased risk of stroke, mortality, metabolic effects (diabetes, weight gain), and acute cardiovascular and pulmonary effects (Reus et al., 2016). In 2015, Health Canada conducted a safety review of aripiprazole (Abilify) and reported that there was a link between ongoing use of this SGA and a heightened risk of two impulse control disorders, problem gambling and hypersexuality. A minority of long-term Abilify users, who had no prior history of impulse control disorders, experienced uncontrollable urges after they began taking the drug. Further, within days to weeks of reducing the dose level or totally discontinuing aripiprazole, the urges stopped (Health Canada, 2015).

There has been a great deal of off-label use of SGAs. Other than being used to treat psychosis, SGAs are now routinely administered,

Table 5.2: Antipsychotic Agents

Type	Drug	Brand Name
First Generation		
butyrophenones	haloperidol	Haldol
phenothiazines	chlorpromazine perphenazine thioridazine trifluoperazine	Largactil, Thorzine Trilafon Mellaril Stelazine
rauwolfia alkaloids	resperpine	Serpasil
thioxanthenes	chlorprothixene flupenthixol fluphenazine thiothixene zuclopenthixol	Tarasan Depixol, Fluanxol Prolixin Navane Acuphase, Clopixol
Second Generation		
	amisulpride aripiprazole asenapine brexpiprazole cariprazine clozepine iloperidone loxepine lurasidone olanzapine paliperidone quetiapine risperidone ziprasidone zotepine	Solian Abilify Saphris Rexulti Vraylar Clozaril Fanapta Loxitane Latuda Zyprexa Invega Seroquel Risperdal Zeldox Lodopin

Source: Adapted from Procyshyn et al., 2017

often by general practitioners, to treat obsessive-compulsive disorder, Tourette's syndrome, autism spectrum disorder, disruptive behaviour disorders, depression, eating disorders, general anxiety syndrome, insomnia, and bipolar disorder, which historically was treated with an entirely different subgroup of psychotherapeutic agents (chapter 5.3).

5.3 MOOD STABILIZERS

Bipolar Disorder

Bipolar disorder was first described in the middle of the 19th century as alternating periods of melancholia and mania. The term *manic-depressive* was applied to those with this condition throughout most of the 20th century, and it was not until the third edition of the American Psychiatric Association's (APA) *Diagnostic and Statistical Manual of Mental Disorders* (DSM), that the diagnosis of bipolar disorder was formalized. Bipolar disorder is a condition where a person moves from feelings of depression, often expressed by feelings of hopelessness, to those of exaggerated well-being or excessive, euphoric views of themselves, their status, and/or their success. These extreme episodes are typically followed by a return to homeostasis, called euthymia. Mania is a specific diagnosis that relates to an episode of persistently elevated or irritable mood and is associated with a decreased need for sleep, excessive talkativeness, racing thoughts, easy distractibility, or grandiosity. Depression is the more common symptom that people seek treatment for, making a proper diagnosis of bipolar condition more difficult as individuals with this diagnosis are less likely to consider their manic stages to be problematic. Bipolar condition is estimated to affect 1–2% of the Canadian population (Noll, 2007).

There are a range of conditions that fall within a diagnosis of bipolar. Bipolar is diagnosed when individuals have experienced at least one episode of mania. The average age of first onset is similar to psychosis, approximately 18 years of age, though there have been some documented cases beginning as late as 65. Bipolar II is diagnosed in those who have had at least one episode of depression and one episode of hypomania but have never experienced an episode of full mania. Hypomania has the same features as mania, but the episode is less severe and does not cause the same degree of social or occupational impairment, and the person can be quite creative and productive, though the nature or pace of the behaviour is out of character for the person. Cyclothymic disorder entails numerous hypomanic episodes and numerous depressive episodes over a two-year period, none of which meet full criteria for either mania or depression. Rapid cycling occurs when a person has had four or more mood episodes (i.e., major depression, mania, or hypomania) within one year. These individuals tend to have poor treatment outcomes. Finally, a mixed episode is when the individual experiences mania and depression during the same period, for a week or more. In a mixed episode, a person could report feeling sad or hopeless with suicidal thoughts, while still feeling highly energized. Outwardly they may appear agitated, with disturbed sleep patterns and a major change in appetite. Individuals with bipolar disorder spend much less time in mania, hypomania, or mixed states than they do in depression (Chiu & Chokka, 2011; Malhi, Adams, & Berk, 2010).

Some individuals with bipolar disorder have increased dopamine transmission in the CNS that affects the limbic system, including the hippocampus, amygdala, and striatum, during periods of mania, while GABA neurotransmission is reduced during periods of depression (Schloesser et al., 2007). Why there is this extreme cycling of neurotransmission is not yet fully understood. The DSM-5 criteria for episodes of mania and depression state that an episode of mania must involve a sustained abnormal mood plus three of the following features present, or four features if the patient's mood is irritable rather than elevated:

1. Inflated self-esteem or grandiosity
2. Increased talkativeness
3. Decreased need for sleep, e.g., is rested after three hours' sleep
4. Easily distracted by unimportant or externally irrelevant stimuli

5. Flight of ideas characterized by a nearly continuous flow of accelerated speech, which abruptly shifts from one topic to another
6. An increase in goal-directed activity, e.g., at work, socially, or sexually; or restlessness, i.e., purposeless activity such as pacing or holding multiple conversations at once
7. Excessive involvement in high-risk activities, e.g., spending money recklessly, sexual indiscretion, or imprudent investments

If the person displays psychotic features or requires hospitalization, then the episode is automatically classified as manic (American Psychiatric Association, 2013).

A major depressive episode is defined by five or more of the following symptoms, present at the same time, for at least a two-week period. At least one of the symptoms must be either a depressed mood or a loss of interest or pleasure:

1. Depressed mood for most of the day, nearly every day
2. Markedly reduced interest or pleasure in all, or almost all, of the day's activities, most of the day, nearly every day
3. Insomnia or hypersomnia, nearly every day
4. Feelings of worthlessness or excessive or inappropriate guilt, nearly every day
5. Significant weight loss when not dieting, or weight gain of more than 5% in a month, or a decrease or increase in appetite nearly every day
6. Psychomotor agitation or retardation nearly every day
7. A decreased ability to think or concentrate, or indecisiveness, nearly every day
8. Recurrent thoughts of death or suicide, or a suicide attempt

Episodes of major depression may last weeks or even months (American Psychiatric Association, 2013).

Overview of Mood Stabilizers

Because bipolar condition, which affects 1% of the Canadian population, has so many distinct manifestations, treatment protocols vary depending upon the nature of the person and their presenting issues. While there are several effective treatments for mania, there are fewer for maintenance of homeostasis and for the depression stage of bipolar disorder. Lithium carbonate, valproate (valproic acid), and carbamazepine have been the traditional responses to pharmacologically treating bipolar disorder (table 5.3); however, there are an increasing number of second-generation antipsychotics being used to address the manic aspect of the disorder (Muralidharan et al., 2013). In fact, SGAs are now recommended when an individual first presents with a manic episode, with valproate being an alternative treatment as it has less risk of adverse motor reactions, followed by carbamazepine. However, neither valproate nor carbamazepine is recommended for women of child-bearing age because of the risks these drugs pose to a fetus, and in those instances, lithium is always prescribed, though recently there has been evidence that it too can contribute to birth defects (appendix B). If the person's mania is still not controlled, it is recommended that benzodiazepines be used along with SGAs. Likewise, if a person has been prescribed an SGA but the mania is not controlled, then the use of valproate or lithium is recommended. If a person presents with depression and is prescribed only antidepressants, there is a risk that the person can shift into a period of instability or even mania. In these situations, antidepressants are to be discontinued and replaced with the traditional bipolar medications, with lithium being the first choice. Likewise, if a person's depression does not lift, then the use of lithium, valproate, or carbamazepine is the next step in the treatment plan (Goodwin et al., 2016).

Lithium Carbonate

Lithium carbonate, first prescribed during the 1950s, is a naturally occurring salt with perceivable effects occurring as soon as one week after first administration. It is used primarily for long-term treatment of bipolar disorder with the goal of preventing further manic and depressive episodes. It is distinct from other mood stabilizers as it also reduces the risk of suicide. Lithium exerts its effects at multiple levels, beginning with clinical changes to mood by counteracting mania and depression and diminishing suicidality. At the neurotransmitter level, lithium inhibits excitatory neurotransmission by decreasing pre-synaptic dopamine activity while promoting inhibitory neutrotransmission by acting on glutamate neurotransmission, which increases both glutamate and GABA levels. Lithium additionally inhibits neurotransmission by also causing more GABA to be released into the synaptic cleft. Lithium use has also been found to provide neuroprotection of the cerebal cortex, producing increased grey matter volumes, in particular in the amygdala, hippocampus, and prefrontal cortical regions of the brain. As a result, lithium can also be prescribed to augment the use of traditional antidepressants when a person is exhibiting aggressive or suicidal behaviour (Malhi et al., 2013; Schloesser et al., 2007).

Lithium, like lead, is a heavy metal, and the same chemical that powers batteries. In individuals exhibiting signs of depression who were prescribed lithium, there were increases in Stages 3 and 4 sleep, while REM sleep decreased, REM latency increased, and REM activity/time spent asleep decreased (Billard, 1987). Side effects of lithium can be unpleasant and include fatigue, headaches, dysphoria, vertigo, nausea, dry mouth (often with a metallic taste), fine motor tremors, slurred speech, and weight gain. Monitoring is essential, as chronic users can have the substance accumulate in their bodies. The effects of lithium intoxication include drowsiness, anorexia, muscle twitching, and vomiting, and at higher levels, convulsions, coma, and potentially death. Thus, levels of the drug in the body must be regularly monitored through blood tests (Alda, 2015; Beaulieu et al., 2008).

Valproate (Valproic Acid)

Valproate, first synthesized in the late 1880s, began to be used in the 1960s, not only to treat bipolar condition but also for epilepsy and migraine headaches. It is among the drugs listed on the World Health Organization's (2014a) list of essential medicines. Valproate is used to help those with bipolar condition maintain stability and has been found to be most useful for persons experiencing rapid cycling and mixed states. It works by stabilizing electrical activity in the brain through blocking the breakdown of GABA, allowing for more of it to remain in the synaptic cleft, aiding in calming the CNS. Side effects may include nausea, vomiting, abdominal cramps, anorexia, diarrhea, indigestion, increased appetite leading to weight gain, sedation, tremors, and decreased liver functioning (Reinares et al., 2013; Salloum et al., 2005). Valproate should not be used during pregnancy due to the severe risks to the fetus (appendix B). Studies examining valproate's effects on REM sleep found no significant impact, though valproate did increase daytime drowsiness and decreased slow-wave sleep (Bazil, 2003).

Carbamazepine

Carbamazepine was the first drug after lithium to be used for long-term treatment of bipolar disorder and is also prescribed to persons with epilepsy, schizophrenia, and fibromyalgia. It has similar effectiveness to lithium for those experiencing an acute manic episode. While the exact mechanism of action of carbamazepine is unknown, its effect is to inhibit the generation of rapid action potentials in the brain, which reduces overall electrical activity in the CNS. The most common side effects of carbamazepine include dizziness, drowsiness, nausea, and vomiting. Other side effects include skin rash, dry mouth, diarrhea, anorexia, constipation, abdominal pain, drowsiness, blurred vision, and ataxia. Use of carbamazepine leads to an increased risk for suicidal thoughts and behaviour compared to other mood stabilizers, and at levels above 24 grams it can be toxic. Like lithium, the use of carbamazepine needs to be carefully monitored (Maan & Saadabadi, 2018). In some users a decrease in REM sleep has been observed along with a shift in wave patterns while sleeping, contributing to daytime drowsiness (Bazil, 2003).

Table 5.3: Mood Stabilizers

Drug	Brand Name
lithium carbonate	Eskalith, Lithane, Lithobid
lithium citrate	Cibalith
carbamazepine	Tegretol
valproate (valproic acid)	Depakene, Epilim

QUIZ

1. Which neurotransmitter does Prozac affect?
2. How does Paxil work?
3. How is Effexor different from Prozac?
4. What are the risks to a fetus if the mother is prescribed antidepressant medication during her pregnancy?
5. What do clozapine, risperidone, and haloperidol have in common?

CASE STUDIES

Julia

Julia, age 52, married Paul when they were both 18. Over the past decade, her mood has steadily worsened, and today she has trouble getting out of bed even after eight or nine hours of sleep, has difficulty finding pleasure in any activity she engages in, is experiencing increasing amounts of guilt over her actions, and has virtually no appetite. Paul finally convinces his wife to see a psychiatrist, and not surprisingly, Dr. Edwards diagnoses depression, prescribing Zoloft for Julia to use. The pharmacist instructs Julia to take one pill in the morning and two in the evening, and to avoid using alcohol or any other psychoactive drug.

Julia takes the drug as prescribed, but after one week, nothing has changed and she feels discouraged. Why is this something she should have expected? What should she do now?

Malcolm

Over the course of his life, Malcolm has used a variety of drugs as a means of self-medicating his undiagnosed mental health issue. He has used alcohol, smoked up to three packs of cigarettes a day, and was a regular cannabis smoker. He has now been placed on Lithane. How is this drug different from the other licit and illicit drugs he has used on his own in the past? What are the pharmacological implications of using this drug versus the others he self-administered in the past?

Jennie

Jennie came to detox one week ago after a serious alcohol binge, which also included taking several hits of acid. Jennie told the counsellor that her diagnosis is borderline schizophrenia and that she also suffers from multiple personality disorder (MPD), something usually associated with severe childhood trauma. During her assessment, Jennie revealed that she was sexually abused as a child, and that her regular doctor has told her that if she takes acid one more time she will die, due to the drug's interaction with medication she is taking for her schizophrenia.

Jennie says that she is addicted to the drugs and alcohol and cannot stop using them on her own, and she would like to go for treatment. She says that she has no friends and has cut off contact with her family; her only supports are her foster mother and her doctor. Jennie has a long history of institutionalization in mental health facilities, none of which were able to help her with her chemical dependencies. Upon working with Jennie, you notice that she may also have a serious eating disorder; every time you see her, she is eating, and every time you speak with her, she tells you that she eats three times as much as the other service users at meals and "raids the fridge" at night.

1. Outline your course of action and explain your rationale.
2. What criteria shaped your plan for Jennie?
3. What pharmacological issues govern your actions?

NOTE

1. For an in-depth examination of specific psychotherapeutic agents, see Procyshyn et al. (2017).

APPENDIX A

Which Neurotransmitters Does a Psychoactive Drug Alter?

Drug	Acetylcholine	Adenosine	Dopamine	Endocannabinoid	Endorphin	GABA	Glutamate	Histamine	Norepinephrine	Serotonin
Alcohol	s	s	s		s	P	s			s
Amphetamines			P						s	s
Antidepressants										
MAOIs			s						s	P
NDRIs			P						P	
SSNRIs									P	P
SSRIs										P
Tricyclic Antidepressants								s	s	P
Antihistamines	s		s					P	s	s
Antipsychotics			P					s		s
Barbiturates						P	s			
Benzodiazpines			s			P				
Caffeine	s	P	s						s	s
Cannabis			s	P	s	s			s	s
Cocaine			P						s	s
Indolealkylamines			s						s	P
Inhalants			s			P	s			s
Ketamine	s		s		s		P		s	s
Khat			P							s
LSD—see Indolealkylamines			s				s		s	P
MDMA—see Phenylethylamines			s						s	P

Drug	Acetylcholine	Adenosine	Dopamine	Endocannabinoid	Endorphin	GABA	Glutamate	Histamine	Norepinephrine	Serotonin
Methamphetamine			P						s	s
Methylenedioxpyrovalerone			P							s
Mood Stabilizers			P			s	s		s	s
Nicotine	P		s						s	s
Non-Barbituruate Sedative-Hypntoics						P				
Opioids	s		s		P	s		s	s	s*
Phencyclidine (PCP)	s						P			
Phenylethylamines			s						s	P

Legend: P = primary effect; s = secondary effect; * = only some

APPENDIX B

Summary of Effects of Psychoactive Drug Consumption during Pregnancy

The risk of major structural or genetic birth defects is approximately 3% of all births, a value that increases with maternal age (Centers for Disease Control and Prevention, 2008). Not only do psychoactive drugs easily pass through the blood-brain barrier, they also readily pass through the placental barrier and reach the embryo. As a result, any psychoactive agent a pregnant woman administers is likely to pass through to the fetus. A baby's body and most internal organs are formed during the first 12 weeks of pregnancy. It is mainly during this time that exposure to recreational drugs could potentially cause birth defects. However, there are a range of physical and cognitive issues associated with the use of various psychoactive drugs during pregnancy as the brain continues to develop right up until the end of pregnancy. It is therefore possible that exposure to certain substances at any stage of pregnancy could have a lasting effect on a child's learning or behaviour. Any psychoactive drug, even those as innocuous as antihistamines and caffeine, has the potential to alter brain development and produce physical changes, which can be short term, such as withdrawal, to life altering (Kabir et al., 2013; Kar et al., 2012). While the great majority of women who conceive while taking psychoactive drugs will deliver a healthy baby, the following section summarizes key empirically demonstrated risks that arise as a result of the consumption of psychoactive substances during pregnancy.

DEPRESSANTS

Alcohol

- Women who are planning a pregnancy or already pregnant are advised to abstain from drinking any alcohol. Binge drinking, which entails consuming four or more drinks per occasion, and regular heavy drinking place a fetus at the greatest risk for severe problems (Brown & Trickey, 2018).
- Risk of adverse birth outcomes, including low birth weight, miscarriage, and premature birth, increases with alcohol consumption over two standard drinks per week but has also been associated with consumption of two units or less per week in the first trimester, with higher levels of consumption correlated with higher risk (Nykjaer et al., 2014; Patra et al., 2011).
- Prenatal ethanol exposure increases drug addiction risk of a child throughout the life cycle. Prenatal ethanol exposure can change the function of dopamine neurons in the ventral tegmental area, increasing the risk of addiction to psychoactive drugs other than alcohol (Brancato, 2018; Wang et al., 2018).
- Alcohol exposure during pregnancy is related to decreased placental weight and a smaller placenta-to-birth weight ratio. Alcohol exposure is also associated with increased risk of placental hemorrhage (Carter et al., 2016).
- Consuming alcohol during pregnancy can cause brain damage to the developing infant, leading to a range of developmental, cognitive, and behavioural problems that can appear at any time during childhood. Fetal alcohol spectrum disorders (FASD) is the umbrella term for the different diagnoses, which include fetal alcohol syndrome (FAS), partial fetal alcohol syndrome, alcohol-related neurodevelopmental disorder (ARND), and alcohol-related birth defects (ARBD). People with FASD often have difficulty in a broad range of areas, including coordination, emotional control, socialization, academic achievement, and maintaining employment (May & Gossage, 2011).

- FAS is the most severe outcome of FASD, with fetal death being a possibility. Children born with FAS have restricted growth, facial abnormalities, and learning and behavioural disorders that may be severe and lifelong. FAS can lead to issues with learning, memory, attention span, communication, vision, or hearing, as well as interpersonal relationship difficulties. Children diagnosed with FAS are easily overstimulated and slow to settle, have difficulties understanding personal boundaries, and have issues with information processing, abstract thinking, and executive function (NOFAS-UK, 2011).
- Individuals with ARND have a range of intellectual disabilities and problems with behaviour and learning. They generally do poorly in school and have difficulties with math, memory, attention, and judgment, and exhibit poor impulse control (NOFAS-UK, 2011).
- Individuals with ARBD might have a range of physical problems, typically with the heart, kidneys, or bones, and often have hearing issues as well (Centers for Disease Control and Prevention, 2018).
- An association was found between maternal alcohol consumption during lactation and later negative effects on child development, namely, reduced abstract reasoning ability at age six to seven, in a dose-dependent manner (Jansson, 2018).
- Figure B.1 highlights the developmental cycle and the risks alcohol consumption poses at various times during gestation.

Antihistamines

- If possible, antihistamine use should not occur during the first trimester of pregnancy (Kar et al., 2012).
- Studies examining the use of H1 blockers during pregnancy indicate that there is no substantive increase in the risk of birth defects or spontaneous abortion. First-generation antihistamine use during pregnancy is recommended over second-generation use due to the lack of adequate long-term studies on potential harmful effects of second-generation antihistamines.
- Chlorpheniramine, hydroxyzine, and dexchlorpheniramine are the antihistamines of choice during pregnancy (Kar et al., 2012).

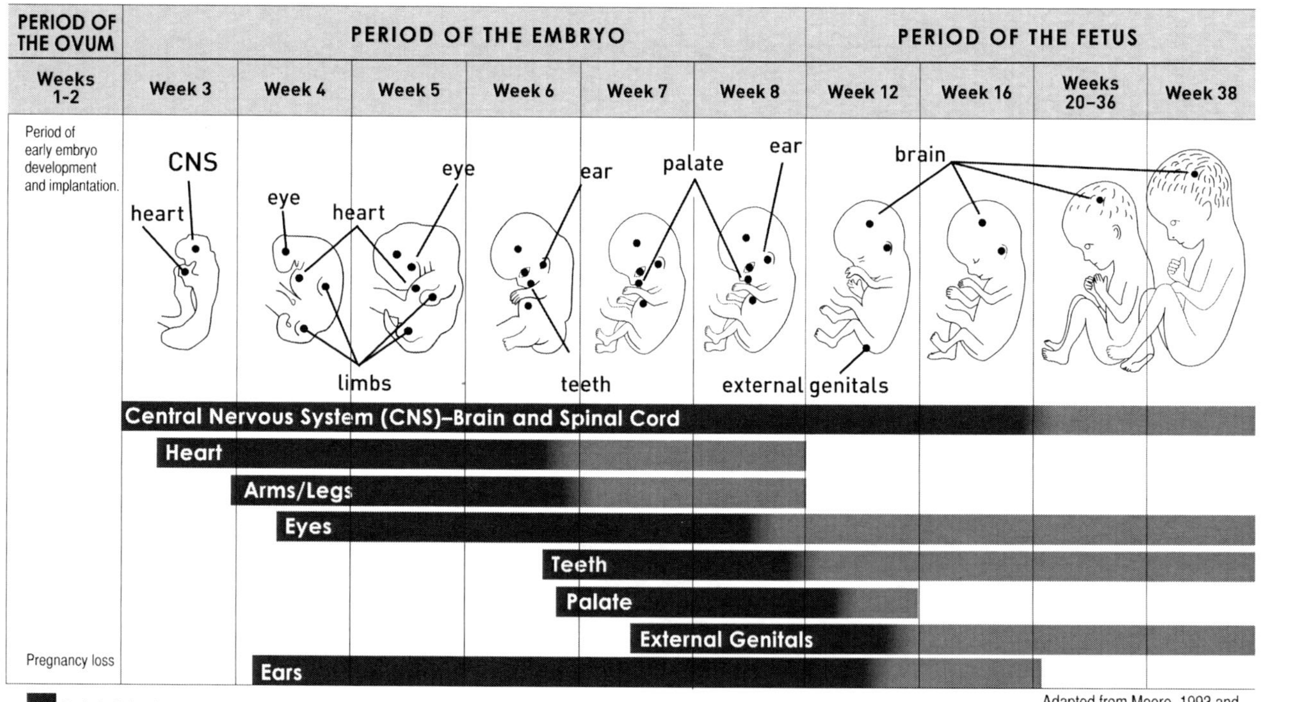

Figure B.1: The Impact of Alcohol Use at Different Points during Pregnancy

Source: https://www.cdc.gov/ncbddd/fasd/documents/fasdbrochure_final.pdf

- If a second-generation H_1 antihistamine is to be used, then loratadine or cetirizine are preferred as they have not been demonstrated to produce any teratogenic (birth defect producing) effects to date (Diav-Citrin et al., 2003; Garbis et al., 2005; Kar et al., 2012).
- All antihistamines are considered safe to use during breastfeeding, as minimal amounts are excreted in the breast milk and would not cause any adverse effects on a breastfeeding infant (So et al., 2010).

Inhalants, Solvents, and Anaesthetic Gases

- There appears to be no association between the use of nitrous oxide as an anaesthetic during pregnancy and fetal malformations (Crawford & Lewis, 1986; Park, Fulton, & Shelley, 1986). However, ongoing occupational exposure to high levels of nitrous oxide can adversely affect a woman's ability to become pregnant (Rowland et al., 1992).
- The risk for pregnancy problems, as well as developmental delays and neurobehavioural difficulties, is higher for the children of women who have been exposed to high concentrations of organic solvents during pregnancy than for those who have not. Toluene is among the most problematic of solvents studied (Hannigan & Bowen, 2010).
- Ongoing use of solvents can lead to the development of fetal solvent syndrome (FSS). Children with FSS have a below-average birth weight, an unusually low level of muscle tone (hypotonia), smaller head circumference, and congenital facial abnormalities. Infants may exhibit physical abnormalities such as smaller faces and jaws, small palpebral fissures (the opening between the eyelids), a thin upper lip, deep-set eyes, and lower-set ears. Other physical anomalies include abnormal scalp hair patterning, down-turned corners of the mouth, blunted fingertips, small fingernails, and urinary tract abnormalities (Bowen, 2011). FSS is also associated with delayed and impaired cognitive development.
- There is increased risk of perinatal death with volatile substance abuse during pregnancy, particularly toluene (Hannigan & Bowen, 2010).
- Withdrawal signs for newborns exposed to concentrations of solvents consist of high-pitched crying, sleeplessness, tremor, hypotonia, and difficulty in feeding (Bowen, 2011).

- Assessments of affected infants documented a host of long-term developmental delays and impairments, including growth delay, hyperactivity, language impairments, and problems with balance as well as walking, and arm/hand movements (Bowen, 2011).
- Major congenital malformations that can occur from even regular occupational exposure to solvents include those of the urinary tract and male genitalia, as well as oral clefts (Cordier et al., 2012; Garlantézec et al., 2009).

Opioids

In Utero

- The probability of high blood pressure, premature labour and rupture of membranes, placental insufficiency, placental abruption, intrauterine growth retardation, and intrauterine death is associated with excessive opioid use during pregnancy (Ross et al., 2015).
- Perinatal heroin and morphine exposure disrupts maturation of the opioid receptor system. Perinatal morphine exposure also induces morphine tolerance (Ross et al., 2015).
- There is limited evidence on the management of heroin addiction during pregnancy. For pregnant women with an opioid use disorder, opioid agonist pharmacotherapy is the recommended therapy (methadone or Suboxone) and is preferable to medically supervised withdrawal, as withdrawal is associated with high relapse rates, which lead to worse outcomes (Gilfillan et al., 2018).
- When compared to women maintained on methadone during pregnancy, women on buprenorphine (Suboxone) had significantly longer gestations, fewer instances of preterm birth, and on average had infants with greater birth weight and head circumference (Meyer et al., 2015; Zedler et al., 2016).

Neonatal Abstinence Syndrome (NAS)

- Withdrawal from opioids of a newborn is called NAS, neonatal abstinence syndrome, and may become apparent anytime during the first week after birth (Kocherlakota, 2014).

- Infants experiencing opioid-induced NAS are irritable; can have feeding, breathing, and sleeping problems; shake or have tremors; cry continually, often at a high pitch; and are more likely to be born with low birth weight and be admitted to a neonatal intensive care unit. They often experience restlessness, tremors and muscle rigidity, fever, sweating, a stuffy nose, sneezing, and diarrhea, and have blotchy skin colouring (Masoumi et al., 2018).
- Infants born with NAS have longer hospital stays than other newborns. However, in the long term there has not yet been demonstrated any long-term cognitive or behavioural abnormalities (Winkelman et al., 2018).
- If non-pharmacological soothing is inadequate to alleviate NAS, infants are typically provided morphine, methadone, or buprenorphine from 1 to 24 weeks (Kocherlakota, 2014), though buprenorphine has been demonstrated to be superior to morphine or methadone for the treatment of opioid-related NAS (Jones et al., 2010; Kraft et al., 2017).
- A Florida study found that the length of hospital stay was shorter for infants exposed to buprenorphine in utero versus methadone (Triplett et al., 2017); likewise, a European study conducted in Norway and the Czech Republic showed a small but not statistically significant difference in neonatal outcomes in favour of buprenorphine compared with methadone (Nechanská et al., 2018).

Child Develoment

- At pre- and elementary school ages, studies have indicated children exposed to heroin in utero show motor and cognitive impairments, inattention, hyperactivity, and a greater risk of ADHD compared to non-exposed children (Ross et al., 2015).
- There has been no evidence of difference in growth patterns between buprenorphine-exposed and non-exposed neonates in terms of hyperactivity, visual/motor impairment, or memory problems, nor is there any indication of an increase in premature birth compared with non-exposed neonates (Ross et al., 2015).

Sedative-Hypnotics

Barbiturates

- In utero, barbiturate effects on neonates include diminished responsiveness, visual inattention, and decreased nutritive sucking (Desmond et al., 1972).
- The majority of infants exposed to barbiturates were full sized and had good one-minute Apgar scores (Desmond et al., 1972). An Apgar score, which assesses Appearance, Pulse, Grimace, Activity, and Respiration, is a method used to quickly summarize the health of a newborn child.
- Episodes of prolonged crying, irritability, and sweating occur during neonatal withdrawal from barbiturates but may not begin for several days post-birth (Desmond et al., 1972).
- Infants whose mothers used barbiturates during pregnancy appear to have a lowered threshold to stimuli, particularly sudden noises, change of orientation in space, cooling, and hunger (Desmond et al., 1972).
- Children exposed to barbiturates in utero have an increased risk of facial dysmorphism, facial clefts, craniofacial abnormalities, congenital heart defects, pre- and postnatal growth deficiency, and developmental delay (Etemad, Moshiri, & Moallem, 2012; Seip, 1976).
- An increased risk of brain tumours was also documented in one study (Gold et al., 1978).

Benzodiazepines

- Use of diazepam during the first trimester of pregnancy was greater among mothers of children born with oral clefts, but the overall risk remains quite low (Iqbal, Sobhan, & Ryals, 2002; Uzun et al., 2010).
- Low birth weight and small head circumference were reported in a study of 17 infants born to women who took diazepam or other benzodiazepines during pregnancy. The weights of these children had normalized by 10 months, but the head circumference was still smaller than expected at 18 months (Laegreid, Hagberg, & Lundberg, 1992).

- Withdrawal does occur, with the most common symptoms being hypertonia (muscle tightness), hyperreflexia (overactive reflexes), restlessness, irritability, abnormal sleep patterns, inconsolable crying, tremors or jerking of the extremities, bradycardia (slow heartbeat), suckling difficulties, apnea, risk of aspiration of feeds, diarrhea, and vomiting. This neonatal withdrawal can appear within a few days to three weeks after birth and can last several months (Iqbal et al., 2002; Uzun et al., 2010).
- The bulk of the evidence indicates that the use of diazepam during gestation has no adverse effects on the child's long-term development. Given the extensive clinical experience, diazepam should be considered safe when used at the lowest possible dosage during pregnancy. Diazepam should be avoided, or the dosage tapered, in the weeks before delivery, if possible, because it may cause neonatal withdrawal syndrome, and floppy infant syndrome (Iqbal et al., 2002).
- While it is comparatively safe to take benzodiazepines during pregnancy compared to barbiturates, it is NOT safe to use these psychoactive agents during lactation as they can cause lethargy, sedation, and weight loss in infants (Iqbal et al., 2002).

Cyclopyrrolones

- It is not yet known if cyclopyrrolones affect fetus development, and so their use is not recommended during pregnancy.
- Use during the last weeks of pregnancy has been known to sedate newborns and may also cause withdrawal symptoms.
- Z-drugs pass into breast milk. Therefore, breastfeeding mothers should avoid using these drugs (Sanofi-Aventis, 2018).

STIMULANTS

Amphetamine

- Amphetamines act directly on both the serotonin and noradrenaline transporters in the placenta, resulting in placental vasoconstriction, which leads to increased rates of premature rupture of membranes, placental abruption and hemorrhage, preterm labour, premature delivery, and intrauterine infections (Ross et al., 2015; Scott & Lust, 2010).

- Amphetamine exposure in pregnancy is associated with higher odds of preterm birth, low birth weight, and small size for gestational age, all of which are associated with a range of short- and long-term illnesses in infants and children (Ladhani, Shah, & Murphy, 2011).
- Neonates exposed to amphetamine in utero display increased physiological stress, lethargy, and lower arousal in the early postpartum period (Scott & Lust, 2010).
- One study found an excess of oral clefts in the offspring of mothers who had amphetamines prescribed in the first 56 days from the last menstrual period (Milkovick & van den Berg, 1977).
- A Swedish study tracked 65 amphetamine-exposed children from birth to age 14 and found a variety of adverse physical, cognitive, emotional, and social effects, including increased prevalence of ADHD, aggression, and learning difficulties attributed to deficits in attention, memory, and motivation (Eriksson, Jonsson, & Zetterstrom, 2000).

Anorexiants

- Case reports of congenital malformations in infants of mothers using dexamphetamine or phenmetrazine exist, but larger empirical studies did not find a statistically significant effect (Källén, Borg, & Reis, 2013).
- An older prospective, observational study of pregnancy and child development examining phenmetrazine found that the severe congenital anomaly rate did not differ from the rate of the group of children whose mothers did not use these drugs (Milkovick & van den Berg, 1977).

Betel

- Babies of women who had chewed betel throughout pregnancy compared to those who had never chewed were more likely to have lower birth weight (Senn et al., 2009) be smaller in size (Yang et al., 2008), and be at greater risk for neonatal jaundice (Costa & Griew, 1982).
- A study of Indigenous women living in Taiwan who chewed betel throughout their pregnancy found premature delivery, stillbirth, and fetal malformation 2.8 times more likely to occur than among a non-using comparison group (Yang et al., 1999).

Caffeine

- Moderate amounts of caffeine during pregnancy do not increase the risks of congenital malformations, miscarriage, or growth retardation (Brent, Christian, & Diener, 2011).
- Consumption of greater than 540 milligrams of caffeine per day is associated with impaired fetal growth, including skeletal development (Bakker et al., 2010).
- Animal studies indicate caffeine use may lead to a decrease in executive function at school age (Ross et al., 2015), though an earlier study did not find any relationship between caffeine consumption and individually administered IQ and attention tests at seven years of age (Barr & Streissguth, 1991).

Cocaine

- Prenatal cocaine exposure affects fetal physical growth and results in an increase of premature birth and generalized growth retardation, including decreased birth weight, shorter body length, and smaller head circumference (Ross et al., 2015).
- Infants aged four to eight months who had been exposed to cocaine in utero showed less arousal, interest, joy, and sadness during learning tasks than non-exposed infants, as well as slower reflexes (Frank et al., 2001).

- At age eight weeks, cocaine-exposed children showed increased heart rate to social stimulation and a higher baseline respiratory rate, but were not more dysregulated in arousal (Frank et al., 2001).
- A significant, stable effect of cocaine exposure on language development was observed over time for all language domains, with cocaine exposure related to poorer language skill performance (Lewis et al., 2007).
- In studies of face-to-face interaction between mothers and infants, heavy prenatal cocaine use correlated with less optimal maternal behaviour and with decreased readiness for interaction among infants at age six months (Frank et al., 2001).
- However, no differences between cocaine-exposed and non-exposed children were found in long-term physical growth, cognitive development, language skills, motor skills, or school performance. Environmental factors had a greater impact on school performance than did in utero cocaine exposure (Hurt et al., 2005; Frank et al., 2001).

Decongestants

- Decongestants should be avoided if possible during all stages of pregnancy as they can reduce blood flow in the placenta and to the baby (United Kingdom Tetralogy Information Service, 2018b).
- First-trimester use of decongestants has been linked with a small risk of specific birth defects—phenylephrine with heart malformation, and phenylpropanolamine with both ear and stomach muscle defects (Yau et al., 2013).
- There has been no observed risk of preterm delivery with the use of decongestants during pregnancy (Hernandez, Mitchell, & Werle, 2010).

Khat (Qat)

- Chewing khat during pregnancy has been associated with inhibition of utero-placental blood flow, leading to the impairment of fetal growth and lower birth weight (Khawaja, Al-Nsour, & Saad, 2008).

- Neonates of mothers who chewed khat during pregnancy also had significant decreases in length, head circumference, and Apgar scores at one and five minutes in comparison with those of mothers who did not chew khat during pregnancy. The severity of each of these neonatal parameters was found to increase in severity with the increased frequency and duration of khat chewing during pregnancy (Hassan, Gunaid, & Murray-Lyon, 2007).
- No significant association between chewing khat and stillbirth or congenital malformations has been reported (Khawaja et al., 2008).
- Nursing mothers in Yemen frequently complained about poor lactation. This may also be associated with khat use, as khat inhibits prolactin secretion (Hassan et al., 2007).
- Women who continue to chew khat after giving birth have been found to have breast milk that contains cathine, which is in turn passed along to infants who are nursing (Hassan et al., 2007).

Methamphetamine

- Methamphetamine use during pregnancy is associated with growth restrictions such as decreased weight, length, and head circumference. Methamphetamine-exposed children scored lower on measures of visual motor integration, attention, verbal memory, and long-term spatial memory. There were no differences among the groups in motor skills, short-delay spatial memory, or measures of non-verbal intelligence. Methamphetamine-exposed children have subtle decreases in size or volume in certain brain regions correlated with poorer sustained attention and delayed verbal memory compared to non-exposed children (Ross et al., 2015).
- Methamphetamine exposure in utero was associated with symptoms of agitation, vomiting, and tachypnea (abnormally rapid breathing) when compared to a non-exposed group (Chomchai et al., 2004).
- Methamphetamine use has been linked with an increased risk of intrauterine passing of meconium, a sign of acute fetal stress and/or hypoxia (Carter et al., 2016).

- There were no differences in cognition between a group of children whose mothers used methamphetamine during pregnancy and a matched-comparison group. There was a subtle exposure effect on fine motor performance on children at one year of age whose mothers used methamphetamine, with the poorest performance observed in the most heavily exposed children. However, by age three no differences in fine motor performance were observed between the two groups (Smith et al., 2011).
- Methamphetamine-exposed children had greater externalizing behavioural problems at age five compared to those not exposed. Parenting stress and psychological symptoms experienced by primary caregivers were associated with increased child behavioural problems, indicating these affected children may have more difficulties negotiating the increasingly complex academic and social demands of school-age children (Ross et al., 2015).

Methylenedioxpyrovalerone (Bath Salts)

- Information regarding the effect of compounds classified as bath salts on pregnant women and fetuses is extremely limited. Only one study summarized the outcomes of six women who used bath salts during pregnancy and this was a preliminary examination. Only two pregnancies resulted in live births, one premature. One of the two infants displayed signs of withdrawal, including jitteriness, hypertonia, and a high-pitched cry (Gray & Holland, 2014).

Methylphenidate (Ritalin and Concerta)

- In the first half of pregnancy there was a 1.3-time increased risk of preeclampsia (high blood pressure in women who have not experienced this prior to pregnancy, high level of protein in the urine that can damage the liver and kidneys, and swelling in the feet, legs, and hands) with methylphenidate users compared to non-users (Cohen et al., 2017).
- Infants exposed during pregnancy more often had central nervous system–related disorders and were more often moderately preterm than non-exposed infants, but there was no increased risk for

congenital malformations or perinatal death (Nörby, Winbladh, & Källén, 2017).

Nicotine (Tobacco)

- Cigarette smoking during pregnancy increases the risk of sudden infant death syndrome (SIDS) (Lee et al., 2018).
- Second-hand smoke exposure during pregnancy increases the risk of infant stillbirth, congenital malformations, low birth weight, and respiratory illnesses (Reece et al., 2018).
- At birth, exposed infants tend to be smaller in body weight, height, and head circumference, effects attributable to third- and possibly second-trimester exposure (Espy et al., 2011).
- Newborns exposed in utero to nicotine are more irritable and have poorer attention than unexposed infants, and they exhibit increased muscle tension, increased tremors and startle responses, and deficient speech processing (Espy et al., 2011).
- Within the first month of life, exposed infants show signs of poorer self-regulation and require more handling by caregivers (Stroud et al., 2009).
- Following birth, the consequences of prenatal nicotine exposure are persistent, with children age six and younger having decreased receptive language skills, which can contribute to language comprehension deficits (Lewis et al., 2007).
- Exposed children also show poorer academic achievement or cognitive scores than peers (Agrawal et al., 2010), including increased diagnosis of ADHD (Lindblad & Hjern, 2010).
- Montgomery and Ekbom (2002) found that children of women who smoked during pregnancy were more likely to develop diabetes later in life than were children of non-smoking mothers.
- Conduct and behavioural disorders are associated with prenatal tobacco exposure, with no level of tobacco exposure appearing to be safe (Ross et al., 2015).
- Secretory Immunoglobulin A (SIgA) plays a critical role in immune functioning by preventing pathogens from adhering to mucosal surfaces, which is how most infectious agents enter the

body, making SIgA a defense against respiratory, intestinal, and urinogenitary infections, as well as periodontal disease. Children who experienced postnatal exposure to a combination of cigarette smoke and cannabis had higher levels of SIgA, increasing the risk of an overactive immune response (Molnar et al., 2018).

HALLUCINOGENS

Dissociative Anaesthetics (Ketamine and Phencyclidine [PCP])

- Ketamine is neurotoxic to the developing mammalian brain. The use of ketamine in pregnant rats was found to affect both learning and memory (Li et al., 2017).
- Data from animal studies suggest that maternal anaesthesia with ketamine during the fetal brain development period can cause fetal brain damage and subsequent neurobehavioural abnormality (Zhao et al., 2014).
- In a single case study, an infant born with ketamine in her system was small for gestational age, exhibited intrauterine growth retardation, hypotonia (floppy baby syndrome), and poor reflex responses (Su, Chang, & Chen, 2010).
- Mvula, Miller, and Ragan (1999) found that PCP use was rarely reported among pregnant women, and in most cases there was greater use of other psychoactive agents.
- Neonatal symptoms of maternal PCP abuse have been observed as jitteriness, hypertonicity (abnormally high tension of the muscles), and vomiting (Strauss, Modanlou, & Bosu, 1981).
- Abnormal neurobehaviour in the newborn period has been observed with maternal PCP use, but mental and psychomotor development was comparable to control infants' development through two years of age (Chasnoff et al., 1986).

Indolealkylamine (LSD-Like)

- There are no published prospective studies that examine fetal outcome following use of LSD in pregnancy. The available data, published mainly during the 1970s, detailed limb, CNS, and vision defects in infants exposed to LSD in utero. The frequencies of spontaneous abortions, premature births, and birth defects in 121 human pregnancies following relatively infrequent, low doses of medically administered lysergic acid diethylamide were within the normal ranges. The incidence of spontaneous abortions was above average for a small sample of 27 pregnancies where LSD was ingested under both medical and non-medical conditions. Spontaneous abortions occurred significantly more frequently when the mother received LSD as opposed to the father only; however, the data do not permit the establishment of a clear causal relationship (Hoyt, 1978; Long, 1972; McGlothlin, Sparkes, & Arnold, 1970).
- There are no reports to date regarding the effects of psilocybin on pregnancy (Scott & Lust, 2010).

Phenylethylamine (Mescaline-Like)

- Studies of babies exposed to MDMA in utero noted premature births, a significantly increased risk of congenital defects, and cardiovascular and musculoskeletal anomalies, as well as congenital cardiac malformation and the risk of spontaneous abortion (Ross et al., 2015).
- The Drugs and Infancy Study found that mothers who took MDMA during the first trimester of pregnancy gave birth to babies with significant gross psychomotor retardation (Parrott et al., 2014).
- A neurobehavioural outcome study suggests that prenatal MDMA exposure predicts poorer infant mental and motor development at 4 and 12 months of age in a dose-dependent manner, with heavier use associated with impaired motor and intellectual development in infants, but whether there are long-lasting changes in neurobehavioural outcomes is not yet known (Singer et al., 2012).

- No studies on other mescaline-like psychoactive agents and pregnancy were located.

Cannabis

- Cannabis has a negative impact on sperm mobility and male reproductive health (Rogers et al., 2017).
- Birth weights for babies of women using cannabis at least once per week before and throughout pregnancy were lower than those of the offspring of non-users (Crume et al., 2018; Fergusson, Horwood, & Northstone, 2002).
- Compared with non-cannabis-using women, babies of women who smoked cannabis during pregnancy were, on average, 375 grams lighter, had a lower gestational age, shorter body length, and were more likely to be small for gestational age and to be admitted to the neonatal intensive care unit (Hayatbakhsh et al., 2012).
- Inhaled Δ9-tetrahydrocannabinol transfers into a mother's breast milk. A maternal dose of 23.2 milligrams of inhaled cannabis leads to an exclusively breastfeeding infant ingesting 2.5% of the maternal dose (Baker et al., 2018).
- As noted in the nicotine section above, children who experienced postnatal exposure to a combination of cigarette smoke and cannabis had an increased risk of an overactive immune response (Molnar et al., 2018).
- An Australian study found that of the 416,834 live births analyzed over a five-year period, there were 2,172 pregnancies in women who were regular cannabis users. The neonates of these women were diagnosed with a higher level of fetal distress than non-using women. One possible explanation proposed was increased fetal hypoxia (oxygen deprivation), as cannabis has been shown to produce carbon monoxide levels five times higher than those produced by cigarette smoking (Burns, Mattick, & Cooke, 2006).
- Newborns exposed to cannabis exhibit a greater likelihood of sleep disturbances, which can continue on for a few months up to three years (Ross et al., 2015).

- Small for gestational age, preterm birth, and neonatal intensive care unit admission are NOT associated with cannabis use (Crume et al., 2018).
- While there are no significant cognitive deficits in children whose mothers used cannabis during pregnancy, issues in verbal and memory tasks, impulsivity, visual-spatial working memory, and abstract reasoning begin to emerge by age four and continue to be evident into adulthood (Ross et al., 2015).
- In the Ottawa Perinatal Prospective Study, there was no increase in major or minor malformations in the offspring of those women who had continued to use marijuana throughout pregnancy; however, an exaggerated startle response and fine tremor was noted in the first week of postnatal life. These children developed normally through infancy, but at 48 months of age impairments were noted in memory and verbal development in children of mothers with heavy cannabis use during pregnancy. Similar effects on verbal memory, abstract reasoning, and mood have been demonstrated in other follow-up studies (Scott & Lust, 2010).
- By age 10 there is a greater risk of issues in abstract and visual reasoning, executive functioning, reading, spelling, hyperactivity, impulsivity, and attention deficits (Porath-Waller, 2016).

PSYCHOTHERAPEUTIC AGENTS

Antidepressants

Norepinephrine-Dopamine Reuptake Inhibitors (NDRIs)

- Bupropion (Welbutrin, Zyban) does not appear to increase the rates of major malformation above baseline levels of non-users (Cole et al., 2006).
- There was NOT a heightened rate of spontaneous abortions among women using bupropion during their pregnancy (Chun-Fai-Chan et al., 2005).

- However, there is still insufficient research to determine if bupropion use is totally safe for a fetus (United Kingdom Tetralogy Information Service, 2018a).

Selective Serotonin-Norepinephrine Reuptake Inhibitors (SSNRIs)

- Duloxetine (Cymbalta) use during pregnancy has been associated with an increased risk of spontaneous abortion, though not with major fetal abnormalities (Andrade, 2014).
- Late-pregnancy exposure to duloxetine is associated with neonatal adaptation syndrome. Symptoms of neonatal adaptation syndrome include: insomnia or somnolence, agitation, tremors, jitteriness, shivering, restlessness, irritability and constant crying, poor feeding, vomiting or diarrhea, poor temperature control, hypoglycemia (low blood sugar), tachypnea (rapid breathing), respiratory distress, nasal congestion, and cyanosis (blue tone to the skin caused by low oxygen levels) (Andrade, 2014).
- Infant exposure to duloxetine in breast milk is less than 1%, making breastfeeding while using the drug not a risk to the infant (Andrade, 2014).

Selective Serotonin Reuptake Inhibitors (SSRIs)

- Continued use of SSRIs during pregnancy has been linked to minor increased risks for prematurity, low Apgar score, hypoglycemia, feeding difficulties, and cerebral excitation (Campagne, 2007; Källén et al., 2013).
- Prenatal exposure to SSRIs is associated with an increased risk of low birth weight and respiratory distress, highlighted by a six-fold increase in the risk for persistent pulmonary hypertension (PPHN) in newborns (Campagne, 2007) even when maternal illness severity is accounted for (Oberlander et al., 2006).
- The use in early pregnancy of citalopram (Celexa, Cipramil) may produce congenital heart defects. No other congenital issues have been reported (Källén & Olausson, 2007).
- Prenatal exposure to SSRIs was associated with an increased risk of speech/language disorders (Brown et al., 2016).

- Late-pregnancy use of SSRIs is associated with increased risk of neonatal adaptation syndrome typically lasting three to five days that may be a result of withdrawal or of excessive serotonin (Källén et al., 2013; Levinson-Castiel et al., 2006; Moses-Kolko et al., 2005).
- No relationship has been found between intellectual disability and maternal antidepressant use during pregnancy (Viktorin et al., 2017).
- No differences in achieving main developmental milestones were found between infants exposed in utero to SSRIs or combined clonazepam-SSRI treatment and non-exposed infants, including language performance and IQ results (Gentile, 2010).
- An American study indicated that there is no significant association between maternal use of SSRIs during pregnancy and autism spectrum disorder in the offspring (Hviid, Melbye, & Pasternak, 2013), whereas a subsequent Canadian study indicated there is (Boukhris et al., 2016). Thus, until a definitive conclusion is agreed upon, this should be considered a risk area.
- Paroxetine (Paxil) does not appear to be associated with an increased risk of cardiovascular defects following use in early pregnancy (Einarson et al., 2008).
- There is currently not enough information to assess whether fluoxetine (Prozac) use in pregnancy is safe for a fetus (United Kingdom Tetralogy Information Service, 2018c), but it has been linked to hypertensive disease of pregnancy and increased numbers of Cesarean deliveries (Yonkers et al., 2017).

Tricyclic Antidepressants (TCAs)

- Källén et al. (2013) linked the TCA clomipramine with an increased risk for congenital malformations, particularly cardiovascular defects.
- There have been no reported negative outcomes with the use of TCAs during pregnancy with regards to long-term cognitive, verbal, and behavioural development (Gentile, 2010).
- However, both duration of depression during pregnancy and the number of depressive episodes after delivery are risk factors for

reduced IQ values and impaired language performance among children (Gentile, 2010).

Antipsychotics

- The overarching concern regarding administering antipsychotics among pregnant women with serious mental illness is, if they discontinue use during pregnancy out of concern for fetal harm, will this jeopardize their own mental health and their ability to care for an infant after delivery.
- Use of second-generation antipsychotics (SGAs) during pregnancy may increase the risk for excessive weight gain and increased serum triglyceride and cholesterol levels among pregnant women (Källén et al., 2013).
- Increased risk of gestational diabetes from the use of SGAs such as olanzapine, quetiapine, risperidone, varipiprazole, and ziprasidone has been reported (Park et al., 2018).
- Data regarding the potential harm of taking clozapine during pregnancy are not unanimous. There are reports of no congenital abnormalities with clozapine, while other studies indicate a risk of congenital malformation. However, breastfeeding is not advised due to the high concentration of clozapine in breast milk leading to increased exposure to clozapine for the newborn (Sethi, 2006).
- Use of both first-generation antipsychotics (FGAs) and SGAs is associated with neonatal complications, including withdrawal symptoms, extrapyramidal signs (impairment of voluntary movements, muscle rigidity, involuntary contractions of muscles in the face, jaw, neck, trunk, pelvis, and extremities), and respiratory problems. SGA use increased the risk for gestational diabetes, resulting in infants who were large for gestational age (Källén et al., 2013).

Mood Stabilizers

- Untreated bipolar disorder is a risk factor for congenital malformations. Abrupt discontinuation of drugs by mothers with bipolar disorder has been shown to lead to a high risk of relapses during pregnancy (Tosato et al., 2017).

- Lithium exposure during the first trimester was associated with an increased risk of major malformations, though there was no greater risk of delivery complications (Munk-Olsen et al., 2018).
- The achievement of principal developmental milestones in babies exposed to lithium during gestation does not appear to be different from that shown by non-exposed comparison children (Gentile, 2010; Källén et al., 2013), though there is a risk for low levels of muscle tone at birth and for cyanosis, which is poor circulation or inadequate oxygenation of the blood (Goodwin et al., 2016).
- The risk of major congenital malformations among infants whose mothers used carbamazepine is 6%. Carbamazepine use has been linked to neonatal bleeding, though this can be addressed with vitamin K injections (Goodwin et al., 2016).
- Valproate (valproic acid) increases the risk of fetal abnormalities to 11%. This includes spina bifida and other neural tube defects, as well as congenital malformations of the heart, oral cleft, genitalia, and limbs, with greater doses associated with a significantly greater risk than lower doses (Etemad et al., 2012).
- Maternal valproate use has been linked to neurodevelopmental delay in children, including a risk of reduced IQ and cognitive fluency, with one-third of children from one study requiring additional educational support in school. By age six, valproate-exposed children continued to demonstrate poor motor performance and impaired neurological outcome, which continued on into adulthood (Gentile, 2010).

REFERENCES

Aarde, S., Huang, P., Creehan, K., Dickerson, T., & Taffe, M. (2013). The novel recreational drug 3,4-methylenedioxypyrovalerone (MDPV) is a potent psychomotor stimulant: Self-administration and locomotor activity in rats. *Neuropharmacology, 71*(2), 130–140.

Abi-Jaude, E., Chen, L., Cheung, P., Bhikram, T., & Sandor, P. (2017). Preliminary evidence on cannabis effectiveness and tolerability for adults with Tourette Syndrome. *The Journal of Neuropsychiatry and Clinical Neurosciences, 29*(4), 391–400.

Advokat, C., Comtay, J., & Julien, R. (2018). *Julien's primer of drug action* (14th ed.). New York: MacMillan Learning.

African Union. (2012). *African Union plan of action on drug control, 2013–2017. Submitted for consideration by the 5th Session of the Africa Union Conference of Ministers of Drug Control (CAMDC5).* Retrieved from: http://sa.au.int/en/sites/default/files/AUPA%20on%20DC%20(2013-2017)%20-%20English_0.pdf

Agrawal, A., Scherrer, J., Grant, J., Sartor, C., Pergadia, M., Duncan, A., Madden, P., Haber, J., Jacob, T., Bucholz, K., & Xian, H. (2010). The effects of maternal smoking during pregnancy on offspring outcomes. *Preventative Medicine, 50*(1), 13–18.

Ailawadhi, S., Sung, K., Carlson, L., & Baer, M. (2007). Serotonin syndrome caused by interaction between citalopram and fentanyl. *Journal of Clinical Pharmacy and Therapeutics, 32*(2), 199–202.

Al-Hairi, Z., & Del Bigio, M. (2010). Brain damage in a large cohort of solvent abusers. *Acta Neuropathologica, 119*(4), 435–445.

Alaggia, R., & Csiernik, R. (2017). Coming home: Rediscovering the family in addiction treatment in Canada. In R. Csiernik & W. Rowe (Eds.), *Responding to the oppression of addiction* (3rd ed.) (pp. 76–94). Toronto: Canadian Scholars' Press.

Alberta Gaming and Liquor Commission. (2018a). *BAC estimation charts.* Retrieved from: http://protect.aglc.ca/siteuploads/document/BAC%20Estimation%20Charts_200806.pdf?v

Alberta Gaming and Liquor Commission. (2018b). *Cannabis staff training.* Edmonton.

Alberti, S., Chiesa, A., Andrisano, C., & Serretti, A. (2015). Insomnia and somnolence associated with second-generation antidepressants during the treatment of major depression: A meta-analysis. *Journal of Clinical Psychopharmacology, 35*(3), 296–303.

Alberts, B., Johnson, A., Lewis, J., Raff, M., Roberts, K., & Walter, P. (2007). *Molecular biology of the cell* (5th ed.). New York: Garland Science.

Alda, M. (2015). Lithium in the treatment of bipolar disorder: Pharmacology and pharmacogenetics. *Molecular psychiatry, 20*(6), 661–670.

Aldington, S., Williams, M., Nowitz, M., Weatherall, M., Pritchard, A., McNaughton, A., Robinson, G., & Beasley, R. (2007). The effects of cannabis on pulmonary structure, functions and symptoms. *Thorax, 62*(12), 1058–1063.

Alessi-Severini, S., Biscontri, R., Collins, D., Kozyrskyj, A., Sareen, J., & Enns, M. (2008). Utilization and costs of antipsychotic agents: A Canadian population-based study, 1996–2006. *Psychiatric Services, 59*(5), 547–553.

Alexander, M., & Stockton, G. (2000). Methylphenidate abuse and psychiatric side effects. *Journal of Clinical Psychiatry, 2*(5), 159–164.

Alford, D., Barry, D., & Fiellin, D. (2013). Treating pain in patients receiving methadone maintenance for opioid dependence. In R. A. Cruciani & H. Knotkova (Eds.), *Handbook of methadone prescribing and buprenorphine therapy* (pp. 31–37). New York: Springer.

Allen, C., & Ivester, J. (2017). Ketamine for pain management: Side effects & potential adverse events. *Pain Management Nursing, 18*(6), 372–377.

Amato, D., Canneva, F., Cumming, P., Maschauer, S., Groos, D., Dahlmanns, J., Grömer, T., Chiofalo, L., Dahlmanns, M., Zheng, F., Kornhuber, J., Prante, O., Alzheimer, C., von Hörsten, S., & Müller, C. (2018). A dopaminergic mechanism of antipsychotic drug efficacy, failure, and failure reversal: The role of the dopamine transporter. *Molecular Psychiatry*. doi:10.1038/s41380-018-0114-5

American Psychiatric Association. (2013). *Diagnostic and statistical manual of mental disorders* (5th ed.). Arlington: American Psychiatric Publishing.

American Psychiatric Association. (2018). *Practice guidelines for the pharmacological treatment of patients with alcohol use disorders*. Washington: APA.

Andersson, K. (2004). Antimuscarinics for treatment of overactive bladder. *The Lancet Neurology, 3*(1), 46–53.

Andrade, C. (2014). The safety of duloxetine during pregnancy and lactation. *Journal of Clinical Psychiatry, 75*(12), e1423–e1427.

Andrews, P., Thomson, J., Amstadter, & Neale, M. (2012). Primum non nocere: An evolutionary analysis of whether antidepressants do more harm than good. *Frontiers in Psychology, 3*, 117. doi:10.3389/fpsyg.2012.00117

Angarita, G., Emadi, N., Hodges, S., & Morgan, P. (2016). Sleep abnormalities associated with alcohol, cannabis, cocaine, and opiate use: A comprehensive review. *Addiction Science & Clinical Practice, 11*, 9. https://doi.org/10.1186/s13722-016-0056-7

Angus, C., Holmes, J., Pryce, R., Meier, P., & Brennan, A. (2016). *Alcohol and cancer trends: Intervention studies.* Sheffield: University of Sheffield and Cancer Research UK.

Antnowicz, J., Metzger, A., & Ramanujam, S. (2011). Paranoid psychosis induced by consumption of methylenedioxypyrovalerone: Two cases. *General Hospital Psychiatry, 33*(6), 640.e5–640.e6.

Arendt, M., Mortensen, P., Rosenberg, R., Pedersen, C., & Waltoft, B. (2008). Familial predisposition for psychiatric disorder: Comparison of subjects treated for cannabis-induced psychosis and schizophrenia. *Archives of General Psychiatry, 65*(11), 1269–1274.

Arroll, B. (2005). Non-antibiotic treatments for upper-respiratory tract infections (common cold). *Respiratory Medicine, 99*(12), 1477–1484.

Ashton, C. (2001). Pharmacology and effects of cannabis: A brief review. *British Journal of Psychiatry, 178*(1), 101–106.

Astley, S. (2010). Profile of the first 1,400 patients receiving diagnostic evaluations for fetal alcohol spectrum disorder at the Washington State Fetal Alcohol Syndrome Diagnostic & Prevention Network. *Canadian Journal of Clinical Pharmacology, 17*(1), e132–e164.

Atalay, H. (2011). Comorbidity of insomnia detected by the Pittsburgh Sleep Quality Index with anxiety, depression and personality disorders. *Israel Journal of Psychiatry and Related Sciences, 48*(1), 54–59.

Aune, D., Schlesinger, S., Norat, T., & Riboli, E. (2018). Tobacco smoking and the risk of atrial fibrillation: A systematic review and meta-analysis of prospective studies. *European Journal of Preventive Cardiology, 25*(13), 1437–1451.

Babor, T., Higgins-Biddle, J., Saunders, J., & Monterra, M. (2001). *AUDIT—The alcohol use disorders identification test: Guidelines for use in primary care.* New York: World Health Organization.

Baker, K., Halliday, G., Hornung, J., Geffen, L., Cotton, R., & Törk, I. (1991). Distribution, morphology and number of monoamine-synthesizing and substance P-containing neurons in the human dorsal raphe nucleus. *Neuroscience, 42*(3), 757–775.

Baker, T., Datta, P., Rewers-Felkins, K., Thompson, H., Kallem, R., & Hale, T. (2018). Transfer of inhaled cannabis into human breast milk. *Obstetrics & Gynecology, 131*(5), 783–788.

Bakker, R., Steegers, E., Obradov, A., Raat, H., Hofman, A., & Jaddoe, V. (2010). Maternal caffeine intake from coffee and tea, fetal growth, and the risks of adverse birth outcomes: The generation R study. *The American Journal of Clinical Nutrition, 91*(6) 1691–1698.

Baldwin, D., Aitchison, K., Bateson, A., Curran, H., Davies, S., Leonard, B., Nutt, D., Stephens, D., & Wilson, S. (2013). Benzodiazepines: Risks and benefits. A reconsideration. *Journal of Psychopharmacology, 27*(11), 967–971.

Balfour, D. (2004). The neurobiology of tobacco dependence: A preclinical perspective on the role of the dopamine projections to the nucleus accumbens. *Nicotine and Tobacco Research, 6*(6), 899–912.

Bar-Lev Schleidera, L., Mechoulamc, R., Ledermanb, V., Hiloub, M., Lencovskya, O., Betzalelb, O., Shbiroa, L., & Novacka, V. (2018). Prospective analysis of safety and efficacy of medical cannabis in large unselected population of patients with cancer. *European Journal of Internal Medicine, 49*(1), 37–43.

Barbanoj, M., Riba, J., Clos, S., Giménez, S., Grasa, E., & Romero, S. (2008). Daytime ayahuasca administration modulates REM and slow-wave sleep in healthy volunteers. *Psychopharmacology, 196*(2), 315–326.

Barker, K., & Hunjadi, D. (2008). Meet Narcan. The amazing drug that helps save overdose patients. *Journal of Emergency Medical Services, 33*(8), 72–76.

Barkin, R., Barkin, S., & Barkin, D. (2006). Propoxyphene (dextropropoxyphene): A critical review of a weak opioid analgesic that should remain in antiquity. *American Journal of Therapeutics, 13*(6), 534–542.

Barnes, M., & Barnes, J. (2016). *Cannabis: The evidence for medical use.* Newcastle upon Tyne: Northumberland, Tyne & Wear NHS Foundation Trust.

Barr, A., Panenka, W., MacEwan, G., Thornton, A., Lang, D., Honer, W., & Lecomtie, T. (2006). The need for speed: An update on methamphetamine addiction. *Journal of Psychiatry and Neuroscience, 31*(5), 301–313.

Barr, H., & Streissguth, A. (1991). Caffeine use during pregnancy and child outcome: A 7-year prospective study. *Neurotoxicology and Teratology, 13*(4), 441–448.

Barson, J., & Leibowitz, S. (2016). Hypothalamic neuropeptide signaling in alcohol addiction. *Progress in Neuro-Psychopharmacology & Biological Psychiatry, 65*, 321–329.

Bart, G., & Walsh, S. L. (2013). Methadone pharmacodynamics and pharmacokinetics. In R. A. Cruciani & H. Knotkova (Eds.), *Handbook of methadone prescribing and buprenorphine therapy* (pp. 59–72). New York: Springer.

Bartels, C., Wagner, M., Wolfsgruber, S., Ehrenreich, H., & Schneider, A. (2018). Impact of SSRI therapy on risk of conversion from mild cognitive impairment to Alzheimer's dementia in individuals with previous depression. *American Journal of Psychiatry, 175*(3), 232–241.

Bassett, J., Gore, J., Kwan, L., Ritch, C., Barocas, D., Penson, D., McCarthy, W., & Saigal, C. (2014). Knowledge of the harms of tobacco use among patients with bladder cancer. *Cancer, 120*(24), 3914–3922.

Baumann, M., Partilla, J., Lehner, K., Thorndike, E., Hoffman, A., Holy, M., Rothman, R., Goldberg, S., Lupica, C., Sittle, H., Brandt, S., Talla, S., Cozzi, N., & Schindler, C. (2012). Powerful cocaine-like actions of 3,4-methylenedioxypyrovalerone (MDPV), a principal constituent of psychoactive "bath salts" products. *Neuropsychopharmacology, 38*(6), 552–562.

Bazil, C. (2003). Effects of antiepileptic drugs on sleep structure. *CNS Drugs, 17*(10), 719–728.

Beaulieu, J., Marion, S., Rodriguiz, R., Medvedev, I., Sotnikova, T., Ghisi, V., Wetsel, W., Lefkowitz, R., Gainetdinov, R., & Caron, M. (2008). A beta-arrestin 2 signaling complex mediates lithium action on behavior. *Cell, 132*(1), 125–136.

Becker-Krail, D., & McClung, C. (2016). Implications of circadian rhythm and stress in addiction vulnerability. *F1000Research, 5*, 59. https://doi.org/10.12688/f1000research.7608.1

Bell, S., Daskalopoulou, M., Rapsomaniki, E., George, J., Britton, A., Bobak, M., Casas, J., Dale, C., Denaxas, S., Shah, A., & Hemingway, H. (2017). Association between clinically recorded alcohol consumption and initial presentation of 12 cardiovascular diseases: Population based cohort study using linked health records. *British Medical Journal, 356*(j909). https://doi.org/10.1136/bmj.j909

Bellone, C., & Gardoni, F. (2015). Modulation of the glutamatergic transmission by dopamine: A focus on Parkinson, Huntington and addiction diseases. *Frontiers in Cellular Neuroscience, 9*, 1–25. doi: 10.3389/fncel.2015.00025

Bents, R., Tokish, J., & Goldberg, L. (2004). Ephedrine, pseudoephedrine, and amphetamine prevalence in college hockey players: Most report performance-enhancing use. *The Physician and Sports Medicine, 32*(9), 30–34.

Berg, B., Pettinati, H., & Volpicelli, B. (1996). A risk-benefit assessment of naltrexone in the treatment of alcohol dependence. *Drug Safety, 15*(4), 274–282.

Bergen-Cico, D., & Macclurg, K. (2016). Kratom (*Mitragyna speciosa*) use, addiction, potential, and legal status. In V. Preedy (Ed.), *Neuropathology of drug addictions and substance misuse: General processes and mechanisms, prescription medications, caffeine and areca, polydrug misuse, emerging addictions and non-drug addictions* (Vol. 3) (pp. 903–911). Cambridge: Academic Press.

Bernstein, E., & Diskant, B. (1982). Phenylpropanolamine: A potentially hazardous drug. *Annals of Emergency Medicine, 11*(6), 311–315.

Berrettini, W., & Lerman, C. (2005). Pharmacotherapy and pharmacogenetics of nicotine dependence. *American Journal of Psychiatry, 162*(8), 1441–1451.

Berteotti, C., Cerri, M., Luppi, M., Silvani, A., & Amici, R. (2015). An overview of sleep physiology and sleep regulation. In A. Guglietta (Ed.), *Drug treatment of sleep disorders* (pp. 3–24). New York: Springer.

Beshears, E., Yeh, S., & Young, N. K. (2005). *Understanding substance abuse and facilitating recovery: A guide for child welfare workers.* Rockville: United States Department of Health and Human Services, Substance Abuse and Mental Health Services Administration.

Bhattacharyya, S., Wilson, R., Appiah-Kusi, E., O'Neill, A., Brammer, M., Perez, J., Murray, R., Allen, P., Bossong, M., & McGuire, P. (2018). Effect of cannabidiol on medial temporal, midbrain, and striatal dysfunction in people at clinical high risk of psychosis: A randomized clinical trial. *Journal of the American Medical Association: Psychiatry.* doi: 10.1001/jamapsychiatry.2018.2309

Biancofiore, G. (2006). Oxycodone controlled release in cancer pain management. *Therapeutics and Clinical Risk Management, 2*(3), 229–234.

Bill C-2: An Act to amend the Controlled Drugs and Substances Act. (2015). Assented to June 18, 2015, 41st Parliament, 2nd session. Retrieved from: the Parliament of Canada website: https://www.parl.ca/Content/Bills/412/Government/C-2/C-2_4/C-2_4.PDF

Billard, M. (1987). Lithium carbonate: Effects on sleep patterns of normal and depressed subjects and its use in sleep-wake pathology. *Pharmacopsychiatry, 20*(5), 195–196.

Bird, S., McAuley, A., Perry, S., & Hunter, C. (2016). Effectiveness of Scotland's national naloxone programme for reducing opioid-related deaths: A before (2006–10) versus after (2011–13) comparison. *Addiction, 111*(5), 883–891.

Birmes, P., Coppin, D., Schmitt, L., & Lauque, D. (2003). Serotonin syndrome: A brief review. *Canadian Medical Association Journal, 168*(11), 1439–1442.

Birnberg, C., & Abitbol, M. (1958). Weight control during pregnancy: A new anorexiant, phenmetrazine hydrochloride. *Obstetrics and Gynecology, 11*(4), 463–467.

Bloomfield, M., Ashok, A., Volkow, N., & Howes, O. (2016). The effects of delta-9-tetraydrocannabinol on the dopamine system. *Nature, 539,* 369–377.

Bogenschutz, M., Forcehimes, A., Pommy, J., Wilcox, C., Barbosa, P., & Strassman, R. (2015). Psilocybin-assisted treatment for alcohol dependence: A proof-of-concept study. *Journal of Psychopharmacology, 29*(3), 289–299.

Bohnert, A., Logan, J., Ganoczy, D., & Dowell, D. (2016). A detailed exploration into the association of prescribed opioid dosage and overdose deaths among patients with chronic pain. *Medical Care, 54*(5), 435–441.

Bonar, E., Cranford, J., Arterberry, J., Walton, M., Bohnert, K., & Ilgen, M. (2019). Driving under the influence of cannabis among medical cannabis patients with chronic pain. *Drug and Alcohol Dependence.* https://doi.org/10.1016/j.drugalcdep.2018.11.016

Bonnet., U., & Preuss, U. (2017). The cannabis withdrawal syndrome: Current insights. *Substance Abuse and Rehabilitation, 8*(1), 9–37.

Borota, D., Murray, E., Keceli, G., Chang, A., Watabe, J., Ly, M., Toscano, J., & Yassa, M. (2014). Post-study caffeine administration enhances memory consolidation in humans. *Nature Neuroscience, 17*(2), 201–203.

Boukhris, T., Sheehy, O., Mottron, L., & Bérard, A. (2016). Antidepressant use during pregnancy and the risk of autism spectrum disorder in children. *Journal of the American Medical Association: Pediatrics, 170*(2), 117–124.

Bourque, J., Afzali, M., & Conrod, P. (2018). Association of cannabis use with adolescent psychotic symptoms. *Journal of the American Medical Association: Psychiatry, 75*(8), 864–866.

Bowen., S. (2011). Two serious and challenging medical complications associated with volatile substance misuse: Sudden sniffing death and fetal solvent syndrome. *Substance Use & Misuse, 46*(sup1), 68–72.

Boyer, E., & Shannon, M. (2005). The serotonin syndrome. *New England Journal of Medicine, 352,* 1112–1120.

Bozarth, M., & Wise, R. (1985). Toxicity associated with long-term intravenous heroin and cocaine self-administration in the rat. *Journal of the American Medical Association*, *254*(1), 81–83.

Brancato, A., Castelli, V., Cavallaro, A., Lavanco, G., Plescia, F., & Cannizzaro, C. (2018). Pre-conceptional and peri-gestational maternal binge alcohol drinking produces inheritance of mood disturbances and alcohol vulnerability in the adolescent offspring. *Frontiers in Psychiatry*. https://doi.org/10.3389/fpsyt.2018.00150

Brands, B., Sproule, B., & Marshman, J. (1998). *Drugs and drug abuse* (3rd ed.). Toronto: Addiction Research Foundation.

Branstetter, S., Horton, W., Mercincavage, M., & Buxton, O. (2016). Severity of nicotine addiction and disruptions in sleep mediated by early awakenings. *Nicotine & Tobacco Research*, *18*(12), 2252–2259.

Breeding, J., & Baughman, F. (2003). Informed consent and the psychiatric drugging of children. *Journal of Humanistic Psychology*, *43*(1), 50–64.

Brennan, R., & Van Hout, M. (2014). Gamma-Hydroxybutyrate (GHB): A scoping review of pharmacology, toxicology, motives for use, and user groups. *Journal of Psychoactive Drugs*, *46*(3), 243–251.

Brent, R., Christian, M., & Diener, R. (2011). Evaluation of the reproductive and developmental risks of caffeine. *Birth Defects Research (Part B), 92*, 152–187.

Brick, J., & Erickson, C. (2013). *Drugs, the brain and behavior.* New York: Routledge.

Bromley, S., Choi, M., & Faruqui, S. (2015). First episode psychosis: An information guide. Toronto: Centre for Addiction and Mental Health.

Brown, A., Gyllenberg, D., Malm, H., McKeague, I., Hinkka-Yli-Salomäki, S., Artama, M., Gissler, M., Cheslack-Postava, K., Weissman, M., Gingrich, J., & Sourander, A. (2016). Association of selective serotonin reuptake inhibitor exposure during pregnancy with speech, scholastic, and motor disorders in offspring. *Journal of the American Medical Association: Psychiatry, 73*(11), 1163–1170.

Brown, R., & Trickey, H. (2018). *Devising and communicating public health alcohol guidance for expectant and new mothers: A scoping report.* London: Alcohol Research UK.

Brown, T., & Alper, K. (2018): Treatment of opioid use disorder with ibogaine: Detoxification and drug use outcomes. *American Journal of Drug and Alcohol Abuse, 44*(1), 24–36.

Burcu, M., Zito, J., Safer, D., Magder, L., dosReis, S., Shaya, F., & Rosenthal, G. (2017). Association of antidepressant medications with incident Type 2 diabetes among Medicaid-insured youths. *Journal of the American Medical Association: Pediatrics, 171*(12), 1200–1207.

Burns, L., Mattick, R., & Cooke, M. (2006). The use of record linkage to examine illicit drug use in pregnancy. *Addiction, 101*(6), 873–882.

Burton, R., & Sheron, N. (2018). No level of alcohol consumption improves health. *Lancet, 392*(10152), 987–988.

Busquets-Garcia, A., Gomis-Gonzajlez, M., Salgado-Mendialda, V., Galera-Lapez, L., Puighermanal, E., Martan-Garcia, E., Maldonado, R., & Ozaita, A. (2017). Hippocampal protein kinase C signaling mediates the short-term memory impairment induced by delta 9-tetrahydrocannabinol. *Neuropsychopharmacology, 43,* 1021–1031.

Busse, J. (2017). *The 2017 Canadian guideline for opioids for chronic non-cancer pain.* Retrieved from: http://nationalpaincentre.mcmaster.ca/documents/Opioid%20GL%20for%20CMAJ_01may2017.pdf

Büttner, A. (2011). Review: The neuropathology of drug abuse. *Neuropathology and Applied Neurobiology, 37*(2), 118–134.

Cadet, J., Bisagno, V., & Milroy, C. (2014). Neuropathology of substance use disorders. *Acta Neuropathology, 127*(1), 91–107.

Caldicott, D., Edwards, N., Kruys, A., Kirkbride, K., Sims, D., Byard, R., Prior, M., & Irvine, R. (2003). Dancing with "death": P-methoxyamphetamine overdose and its acute management. *Journal or Toxicology and Clinical Toxicology, 41*(2), 143–154.

Calipari, E., Ferris, M., Melchior, J., Bermejo, K., Salahpour, A., Roberts, D., & Jones, S. (2012). Methylphenidate and cocaine self-administration produce distinct dopamine terminal alterations. *Addiction Biology, 19*(2), 145–155.

Cameron, K., Kolanos, R., Verkariva, R., Felice, L., & Glennon, R. (2013). Mephedrone and methylenedioxypyrovalerone (MDPV), major constituents of "bath salts," produce opposite effects at the human dopamine transporter. *Psychopharmacology, 227*(3), 493–499.

Campagne, D. (2007). Fact: Antidepressants and anxiolytics are not safe during pregnancy. *European Journal of Obstetrics & Gynecology and Reproductive Biology, 135*(2), 145–148.

Canadian Cancer Society. (1987). *Don't get pinched.* Ottawa: Author.

Canadian Centre for Occupational Health and Safety. (2018). *What is a LD_{50} and LC_{50}?* Retrieved from: https://www.ccohs.ca/oshanswers/chemicals/ld50.html

Canadian Centre on Substance Abuse. (2006). *Youth volatile solvent abuse.* Ottawa: Author.

Canadian Centre on Substance Abuse. (2012). *Bath salts.* Ottawa: Author.

Canadian Centre on Substance Abuse. (2016). *Novel synthetic opioids in counterfeit pharmaceuticals and other illicit street drugs.* Ottawa: Author.

Canadian Institute for Health Information. (2017). *Alcohol harm in Canada: Examining hospitalizations entirely caused by alcohol and strategies to reduce alcohol harm.* Ottawa: Author.

Canadian Pharmacists Association. (2017). *Compendium of pharmaceuticals and specialities (CPS).* Toronto: Author.

Canadian Substance Use Costs and Harms Scientific Working Group. (2018). *Canadian substance use costs and harms (2007–2014).* Ottawa: Canadian Centre on Substance Use and Addiction.

Cantu, C., Arauz, A., Murillo-Bonilla, L., Lopez, M., & Barinagarrementeria, F. (2003). Stroke associated with sympathomimetics contained in over-the-counter cough and cold drugs. *Stroke, 34*(7), 1667–1672.

Canuso, C., Singh, J., Fedgchin, M., Alphs, L., Lane, R., Lim, P., Pinter, C., Hough, D., Sanacora, G., Manji, H., & Drevets, W. (2018). Efficacy and safety of intranasal esketamine for the rapid reduction of symptoms of depression and suicidality in patients at imminent risk for suicide: Results of a double-blind, randomized, placebo-controlled study. *American Journal of Psychiatry, 175*(7), 620–630.

Carbonaro, T., Bradstreet, M., Barrett, F., MacLean, K., Jesse, R., Johnson, M., & Griffiths, R. (2016). Survey study of challenging experiences after ingesting psilocybin mushrooms: Acute and enduring positive and negative consequences. *Journal of Psychopharmacology*, *30*(12), 1268–1278.

Carelli, R. (2002). The nucleus accumbens and reward: Neurophysiologyical investigations in behaving animals. *Behavioral and Cognitive Neuroscience Review*, *1*(4), 281–296.

Carelli, R., & Deadwyler, S. (1994). A comparision of nucleus accumbens neuronal firing patterns during cocaine self-administration and water reinforcement in rats. *The Journal of Neruroscience*, *14*(12), 7735–7746.

Carelli, R., Ijames, S., & Crumling, A. (2000). Evidence that separate neural circuits in the nucleus accumbens encode cocaine versus "natural" (water and food) reward. *The Journal of Neruroscience*, *20*(11), 4355–4266.

Carhart-Harris, R., Bolstridge, M., Rucker, J., Day, C., Erritzoe, D., Kaelen, M., & Nutt, D. (2016). Psilocybin with psychological support for treatment-resistant depression: An open-label feasibility study. *Lancet Psychiatry*, *7*, 619–627.

Carhart-Harris, R., Erritzoe, D., Williams, T., Stone, J., Reed, L., Colasanti, A., Tyacke, R., Leech, R., Malizia, A., Murphy, K., Hobden, P., Evans, J., Feilding, A., Wise, R., & Nutt, D. (2012). Neural correlates of the psychedelic state as determined by fMRI studies with psilocybin. *Proceedings of the National Academy of Sciences, 109*(6), 2138–2143.

Carhart-Harris, R., Kaelen, M., Bolstridge, M., Williams, T., Williams, L., Underwood, R., Fielding, A., & Nutt, D. (2016). The paradoxical psychological effects of lysergic acid diethylamide (LSD). *Psychological Medicine, 46*(7), 1379–1390.

Carhart-Harris, R., Muthukumaraswamy, S., Roseman, L., Kaelen, M., Droog, W., & Nutt, D. (2016). Neural correlates of the LSD experience revealed by multimodal neuroimaging. *Proceedings of the National Academy of Sciences, 113*(17), 4853–4858.

Carhart-Harris, R., & Nutt, D. (2017). Serotonin and brain function: A tale of two receptors. *Journal of Psychopharmacology, 31*(9), 1091–1120.

Carr, G. (2011). Alcoholism: A modern look at an ancient illness. *Primary Care: Clinics in Office Practice, 38*(1), 9–21.

Carr, G., Maltese, F., Sibley, D., Weinberger, D., & Papaleo, F. (2017). The dopamine D_5 receptor is involved in working memory. *Frontiers in Pharmacology, 8*. https://doi.org/10.3389/fphar.2017.00666

Carroll, M. (1985). *PCP: The dangerous angel.* New York: Chelsea House Publishers.

Carroll, M. (1990). PCP and hallucinogens. *Advances in alcohol and substance abuse, 9*(1/2), 167–190.

Carroll, M., & Gallo, G. (1985). *Quaaludes.* New York: Chelsea House Publishers.

Carter, R., Wainwright, H., Molteno, C., Georgieff, M., Dodge, N., Warton, F., Meintjes, E., Jacobson, J., & Jacobson, S. (2016). Alcohol, methamphetamine, and marijuana exposure have distinct effects on the human placenta. *Alcoholism: Clinical and Experimental Research, 40*(4), 753–764.

Carvalho, F. (2003). The toxicological potential of khat. *Journal of Ethnopharmacology, 87*(1), 1–2.

Cascade, E., & Kalali, A. (2008). Use of benzodiazepines in the treatment of anxiety. *Psychiatry, 5*(9), 21–22.

Catino, A., Misino, A., Logroscino, A., Montagna, E., & Galetta, D. (2017). Cancer, heart diseases, and common risk factors: Smoke. In C. Lestuzzi, S. Oliva, & F. Ferraù (Eds.), *Manual of Cardio-oncology* (pp. 15–28). New York: Springer.

Caulfield, A. (2015). Do the risks of khat-induced dependence and psychosis warrant the 2014 UK ban? *Drug Science, Policy and Law, 2*, 1–8.

Caviness, C., & Anderson, B. (2018). Impact of nicotine and other stimulants on sleep in young adults. *Journal of Addiction Medicine.* doi:10.1097/ADM.0000000000000481

Center for Behavioral Health Statistics and Quality. (2014, March 13). 1 in 10 energy drink–related emergency department visits result in hospitalization. *The DAWN Report.* Rockville: Substance Abuse and Mental Health Services Administration.

Centers for Disease Control and Prevention. (2008). Update on overall prevalence of major birth defects—Atlanta, Georgia, 1978–2005. *Morbidity and Mortality Weekly Report, 57*, 1–5.

Centers for Disease Control and Prevention. (2018). *Fetal alcohol spectrum disorders.* Retrieved from: https://www.cdc.gov/ncbddd/fasd/facts.html

Centre for Addiction and Mental Health. (2006). *About cocaine.* Toronto: Author.

Centre for Addiction and Mental Health. (2012). Benzodiazepines: Psychiatric medication. Retrieved from: http://www.camh.ca/en/hospital/health_information /a_z_mental_health_and_addiction_information/Benzodiazepines/Pages/default.aspx

Chan, J., Trinder, J., Andrews, H., Colrain, I., & Nichols, C. (2013). The acute effects of alcohol on sleep architecture in late adolescence. *Alcoholism: Clinical and Experimental Research, 37*(10), 1720–1728.

Chang, Y., Cho, Y., Kim, Y., Sung, E., Ahn, J., Jung, H., Yun, K., Shin, H., & Ryu, S. (2018). Non-heavy drinking and worsening of non-invasive fibrosis markers in nonalcoholic fatty liver disease: A cohort study. *Hepatology*. https://doi.org/10.1002/hep.30170

Chao, M., Bi, K., Zhang, M., Su, D., Fan, X., Ji, W., & Chen, X. (2010). Toxicology effects of morning glory seed in rat: A metabonomic method for profiling of urine metabolic changes. *Journal of Ethnopharmacology, 130*(1), 134–142.

Chasnoff, I., Burns, K., Burns, W., & Schnoll, S. (1986). Prenatal drug exposure: Effects on neonatal and infant growth and development. *Neurobehavioral Toxicology and Teratology, 8*(4), 357–362.

Cheng, H., Kellar, D., Lake, A., Finn, P., Rebec, G., Dharmadhikari, S., Dydak, U., & Newman, S. (2018). Effects of alcohol cues on MRS glutamate levels in the anterior cingulate. *Alcohol and Alcoholism, 53*(1), 209–215.

Chenier, N. (2001). *Substance abuse and public policy.* Ottawa: Government of Canada.

Cheung, J., Mann, R., Ialomiteanu, A., Stodutl, G., Chan, V., Ala-Leppilampi, K., & Rehm, J. (2010). Anxiety and mood disorders and cannabis use. *The American Journal of Drug and Alcohol Abuse, 36*(2), 118–122.

Chief Public Health Officer of Canada. (2016). *Alcohol consumption in Canada.* Ottawa: Public Health Agency of Canada.

Chikahisa, S., Kodama, T., Soya, A., Sagawa, Y., Ishimaru, Y., Hiroyoshi, S., & Seiji, N. (2013). Histamine from brain resident MAST cells promotes wakefulness and modulates behavioral states. *PLoS ONE 8*(10), e78434. doi:10.1371/journal.pone.0078434

Chiu, J., & Chokka, P. (2011). Prevalence of bipolar disorder symptoms in primary care: A Canadian study. *Canadian Family Physician, 57*(2), e58–e67.

Choi, D., Choi, S., & Park, S. (2018). Effect of smoking cessation on the risk of dementia: A longitudinal study. *Annals of Clinical and Transnational Neurology, 5*(10), 1192–1199.

Chomchai, C., Na Manorom, N., Watanarungsan, P., Yossuck, P., & Chomchai, S. (2004). Methamphetamine abuse during pregnancy and its health impact on neonates born at Siriraj Hospital, Bangkok, Thailand. *Southeast Asian Journal of Tropical Medicine and Public Health, 35*(1), 228–231.

Chorniy, A., & Kitahima, L. (2016). Sex, drugs, and ADHD: The effects of ADHD pharmacological treatment on teens' risky behaviors. *Labour Economics, 43(1),* 87–105.

Chow, A., Benninger, M., Brook, I., Brozek, J., Goldstein, E., Hicks, L., Pankey, G., Seleznick, M., Volturo, G., Wald, E., & File, T. (2012). IDSA clinical practice guideline for acute bacterial rhinosinusitis in children and adults. *Clinical Infectious Diseases, 54*(8), e72–e112.

Chun-Fai-Chan, B., Koren, G., Fayez, I., Kalra, S., Voyer-Lavigne, S., Boshier, A., Shakir, S., & Einarson, A. (2005). Pregnancy outcome of women exposed to bupropion during pregnancy: A prospective comparative study. *American Journal of Obstetrics and Gynecology, 192*(3), 932–936.

Church, D., & Church, M. (2011). Pharmacology of antihistamines. *World Allergy Organization Journal, 4*(S3), S22–S27.

Church, M., Maurer, M., Simons, F., Bindslev-Jensen, C., van Cauwenberge, P., Bousquet, J., Holgate, S., & Zuberbier, T. (2010). Risk of first-generation H_1-antihistamines: A GA^2LEN position paper. *Allergy, 65*(4),459–466.

Ciccarone, D. (2011). Stimulant abuse: Pharmacology, cocaine, methamphetamine, treatment, attempts at pharmacotherapy. *Primary Care, 38*(1), 41–58.

Ciechanowski, P. (2012). Exposure assessment report: Risks to toluene exposure and adverse health outcomes. Retrieved from: http://ssrn.com/abstract=2312788.

Cipriani, A., Furukawa, T., Salanti, G., Chaimani, A., Atkinson, L., Ogawa, Y., Leucht, S., Ruhe, H., Turner, E., Higgins, J., Egger, M., Takeshima, N., Hayasaka, Y., Imai, H., Shinohara, K., Tajika, A., Ioannidis, J., & Geddes, J. (2018). Comparative efficacy and acceptability of 21 antidepressant drugs for the acute treatment of adults with major depressive disorder: A systematic review and network meta-analysis. *Lancet, 391*(10128), 1357–1366.

Ciraulo, D., & Oldham, M. (2014). Sedative-hypnotics. In B. Mardas and M. Kuhar (Eds.), The effects of drug abuse on the human nervous system (pp. 492–532). Waltham: Academic Press.

Cohen, J., Hernández-Díaz, S., Bateman, B., Park, Y., Desai, R., Gray, K., Patorno, E., Mogun, H., & Huybrechts, K., (2017). Placental complications associated with psychostimulant use in pregnancy. *Obstetrics & Gynecology, 130*(6), 1192–1201.

Cohrs, S. (2008). Sleep disturbances in patients with schizophrenia. *CNS Drugs, 22*(11), 939–962.

Cole, J., Mocell, J., Haight, B., Cosmatos, I., Stoler, J., & Walker, A. (2006). Bupropion in pregnancy and the prevalence of congenital malformations. *Pharmacoepidemilogy and Drug Safety, 16*(5), 474–484.

Colon-Perez, L., Tran, K., Thompson, K., Pace, M., Blum, K., Goldberger, B., Gold, M., Bruijnzeel, A., Setlow, B., & Febo, M. (2016). The psychoactive designer drug and bath salt constituent MDPV causes widespread disruption of brain functional connectivity. *Neuropsychopharmacology, 41*(9), 2352–2365.

Colzato, L., Ruiz, M., van den Wildenberg, W., & Hommel, B. (2011). Khat use is associated with impaired working memory and cognitive flexibility. *PLoS ONE 6*(6), e20602. doi:10.1371/journal.pone.0020602

Conference Board of Canada. (2017). *The costs of tobacco use in Canada, 2012.* Ottawa: Author.

Connor, J. (2017). Alcohol consumption as a cause of cancer. *Addiction, 112*(2), 222–228.

Conroy, D., Kurth, M., Strong, D., Brower, K., & Stein, M. (2016). Marijuana use patterns and sleep among community-based young adults. *Journal of Addictive Diseases, 35*(2), 135–143.

Contet, C., Kieffer, B., & Befort, K. (2004). Mu opioid receptor: A gateway to drug addiction. *Current Opinions in Neurobiology, 14*(3), 370–378.

Cooper, W., Habel, L., Sox, C., Chan, K., Arbogast, P., Cheetham, T., Murray, K., Quinn, V., Stein, C., Callahan, S., Fireman, B., Fish, F., Kirshner, H., O'Duffy, A., Connell, F., & Ray, W. (2011). ADHD drugs and serious cardiovascular events in children and young adults. *New England Journal of Medicine, 365*(20), 1896–1904.

Cordier, S., Garlantézec, R., Labat, L., Rouget, F., Monfort, C., Bonvallot, N., Roig, B., Pulkkinen, J., Chevrier, C. & Multigner, L. (2012). Exposure during pregnancy to glycol ethers and chlorinated solvents and the risk of congenital malformations. *Epidemiology, 23*(6), 806–812.

Costa, C., & Griew, A. (1982). Effects of betel chewing on pregnancy outcome. *ANZOG, 22*(1), 22–24.

Crain, T., & Barber, L. (2018). *Sick, unsafe, and unproductive: Poor employee sleep is bad for business.* Bowling Green: Society for Industrial and Organizational Psychology.

Crawford, J., & Lewis, M. (1986). Nitrous oxide in early human pregnancy. *Anaesthesia, 41*(9), 900–905.

Croche, S., Alonso, S., & Loscertales, A. (2011). Accidental cannabis poisoning in children: Report of four cases in a tertiary care center from southern Spain. *Archivos Argentinos de Pediatria, 109*(1), 4–7.

Cruickshank, C., & Dyer, K. (2009). A review of the clinical pharmacology of methamphetamine. *Addiction, 104*(7), 1085–1099.

Crume, T., Juhl, A., Brooks-Russell, A., Hall, K., Wymore, E., & Borgelt, L. (2018). Cannabis use during the perinatal period in a state with legalized recreational and medical marijuana: The association between maternal characteristics, breastfeeding patterns, and neonatal outcomes. *The Journal of Pediatrics, 197*(1), 90–96.

Cruz, M. (2011). Lurasidone HCl (Latuda), an oral, once-daily atypical antipsychotic agent for the treatment of patients with schizophrenia. *Pharmacy and Therapeutics, 36*(8), 489–492.

Cservenka, A., & Brumback, T. (2017). The burden of binge and heavy drinking on the brain: Effects on adolescent and young adult neural structure and function. *Frontiers of Psychology, 8*(1111). doi:10.3389/fpsyg.2017.01111

Csiernik, R. (2016). *Substance use and abuse: Everything matters* (2nd ed.). Toronto: Canadian Scholars' Press.

Csiernik, R., & Rowe, W. (2017). Creating a holistic understanding of addiction. In R. Csiernik & W. S. Rowe (Eds.), *Responding to the oppression of addiction: Canadian social work perspectives* (3rd ed.) (pp. 7–26). Toronto: Canadian Scholars' Press.

Cuijpers, P., van Straten, A., Schuurmans, J., Oppen, P., Hoolon, S., & Andersson, G. (2010). Psychotherapy for chronic major depression and dysthymia: A meta-analysis. *Clinical Psychology Review, 30*(1), 51–62.

Curran, V., Freeman, T., Mokrysz, C., Lewis, D., Morgan, C., & Parsons, L. (2016). Keep off the grass? Cannabis, cognition and addiction. *Nature Reviews: Neuroscience, 17,* 293–306.

Currie, C. (2013). Epidemiology of adolescent Salvia divinorum use in Canada. *Drug and alcohol dependency, 128*(1–2), 166–170.

Cuttlera, C., Spradlina, A., & McLaughlin, R. (2018). A naturalistic examination of the perceived effects of cannabis on negative affect. *Journal of Affective Disorders, 235,* 198–205.

Danforth, A., Grob, C., Struble, C., Feduccia, A., Walker, N., Jerome, L., Yazar-Klosinski, B., & Emerson, A. (2018). Reduction in social anxiety after MDMA-assisted psychotherapy with autistic adults: A randomized, double-blind, placebo-controlled pilot study. *Psychopharmacology, 235*(11), 3137–3148.

Danforth, A., Struble, C., Yazar-Klosinski, B., & Grob, C. (2015). MDMA-assisted therapy: A new treatment model for social anxiety in autistic adults. *Progress in Neuropsychopharmacology and Biological Psychiatry, 64*(3), 237–249.

Daniali, S., Madjd, Z., Shahbazi, A., Niknazar, S., & Shahbazzadeh, D. (2013). Chronic Ritalin administration during adulthood increases serotonin pool in rat medial frontal cortex. *Iranian Biomedical Journal, 17*(3), 134–139.

Daniel, M., Martin, A., & Carter, J. (1992). Opiate receptor blockade by naltrexone and mood state after acute physical activity. *British Journal of Sports Medicine 26*(2), 111–115.

De Sutter, A., van Driel, M., Kumar, A., Lesslar, O., & Skrt, A. (2012). Oral antihistamine-decongestant-analgesic combinations for the common cold. *Cochrane Database of Systematic Reviews, 2*. Art. No.: CD004976. doi:10.1002/14651858.CD004976.pub3

de Vocht, F., Sobala, W., Wilczynska, U., Kromhout, H., Szeszenia-Dabrowska, N., & Peplonska, B. (2009). Cancer mortality and occupational exposure to aromatic amines and inhalable aerosols in rubber tire manufacturing in Poland. *Cancer Epidemiology, 33*(2), 94–102.

Degenhardt, L., Charlson, F., Mathers, B., Hall, W., Flaxman, A., Johns, N., & Vos, T. (2014). The global epidemiology and burden of opioid dependence: Results from the global burden of disease 2010 study. *Addiction, 109*(8), 1320–1333.

den Hollander, B., Schouw, M., Groot, P., Huisman, H., Caan, M., Barkhof, F., & Liesbeth, R. (2012). Preliminary evidence of hippocampal damage in chronic users of ecstasy. *Journal of Neurology, Neurosurgery and Psychiatry, 83*(1), 83–85.

deShazo, R., Parker, S., Williams, D., Ingram, J., Elsohly, M., Rodenmeyer, K., & McCullouch, K. (2018). Marijuana's effects on brain structure and function: What do we know and what should we do? A brief review and commentary. *The American Journal of Medicine*. https://doi.org/10.1016/j.amjmed.2018.09.006

Desmond, M., Schwanecke, R., Wilson, G., Yasunaga, S., & Burgdorff, I. (1972). Maternal barbiturate utilization withdrawal symptomatology. *The Journal of Pediatrics, 80*(2), 190–197.

Devilbiss, D., & Berridge, C. (2008). Cognition-enhancing doses of methylphenidate preferentially increase prefrontal cortex neuronal responsiveness. *Biological Psychiatry, 64*(7), 626–635.

Dhaifalaha, I., & Šantavýb, J. (2004). Khat habit and its health effect: A natural amphetamine. *Biomedical Papers, 148*(1), 11–15.

Dhalla, I., Mamdani, M., Sivilotti, M., Kopp, A., Qureshi, O., & Juurlink, D. (2009). Prescribing of opioid analgesics and related mortality before and after the introduction of long-acting oxycodone. *Canadian Medical Association Journal, 181*(12): 891–896.

Diav-Citrin, O., Shechtman, S., Aharonovich, A., Moerman, L., Aron, J., Wajnberg, R., & Ornov, A. (2003). Pregnancy outcome after gestational exposure to loratadine or antihistamines: A prospective controlled cohort study. *Journal of Allergy and Clinical Immunology, 111*(6), 1239–1243.

Diekelmann, S., & Born, J. (2010). The memory function of sleep. *Nature Reviews: Neuroscience, 11*(1), 114–126.

Dimsdale, J., Norman, D., DeJardin, D., & Wallace, M. (2007). The effect of opioids on sleep architecture. *Journal of Clinical Sleep Medicine, 3*(1), 33–36.

Ding, Y., Chi, H., Grady, D., Morishima, A., Kidd, J., Kidd, K., Flodman, P., Spence, M., Schuck, S., Swanson, J., Zhang, Y., & Moyzis, R. (2002). Evidence of positive selection acting at the human dopamine receptor D4 gene locus.

Proceedings of the National Academy of Sciences of the United States of America, 99(1), 309–314.

Dingwall, K., Maruff, P., Fredrickson, A., & Cairney, S. (2011). Cognitive recovery during and after treatment for volatile solvent abuse. *Drug and Alcohol Dependence, 118*(1), 180–185.

Diver, W., Jacobs., E., & Gapstur, S. (2018). Secondhand smoke exposure in childhood and adulthood in relation to adult mortality among never smokers. *American Journal of Preventive Medicine, 55*(3), 345–352.

Doblin, S. (2002). A clinical plan for MDMA (ecstasy) in the treatment of post-traumatic stress disorder (PTSD): Partnering with the FDA. *Journal of Psychoactive Drugs, 34*(2), 185–194.

Dobrescu, A., Bhandari, A., Sutherland, G., & Dinh, T. (2017). *The costs of tobacco use in Canada, 2012.* Ottawa: The Conference Board of Canada.

Dorland, W. A. N. (2012). *Dorland's illustrated medical dictionary.* New York: Elsevier.

dos Santos, R. (2013). Safety and side effects of ayahuasca in humans—an overview focusing on developmental toxicology. *Journal of Psychoactive Drugs, 45*(1), 68–78.

dos Santos, R., Bouso, J., & Hallak, J. (2017). Ayahuasca, dimethyltryptamine, and psychosis: A systematic review of human studies. *Therapeutic Advances in Psychopharmacology, 7*(4), 141–157.

Drake, C., Roehrs, T., Shambroom, J., & Roth, T. (2013). Caffeine effects on sleep taken 0, 3, or 6 hours before going to bed. *Journal of Clinical Sleep Medicine, 9*(11), 1195–1200.

Drapeau, C., & Nadorff, M. (2017). Suicidality in sleep disorders: Prevalence, impact, and management strategies. *Nature and Science of Sleep, 9*, 213–226.

Drug Enforcement Administration. (2013). *Desomorphine.* Retreived from http://www.deadiversion.usdoj.gov/drug_chem_info/desomorphine.pdf

Duman, R., & Aghajanian, G. (2012). Synaptic dysfunction in depression: Potential therapeutic targets. *Science, 388*(6103), 68–72.

Dunleavy, D., Brezinova, V., Oswald, I., Maclean, A., & Tinker, M. (1972). Changes during weeks in effects of tricyclic drugs on the human sleeping brain. *The British Journal of Psychiatry, 120*(559), 663–672.

Dusunen, A. (2018). The effect of heroin use disorder on the sexual functions of women. *The Journal of Psychiatry and Neurological Sciences, 31*(3), 238–245.

Dziegielewski, S. (2005). *Understanding substance addictions.* Chicago: Lyceum Books.

Einarson, A., Pistelli, A., DeSantis, M., Malm, H., Paulus, W., Panchaud, A., Kennedy, D., Einarson, T., & Koren, G. (2008). Evaluation of the risk of congenital cardiovascular defects associated with use of Paroxetine during pregnancy. *American Journal of Psychiatry, 165*(6), 749–752.

El-Alfy, A., Wilson, L., ElSohly, M., & Abourashed, E. (2009). Towards a better understanding of the psychopharmacology of nutmeg: Activities in the mouse tetrad assay. *Journal of ethnopharmacology, 126*(2), 280–286.

El-Hadidy, M., & Helaly, A. (2015). Medical and psychiatric effects of long-term dependence on high dose of tramadol. *Substance Use & Misuse, 50*(5), 582–589.

Eli Lilly and Company. (2016). Strattera® (atomoxetine HCl): Warning. Retrieved from: http://www.fda.gov/ohrms/dockets/dockets/06p0209/06P-0209-EC3-Attach-1.pdf

Elikkottil, J., Gupta, P., & Gupta, K. (2009). The analgesic potential of cannabinoids. *Journal of Opioid Management, 5*(6), 341–357.

Engelhardt, H., Smits, R., Leurs, R., Haaksma, E., & de Esch, I. (2009). A new generation of anti-histamines: Histamine H_4 receptor antagonists on their way to the clinic. *Current Opinion in Drug Discovery & Development, 2009, 12*(5), 628–643.

Englund, A., Morrison, P., Nottage, J., Hague, D., Kane, F., Bonaccorso, S., Stone, J., Reichenberg, A., Brenneisen, R., Holt, D., Feilding, A., Walker, L., Murray, R., & Kapur, S. (2013). Cannabidiol inhibits THC-elicited paranoid symptoms and hippocampal-dependent memory impairment. *Journal of Psychopharmacology, 27*(1), 19–27.

Erickson, C., McLeod, R., Mingo, G., Egan, R., Pedersen, O., & Hey, J. (2001). Comparative oral and topical decongestant effects of phenylpropanolamine and d-pseudoephedrine. *American Journal of Rhinology, 15*(2), 83–90.

Eriksson, M., Jonsson, B., & Zetterstrom, R. (2000). Children of mothers abusing amphetamine: Head circumference during infancy and psychosocial development until 14 years of age. *Acta Paediatrica, 89*(12), 1474–1478.

Ersche, K., Barnes, A., Jones, P., Morein-Zamir, S., Robbins, T., & Bullmore, E. (2011). Abnormal structure of frontostriatal brain systems is associated with aspects of impulsivity and compulsivity in cocaine dependence, *Brain, 134*(7), 2013–2024.

Esbenshade, T., Browman, K., Bitner, R., Strakhova, M., Cowart, M., & Brioni, J. (2008). The histamine H3 receptor: An attractive target for the treatment of cognitive disorders. *British Journal of Pharmacology, 154*(6), 1166–1181.

Espy, K., Fang, H., Johnson, C., Stopp, C., & Wiebe, S. (2011). Prenatal tobacco exposure: Developmental outcomes in the neonatal period. *Developmental Psychology, 74*(1), 153–156.

Etemad, L., Moshiri, M., & Moallem, S. (2012). Epilepsy drugs and effects on fetal development: Potential mechanisms. *Journal of Research in Medical Sciences: The Official Journal of Isfahan University of Medical Sciences, 17*(9), 876–881.

Etienne, H., Desprez, T., Serrat, R., Bellocchio, L., Soria-Gomez, E., & Marsicano, G. (2016). A cannabinoid link between mitochondria and memory. *Nature, 539,* 555–559.

Ettensohn, M., Markey, S., & Levine, S. (2018). Considering ketamine for treatment of comorbid pain, depression, and substance use disorders. *Psychiatric Annals, 48*(4), 180–183.

European Monitoring Centre for Drugs and Addiction. (2008a). *GHB and its precursor GBL: An emerging trend case study.* Luxembourg: Office for Official Publications of the European Communities.

European Monitoring Centre for Drugs and Addiction. (2008b). *Monitoring the supply of cocaine to Europe.* Luxembourg: Office for Official Publications of the European Communities.

European Monitoring Centre for Drugs and Drug Addiction. (2009). *Preventing later substance use disorders in at-risk children and adolescents: A review of the theory and evidence base of indicated prevention.* Luxembourg: Office for Official Publications of the European Communities.

European Monitoring Centre for Drugs and Drug Addiction. (2011). *Salvia divinorium.* Retrieved from: http://www.emcdda.europa.eu/publications/drug-profiles/salvia

European Monitoring Centre for Drugs and Drug Addiction. (2013). *Heroin.* Retrieved from: http://www.emcdda.europa.eu/publications/drug-profiles/heroin

European Monitoring Centre for Drugs and Drug Addiction. (2015a). *Barbiturates.* Retrieved from: http://www.emcdda.europa.eu/publications/drug-profiles/barbiturates

European Monitoring Centre for Drugs and Drug Addiction. (2015b). *Benzodiazepines drug profile.* Retrieved from: http://www.emcdda.europa.eu/publications/drug-profiles/benzodiazepine

European Monitoring Centre for Drugs and Drug Addiction. (2017a). *Carfentanil.* Retrieved from: http://www.emcdda.europa.eu/system/files/publications/6502/2017.6256_EN_04-WEB.pdf

European Monitoring Centre for Drugs and Drug Addiction. (2017b). *Furanylfentanyl.* Retrieved from: http://www.emcdda.europa.eu/system/files/publications/6712/20176480_TDAK17002ENN_PDF.pdf

European Monitoring Centre for Drugs and Drug Addiction. (2018a). *4F-iBF.* Retrieved from: http://www.emcdda.europa.eu/system/files/publications/9123/Risk%20assessment%204F-iBF.pdf

European Monitoring Centre for Drugs and Addiction. (2018b). *Captagon: Understanding today's illicit market.* Retrieved from: http://www.emcdda.europa.eu/system/files/publications/9783/20184976_TDAU18002ENN_PDF.PDF

European Monitoring Centre for Drugs and Drug Addiction. (2018c). *Cyclopropylfentanyl.* Retrieved from: http://www.emcdda.europa.eu/system/files/publications/9607/Risk%20assessment%20cyclopropylfentanyl.pdf

European Monitoring Centre for Drugs and Drug Addiction. (2018d). *Methoxyacetylfentanyl.* Retrieved from: http://www.emcdda.europa.eu/system/files/publications/9606/Risk%20assessment%20methoxyacetylfentanyl.pdf

Evans, E., & Sullivan, M. (2014). Abuse and misuse of antidepressants. *Substance abuse and rehabilitation, 5(1)*, 107–120.

Everson, C. (1993). Sustained sleep deprivation impairs host defence. *American Journal of Physiology: Regulatory, Integrative and Comparative Physiology, 265*(5), R1148–R1154.

Everson, C., & Szabo, A. (2009). Recurrent restriction of sleep and inadequate recuperation induce both adaptive changes and pathological outcomes. *American Journal of Physiology: Regulatory, Integrative and Comparative Physiology, 297*(5), R1430–R1440.

Ezquerra-Romano, I., Lawn, W., Krupitsky, E., & Morgan, C. (2018). Ketamine for the treatment of addiction: Evidence and potential mechanisms. *Neuropharmacology, 142*(1), 72–82.

Fabry, D., Davila, E., Arheart, K., Serdar, B., Dietz, N., Bandiera, F., & Lee, D. J. (2010). Secondhand smoke exposure and the risk of hearing loss. *Tobacco control, 20*(1), 82–85.

Fadiman, J. (2011). *The psychedelic explorer's guide: Safe, therapeutic, and sacred journeys.* New York: Simon and Schuster.

Fagerstrom, K. (2018). A comparison of dependence across different types of nicotine containing products and coffee. *International Journal of Environmental Research and Public Health, 15*, 1609. doi:10.3390/ijerph15081609

Faraone, S., Biederman, J., Morley, C., & Spencer, T. (2008). Effects of stimulants on height and weight: A review of the literature. *Journal of the American Academy of Child and Adolescent Psychiatry, 47*(9), 994–1009.

Feduccia, A., & Mithoefer, M. (2018). MDMA-assisted psychotherapy for PTSD: Are memory reconsolidation and fear extinction underlying mechanisms? *Progress in Neuro-Psychopharmacology and Biological Psychiatry, 84*(A), 221–228.

Feinberg, I., & Campbell, I. (1993). Ketamine administration during waking increases delta EEG intensity in rat sleep. *Neuropsychopharmacology, 9*(1), 41–48.

Ferguson, D., & Boden, J. (2008). Cannabis use and later life outcome. *Addiction, 103*(6), 969–976.

Fergusson, D., Horwood, L., & Northstone, K. (2002). Maternal use of cannabis and pregnancy outcome. *BJOG: An International Journal of Obstetrics and Gynaecology, 109*(1), 21–27.

Fernandez, J., & Francis, E. (2012). Propylhexedrine: A vintage drug of abuse, rediscovered. *Journal of Psychoactive Drugs, 44*(3), 277–279.

Fernandez-Ruis, J., Romero, J., & Ramos, A. (2015). Endocannabinoids and neurodegenerative disorders: Parkinson's disease, Huntington's Chorea,

Alzheimer's disease and others. *Handbook of Experimental Pharmacology, 231,* 233–259.

Ferré, S., Diamond, I., Goldberg, S. R., Yao, L., Hourani, S. M. O., Huang, Z. L., Urade, Y., & Kitchen, I. (2007). Adenosine A_{2A} receptors in ventral striatum, hypothalamus and nociceptive circuitry. Implications for drug addiction, sleep and pain. *Progress in Neurobiology, 83*(5), 332–347.

Finckh, A., Dehler, S., Costenbader, K., & Gabay, C. (2007). Cigarette smoking and radiographic progression in rheumatoid arthritis. *Annals of the Rheumatic Diseases, 66*(8), 1066–1071.

Fingleton, N., Matheson, C., & Jaffray, M. (2015). Changes in mental health during opiate replacement therapy: A systematic review. *Drugs: Education, Prevention and Policy, 22*(1), 1–18.

Fischer, B., & Rehm, J. (2009). Deaths related to the use of prescription opioids. *Canadian Medical Association Journal, 181*(12), 881–882.

Fiz, J., Duran, M., Capella, D., Carbonell, J., & Farre, M. (2011). Cannabis use in patients with fibromyalgia: Effect on symptoms relief and health-related quality of life. *PLoS One, 6*, e18440. doi:10.1371/journal.pone.0018440

Floraa, M., Mascie-Taylorb, C., & Rahmanc, M. (2012). Betel quid chewing and its risk factors in Bangladeshi adults. *WHO South-East Asia Journal of Public Health, 1*(2), 169–181.

Fontanill, D., Johannessen, M., Hajipour, A., Cozzi, N., Jackson, M., & Ruoho, A. (2009). The hallucinogen N,N-Dimethyltryptamine (DMT) is an endogenous sigma-1 receptor regulator. *Science, 323*(5916), 934–937.

Food and Drug Administration. (2018). *Statement from FDA Commissioner Scott Gottlieb, M.D., on new warning letters FDA is issuing to companies marketing kratom with unproven medical claims; and the agency's ongoing concerns about kratom.* Retrieved from: https://www.fda.gov/NewsEvents/Newsroom/PressAnnouncements/ucm620106.htm

Frank, D., Augustyn, M., Grant Knight, W., Pell, T., & Zuckerman, B. (2001). Growth, development, and behavior in early childhood following prenatal cocaine exposure: A systematic review. *Journal of the American Medical Association, 285*(12), 1613–1625.

Fredholm, B., Gustafsson, L., Hedqvist, P., Sollevi, A., Berne, R., Rall, T., & Rubio, R. (1983). Adenosine in the regulation of neurotransmitter release in the peripheral nervous system. *Regulatory Function of Adenosine: Proceedings of the International Symposium on Adenosine*, Charlottesville, Virginia, June 7–11, 1982.

Fride, E., Bregman, T., & Kirkham, T. (2005). Endocannabinoids and food intake: Newborn suckling and appetite regulation in adulthood. *Experimental Biology and Medicine, 230*(4), 225–234.

Fudala, P. (2006). Development of opioid formulations with limited diversion and abuse potential. *Drug and Alcohol Dependence, 83*(S1), S40–S47.

Gable, R. (2004). Comparison of acute lethal toxicity of commonly abused psychoactive substances. *Addiction, 99*(6), 686–696.

Gable, R. (2006). Risk assessment of ritual use of oral dimethyltryptamine (DMT) and harmala alkaloids. *Addiction, 102*(1), 24–34.

Gafoor, R., Booth, H., & Gulliford, M. (2018). Antidepressant utilisation and incidence of weight gain during 10 years' follow-up: Population based cohort study. *British Medical Journal, 361*, k1951. doi:10.1136/bmj.k1951

Gage, S., Jones, H., Taylor, A., Burgess, S., Zammit, S., & Munafo, M. (2017). Investigating causality in associations between smoking initiation and schizophrenia using Mendelian randomization. *Scientific Reports, 7*(40653). https://doi.org/10.1038/srep40653

Gahr, M., Freudenmann, R., Hiemke, C., Gunst, I., Connemann, B., & Schonfeldt-Lecuona, C. (2012). Krokodil: Revival of an old drug with new problems. *Substance Use and Misuse, 47*(7), 861–863.

Gainetdinov, R., Mohn, A., Bohn, L., & Caron, M. (2001). Glutamatergic modulation of hyperactivity in mice lacking the dopamine transporter. *Proceedings of the National Academy of Science, 98*(20), 11047–11054.

Galbis-Reig, D. (2016). A case report of kratom addiction and withdrawal. *Wisconsin Medical Journal, 115*(1), 49–52.

Galletly, C., Suetani, S., & Dark, F. (2018). Medication discontinuation in first episode psychosis: Thinking about the offset of psychotic disorders. *Australian & New Zealand Journal of Psychiatry, 52*(9), 819–821.

Garbis, H., Elefant, E., Diav-Citrin, O., Mastroiacovo, P., Schaefer, C., & Mathieu-Nolf, M. (2005). Pregnancy outcome after exposure to ranitidine and other H2-blockers: A collaborative study of the European Network of Teratology Information Services. *Reproductive Toxicology, 19*(4), 453–458.

Garbutt, J. (2010). Efficacy and tolerability of naltrexone in the management of alcohol dependence. *Current Pharmacological Design, 16*(19), 2091–2097.

Garlantézec, R., Monfort, C., Rouget, F., & Cordier, S. (2009). Maternal occupational exposure to solvents and congenital malformations: A prospective study in the general population. *Occupational and Environmental Medicine, 66*(7), 456–463.

Gass, J. (2008). *Quaaludes.* New York: Chelsea House.

Gasser, P., Kirchner, K., & Passie, T. (2015). LSD-assisted psychotherapy for anxiety associated with a life-threatening disease: A qualitative study of acute and sustained subjective effects. *Journal of Psychopharmacology, 29*(1), 57–68.

GBD 2016 Alcohol Collaborators. (2018). Alcohol use and burden for 195 countries and territories, 1990–2016: A systematic analysis for the Global Burden of Disease Study 2016. *Lancet.* http://dx.doi.org/10.1016/S0140-6736(18)31310-2

Gentile, S. (2010). Neurodevelopmental effects of prenatal exposure to psychotropic mediations. *Depression and Anxiety, 27*(7), 675–686.

Ghasemiesfe, M., Ravi, D., Vali, M., Korenstein, D., Arjomandi, M., Frank, J., Austin, P., & Keyhani, S. (2018). Marijuana use, respiratory symptoms, and pulmonary function: A systematic review and meta-analysis. (2018). *Annals of Internal Medicine, 169*(2), 106–115.

Ghoneim, M., & Mewaldt, S. (1975). Effects of diazepam and scopolamine on storage, retrieval and organizational processes in memory. *Psychopharmacologia, 44*(3), 257–262.

Gilfillan, K., Dannatt, L., Stein, D., & Vythilingum, B. (2018). Heroin detoxification during pregnancy: A systematic review and retrospective study of the management of heroin addiction in pregnancy. *South African Medical Journal, 108*(2), 111–117.

Gill, N., Shield, A., Blazevich, A., Zhou, S., & Weatherby, R. (2000). Muscular and cardiorespiratory effects of pseudoephedrine in human athletes. *British Journal of Clinical Pharmacology, 50*(3), 205–213.

Gilman, J., Kuster, J., Lee, S., Lee, M., Kim, B., Makris, N., van der Kouwe, A., Blood, A., & Breiter, H. (2014). Cannabis use is quantitatively associated with nucleus accumbens and amygdala abnormalities in young adult recreational users. *Journal of Neuroscience, 34*(16), 5529–5538.

Giordano, L. (2013). Brain buzz: Effects of caffeine, nicotine, alcohol and drugs on learning. Retrieved from: http://www.yale-university.com/ynhti/curriculum/units/2009/4/09.04.05.x.html

Goff, D., Falkai, P., Fleischhacker, W., Girgis, R., Kahn, R., Uchida, H., Zhao, J., & Lieberman, J. (2017). The long-term effects of antipsychotic medication on clinical course in schizophrenia. *American Journal of Psychiatry, 174*(9), 840–849.

Golan, D. (Ed.). (2016). *Principles of pharmacology: The pathophysiologic basis of drug therapy* (4th ed.). Philadelphia: Lippicott, Williams and Wilkins.

Gold, E., Gordis, L., Tonascia, J., & Szklo, M. (1978). Increased risk of brain tumors in children exposed to barbiturates. *JNCI: Journal of the National Cancer Institute, 61*(4), 1031–1034.

Goldman, S., Galarneau, D., & Friedman, R. (2007). New onset LSD flashbacks triggered by the use of SSRIs. *The Ochsner Journal, 7*(1), 37–39.

Goldstein, E. (2010). *Sensation and perception* (8th ed.). Belmont, CA: Wadsworth Publishing Company.

González-Pinto, A., Vega, P., Ibáñez, B., Mosquera, F., Barbeito, S., Gutiérrez, M., & Vieta, E. (2008). Impact of cannabis and other drugs on age at onset of psychosis. *Journal of Clinical Psychiatry, 69*(8), 1210–1216.

Goodwin, G., Haddad, P., Ferrier, I., Aronson, J., Barnes, T., Cipriani, A., Coghill, D., Fazel, S., Geddes, J., Grunze, H., Holmes, E., Howes, O., Hudson, S., Hunt, N., Jones, I., Macmillan, I., McAllister-Williams, H., Miklowitz, D., Morriss, R., Munafò, M., Paton, C., Saharkian, B., Saunders, K., Sinclair,

J., Taylor, D., Vieta, E., & Young, A. (2016). Evidence-based guidelines for treating bipolar disorder: Revised third edition recommendations from the British Association for Psychopharmacology. *Journal of Psychopharmacology, 30*(6), 495–553.

Government of Canada. (2009). *Guidance document for practitioners. File Number 00-102841-266.* Ottawa: Government of Canada.

Government of Canada. (2013). *Darvon-N (dextropropoxyphene): Recall and withdrawal in Canada.* Retrieved from: http://healthycanadians.gc.ca/recall-alert-rappel-avis/hc-sc/2010/16115a-eng.php

Government of Canada. (2015). *Order Amending Schedule IV to the Controlled Drugs and Substances Act (Salvia Divinorum).* Retrieved from: http://gazette.gc.ca/rp-pr/p2/2015/2015-08-12/html/sor-dors209-eng.html

Government of Canada. (2018). Overview of national data on opioid-related harms and deaths. Retrieved from: https://www.canada.ca/en/health-canada/services/substance-use/problematic-prescription-drug-use/opioids/data-surveillance-research/harms-deaths.html

Gowing, L., Ali, R., Allsop, S., Marsden, J., Turf, E., West, R., & Witton, J. (2015). Global statistics on addictive behaviours: 2014 status report. *Addiction, 110*(6), 904–919.

Grape, S., Schug, B., & Schug, S. (2010). Formulations of fentanyl for the management of pain. *Drugs, 70*(1), 57–72.

Graves, D. (2018). Cannabis shenanigans: Advocating for the restoration of an effective treatment of pain following spinal cord injury. *Spinal Cord Series and Cases, 4*(1), https://doi.org/10.1038/s41394-018-0096-1

Gray, B., & Holland, C. (2014). Implications of psychoactive bath salts use during pregnancy. *Nursing for Women's Health, 18*(3), 220–230.

Greer, G., Grob, C., & Halberstadt, A. (2014). PTSD symptom reports of patients evaluated for the New Mexico medical cannabis program. *Journal of Psychoactive Drugs, 46*(1), 73–77.

Grella, S., Funka, D., Coena, K., Li, A., & Lêa, A. (2014). Role of the kappa-opioid receptor system in stress-induced reinstatement of nicotine seeking in rats. *Behavioural Brain Research, 265*, 188–197.

Gresser, E. (2013, August 14). World drug trade: $50 billion? *Progressive Economy.* Retrieved from: http://progressive-economy.org/2013/08/14/world-drug-trade-50-billion/

Griffiths, R., Johnson, M., Richards, W., Richards, B., McCann, U., & Jesse, R. (2011). Psilocybin occasioned mystical-type experiences: Immediate and persisting dose-related effects. *Psychopharmacology, 218*(4), 649–665.

Grob, C., Danforth, A., Chopra, G., Hagerty, M., McKay, C., Halberstadt, A., & Greer, G. (2011). Pilot study of psilocybin treatment for anxiety in patients with advanced-stage cancer. *Archives of General Psychiatry, 68*(1), 71–78.

Grond, S., & Sablotzki, A. (2004). Clinical pharmacology of Tramadol. *Clinical Pharmacokinetics, 43*(13), 879–923.

Grunder, G., Hippius, H., & Carlsson, A. (2009). The atypicality of antipsychotics: A concept re-examined and re-defined. *Nature Reviews Drug Discovery, 8*(2), 197–202.

Gupta, B., & Gupta, U. (1999). *Caffeine and behaviour: Current views and research trends.* New York: CRC Press.

Gupta, P., & Ray, C. (2004). Epidemiology of betel quid usage. *Annals of Academy of Medicine, 33*(S-4), 31–36.

Guzman, F. (2012). First generation anti-psychotics: An introduction. Retrieved from: http://psychopharmacologyinstitute.com/antipsychotics/first-generation-antipsychotics/

Hall, R., & Zisook, S. (1981). Paradoxical reactions to benzodiazepines. *British Journal of Clinical Pharmacology, 11*(S1), 99S–104S.

Hall, W. (2015). What has research over the past two decades revealed about the adverse health effects of recreational cannabis use? *Addiction, 110*(1), 19–35.

Hall, W., & Degenhardt, L. (2009). Adverse health effects of non-medical cannabis use. *Lancet, 374,* 1383–1391.

Halpern, J., & Pope, H. (2003). Hallucinogen persisting perception disorder: What do we know after 50 years. *Drug and Alcohol Dependency, 69*(1), 109–119.

Hancock, S., & McKim, W. (2018). *Drugs and behaviour: An introduction to behavioral pharmacology* (8th ed.). New York: Pearson.

Handford, C., Kahan, M., Srivastava, A., Cirone, S., Sanhera, S., & Palda, V. (2011). *Buprenorphine/Naloxone for opioid dependence.* Toronto: Centre for Addiction and Mental Health.

Hannigan, J., & Bowen, S. (2010). Reproductive toxicology and teratology of abused toluene. *Systems Biology in Reproductive Medicine, 56*(2), 184–200.

Harris, R., & Buck, K. (1990). The process of alcohol tolerance and dependence. *Alcohol Health and Research World, 14*(2), 105–109.

Hasler, B., Kirisci, L., & Clark, D. (2016). Restless sleep and variable sleep timing during late childhood accelerate the onset of alcohol and other drug involvement. *Journal of Studies on Alcohol and Drugs, 77*(4), 649–655.

Hasler, B., Smith, L., Cousins, J., & Bootzins, R. (2012). Circadian rhythms, sleep, and substance abuse. *Sleep Medicine Reviews, 16*(1), 67–81.

Hassan, N., Gunaid, A., & Murray-Lyon, I. (2007). Khat (Catha edulis): Health aspects of khat chewing. *Eastern Mediterranean Health Journal, 13*(3), 706–718.

Hayatbakhsh, M., Flenady, V., Gibbons, K., Kingsbury, A., Hurrion, E., Mamun, A., & Najman, J. (2012). Birth outcomes associated with cannabis use before and during pregnancy. *Pediatric Research, 71*(2), 215–219.

Haydar, S., & Dunlop, J. (2010). Neuronal nicotinic acetylcholine receptors—targets for the development of drugs to treat cognitive impairment associated with schizophrenia and Alzheimer's disease. *Current Topics in Medicinal Chemistry, 10*(2), 144–152.

Health Canada. (2014). *IMOVANE (zopiclone)—new dosage recommendations to minimize the risk of next-day impairment.* Retrieved from: http://healthycanadians.gc.ca/recall-alert-rappel-avis/hc-sc/2014/42255a-eng.php

Health Canada. (2015). *Summary of safety review: Abilify and Abilify Maintena (aripiprazole)—evaluating the risk of certain impulse control behaviours.* Retrieved from: https://www.canada.ca/en/health-canada/services/drugs-health-products/medeffect-canada/safety-reviews/summary-safety-review-abilify-abilify-maintena-aripiprazole-evaluating-risk-certain-impulse-control-behaviours.html

Health Canada. (2016). *Summary of safety review: Methylphenidate.* Retrieved from: https://hpr-rps.hres.ca/reg-content/summary-safety-review-detail.php?linkID=SSR00033

Healy, D., Le Noury, J., & Derelie, M. (2017). Enduring sexual dysfunction after treatment with antidepressants, 5α-reductase inhibitors and isotretinoin: 300 cases. *International Journal of Risk and Safety Medicine, 29*(3–4), 125–134.

Heikkinen, N., Niskanen, E., Könönen, M., Tolmunen, T., Kekkonen, V., Kivimäki, P., Tanila, H., Laukkanen, E., & Vanninen, R. (2017). Alcohol consumption during adolescence is associated with reduced grey matter volumes. *Addiction, 112*(4), 604–613.

Heinen, M., Verhage, B., Ambergen, T., Goldbohm, R., & van den Brandt, P. (2009). Alcohol consumption and risk of pancreatic cancer in the Netherlands cohort study. *American Journal of Epidemiology, 169*(10), 1233–1242.

Heisler, L., & Tecott, L. (2000). A paradoxical locomotor response in serotonin 5-HT (2C) receptor mutant mice. *Journal of Neuroscience, 20*(8), 1–5.

Hejja, P., & Galloon, S. (1975). A consideration of ketamine dreams. *Canadian Anesthetic Society Journal, 22*(1), 100–105.

Hemby, S., McIntosh, S., Leon, F., Cutler, S., & McCurdy, C. (2018). Abuse liability and therapeutic potential of the *Mitragyna speciosa* (kratom) alkaloids mitragynine and 7-hydroxymitragynine. *Addiction Biology.* https://doi.org/10.1111/adb.12639

Hendeles, L. (1993). Selecting a decongestant. *Pharmacotherapy: The Journal of Pharmacology and Drug Therapy, 13*(6S), 129S–134S.

Hermanns-Clausen, M., Kneisel, S., Szabo. B., & Auwärter, V. (2013). Acute toxicity due to the confirmed consumption of synthetic cannabinoids: Clinical and laboratory findings. *Addiction, 108*(3), 534–544.

Hernandez, R., Mitchell, A., & Werle, M. (2010). Decongestant use during pregnancy and its association with preterm delivery. *Birth Defects Research (Part A) 88*(9), 707–761.

Herrero, L., Chaucer, B., Singh, S., Deshpande, V., & Patel, S. (2016). Acute pancreatitis secondary to marijuana consumption. *Journal of the Pancreas, 17*(3), 322–323.

Herrmann, E., Johnson, P., Bruner, N., Vandrey, R., & Johnson, M. (2017). Morning administration of oral methamphetamine dose-dependently disrupts nighttime sleep in recreational stimulant users. *Drug and Alcohol Dependency, 178*, 291–295.

Herzog, T., Murphy, K., Little, M., Suguitan, G., Pokhrel, P., & Kawamoto, C. (2014). The Betel Quid Dependence Scale: Replication and extension in a Guamanian sample. *Drug and Alcohol Dependence, 138*, 154–160.

Hickman, M., Steer, C., Tilling, K., Lim, A., Marsden, J., Millar, T., Strang, J., Tefler, M., Vicerman, P., & Macleod, J. (2018). The impact of buprenorphine and methadone on mortality: A primary care cohort study in the United Kingdom. *Addiction, 113*(8), 1461–1476.

Hieronymus, F., Lisinski, A., Nilsson, S., & Eriksson, E. (2018). Efficacy of selective serotonin reuptake inhibitors in the absence of side effects: A mega-analysis of citalopram and paroxetine in adult depression. *Molecular Psychiatry, 23*(8), 1731–1736.

Hill, M., Campolongo, P., Yehuda, R., & Patel, S. (2018). Integrating endocannabinoid signaling and cannabinoids into the biology and treatment of posttraumatic stress disorder. *Neuropsychopharmacology, 43*(1), 80–102.

Hillhouse, T., & Porter, J. (2015). A brief history of the development of antidepressant drugs: From monoamines to glutamate. *Experimental and clinical psychopharmacology, 23*(1), 1–21.

Hirayama, T. (1981). Non-smoking wives of heavy smokers have a higher risk of lung cancer: A study from Japan. *British Medical Journal, 282*(6259), 183–185.

Hodges, K., Hancock, S., Currell, K., Hamilton, B., & Jeukendrup, A. (2006). Pseudoephedrine enhances performance in 1500-m runners. *Medical Science in Sports and Exercise, 38*(2), 329–333.

Holden, S. (2013). Fresh fears over PMA being used in ecstasy pills. Retrieved from: http://www.bbc.co.uk/newsbeat/23618912

Holder, M., Veichweg, S., & Mong, J. (2015). Methamphetamine-enhanced female sexual motivation is dependent on dopamine and progesterone signaling in the medial amygdala. *Hormones and Behavior, 67*(1), 1–11.

Holitzki, H., Dowsett, L., Spackman, E., Noseworthy, T., & Clement, F. (2017). Health effects of exposure to second- and third-hand marijuana smoke: A systematic review. *Canadian Medical Association Journal—Open, 5*(4), E814–E822.

Holler, J., Vorce, S., McDonough-Bender, P., Magluilo, J., Solomon, C., & Levine, B. (2011). A drug toxicity death involving propylhexedrine and mitragynine. *Journal of Analytical Toxicology, 35*(1), 54–59.

Hong, D., Flood, P., & Diaz, G. (2008). The side effects of morphine and hydromorphone patient-controlled analgesia. *Anesthesia and Analgesia, 107*(4), 1384–1389.

Howard, M., & Garland, E. (2012). Volatile substance misuse. *CNS Drugs, 26*(11), 927–935.

Hoyt, C. (1978). Optic disc anomalies and maternal ingestion of LSD. *Journal of Pediatric Ophthalmology and Strabismus, 15*(5), 286–289.

Hsu, W., Chiu, N., Liu, J., Wang, C., Chang, T., Liao, Y., & Kuo, P. (2012). Sleep quality in heroin addicts under methadone maintenance treatment. *Acta Neuropsychiatrica, 24*(6), 356–360.

Hua, T., Vemuri, K., Pu, M., Qu, L., Han, G. W., Wu. Y., Zhao, S., & Liu, Z. (2016). Crystal structure of the human cannabinoid receptor CB. *Cell, 167*(3), 750–762.

Huang, X., Chen, Y., Shen, Y., Cao, X., Li, A., Liu, Q., Li, Z., Zhang, L., Dai, W., Tan, T., Arias-Carrion, O., Xue, Y., Su, H., & Yuan, T. (2017). Methamphetamine abuse impairs motor cortical plasticity and function. *Molecular Psychiatry, 22*(9),1274–1281.

Huestis, M. (2009). Human cannabinoid pharmacokinetics. *Chemistry and Biodivesity, 4*(8), 1770–1804.

Hulka, L., Scheidegger, M., Vonmoos, M., Preller, K., Baumgartner, M., Herdener, M., Seifritz, E., Henning, A., & Quednow, B. (2016). Glutamatergic and neurometabolic alterations in chronic cocaine users measured with ^{1}H-magnetic resonance spectroscopy. *Addiction Biology, 21*(1), 205–217.

Hunter, K., & Ochoa, R. (2006). Campral for treatment of alcoholism. *American Family Physician, 74*(4), 645–646.

Hurt, H., Brodsky, N., Roth, H., Malmud, E., & Giannetta, J. (2005). School performance of children with gestational cocaine exposure. *Neurotoxicology and Teratology, 27*(2), 203–211.

Hviid, A., Melbye, M., & Pasternak, B. (2013). Use of selective serotonin reuptake inhibitors during pregnancy and risk of autism. *New England Journal of Medicine, 369*(25), 2406–2415.

Iadarola, N., Niciu, M., Richards, E., Vande Voort, J., Ballard, E., Lundin, N., Nugent, A., Machado-Vieira, R., & Zarate, C. (2015). Ketamine and other

N-methyl-D-aspartate receptor antagonists in the treatment of depression: A perspective review. *Therapeutic Advances in Chronic Disease, 6*(3), 97–114.

Inaba, D., & Cohen, W. (2011). *Uppers, downers, all arounders.* Medford: CNS Productions.

Institute of Medicine. (2009). Secondhand smoke exposure and cardiovascular effects: Making sense of the evidence. Washington: Author.

Iqbal, M., Sobhan, T., & Ryals, T. (2002). Effects of commonly used benzodiazepines on the fetus, the neonate, and the nursing infant. *Psychiatric Services, 53*(1), 39–49.

Irwin, M., Bjurstrom, M., & Olmstead, R. (2016). Polysomnographic measures of sleep in cocaine dependence and alcohol dependence: Implications for age-related loss of slow wave, Stage 3 sleep. *Addiction, 111*(6), 1084–1092.

Jankowiak, W., & Bradburd, D. (2003). *Drugs, labor and colonial expansion.* Tucson: University of Arizona Press.

Jansson, L. (2018). Maternal alcohol use during lactation and child development. *Pediatrics, 142*(2), e20181377.

Jayasekara, H., MacInnis, R., Room, R., & English, D. (2015). Long-term alcohol consumption and breast, upper aero-digestive tract and colorectal cancer risk: A systematic review and meta-analysis. *Alcohol and Alcoholism, 51*(3), 315–330.

Jinwala, F., & Gupta, M. (2012). Synthetic cannabis and respiratory depression. *Journal of Child and Adolescent Psychopharmacology, 22*(6), 459–462.

Johansen, S., Hansen, A., Muller, I., Lundemose, J., & Franzmann, M. (2003). Three fatal cases of PMA and PMMA poisoning in Denmark. *Journal of Analytical Toxicology, 27*(4), 253–256.

Johnson, B., Rosenthal, N., Capece, J., Wiegand, F., Mao, L., Bevers, K., McKay, A., Ait-Daoud, N., Anton, R., Ciraulo, D., Kranzler, H., Mann, K., O'Malley, S., & Swift, R. (2007). Topiramate for treating alcohol dependence: A randomized controlled trial. *Journal of the American Medical Association, 298*(14), 1641–1651.

Johnson, D. (1991). Pharmacology and safety of phenylpropanolamine. *Drug Development Research, 22*(2), 197–207.

Johnson, D., & Hricik, J. (1993). The pharmacology of α-adrenergic decongestants. *Pharmacotherapy: The Journal of Pharmacology and Drug Therapy, 13*(6S), 110S–115S.

Johnson, M., Garcia-Romeu, A., Cosimano, M., & Griffiths, R. (2014). Pilot study of the 5-HT2AR agonist psilocybin in the treatment of tobacco addiction. *Journal of Psychopharmacology, 28*(11), 983–992.

Johnstad, P. (2018). Powerful substances in tiny amounts: An interview study of psychedelic microdosing. *Nordic Studies on Alcohol and Drugs, 35*(1), 39–51.

Jones, H., Kaltenbach, K., Heil, S., Stine, S., Coyle, M., Arria, A., O'Grady, K., Selby, P., Martin, P., & Gischer, G. (2010). Neonatal abstinence syndrome after methadone or buprenorphine exposure. *New England Journal of Medicine, 363*(24), 2320–2331.

Joy, J., Watson, S., & Benson Jr., J. (1999). *Marijuana and medicine: Assessing the scientific base.* Washington: National Academy Press.

Kaar, S., Ferris, J., Waldron, J., Devaney, M., Ramsey, J., & Winstock, A. (2016). Up: The rise of nitrous oxide abuse. An international survey of contemporary nitrous oxide use. *Journal of Psychopharmacology, 30*(4), 395–401.

Kabir, Z., McCarthy, D., Bhide, P., & Kosofsky, B. (2013). Cup of Joe: A brain development "no"? *Science Translational Medicine, 5*(197), 1–3.

Kalant, H. (2001). The pharmacology and toxicology of "ecstasy" (MDMA) and related drugs. *Canadian Medical Association, 165*(7), 917–928.

Kales, A., Bixler, E., Vela-Bueno, A., Soldatos, C., & Manfredi, R. (1987). Alprazolam: Effects on sleep and withdrawal phenomena. *The Journal of Clinical Pharmacology, 27*(7), 508–515.

Kalinin, S., González-Prieto, M., Scheiblich, H., Lisi, L., Kusumo, H., Heneka, M., Madrigal, J., Pandey, S., & Feinstein, D. (2018). Transcriptome analysis of alcohol-treated microglia reveals downregulation of beta amyloid phagocytosis. *Journal of Neuroinflammation, 15*(1). https://doi.org/10.1186/s12974-018-1184-7

Källén, B., Borg, N., & Reis, M. (2013). The use of central nervous system active drugs during pregnancy. *Pharmaceuticals, 6*(10), 1221–1286.

Källén B., & Olausson, P. (2007). Maternal use of selective serotonin re-uptake inhibitors in early pregnancy and infant congenital malformations. *Birth Defects Research, 79*(4), 301–308.

Kalpaklioglu, F., & Baccioglu, A. (2012). Efficacy and safety of H_1 antihistamines: An update. *Anti-Inflammatory & Anti-Allergy Agents in Medicinal Chemistry, 11*(3), 230–237.

Kalso, E. (2005). Oxycodone. *Journal of Pain and Symptom Management, 29*(5), 47–56.

Kanfer, I., Dowse, R., & Vuma, V. (1993). Pharmacokinetics of oral decongestants. *Pharmacotherapy: The Journal of Pharmacology and Drug Therapy, 13*(6S), 116S–128S.

Kaplan, K., McQuaid, J., Batki, S., & Rosenlicht, N. (2014). Behavioral treatment of insomnia in early recovery. *Journal of Addiction Medicine, 8*(6), 395–398.

Kar, S., Krishnan, A., Preetha, K., & Mohankar, A. (2012). A review of antihistamines used during pregnancy. *Journal of Pharmacology & Pharmacotherapeutics, 3*(2), 105–108.

Karma, S., Ducharme, S., Corley, J., Chouinard-Decorte, F., Starr, J., Wardlaw, J., Batsin, M., & Deary, I. (2015). Cigarette smoking and thinning of the brain's cortex. *Molecular Psychiatry, 20*(6), 778–785.

Katzung, B. (2007). *Basic & clinical pharmacology* (10th ed.). Toronto: McGraw Hill Medical.

Kellen, A., Powers, L., & Birnbaum, L. (2017). Drug use, addiction and the criminal justice system. In R. Csiernik & W. Rowe (Eds.), *Responding to the oppression of addiction* (3rd ed.) (pp. 260–280). Toronto: Canadian Scholars' Press.

Kerensky, T., & Walley, A. (2017). Opioid overdose prevention and naloxone rescue kits: What we know and what we don't know. *Addiction Science and Clinical Practice, 12*(4). https://doi.org/10.1186/s13722-016-0068-3

Kernan, W., Viscoli, C., Brass., L., Broderick, J., Brott, T., Feldman, E., Morgenstern, L., Wilterdink, J., & Horwitz, R. (2000). Phenylpropanolamine and the risk of hemorrhagic stroke. *New England Journal of Medicine, 343*(25), 1826–1832.

Kerrigan, S., & Lindsey, T. (2005). Fatal caffeine overdose: Two case studies. *Forensic Science International, 153*(1), 67–69.

Ketcherside, A., Matthews, I., & Filbey, F. (2013). The serotonin link between alcohol use and affective disorders. *Journal of Addiction Prevention, 1*(2), 3(1–5).

Khaled, A. (2013). The effect of illicit trade in narcotics on global economy. *Annals of the University of Oradea, Economic Science Series, 22*(1), 21–27.

Khatib, M., Jarra, Z., Bizrah, M., & Checinski, K. (2013). Khat: Social habit or cultural burden? A survey and review. *Journal of Ethnicity in Substance Abuse, 12*(2), 140–153.

Khawaja, M., Al-Nsour, M., & Saad, G. (2008). Khat (Catha edulis) chewing during pregnancy in Yemen: Findings from a national population survey. *Maternal and Child Health Journal, 12*(3), 308–312.

King, C., & Holmes, A. (2015). Cannabinoid hyperemesis syndrome. *Canadian Medical Association Journal, 187*(5), 355.

Kirby, L., Zeeb, F., & Winstanley, C. (2011). Contributions of serotonin in addiction vulnerability. *Neuropharmacology 61*(3), 421–432.

Kish, S., Fitzmaurice, P., Chang, L., Furukawa, Y. ,& Tong, J. (2010). Low striatal serotonin transporter protein in a human polydrug MDMA (ecstasy) user: A case study. *Journal of Psychopharmacology, 24*(2), 281–284.

Klinkenberg, I., & Blokland, A. (2010). The validity of scopolamine as a pharmacological model for cognitive impairment: A review of animal behavioral studies. *Neuroscience and Biobehavioral Review, 34*(8), 1307–1350.

Kocherlakota, P. (2014). Neonatal abstinence syndrome. *Pediatrics, 134*(2), e547–e561.

Koenig, X., & Hilber, K. (2015). The anti-addiction drug ibogaine and the heart: A delicate relation. *Molecules*, *20*(2), 2208–2228.

Kolb, B., Li, Y., Robinson, T., & Parker L. (2018). THC alters morphology of neurons in medial prefrontal cortex, orbital prefrontal cortex, and nucleus accumbens and alters the ability of later experience to promote structural plasticity. *Synapse, 72*(3), e22022. https://doi.org/10.1002/syn.22020

Kosten, T., & George, T. (2002). The neurobiology of opioid dependence: Implications for treatment. *Science & Practice Perspectives*, *1*(1), 13–20.

Koukouli, F., Rooy, M., Tziotis, D., Sailor, K., O'Neill, H., Levenga, J., Witte, M., Nilges, M., Changeux, J., Hoeffer, C., Stitzel, J., Gutkin, B., DiGregorio, D., & Maskos, U. (2017). Nicotine reverses hypofrontality in animal models of addiction and schizophrenia. *Nature Medicine*, *23*(3), 347–354.

Kozlowski, L., Wilkinson, A., Skinner, W., Kent, C., Franklin, T., & Pope, M. (1989). Comparing tobacco cigarette dependence with other drug dependencies greater or equal "difficulty quitting" and "urges to use," but less "pleasure" from cigarettes. *Journal of the American Medical Association, 261*(6), 898–901.

Kraehenmann, R., Schmidt, A., Friston, K., Preller, K., Seifritz, E., & Vollenweider, F. (2015). The mixed serotonin receptor agonist psilocybin reduces threat-induced modulation of amygdala connectivity. *NeuroImage. Clinical*, *11*(1), 53–60.

Kraft, W., Adeniyi-Jones, S., Chervoneva, I., Greenspan, J., Abatemarco, D., Kaltenbach, K., & Ehrlich, M. (2017). Buprenorphine for the treatment of the neonatal abstinence syndrome. *The New England Journal of Medicine*, *376*(24), 2341–2348.

Krampe, H., & Hannelore, E. (2010). Supervised disulfiram as adjunct to psychotherapy in alcoholism treatment. *Current Pharmaceutical Design*, *16*(19), 2076–2090.

Krawczyk, M., Mason, X., DeBacker, J., Sharma, R., Normandeau, C., Hawken, E., Di Prospero, C., Chiang, C., Martinez, A., Jones, A., Doudnikoff, E., Caille, S., Bezard, E., Georges, F., & Dumont, E. (2013). D1 dopamine receptor mediated LTP at GABA synapses encodes motivation to self-administer cocaine in rats. *The Journal of Neuroscience, 33*(29), 11960–11971.

Krebs, T., & Johansen, P. (2012). Lysergic acid diethylamide (LSD) for alcoholism: Meta-analysis of randomized controlled trials. *Journal of Psychopharmacology*, *26*(7), 994–1002.

Krishnarajan, D., Varadharajan, V., Gobi, N., Gowtham, D., Srinivas, G., & Vasudevan, P. (2016). Recent approaches of transdermal drug delivery system: A review. *Pharmaccophore, 7*(4), 6–12.

Krystal A. (2010). Antidepressant and antipsychotic drugs. *Sleep Medicine Clinics*, *5*(4), 571–589.

Kyle, P., Iverson, R., Gajaogowni, R., & Spencer, L. (2011). Illicit bath salts: Not for bathing. *Journal of the Mississippi State Medical Association, 52*(12), 375–377.

Lachenmeier, D., Kanteres, F., & Rehm, J. (2009). Carcinogenicity of acetaldehyde in alcoholic beverages: Risk assessment outside ethanol metabolism. *Addiction, 104*(4), 533–550.

Lader M. (2011). Benzodiazepines revisited—will we ever learn? *Addiction, 106*(12), 2086–2109.

Ladhani, N., Shah, P., & Murphy, K. (2011). Prenatal amphetamine exposure and birth outcomes: A systematic review and metaanalysis. *American Journal of Obstetrics and Gynecology, 205*(219), e1–7.

Laegreid, L., Hagberg, G., & Lundberg, A. (1992). The effect of benzodiazepines on the fetus and the newborn. *Neuropediatrics, 23*(1), 18–23.

Lafaye, G., Desterke, C., Marulaz, L., & Benyamina, A. (2018). Cannabidiol affects circadian clock core complex and its regulation in microglia cells. *Addiction Biology*. doi:10.1111/adb.12660

Lakhan, S., & Rowland, M. (2009). Whole plant cannabis extracts in the treatment of spasticity in multiple sclerosis: A systematic review. *BMC Neurology, 9*(59). doi:10.1186/1471-2377-9-59

Lalanne, L., Ayranci, G., Kieffer, B., & Lutz, P. (2014). The kappa opioid receptor: From addiction to depression, and back. *Frontiers in Psychiatry, 5*. doi:10.3389/fpsyt.2014.00170

Lamberti, M., Siracusano, R., Italiano, D., Alosi, N., Cucinotta, F., Di Rosa, G., Germanò, E., Spina, E., & Gagliano, A. (2016). Head-to-head comparison of aripiprazole and risperidone in the treatment of ADHD symptoms in children with autistic spectrum disorder and ADHD: A pilot, open-label, randomized controlled study. *Paediatric Drugs, 18*(4), 319–329.

Lange, S., Probst, C., Gmel, G., Rehm, J., Burd, L., & Popova, S. (2017). Global prevalence of fetal alcohol spectrum disorder among children and youth: A systematic review and meta-analysis. *JAMA Pediatrics, 171*(10), 948–956.

Lappin, J., Darke, S., & Farrell, M. (2017). Stroke and methamphetamine use in young adults: A review. *Journal of Neurology Neurosurgery and Psychiatry, 88*(12), 1079–1091.

Lappin, J., Sara, G., & Farrell, M. (2017). Methamphetamine-related psychosis: An opportunity for assertive intervention and prevention. *Addiction, 112*(6), 927–928.

Large, M., Sharma, S., Compton, M., Slade, T., & Nielssen, N. (2011). Cannabis use and earlier onset of psychosis: A systematic meta-analysis. *Archives of General Psychiatry, 68*(6), 555–561.

Larochelle, M., Zhang, F., Ross-Degnan, D., & Wharam, J. (2015). Rates of opioid dispensing and overdose after introduction of abuse-deterrent extended-release oxycodone and withdrawal of propoxyphene. *JAMA Internal Medicine, 175*(6), 978–987.

Lauritsen, K., & Rosenberg, H. (2016). Comparison of outcome expectancies for synthetic cannabinoids and botanical marijuana. *American Journal of Drug and Alcohol Abuse, 42*(4), 377–384.

Lavretsky, H., Reinlieb, M., St Cyr, N., Siddarth, P., Ercoli, L., & Senturk, D. (2015). Citalopram, methylphenidate, or their combination in geriatric depression: A randomized, double-blind, placebo-controlled trial. *The American Journal of Psychiatry, 172*(6), 561–569.

Lawson, J., & Scheffer, I. (2018). Therapeutic use of medicinal cannabis in difficult to manage epilepsy. *British Journal of Pharmacology*. https://doi.org/10.1111/bcp.13711

Le Dain Commission. (1972). *Final report of the Commission of Inquiry into the non-medical use of drugs*. Ottawa: Information Canada.

Le Garrec, S., Dauger, S., & Sachs, P. (2014). Cannabis poisoning in children. *Intensive Care Medicine, 40*(9), 1394–1395.

Lee, H., & Roth, B. (2012). Neural correlates of the psychedelic state as determined by fMRI studies with psilocybin. *Proceedings of the National Academy of Sciences, 109*(6), 1820–1821.

Lee, M., & Shlain, B. (2001). *Acid dreams: The complete social history of LSD*. London: MacMillan.

Lee, S., Sirieix, C., Nattie, E., & Li, A. (2018). Pre- and early postnatal nicotine exposure exacerbates autoresuscitation failure in serotonin-deficient rat neonates. *The Journal of Physiology*. https://doi.org/10.1113/JP275885

Legriel, S., Bruneel, F., Sprewux-Varoquaux, O., Birenbaum, A., Chadenat, M., Mignon, F., & Bedos, J. (2008). Lysergic acid amide-induced posterior reversible encephalopathy syndrome with status epilepticus. *Neurocritical Care, 9*(2), 247–252.

Leone. S., & Ferrari, A. (2018). Krokodil: The drug that kills. *Journal of Addiction and Recovery, 1*, 1005. Retrieved from: https://meddocsonline.org/journal-of-addiction-recovery/Krokodil-The-drug-that-kills.pdf

Leucht, S., Leucht, C., Huhn, M., Chaimani, A., Mavridis, D., Helfer, B., Samara, M., Rabaioli, M., Bächer, S., Cipriani, A., Geddes, J., Salanti, G., & Davis, J. (2017). Sixty years of placebo-controlled antipsychotic drug trials in acute schizophrenia: Systematic review, bayesian meta-analysis, and meta-regression of efficacy predictors. *American Journal of Psychiatry, 174*(10), 927–942.

Leurs, R., Chazot, P. L., Shenton, F. C., Lim, H. D., & de Esch, I. J. (2009). Molecular and biochemical pharmacology of the histamine H4 receptor. *British Journal of Pharmacology, 157*(1), 14–23.

Leurs, R., Church, M., & Tagliatatela, M. (2002). H_1-antihistamines: Inverse agonism, anti-inflammatory actions and cardiac effects. *Clinical and Experimental Allergy, 32*(4), 489–498.

Levine, M., Phelan, E., Balderson, B., & Wagner, E. (2007). Collaborative treatment planning for older patients in primary care. *Generations, 30*(3), 83–85.

Levinson-Castiel, R., Merlob, P., Linder, N., Sirota, L., & Klinger, G. (2006). Neonatal abstinence syndrome after in utero exposure to selective serotonin reuptake inhibitors in term infants. *Archives of Pediatric and Adolescent Medicine, 160*(2), 173–176.

Lewis, B., Kirchner, H., Short, E., Minnes, S., Weishampel, P., Satayathum, S., & Singer, L. (2007). Prenatal cocaine and tobacco effects on children's language trajectories. *Pediatrics, 120*(1), e78–e85.

Li, Y., Li, X., Guo, C., Li, L., Wang, Y., Zhang, Y., Chen, Y., Liu, W., & Gao, L. (2017). Long-term neurocognitive dysfunction in offspring via NGF/ERK/CREB signaling pathway caused by ketamine exposure during the second trimester of pregnancy in rats. *Oncotarget, 8*(19), 30956–30970.

Liao, Y., Tang, J., Liu, T., Chen, X., Luo, T., & Hao, W. (2011). Sleeping problems among Chinese heroin-dependent individuals. *The American Journal of Drug and Alcohol Abuse, 37*(3), 179–183.

Lin, D., Liu, H., & Yin, H. (2007). Recent paramethoxymethamphetamine (PMMA) deaths in Taiwan. *Journal of Analytical Toxicology, 31*(2), 109–113.

Lindblad, F., & Hjern, A. (2010). ADHD after fetal exposure to maternal smoking. *Nicotine Tobacco Research, 12*(4), 408–415.

Ling, L., Marchant, C., Buckley, N., Prior, M., & Irvine, R. (2001). Poisoning with the recreational drug paramethoxyamphetamine (death). *Medical Journal of Australia, 174*(9), 453–455.

Liu, W. (2014). Histamine H4 receptor antagonists for the treatment of inflammatory disorders. *Drug Discoveries Today, 19*(8), 1222–1225.

Llewellyn, D., Lang, I., Langa, K., Naughton, F., & Matthews, F. (2009). Exposure to second hand smoke and cognitive impairment in non-smokers: National cross-sectional study with cotinine measurement. *British Medical Journal, 338*, 632–634. doi:10.1136/bmj.b462

Logan, R., Hasler, B., Forbes, E., Franzen, P., Torregrossa, M., Huang, Y., Buysse, D., Clark, D., & McClung, C., (2018). Impact of sleep and circadian rhythms on addiction vulnerability in adolescents. *Biological psychiatry, 83*(12), 987–996.

Loizaga-Velder, A., & Verres, R. (2014). Therapeutic effects of ritual ayahuasca use in the treatment of substance dependence—qualitative results. *Psychoactive Drugs, 46*(1), 63–72.

Long, S. (1972). Does LSD induce chromosomal damage and malformations? A review of the literature. *Teratology, 6*(1), 75–90.

Lorenzetti, V., Solowij, N., Whittle, S., Fornito, A., Lubman, D., Pantelis, C., & Yucel, M. (2015). Gross morphological brain changes with chronic heavy cannabis use. *British Journal of Psychiatry, 206*(1), 77–78.

Lowinson, J., Ruiz, P., Millman, R., & Langrod, J. (2011). *Substance abuse: A comprehensive textbook* (2nd ed.). Hagerstown: Williams & Wilkens.

Loy, H., Merry, S., Hetrick, S., & Stasiak, K. (2012). Atypical antipsychotics for disruptive behaviour disorders in children and youths. *Cochrane Database of Systematic Reviews,* Issue 9. Art. No.: CD008559. doi:10.1002/14651858.CD008559.pub2

Lurie, Y., Gopher, A., Lavon, O., Almog, S., Sulimani, L., & Bentur, Y. (2012). Severe paramethoxymethamphetamine (PMMA) and paramethoxyamphetamine (PMA) outbreak in Israel. *Clinical Toxicology, 50*(1), 39–43.

Luscher, C. (2016). The emergence of a circuit model for addiction. *Annual Review of Neuroscience, 39*, 257–276.

Lutfy, K., & Cowan, A. (2004). Buprenorphine: A unique drug with complex pharmacology. *Current neuropharmacology, 2*(4), 395–402.

Lutz, P., & Kieffer, B. (2013). The multiple facets of opioid receptor function: Implications for addiction. *Current Opinion in Neurobiology*, *23*(4), 473–479.

Lyall, L., Wyse, C., Graham, N., Ferguson, A., Lyall, D., Cullen, B., Celis Morles, C., Biello, S., & Smith, D. (2018). Association of disrupted circadian rhythmicity with mood disorders, subjective wellbeing, and cognitive function: A cross-sectional study of 91 105 participants from the UK Biobank. *The Lancet. Psychiatry, 5*(6), 507–514.

Maan, J., & Saadabadi, A. (2018). *Carbamazepine.* Treasure Island: StatPearls Publishing. Retrieved from: https://www.ncbi.nlm.nih.gov/books/NBK482455/

Macher, A., & Penders, T. (2012). False-positive phencyclidine immunoassay results caused by 3,4-methylenedioxypyrovalerone (MDPV). *Drug Testing and Analysis, 5*(2), 130–132.

Madadi, P., & Koren, G. (2008). Pharmacogenetic insights into codeine analgesia: Implications to pediatric codeine use. *Pharmacogenomics, 9*(9), 1267–1284.

Maertens, R., White, P., Rickert, W., Levasseur, G., Douglas, G., Bellier, P., & Desjardins, S. (2009). The genotoxicity of mainstream and sidestream marijuana and tobacco smoke condensates. *Chemical Research in Toxicology*, *22*(8), 1406–1414.

Mahendran, R., Lim, H., Tan, J., Chua, S., & Winslow, M. (2016). *Salvia divinorum*: An overview of the usage, misuse, and addiction processes. *Asia-Pacific Psychiatry, 8*(1), 23–31.

Maillet, E., & Friedhoff, L. (2015). Low dose administration of ibogaine for treating nicotine addiction and preventing relapse of nicotine use. *US Patent App. 14/635,773, 2015.*

Maillet, E., Milon, N., Heghinian, M., Fishback, J., Schürer, S., Garamszegi, N., & Mash, D. (2015). Noribogaine is a G-protein biased κ-opioid receptor agonist. *Neuropharmacology, 99,* 675–688.

Maisel, N., Blodgett, J., Wilbourne, P., Humphreys, K., & Finney, J. (2012). Meta-analysis of naltrexone and acamprosate for treating alcohol use disorders: When are these medications most helpful? *Addiction, 108*(2), 275–293.

Malaysia Ministry of Health. (2013). *Pain management handbook.* Retrieved from: http://hsajb.moh.gov.my/versibaru/uploads/anaes/Pain_Management_Handbook_compile.pdf

Malhi, G., Adams, D., & Berk, M. (2010). The pharmacological treatment of bipolar disorder in primary care. *Medical Journal of Australia, 193*(4), S24–S30.

Malhi, G., Tanious, M., Das, P., Coulston, C., & Berk, M. (2013). Potential mechanisms of action of lithium in bipolar disorder. *CNS Drugs, 27*(2), 135–153.

Malik, P., Gasser, R., Kemmler, G., Moncayo, R., Finkenstedt, G., Kurz, M., & Fleischhacker, W. (2008). Low bone mineral density and impaired bone metabolism in young alcoholic patients without liver cirrhosis: A cross-sectional study. *Alcoholism: Clinical and Experimental Research, 33*(2), 375–381.

Malyshevskaya, O., Aritake, K., Kaushik, M., Uchiyama, N., Cherasse, Y., Kikura-Hanajiri, R., & Urade, Y. (2017). Natural (Δ^9-THC) and synthetic (JWH-018) cannabinoids induce seizures by acting through the cannabinoid CB_1receptor. *Scientific Reports, 7*(1), 10516. doi:10.1038/s41598-017-10447-2

Mammen, G., Rueda, S., Roerecke, M., Bonato, S., Lev-Ran, S., & Rehm, J. (2018). Association of cannabis with long-term clinical symptoms in anxiety and mood disorders: A systematic review of prospective studies. *The Journal of Clinical Psychiatry, 79*(4), pii:17r11839. doi:10.4088/JCP.17r11839

Manza, P., Tomsi, D., & Volkow, N. (2018). Subcortical local functional hyperconnectivity in cannabis dependence. *Biological Psychiatry: Cognitive Neuroscience and Neuroimaging, 3*(3), 285–293.

Márquez, J., Campos-Sandoval, J., Peñalver, A., Mates, J., Segura, J., Blanco, E., Alonso, F., & Rodrigues de Fonseca, F. (2017). Glutamate and brain glutaminases in drug addiction *Neurochemical Research, 42*(3), 846–857.

Martin, B., & Wiley, J. (2004). Mechanism of action of cannabinoids: How it may lead to treatment of cachexia, emesis, and pain. *The Journal of Supportive Oncology, 2*(4), 305–314.

Martins, S., & Alexandre, P. (2009). The association of ecstasy use and academic achievement among adolescents in two U.S. national surveys. *Addictive Behaviors, 34*(1), 1–124.

Marwaha, S., Winsper, C., Bebbington, P., & Smith, D. (2017). Cannabis use and hypomania in young people: A prospective analysis, *Schizophrenia Bulletin*, sbx158. https://doi.org/10.1093/schbul/sbx158

Masoumi, Z., Shayan, A., Azizi, S., & Sadeghian, A. (2018). Incidence of complications among infants born from addicted mothers in Fatemieh hospital in Shahroud City, Iran. *Journal of Biostatistics and Epidemiology, 4*(1), 24–29.

Mattick, R., Kimber, J., Breen, C., & Davoli, M. (2014). Buprenorphine maintenance versus placebo or methadone maintenance for opioid dependence. *Cochrane Database of Systemic Reviews, 2*. doi:10.1002/14651858.CD002207.pub4

May, P., & Gossage, J. (2011). Maternal risk factors for fetal alcohol spectrum disorders. *Alcohol Research and Health, 34*(1), 16–23.

McCall, W., Benca, R., Rosenquist, P., Riley, M., McCloud, L., Newman, J., Case, D., Rumble, M., & Krystal, A. (2016). Hypnotic medications and suicide: Risk, mechanisms, mitigation and the FDA. *American Journal of Psychiatry, 174*(1), 18–25.

McCann, U., Sgambati, F., Schwartz, A., & Ricaurte, G. (2009). Sleep apnea in young abstinent recreational MDMA ("ecstasy") consumers. *Neurology, 73*(23), 2011–2017.

McCarthy, D., Mycyk, M., & DesLauriers, C. (2006). Hospitalization for caffeine abuse is associated with concomitant abuse of other pharmaceutical products. *Annals of Emergency Medicine, 48*(4), 101.

McClean, J., Anspikian, A., & Tsuang, J. (2012). Bath salt use: A case report and review of the literature. *Journal of Dual Diagnosis, 8*(3), 250–256.

McDonald, R., Campbell, N., & Strang, J. (2017). Twenty years of take-home naloxone for the prevention of overdose deaths from heroin and other opioids: Conception and maturation. *Drug and Alcohol Dependence, 178*(1), 176–187.

McGlothlin, W., Sparkes, R., & Arnold, D. (1970). Effect of LSD on human pregnancy. *Journal of the American Medical Association, 212*(9), 1483–1487.

McInnis, O., & Plecas, D. (2016). *Respiratory effects of cannabis smoking: An update.* Ottawa: Canadian Centre on Substance Abuse.

Mechoulan, R., & Parker, L. (2013). The endocannabinoid system and the brain. *Annual Review of Psychology, 64*, 21–47.

Mehra, R., Moore, B., Crothers, K., Tetrault, J., & Fiellin, D. (2006). The association between marijuana smoking and lung cancer. *Archives of Internal Medicine, 166*(13), 1359–1367.

Meier, M., Caspi, A., Ambler, A., Harrington, H., Houts, R., Keefe, R., McDonald, K., Ward, A., Poulton, R., & Moffitt, T. (2012). Cannabis use and neuropsychological decline. *Proceedings of the National Academy of Sciences*, 201206820. doi:10.1073/pnas.1206820109

Meier, M., Caspi, A., Cerdá, M., Hancox, R., Harrington, H., Houts, R., Poulton, R., Ramrakha, S., Thomson, W., & Moffitt, T. (2016). Associations between cannabis use and physical health problems in early midlife: A longitudinal comparison of persistent cannabis vs tobacco users. *Journal of the American Medical Association: Psychiatry, 73*(7), 731–740.

Melis, M., & Argiolas, A. (1995). Dopamine and sexual behavior. *Neuroscience & Biobehavioral Reviews, 19*(1), 19–38.

Meltzer E., & Hamilos, D. (2011). Rhinosinusitis. *Mayo Clinic Proceedings, 86*(5), 427–443.

Meston, C., & Frohlich, P. (2000). The neurobiology of sexual function. *Archives of General Psychiatry, 57*(11), 1012–1030.

Meyer, M., Johnston, A., Crocker, A., & Heil, S. (2015). Methadone and buprenorphine for opioid dependence during pregnancy: A retrospective cohort study. *Journal of Addiction Medicine, 9*(1), 81–86.

Mike, T., Shaw, D., Forbes, E., Sitnick, S., & Hasler, B. P. (2016). The hazards of bad sleep—sleep duration and quality as predictors of adolescent alcohol and cannabis use. *Drug and Alcohol Dependence, 168*, 335–339.

Milkovick, L., & van den Berg, B. (1977). Effects of antenatal exposure to anorectic drugs. *American Journal of Obstetrics & Gynecology, 129(*6), 637–642.

Miller, M., Swanson, S., Azrael, D., Pate, V., & Stürmer, T. (2014). Antidepressant dose, age, and the risk of deliberate self-harm. *JAMA Internal Medicine, 174*(6), 899–909.

Milne, M., Crouch, B., & Carabati, E. (2009). Buprenorphine for opioid dependence. *Journal of Pain & Palliative Care Pharmacotherapy, 23*(2), 153–155.

Minozzi, S., Amato, L., Vecchi, S., Davoli, M., Kirchmayer, U., & Verster, A. (2011). Oral naltrexone maintenance treatment for opioid dependence. *Cochrane Database of Systematic Reviews, 4*, CD001333.

Mir, A., Obafemi, A., Young, A., & Kane, C. (2011). Myocardial infarction associated with use of the synthetic cannabinoid K2. *Pediatrics, 128*(6), e1622–e1627.

Mirmiran, M., Scholtens, J., van de Poll, N., Uylings, H., van der Gugten, J., & Boer, G. (1983). Effects of experimental suppression of active REM sleep during early development upon adult brain and behaviour in the rat. *Brain Research, 283*(2–3), 277–286.

Mithoefer, M., Mithoefer, A., Feduccia, A., Jerome, L., Wagner, M., Wymer, J., Holland, J., Hamilton, S., Yazar-Klosinski, B., Emerson, A., & Doblin, R. (2018). 3,4-methylenedioxymethamphetamine (MDMA)-assisted psychotherapy for post-traumatic stress disorder in military veterans, firefighters, and police officers: A randomised, double-blind, dose-response, phase 2 clinical trial. *Lancet Psychiatry, 5*(6), 486–497.

Mizrachi, Z., Segev, A., & Akirav, I. (2016). Cannabinoids and post-traumatic stress disorder: Clinical and preclinical evidence for treatment and prevention. *Behavioural Pharmacology, 27*(7), 561–569.

Molnar, D., Granger, D., Shisler, S., & Eiden, D. (2018). Prenatal and postnatal cigarette and cannabis exposure: Effects on secretory immunoglobulin A in early childhood. *Neuortoxicology and Teratology, 67*(1), 31–36.

Montgomery, S., & Ekbom, A. (2002). Smoking during pregnancy and children's risk of diabetes. *British Medical Journal, 324*(7328), 26–27.

Monti, J., BaHammam, A., Pandi-Perumal, S., Bromundt, V., Spence, D., Cardinali, D., & Brown, G. (2013). Sleep and circadian rhythm dysregulation in schizophrenia. *Progress in neuro-psychopharmacology & biological psychiatry, 43*(3), 209–216.

Moore, J., & Kelz, M. (2009). Opiates, sleep, and pain: The adenosinergic link. *Anesthesiology, 111*(6), 1175–1176.

Morgan, C., & Curran, H. V. (2008). Effects of cannabidiol on schizophrenia-like symptoms in people who use cannabis. *British Journal of Psychiatry, 192*(4), 306–307.

Morgan, C., & Curran, H. V. (2012). Ketamine use: A review. *Addiction, 107*(1), 27–38.

Morgan, P., & Malison, R. (2007). Cocaine and sleep: Early abstinence. *Scientific World Journal, 7*, 223–230.

Morgan, W. (1990). Abuse potential of barbiturates and other sedative-hypnotics. *Advances in Alcohol and Substance Abuse, 9*(1/2), 67–82.

Moses-Kolko, E., Bogen, D., Perel, J., Bregar, A., Uhl, K., Levin, B., & Wisner, K. (2005). Neonatal signs after late in utero exposure to serotonin reuptake inhibitors: Literature review and implications for clinical applications. *Journal of the American Medical Association, 293*(19), 2372–2383.

Müller, C., Geisel, O., Pelz, P., Higl, V., Krüger, J., Stickel, A., Beck, A., Wernecke, K., Hellweg, R., & Heinz, A. (2015). High-dose baclofen for the treatment of alcohol dependence (BACLAD study): A randomized, placebo-controlled trial. *European Neuropsychopharmacology, 25*(8), 1167–1177.

Muller, F., Lenz, C., Dolder, P., Harder, S., Schmid, Y., Lang, U., Liechti, M., & Borgwardt, S. (2017). Acute effects of LSD on amygdala activity during processing of fearful stimuli in healthy subjects. *Translational Psychiatry, 7*, e1084. doi:10.1038/tp.2017.54

Munk-Olsen, T., Liu, X., Viktorin, A., Brown, H., Di Florio, A., D'Onofrio, B., Gomes, T., Howard, L., Khalifeh, H., Krohn, H., Larsson, H., Lichtenstein, P., Taylor, C., Van Kamp, I., Wesseloo, R., Meltzer-Brody, S., Vigod, S., & Bergink, V. (2018). Maternal and infant outcomes associated with lithium use in pregnancy. An international collaboration combining data from 6 cohort studies using meta-analysis covering 727 lithium exposed pregnancies and 21,397 bipolar or major depressive disorder reference pregnancies. *Lancet Psychiatry, 5*(8), 644–652.

Muñoz-Cuevas, F., Athilingam, J., Piscopo, D., & Wilbrecht, L. (2013). Cocaine-induced structural plasticity in frontal cortex correlates with conditioned place preference. *Nature Neuroscience, 16*(10), 1367–1369.

Munzar, P., Tanda, G., Justinova, Z., & Goldberg, S. (2004). Histamine H3 receptor antagonists potentiate methamphetamine self-administration and methamphetamine-induced accumbal dopamine release. *Neuropsychopharmacology, 29*(4), 705–717.

Muralidharan, K., Ali, M., Silveira, L., Bond, D., Fountoulakis, K., Lam, R., & Yatham, L. (2013). Efficacy of second-generation antipsychotics in treating acute mixed episodes in bipolar disorder: A meta-analysis of placebo-controlled trials. *Journal of Affective Disorders, 150*(2), 408–414.

Murray, B., Murphy, C., & Beuhler, M. (2012). Death following recreational use of designer drug "bath salts" containing 3,4-Methylenedioxypyrovalerone (MDPV). *Journal of Medical Toxicology, 8*(1), 69–75.

Mvula, M., Miller, J., & Ragan, F. (1999). Relationship of phencyclidine and pregnancy outcome. *The Journal of Reproductive Medicine, 44*(12), 1021–1024.

Nagarkatti, P., Pandey, R., Rieder, S., Hegde, V., & Nagarkatti, M. (2009). Cannabinoids as novel anti-inflammatory drugs. *Future Medicinal Chemistry, 1*(7), 1333–1349. https://doi.org/10.4155/fmc.09.93

Nakajima, S., Gerretsem, P., Takeuchi, H., Caravaggio, F., Chow, T., Le Foll, B., Mulsant, B., Pollock, B., & Graff-Guerrero, A. (2013). The potential role of dopamine D_3 receptor neurotransmission in cognition. *European Neuropsychopharmacology: The Journal of the European College of Neuropsychopharmacology, 23*(8), 799–813.

National Academies of Sciences, Engineering, and Medicine. (2017). *The health effects of cannabis and cannabinoids: The current state of evidence and recommendations for research.* Washington: National Academies Press.

National Highway Traffic Safety Administration. (2014). *Drugs and human performance facts sheets.* Washington: United States Department of Transportation.

National Institute on Alcohol Abuse and Alcoholism. (2005). *Helping patients who drink too much: A clinician's guide* (NIH Publication No. 07-3769). Washington: US Department of Health and Human Services, National Institutes of Health. Retrieved from: http://pubs.niaaa.nih.gov/publications/Practitioner/CliniciansGuide2005/guide.pdf

National Institute on Drug Abuse. (2007). *The neurobiology of addiction: Section III—the action of heroin.* Retrieved from: https://www.drugabuse.

gov/publications/teaching-packets/neurobiology-drug-addiction/section-iii-action-heroin-morphine

National Institute on Drug Abuse. (2008). Brain pathways are affected by drugs of abuse. Retrieved from: http://www.drugabuse.gov/publications/addiction-science/why-do-people-abuse-drugs/brain-pathways-are-affected-by-drugs-abuse

National Institute on Drug Abuse. (2012a). Fentanyl. Retrieved from: http://www.drugabuse.gov/drugs-abuse/fentanyl

National Institute on Drug Abuse. (2012b). *Principles of drug addiction treatment: A research-based guide* (3rd ed.). Rockville: U.S. Department of Health and Human Services, Substance Abuse and Mental Health Services Administration.

Navari, R., & Province, P. (2006). Emerging drugs for chemotherapry-induced emesis. *Expert Opinion on Emerging Drugs, 11*(1), 137–151.

Nechanská, B., Mravčík, V., Skurtveit, S., Lund, I., Gabrhelík, R., Engeland, A., & Handal, M. (2018). Neonatal outcomes after fetal exposure to methadone and buprenorphine: National registry studies from the Czech Republic and Norway. *Addiction, 113*(7), 1286–1294.

Nelemans, S., Hale, W., Raaijmakers, Q., Branje, S., van Lier, P., & Meeus, W. (2016). Longitudinal associations between social anxiety symptoms and cannabis use throughout adolescence: The role of peer involvement. *European Child and Adolescent Psychiatry, 25*(5), 483–492.

Nelson, L., & Schwaner, R. (2009). Transdermal fentanyl: Pharmacology and toxicology. *Journal of medical toxicology, 5*(4), 230–241.

Neu, P. (2018). Course and complications of GHB detoxification treatment: A 1-year case series. *Der Nervenarzt*. doi:10.1007/s00115-018-0636-8

New Advent. (2009). St. Barbara. Retrieved from: http://www.newadvent.org/cathen/02284d.htm

Newcomer, J. (2005). Second-generation (atypical) antipsychotics and metabolic effects: A comprehensive literature review. *CNS Drugs, 19*(S1), 1–93.

NOFAS-UK. (2011). Foetal alcohol spectrum disorder (FASD): Information for parents, carers and professionals. Retrieved from: http://www.nofasuk.org/documents/2011.331%20NOFAS%20Factsheets%20Generic%20Final.pdf

Noll, R. (2007). *The encylopedia of schizophrenia and other psychotic disorders* (3rd ed.). New York: Facts On File.

Noller, G., Frampton, C., & Yazar-Klosinski, B. (2018). Ibogaine treatment outcomes for opioid dependence from a twelve-month follow-up observational study. *American Journal of Drug and Alcohol Abuse, 44*(1), 37–46.

Nörby, U., Winbladh, B., & Källén, K. (2017). Perinatal outcomes after treatment with ADHD medication during pregnancy. *Pediatrics, 140*(6), e20170747.

Nu-Pharm. (2009). *Product monograph: Nu-Zopiclone.* Richmond Hill: Nu Pharma Inc.

Nuutinen, S., & Panula, P. (2010). Histamine in neurotransmission and brain diseases. In R. Thurmond (Ed.), *Histamine in inflammation (Advances in experimental medicine and biology)* (Vol. 709) (pp. 95–108). Boston: Springer.

Nykjaer, C., Alwan, N., Greenwood, D., Simpson, N., Hay, A., White, K., & Cade, J. (2014). Maternal alcohol intake prior to and during pregnancy and risk of adverse birth outcomes: Evidence from a British cohort. *Journal of Epidemiology & Community Health, 68*(6), 542–549.

Oberg, M., Jaakkola, M., Woodward, A., Peruga, A., & Pruss-Ustun, A. (2011). Worldwide burden of disease from exposure to second-hand smoke. A retrospective analysis of data from 192 countries. *The Lancet, 377*(9760), 139–146.

Oberlander, T., Warburton, W., Misri, S., Aghajanian, J., & Hertzman, C. (2006). Neonatal outcomes after prenatal exposure to selective serotonin reuptake inhibitor antidepressants and maternal depression using population-based linked health data. *Archives of General Psychiatry, 63*(8), 898–906.

Office of National Statistics. (2018). *Deaths related to volatile substances and helium in Great Britain: 2001 to 2016.* Retrieved from: https://www.ons.gov.uk/peoplepopulationandcommunity/birthsdeathsandmarriages/deaths/articles/deathsrelatedtovolatilesubstancesandheliumingreatbritain/2001to2016registrations

O'Malley, S., Jaffe, A., Chang, G., Schottenfeld, R., Meyer, R., & Rounsaville, B. (1992). Naltrexone and coping skills therapy for alcohol dependence. *Archives of General Psychiatry, 49*(11), 881–887.

O'Neill, D., Britton, A., Brunner, E., & Bell, S. (2017). Twenty-five-year alcohol consumption trajectories and their association with arterial aging: A prospective cohort study. *Journal of the American Heart Association, 6*(2), e005288. doi:10.1161/JAHA.116.005288

Orman, J., & Keating, G. (2009). Spotlight on buprenorphine/naloxone in the treatment of opioid dependence. *CNS Drugs, 23*(10), 899–902.

Osorio, F., Sanches, R., Macedo, L., Santos, R., Maia de Oliveira, J., Wichert-Ana, L., Araujo, D., Riba, J., Crippa, J., & Hallak J. (2015). Antidepressant effects of a single dose of ayahuasca in patients with recurrent depression: A preliminary report. *Brazilian Journal of Psychiatry, 37*(1), 13–20.

Ot'alora G., Grigsby, J., Poulter, B., Van Derveer, J., Giron, S., Jerome, L., Feduccia, A., Hamilton, S., Yazar-Klosinski, B., Emerson, A., Mithoefer, M., & Doblin, R. (2018). 3,4-Methylenedioxymethamphetamine-assisted psychotherapy for treatment of chronic posttraumatic stress disorder: A randomized phase 2 controlled trial. *Journal of Psychopharmacology, 32*(12), 1295–1307.

Padala, P., Padala, K., Lensing, S., Ramirez, D., Monga, V., Bopp, M., Roberson, P., Dennis, R., Petty, F., & Sullivan, D. (2018). Methylphenidate for apathy in community-dwelling older veterans with mild Alzheimer's disease: A double-blind, randomized, placebo-controlled trial. *American Journal of Psychiatry, 175*(2), 159–168.

Pagel, J. F., & Parnes, B. L. (2001). Medications for the treatment of sleep disorders: An overview. *Journal of Clinical Psychiatry, 3*(3), 118–125.

Palpacuer, C., Duprez, R., Huneau, A., Locher, C., Boussageon, R., Laviolle, B., & Naudet, F. (2018). Pharmacologically controlled drinking in the treatment of alcohol dependence or alcohol use disorders: A systematic review with direct and network meta-analyses on nalmefene, naltrexone, acamprosate, baclofen and topiramate. *Addiction, 113*(2), 220–237.

Pandey, R., Gurumurthy, Narang, P., Remedios, K., Kadam, K., Murugappan, M., Sridhar, A., & Galinski, J. (2018). Nicotinic receptor up regulation and nicotine addiction: A review of mechanisms. *Chronicles of Pharmaceutical Science, 2*(3), 572–580.

Papenberg, G., Backman, L., Fratiglioni, L., Laukka, E., Fastborn, J., & Johnell, K. (2017). Anticholinergic drug use is associated with episodic memory decline in older adults without dementia. *Neurobiology of Aging, 55*(1), 27–32.

Parekh, P., Ozburn, A., & McClung, C. (2015). Circadian clock genes: Effects on dopamine, reward and addiction. *Alcohol, 49*(4), 341–349.

Park, G., Fulton, I., & Shelley, M. (1986). Normal pregnancy following nitrous oxide exposure in the first trimester. *British Journal of Anaesthesia*, *58*(5), 576–581.

Park, Y., Hernandez-Diaz, S., Bateman, B., Cohen, J., Desai, R., Patorno, E., Glynn, R., Cohen, L., Mogun, H., & Huybrechts, K. (2018). Continuation of atypical antipsychotic medication during early pregnancy and the risk of gestational diabetes. *The American Journal of Psychiatry*. https://doi.org/10.1176/appi.ajp.2018.17040393

Parrott, A., Moore, D., Turner, J., Goodwin, J., Min, M., & Singer, L. (2014). MDMA and heightened cortisol: A neurohormonal perspective on the pregnancy outcomes of mothers used "Ecstasy" during pregnancy. *Human Psychopharmacology: Clinical and Experimental, 29*(1), 1–7.

Parvaz, M., Moeller, S., d'Oleire Uquillas, F., Pflumm, A., Maloney, T., Alia-Klein, N., & Goldstein, R. (2017). Prefrontal gray matter volume recovery in treatment-seeking cocaine-addicted individuals: A longitudinal study. *Addiction Biology, 22*(5), 1391–1401.

Pase, M., Himali, J., Grima, N., Beiser, A., Satizabal, C., Aparicio, H., Thomas, R., Gottlieb, D., Auerbach, S., & Seshadri, S. (2017). Sleep architecture and the risk of incident dementia in the community. *Neurology, 89*(12), 1244–1250.

Passie, T., Halpern, J., Stichtenoth, D., Emrich H., & Hintzen, A. (2008). The pharmacology of lysergic acid diethylamide: A review. *CNS Neuroscience and Therapeutics, 4*(4), 295–314.

Patel, R., Reiss, P., Shetty, H., Broadbent, M., Stewart, R., McGuire, P., & Taylor, M. (2015). Do antidepressants increase the risk of mania and bipolar disorder in people with depression? A retrospective electronic case register cohort study. *BMJ Open, 5*(12), e008341.

Patra, J., Bakker, R., Irving, H., Jaddoe, V., Malini, S., & Rehm, J. (2011) Dose-response relationship between alcohol consumption before and during pregnancy and the risks of low birth weight, preterm birth and small for gestational age (SGA)—a systematic review and meta-analyses. *BJOG: An International Journal of Obstetrics and Gynaecology, 118*(12), 1411–1421.

Paul, S. (2006). Alcohol-sensitive GABA receptors and alcohol antagonists. *Proceedings of the National Academy of Science, 103*(22), 8307–8308.

Pellissier, L., Pujol, C., Becker, J., & Le Merrer, J. (2016) Delta opioid receptors: Learning and motivation. In *Handbook of experimental pharmacology* (pp. 1–34). Berlin: Springer.

Pereira., J., Lawlor, P., Vigano, A., Dorgan, M., & Bruera, E. (2001). Equianalgesic dose ratios for opioids: A critical review and proposals for long-term dosing. *Journal of Pain Symptom Management, 22*(2), 672–687.

Pérez-Mañá, C., Castells, X., Torrens, M., Capellà, D., & Farre, M. (2013). Efficacy of psychostimulant drugs for amphetamine abuse or dependence. *Cochrane Database of Systematic Reviews,* Issue 9. Art. No.: CD009695. doi:10.1002/14651858.CD009695.pub2

Perucca, E., Gram, L., Avanzini, G., & Dulac, O. (1998). Antiepileptic drugs as a cause of worsening seizures. *Epilepsia, 39*(1), 5–17.

Petroff, O. (2002). GABA and glutamate in the human brain. *Neuroscientist, 8*(6), 562–573.

Phillips, A., Strobl, R., Grill, E., & Laux, G. (2018). Anticholinergic and sedative medications and the risk of vertigo or dizziness in the German primary care setting: A matched case-control study from the CONTENT registry. *Pharmacoepidemiology and Safety, 27*(8), 912–920.

Piper, B. (2006). A developmental comparison of the neurobehavioral effects of ecstasy (MDMA). *Neurotoxicology and Teratology, 29*(2), 288–300.

Porath-Waller, A. (2016). *Clearing the smoke on cannabis: Maternal cannabis use during pregnancy—an update.* Ottawa: Canadian Centre on Substance Abuse.

Pottie, K., Thompson, W., Davies, S., Grenier, J., Sadowski, C., Welch, V., Holbrook, A., Boyd, C., Swenson, R., Ma, A., & Farrell, B. (2018). Deprescribing benzodiazepine receptor agonists: Evidence-based clinical practice guideline. *Canadian Family Physician, 64*(5), 339–351.

Pradham, S. (1984). Phencyclidine (PCP): Some human studies. *Neuroscience and Biobehavioral Reviews, 8*(4), 493–501.

Prahham, A., Befort, K., Nozaki, C., Gavériaux-Ruff, C., & Keiffer, B. (2011). The delta opioid receptor: An evolving target for the treatment of brain disorders. *Trends in Pharmacological Science*, *32*(10), 581–590.

Preller, K., Schilbach, L., Pokorny, T., Flemming, J., Seifritz, E., & Vollenweider, F. (2018). Role of the 5-HT_{2A} receptor in self- and other-initiated social interaction in lysergic acid diethylamide-Induced states: A pharmacological fMRI study. *Journal of Neuroscience, 38*(14), 3603–3611.

Prochazkova, L., Lippelt, D., Colzato, L., Kuchar, M., Sjoerds, Z., & Hommel, B. (2018). Exploring the effect of microdosing psychedelics on creativity in an open-label natural setting. *Psychopharmacology, 235*(12), 3401–3413.

Procyshyn, R., Bezchlibnyk-Butler, K., & Jeffries, J. (2017). *Clinical handbook of psychotropic drugs* (22nd ed.). Ashland: Hogrefe & Huber Publishers.

Prosser, J., & Nelson, L. (2012). The toxicology of bath salts: A review of synthetic cathinones. *Journal of Medical Toxicology, 8*(1), 33–42.

Pullen, L., Abbott, A., Lawhorn, A., & Harder, S. (2018). A review of the use of oral and injectable naltrexone for alcohol and opioid addiction treatment. *Mental Health Practice*. doi:10.7748/mhp.2018.e1263

Purdue Pharma. (2004). *Palladone*. Stamford: Author.

Queiroz, C., Tiba, P., Moreira, K., Guidine, P., Rezende, G., Moraes, M., Prado, M., Prado, V., Tufik, S., & Mello, L. (2013). Sleep pattern and learning in knockdown mice with reduced cholinergic neurotransmission. *Brazilian Journal of Medical and Biological Research*, *46*(10), 844–854.

Quinn, P., Chang, Z., Hur, K., Gibbons, R., Lahey, B., Rickert, M., Sjölander, A., Lichtenstein, P., Larsson, H., & D'Onofrio, B. (2017). ADHD medication and substance-related problems. *American Journal of Psychiatry, 174*(9), 877–885.

Ragia, G., & Manolopoulos, V. (2014). Pharmacgenomics of alcohol addiction: Personalizing pharmacologic treatment of alcohol dependence. *Hospital Pharmacology, 1*(3), 147–167.

Rahman, S. (2015). Targeting brain nicotinic acetylcholine receptors to treat major depression and co-morbid alcohol or nicotine addiction. *CNS & Neurological Disorders—Drug Targets, 14*(5), 647–653.

Raman-Wilms, L. (2014). *Canadian Pharmacists Association guide to drugs in Canada* (4th ed.). Toronto: Dorling Kindersley.

Rampino, A., Marakhovskaia, A., Beaulieu, J., & Silva, T. (2019). Antipsychotic drug responsiveness and dopamine receptor signaling; old players and new prospects. *Frontiers of Psychiatry*. doi:10.3389/fpsyt.2018.00702

Ranganathan, M., & D'Souza, D. (2006). The acute effects of cannabinoids on memory in humans: A review. *Psychopharmacology, 188*(4), 425–444.

Reece, A., Norman, A., & Hulse, G. (2016). Cannabis exposure as an interactive cardiovascular risk factor and accelerant of organismal ageing: A longitudinal study. *British Medical Journal Open, 6,* e011891. doi:10.1136/bmjopen-2016-011891

Reece, S., Morgan, C., Parascandola, M., & Siddiqi, K. (2018). Second hand smoke exposure during pregnancy: A cross-sectional analysis of data from Demographic and Health Survey from 30 low-income and middle-income countries. *Tobacco Control.* doi:10.1136/tobaccocontrol-2018-054288

Rehm, J., Baliunas, D., Brochu, S., Fischer, B., Gnam, W., Patra, J., & Single, E. (2006). *The costs of substance abuse in Canada, 2002.* Ottawa: Canadian Centre on Substance Abuse.

Reinares, M., Rosa, A., Franco, C., Goikolea, J., Fountoulakis, K., Siamouli, M., Gonda, X., Franqou, S., & Vieta, E. (2013). A systematic review on the role of anticonvulsants in the treatment of acute bipolar depression. *The International Journal of Neuropsychopharmacology, 16*(2), 485–496.

Reinoso-Suarez, F., De Andres, I., Rodrigo-Angulo, M. L., De la Roza, C., Nunez, A., & Garzon, M. (1999). The anatomy of dreaming and REM sleep. *European Journal of Anatomy, 3*(3), 163–175.

Reus, V., Fochtmann, L., Eyler, A., Hilty, D., Horvitz-Lennon, M., Jibson, M., Lopez, O., Mahoney, J., Pasic, J., Tan, Z., Wills, C., Rhoads, R., & Yager, J. (2016). The American Psychiatric Association Practice Guideline on the use of antipsychotics to treat agitation or psychosis in patients with dementia. *American Journal of Psychiatry, 173*(5), 543–546.

Rigg, K., & Sharp, A. (2018). Deaths related to MDMA (ecstasy/molly): Prevalence, root causes, and harm reduction interventions. *Journal of Substance Use, 23*(4), 345–352.

Risser, D., Honigschnabl, S., Stichenwerth, M., Pfundl, S., Sebald, D., Kaff, A., & Bauer, G. (2001). Mortality of opiate users in Vienna, Austria. *Drug and Alcohol Dependence, 64*(3), 251–256.

Ritz, B., Ascherio, A., Checkoway, H., Marder, K., Nelson, L., Rocca, W., & Gorell, J. (2007). Pooled analysis of tobacco use and risk of Parkinson disease. *Archives of Neurology, 64*(7), 990–997.

Robbins, T., & Sahakian, B. (1979). "Paradoxical" effects of psychomotor stimulant drugs in hyperactive children from the standpoint of behavioural pharmacology. *Neuropharmacology, 18*(12), 931–950.

Robson, P. (2014). Therapeutic potential of cannabinoid medicines. *Drug Testing and Analysis, 6*(1-2), 24–30.

Rogers, G., Elston, J., Garside, R., Roome, C., Taylor, R., Younger, P., & Somerville, M. (2009). The harmful health effects of recreational ecstasy: A systematic review of observational evidence. *Health Technology Assessment, 13*(6), 1–354.

Rogers, M., Rajanahally, S., Brisbane, W., Ostrowski, K., Lendvay, T., & Walsh, T. (2017). Relationship between cannabis and male reproductive health: A systematic review. *Fertility and Sterility, 108*(3), e131–e132.

Roncero, C., Grau-Lopez, L., Diaz-Moran, S., Miquel, L., Martinez-Luna, N., & Casas, M. (2012). Evaluation of sleep disorders in drug dependent inpatients. *Medicina Clinica, 138*(8), 332–335.

Rose, A., & Jones, A. (2018). Baclofen: Its effectiveness in reducing harmful drinking, craving, and negative mood. A meta-analysis. *Addiction, 113*(8), 1396–1406.

Roseman, L., Demetriou, L., Wall, M., Nutt, D., & Carhart-Harris, R. (2017). Increased amygdala responses to emotional faces after psilocybin for treatment-resistant depression. *Neuropharmacology, 142*(3), 263–269.

Rosenbaum, C., Carreiro, S., & Babu, K. (2012). Here today, gone tomorrow . . . and back again? A review of herbal marijuana alternatives (K2, Spice), synthetic cathinones (bath salts), kratom, Salvia divinorum, methoxetamine, and piperazines. *Journal of Medical Toxicology, 8*(1), 15–32.

Ross, E., Graham, D., Money, K., & Stanwood, G. (2015). Developmental consequences of fetal exposure to drugs: What we know and what we still must learn. *Neuropsychopharmacology Reviews, 40*, 61–87.

Ross, E., Reisfield, G., Watson, M., Chronister, C., & Goldberger, B. (2012). Psychoactive "bath salts" intoxication with methylenedioxypyrovalerone. *The Amercian Journal of Medicine, 125*(9), 854–858.

Roth, A., & Fonagy, P. (2005). *What works for whom? A critical review of psychotherapy research.* New York: Guilford Press.

Roth, B., Baner, K., Westkaemper, R., Siebert, D., Rice, K., Steinberg, S., & Rothman, R. (2002). Salvinorin A: A potent naturally occurring nonnitrogenous kappa opioid selective agonist. *Proceedings of the Natural Academy of Science, 99*(18), 11934–11939.

Roth, B., Gibbons, S., Arunotayanun, W., Huang, X., Setola, V., Treble, R., & Iversen, L. (2013). The ketamine analogue methoxetamine and 3- and 4-methoxy analogues of phencyclidine are high affinity and selective ligands for the glutamate NMDA receptor. *PLoS One, 8*(3), e59334.

Roth, T., Hartse, K., Saab, P., Piccione, P., & Kramer, M. (1980). The effects of flurazepam, lorazepam, and triazolam on sleep and memory. *Psychopharmacology 70*(3), 231–237.

Rowland, A., Day Baird, D., Weinberg, C., Shore, D., Shy, C., & Wilcox, A. (1992). Reduced fertility among women employed as dental assistants exposed to high levels of nitrous oxide. *The New England Journal of Medicine, 327*(14), 993–997.

Rubi, L., Eckert, D., Boehm, S., Hilber, K., & Koenig, X. (2016). Anti-addiction drug ibogaine prolongs the action potential in human induced pluripotent stem cell-derived cardiomyocytes. *Cardiovascular toxicology, 17*(2), 215–218.

Rucker, J., Iliff, D., & Nutt, J. (2018). Psychiatry & the psychedelic drugs. Past, present & future. *Neuropharmacology, 142*, 200–281.

Rush, B., Urbanoski, K., Bassani, D., Castel, S., Wild, T. C., Strike, C., Kimberley, D., & Somers, J. (2008). Prevalence of co-occurring substance use and other mental disorders in the Canadian population. *Canadian Journal of Psychiatry, 53*(12), 800–809.

Russolillo, A., Moniruzzaman, A., & Somers, J. (2018). Methadone maintenance treatment and mortality in people with criminal convictions: A population-based retrospective cohort study from Canada. *PLoS Med 15*(7), e1002625. https://doi.org/10.1371/journal.pmed.1002625

Ruxton, C. (2008). The impact of caffeine on mood, cognitive function, performance and hydration: A review of benefits and risks. *Nutrition Bulletin, 33*(1), 15–25.

Sabanaygam, C., & Shankar, A. (2011). The association between active smoking, smokeless tobacco, second-hand smoke exposure and insufficient sleep. *Sleep Medicine, 12*(1), 7–11.

Safer, D., & Allen, R. (1971). The central effects of scopolamine in man. *Biological Psychiatry, 3*(4), 347–355.

Salloum, I., Cornelius, J., Daley, D., Kirisci, L., & Himmelhoch, J. (2005). Efficacy of valproate maintenance in patients with bipolar disorder and alcoholism. *Archives of General Psychiatry, 62*(1), 37–45.

Sanacora, G., Treccani, G., & Popoli, M. (2012). Towards a glutamate hypothesis of depression: An emerging frontier of neuropsychopharmacology for mood disorders. *Neuropharmacology, 62*(1), 63–77.

Sanches, R., de Lima Osório, F., Dos Santos, R., Macedo, L., Maia-de-Oliveira, J., Wichert-Ana, L., de Araujo, D., Riba, J., Crippa, J., & Hallak, J. (2016). Antidepressant effects of a single dose of ayahuasca in patients with recurrent depression: A SPECT study. *Journal of Clinical Psychopharmacology, 36*(1), 77–81.

Sangal, R., Owens., J., Allen, A., Sutton, V., Schuh, K., & Kelsey, D. (2006). Effects of atomoxetine and methylphenidate on sleep in children with ADHD. *Sleep, 29*(12), 1573–1585.

Sanofi-Aventis. (2018). *Imovane (Zopiclone).* Retrieved from: http://products.sanofi.ca/en/imovane.pdf

Santamarina-Rubio, E., Perez, K., Ricart, I., Rodriguez-Sanz, A., Rodriguez-Martos, M., Brugal, T., & Suelves, J. (2009). Substance use among road traffic casualties admitted to emergency departments. *Injury Prevention, 15*(1), 87–94.

Sanyal, C., Asbridge, M., Kisely, S., Sketris, I., & Andreou, P. (2011). The utilization of antidepressants and benzodiazepines among people with major depression in Canada. *Canadian Journal of Psychiatry, 56*(11), 667–676.

Schierenbeck, T., Riemann, D. Berger, M., & Hornyak, M. (2008). Effect of illicit recreational drugs upon sleep: Cocaine, ecstasy and marijuana. *Sleep Medicine Reviews, 12*(5), 381–389.

Schimmelmann, B., Conus, P., Cotton, S., Kupferschmid, S., McGorry, P., & Lambert, M. (2012). Prevalence and impact of cannabis use disorders in adolescents with early onset first episode psychosis. *European Psychiatry, 27*(6), 463–469.

Schizophrenia Commission. (2012). *The abandoned illness: A report by the Schizophrenia Commission.* London: Rethink Mental Illness.

Schloesser, R., Huang, J., Klein, P., & Manj, H. (2007). Cellular plasticity cascades in the pathophysiology and treatment of bipolar disorder. *Neuropsychopharmacology, 33*(1), 110–133.

Schoeler, T., Monk, A., Sami, M., Klamerus, E., Foglia, E., Brown, R., Camuri, G., Altamura, A., Murray, R., & Bhattacharyya, S. (2016). Continued versus discontinued cannabis use in patients with psychosis: A systematic review and meta-analysis. *Lancet Psychiatry, 3*(3), 215–225.

Schooler, N., Goldberg, S., Boothe, H., & Cole, J. (1967). One year after discharge: Community adjustment of schizophrenic patients. *American Journal of Psychiatry, 123*(8), 986–995.

Schwenk, E., Viscusi, E., Buvanendran, A., Hurley, R., Wasan, A., Narouze, S., Bhatia, A., Davis, F., Hooten, W., & Cohen, S. (2018). Consensus guidelines on the use of intravenous ketamine infusions for acute pain management from the American Society of Regional Anesthesia and Pain Medicine, the American Academy of Pain Medicine, and the American Society of Anesthesiologists. *Regional Anesthesia and Acute Pain Medicine, 43*(5), 456–466.

Scofield, M., Heinsbroek, J., Gipson, C., Kupchik, Y., Spencer, S., Smith, A., Roberts-Wofe, D., & Kalivas, P. (2016). The nucleus accumbens: Mechanisms of addiction across drug classes reflect the importance of glutamate homeostasis. *Pharmacological Reviews, 68*(3), 816–871.

Scott, K., & Lust, K. (2010). Illicit substance use in pregnancy—a review. *Obstetric Medicine, 3*(3): 94–100.

Scott, L., Figgitt, D., Keam, S., & Waugh, J. (2005). Acamprosate. *CNS Drugs, 19*(5), 445–464.

Seeman, P. (2013a). Are dopamine D2 receptors out of control in psychosis? *Progress in Neuro-Psychopharmacology & Biological Psychiatry, 46*(2), 146–152.

Seeman, P. (2013b). An agonist at glutamate and dopamine D2 receptors, LY404039. *Neuropharmacology, 66*(1), 87–88.

Seip, M. (1976). Growth retardation, dysmorphic facies and minor malformations following massive exposure to phenobarbitone in utero. *Acta Paediatrica, 65*(4), 617–621.

Self, D. (1999). Anandamide: A candidate neurotransmitter heads for the big leagues. *Nature Neuroscience, 2*(4), 304–305.

Senn, M., Baiwog, F., Winmai, J., Mueller, I., Rogerson, S., & Senn, N. (2009). Betel nut chewing during pregnancy, Madang province, Papua New Guinea. *Drug and Alcohol Dependence, 105*(1–2), 126–131.

Serretti, A., & Mandelli, L. (2010). Antidepressants and body weight: A comprehensive review and meta-analysis. *Journal of Clinical Psychiatry, 71*(10), 1259–1272.

Sethi, S. (2006). Clozapine in pregnancy. *Indian Journal of Psychiatry, 48*(3), 196–197.

Shen, Y., Cao, X., Shan, C., Dai, W., & Yuan, T. (2017). Heroin addiction impairs human cortical plasticity. *Biological Psychiatry, 81*(7), e49–e50.

Short, B., Fong, J., Galvez, V., Shelker, W., & Loo, C. (2017). Side-effects associated with ketamine use in depression: A systematic review. *Lancet Psychiatry, 5*(1), 65–78.

Silins, E., Horwood, L., Patton, G., Fergusson, D., Olsson, C., Hutchinson, D., Spry, E., Toumbourou, J., Degenhardt, L., Swift, W., Coffey, C., Tait, R., Letcher, P., Copeland, J., & Mattick, R. (2014). Young adult sequelae of adolescent cannabis use: An integrative analysis. *Lancet Psychiatry, 1*(4): 286–293.

Simons F. (2003). Antihistamines. In *Middleton's allergy: Principles and practice* (6th ed.) (pp. 834–869). New York: Mosby.

Simou, E., Britton, J., & Leonardi-Bee, J. (2018). Alcohol and the risk of pneumonia: A systematic review and meta-analysis. *BMJ Open 8*(8), e022344. doi:10.1136/bmjopen-2018-022344

Simpson, C. (2015, January 3). 30 fatalities linked to ecstasy-like pills. *The Irish Times*. Retrieved from: http://www.irishnews.com/news/2015/01/03/news/30-fatalities-linked-to-ecstasy-like-pills-112119/

Singer, L., Moore, D., Fulton, S., Goodwin, J., Turner, J., Min, M., & Parrott, A. (2012). Neurobehavioral outcomes of infants exposed to MDMA (Ecstasy) and other recreational drugs during pregnancy. *Neurotoxicology & Teratology, 34*(3), 303–310.

Singer, S., Rossi, S., Verzosa, S., Hahim, A., Lonow, R., Cooper, T., Sershen, H., & Laitha, A. (2004). Nicotine-induced changes in neurotransmitter levels in brain areas associated with cognitive function. *Neurochemical Research, 29*(9), 1779–1792.

Singh, J., Fedgchin, M., Daly, E., Xi, L., Melman, C., De Bruecker, G., Tadic, A., Sienaert, P., Wiegand, F., Manji, H., Drevets, W., & Van Nueten, L. (2016). Intravenous esketamine in adult treatment-resistant depression: A double-blind, double-randomization, placebo-controlled study. *Biological Psychiatry, 80*(6), 424–431.

Single, E., Robson, L., Xie, X., & Rehm, J. (1996). *The cost of substance abuse in Canada*. Ottawa: Canadian Centre on Substance Abuse.

Sirohi, S., Dighe, S., Madia, P., & Yoburn, B. (2009). The relative potency of inverse opioid agonists and a neutral opioid antagonist in precipitated withdrawal and antagonism of analgesia and toxicity. *Journal of Pharmacology and Experimental Therapeutics, 330*(2), 513–519.

Slater, J., Zechnich, A., & Haxby, D. (1999). Second-generation antihistamines. *Drugs, 57*(1), 47–57.

Slemmer, J., Martin, B., & Damaj, M. (2000). Bupropion is a nicotinic antagonist. *Journal of Pharmacology and Experimental Therapeutics, 295*(1), 321–327.

Smart, G., & Storm, T. (1964). The efficacy of LSD in the treatment of alcoholism. *Quarterly Journal in the Studies of Alcohol, 25*, 333–338.

Smetanin, P., Stiff, D., Briante, C., Adair, C. , Ahmad, S., & Khan, M. (2011). *The life and economic impact of major mental illnesses in Canada: 2011 to 2041.* Ottawa: Risk Analytica on behalf of the Mental Health Commission of Canada.

Smith, D., Raswyck, E., & Davidson, L. (2014). From Hofmann to the Haight Ashbury, and into the future: The past and potential of lysergic acid diethlyamide. *Journal of Psychoactive Drugs, 46*(1), 3–10.

Smith, G., Barrett, F., Joo, J., Nassery, N., Savonenko, A., Sodums, D., Marano, C., Munro, C., Brandt, J., Kraut, M., Zhou, Y., Wong, D., & Workman, C. (2017). Molecular imaging of serotonin degeneration in mild cognitive impairment. *Neurobiology of disease, 105*(1), 33–41.

Smith, H. (2009). Opioid metabolism. *Mayo Clinic Procedures, 84*(7), 613–624.

Smith, L., LaGasse, L., Derauf., C., Newman, E., Shah, R., Haning, W., Arria, A., Huestis, M., Strauss, A., Della Grotta, S., Dansereau, L., Lin, H., & Lester, B. (2011). Motor and cognitive outcomes through three years of age in children exposed to prenatal methamphetamine. *Neurotoxicology and Teratology, 33*(1), 176–184.

Smith, M. (2018, August 14). Fentanyl used to execute Nebraska inmate, in a first for U.S. *New York Times*. Retrieved from: https://www.nytimes.com/2018/08/14/us/carey-dean-moore-nebraska-execution-fentanyl.html

So, M., Bozzo, P., Inoue, M., & Einarson, A. (2010). Safety of antihistamines during pregnancy and lactation. *Canadian Family Physician, 56*(5), 427–429.

Society for the Study of Addiction. (2016). *Novel psychoactive substances.* Retrieved from: https://www.addiction-ssa.org/images/uploads/Clin_111_Novel_Psychoative_SubstancesupdatedAug16.pdf

Sophocleous, A., Robertson, R., Ferreira, N., McKenzie, J., Fraser, W., & Ralston, S. (2017). Heavy cannabis use is associated with low bone mineral density and an increased risk of fractures. *American Journal of Medicine, 130*(2), 214–221.

Spadari, M., Glaizal, M., Tichadou, L., Blanc, I., Drouet, G., Aymard, I., De Haro, L., Hayek-Lanthois, M., & Arditti, J. (2009). Accidental cannabis poisoning in children: Experience of the Marseille poison center. *Presse Medicale, 38*(11), 1563–1567.

Special Advisory Committee on the Epidemic of Opioid Overdoses. (2018). *National report: Apparent opioid-related deaths in Canada (January 2016 to December 2017).* Ottawa: Public Health Agency of Canada.

Special Committee on Non-Medical Use of Drugs. (2002). *Policy for the new millennium: Working together to redefine Canada's drug strategy.* Ottawa: Public Works and Government Services Canada.

Spinella, M. (2001). *The psychopharmacology of herbal medicine.* Boston: Massachusetts Institute of Technology.

Spinks, A., & Wasiak, J. (2011). Scopolamine (hyoscine) for preventing and treating motion sickness. *Cochrane Databse of Systemic Reviews, 6.* Art No. CD002851. doi:10.1002/14651858.CD002851.pub4

Sproule, B. (2004). *Pharmacology and drug abuse* (2nd ed.). Toronto: Centre for Addiction and Mental Health.

Sproule, B., Brands, B., Li, S., & Catz-Biro, L. (2009). Changing patterns in opioid addiction: Characterizing users of oxycodone and other opioids. *Canadian Family Physician*, *55*(1), 68–69.

Srisurapanont, M., & Jarusuraisin, N. (2005). Naltrexone for the treatment of alcoholism: A meta-analysis of randomized controlled trials. *The International Journal of Neuropsychopharmacology*, *8*(2), 267–280.

Srivastava, A., & Kahan, M. (2006). Methadone induction doses: Are our current practices safe? *Journal of Addictive Diseases*, *25*(3), 5–13.

Stahl, S. (2017). Dazzled by the dominions of dopamine: Clinical roles of D3, D2, and D1 receptors. *CNS Spectrum, 22*(4), 305–311.

Stebner, B. (2012, May 12). The most dangerous drug in the world: "Devil's Breath" chemical from Colombia can block free will, wipe memory and even kill. *Daily Mail.* Retrieved from: http://www.dailymail.co.uk/news/article-2143584/Scopolamine-Powerful-drug-growing-forests-Colombia-ELIMINATES-free-will.html

Steiger, A. (2010). Sleep cycle. *Corsini Encyclopedia of Psychology*, 1–2. doi:10.1002/9780470479216.corpsy0879

Stith, S., Vigil, J., Brockelman, F., Keeling, K., & Hall, B. (2018). Patient-reported symptom relief following medical cannabis consumption. *Frontiers in Pharmacology*, *9*, 916. doi:10.3389/fphar.2018.00916

Stockings, E., Zagic, D., Campbell, G., Weier, M., Hall, W., Nielsen, S., Herkes, G., Farrell, M., & Degenhardt, L. (2018). Evidence for cannabis and cannabinoids for epilepsy: A systematic review of controlled and observational evidence. *Journal of Neurology, Neurosurgery and Psychiatry, 89*(7), 741–753.

Stoeber, M., Jullié, D., Lobingier, B., Laeremans, T., Steyaert, J., Schiller, P., Manglik, A., & von Zastrow, M. (2018). A genetically encoded biosensor reveals location bias of opioid drug action. *Neuron, 98*(5), 963–976.

Storr, M., Devlin, S., Kaplan, G., Panaccione, R., & Andrews, C. (2014). Cannabis use provides symptom relief in patients with inflammatory bowel disease but is associated with worse disease prognosis in patients with Crohn's disease. *Inflammatory Bowel Diseases, 20*(3), 472–480.

Stowie, A., Prosser, R., & Glass, J. (2015). Cocaine modulation of the mammalian circadian clock: Potential therapeutic targets. *Therapeutic Targets for Neurological Diseases, 2, e607.* doi:10.14800/ttnd.607

Strauss, A., Modanlou, H., & Bosu, S. (1981). Neonatal manifestations of maternal phencyclidine (PCP) abuse. *Pediatrics, 68*(4), 550–552.

Stroud, L., Paster, R., Papandonatos, G., Niaura, R., Salisbury, A., Battle, C., Lagasse, L., & Lester, B. (2009). Maternal smoking during pregnancy and newborn neurobehavior: Effects at 10 to 27 days. *The Journal of Pediatrics, 154*(1), 10–16.

Su, P., Chang, Y., & Chen, J. (2010). Infant with in utero ketamine exposure: Quantitative measurement of residual dosage in hair. *Pediatrics & Neonatology, 51*(5), 279–284.

Sue, D., Sue, D., Sue, D., & Sue, S. (2011). *Understanding abnormal behaviour* (10th ed.). Toronto: Houghton Mifflin.

Suhaimi, M. Z., Sanip, Z., Jan, H. J., & Yusoff, H. M. (2016). Leptin and calorie intake among different nicotine dependent groups. *Annals of Saudi Medicine, 36*(6), 404–408.

Sulzer, D., Sonders, M., Poulsen, N., & Galli, A. (2005). Mechanisms of neurotransmitter release by amphetamines: A review. *Progress in Neurobiology, 75*(6), 406–433.

Sumnall, H., Woolfall, K., Cole, J., Mackridge, A., & McVeigh, J. (2008). Diversion and abuse of methylphenidate in light of new guidance. *British Medical Journal, 337*, a2287.

Svatikova, A., Covassin, N., Somers, K. R., Somers, K. V., Soucek, F., Kara, T., & Bukartyk, J. (2015). A randomized trial of cardiovascular responses to energy drink consumption in healthy adults. *Journal of the American Medical Association, 314*(19), 2079–2082.

Sylvestre, M., Abrahamowicz, M., Čapek, R., & Tamblyn, R. (2012). Assessing the cumulative effects of exposure to selected benzodiazepines on the risk of fall-related injuries in the elderly. *International Psychogeriatrics, 24*(4), 577–586.

Takagi, M., Lubman, D., & Yu, M. (2011). Solvent-induced leukoencephalopathy: A disorder of adolescence? *Substance Use and Misuse, 45*(1), 95–98.

Tanguay, H., Zadra, A., Good, D., & Leri, F., (2015). Relationship between drug dreams, affect, and craving during treatment for substance dependence. *Journal of Addiction Medicine, 9*(2), 123–129.

Tanner, G., Bordon, N., Conroy, S., & Best, D. (2011). Comparing methadone and Suboxone in applied treatment settings: The experiences of maintenance patients in Lanarkshire. *Journal of Substance Abuse*, *16*(3), 171–178.

Tapiainen, V., Taipale, H., Tanskanen, A., Tiihonen, J., Hartikainen, S., & Tolppanen, A. (2018). The risk of Alzheimer's disease associated with benzodiazepines and related drugs: A nested case–control study. *Acta Psychiatrica Scandinavica, 138*(2), 91–100.

Tarr, B., Launay, J., Benson, C., & Dunbar, R. (2017). Naltrexone blocks endorphins released when dancing in synchrony. *Adaptive Human Behavior and Physiology, 3*(3), 241–254.

Tecce, J., & Cole, J. (1974). Amphetamine effects in man: Paradoxical drowsiness and lowered electrical brain activity (CNV). *Science*, *185*(4149), 451–453.

Terbeck, S., Akkus, F., Chesterman, L., & Hasler, G. (2015). The role of metabotropic glutamate receptor 5 in the pathogenesis of mood disorders and addiction: Combining preclinical evidence with human Positron Emission Tomography (PET) studies. *Frontiers in Neuroscience, 9*. doi:10.3389/fnins.2015.00086

Thapar, A., Fowler, T., Rice, F., Scourfield, J., van den Bree, M., Thomas, H., & Hay, D. (2003). Maternal smoking during pregnancy and attention deficit hyperactivity disorder symptoms in offspring. *American Journal of Psychiatry, 160*(11), 1985–1989.

Thomas-MacLean, R., Stoppard, J., Meidema, B., & Tatemichi, S. (2005). Diagnosing depression: There is no blood test. *Canadian Family Physician*, *51*(8), 1102–1110.

Thurmond, R. (2015). The histamine H4 receptor: From orphan to the clinic. *Frontiers in Pharmacology, 6*. doi:10.3389/fphar.2015.00065

Tomkins, D., & Sellers, E. (2001). Addiction and the brain: The role of neurotransmitters in the cause and treatment of drug dependence. *Canadian Medical Association Journal*, *164*(6), 817–821.

Tosato, S., Albert, U., Tomassi, S., Iasevoli, F., Carmassi, C., Ferrari, S., Nanni, M., Nivoli, A., Volpe, U., Atti, A., & Fiorillo, A. (2017). A systematized review of atypical antipsychotics in pregnant women: Balancing between risks of untreated illness and risks of drug-related adverse effects. *Journal of Clinical Psychiatry, 78*(5), e477–e489.

Toubia, T., & Khalife, T. (2018). The endogenous opioid system. *Clinical Obstetrics and Gynecology*. doi:10.1097/GRF.0000000000000409

Trafton, J., & Ramani, A. (2009). Methadone: A new old drug with promises and pitfalls. *Current Pain and Headache Reports, 13*(1), 24–30.

Trescot, A., Datta, S., Lee, M., & Hansen, H. (2008). Opioid pharmacology. *Pain Physician, 11,* S133–S153.

Trifilieff, P., Ducrocq, F., van der Veldt, S., & Martinez, D. (2017). Blunted dopamine transmission in addiction: Potential mechanisms and implications for behavior. *Seminars in Nuclear Medicine, 47*(1), 64–74.

Triplett, K., Goodin, A., Delcher, C., Brown, J., & Roussos-Ross, K. (2017). Opioid drug exposures and health care utilization measures associated with neonatal abstinence syndrome in Florida, 2011–2015. *Journal of Gynecology & Obstetrics, 1*(4), 018.

Tunnicliff, G. (1997). Sites of action of gamma-hydroxybutyrate (GHB)—a neuroactive drug with abuse potential. *Clinical Toxicology, 35*(6), 581–590.

Turner, E., Matthews, A., Linardardatos, E., Tell, R., & Rosthenthal, R. (2008). Selective publication of antidepressant effectiveness and its influence on apparent efficacy. *New England Journal of Medicine, 358*(3), 252–260.

Tzu-Chin, W., Tashkin, D., Djahed, B., & Rose, J. (1988). Pulmonary hazards of smoking marijuana as compared with tobacco. *New England Journal of Medicine, 318*(6), 347–351.

Uchiyama, N., Kihura-Hanjiri, R., Kawahara, N., & Goda, Y. (2009). Identification of a cannabiminmetic indole as a designer drug in a herbal product. *Forensic Toxicology, 2*(1), 61–66.

Umbricht A., & Velez, M. (2015). Benzodiazepine abuse and addiction. In N. el-Guebaly, G. Carrà, & M. Galanter (Eds.), *Textbook of addiction treatment: International perspectives* (pp. 345–365). Milano: Springer.

United Kingdom Tetralogy Information Service. (2018a). *Bupropion.* Retrieved from: http://www.medicinesinpregnancy.org/Medicine--pregnancy/Bupropion/

United Kingdom Tetralogy Information Service. (2018b). *Decongestants.* Retrieved from: http://www.medicinesinpregnancy.org/Medicine--pregnancy/Decongestants/

United Kingdom Tetralogy Information Service. (2018c). *Fluoxetine.* Retrieved from: http://www.medicinesinpregnancy.org/Medicine--pregnancy/Fluoxetine/

United Nations Office on Drugs and Crime. (2013). *The challenge of new psychoactive drugs.* Vienna: United Nations.

United Nations Office on Drugs and Crime. (2016). *Terminology and information on drugs* (3rd ed.). Vienna: United Nations.

United Nations Office on Drugs and Crime. (2017). *Global synthetic drugs assessment.* Vienna: United Nations.

United Nations Office on Drugs and Crime. (2018). *2018 world drug report.* Vienna: United Nations.

United States Food and Drug Administration. (2016). *Phenylpropanolamine (PPA) information page.* Retrieved from: https://www.fda.gov/Drugs/DrugSafety/InformationbyDrugClass/ucm150738.htm

Uzun, S., Kozumplik, O., Jakovljević, M., & Sedić, B. (2010). Side effects of treatment with benzodiazepines. *Psychiatria Danubina, 22*(1), 90–93.

Vallance, J., Gardiner, P., Lynch, B., D'Silva, A., Boyle, T., Taylor, L., Johnson, S., Buman, M., & Owen, N. (2018). Evaluating the evidence on sitting, smoking, and health: Is sitting really the new smoking? *American Journal of Public Health, 108*(11), 1478–1482.

Van Dam, N., Bed, G., & Earleywine, M. (2012). Characteristics of clinically anxious versus non-anxious regular, heavy marijuana users. *Addictive Behaviors, 37*(11), 1217–1223.

van Ours, J., & Williams, J. (2009). Cannabis use and mental health problems (Discussion paper). Tilburg University, The Netherlands.

Vandrey, R., Budney, A., Hughes, J., & Liguori, A. (2008). A within subject comparison of withdrawal symptoms during abstinence from cannabis, tobacco and both substances. *Drug and Alcohol Dependence, 92*(1–3), 48–54.

Vaquero, L., Sampedro, F., de los Cobos, J., Batlle, F., Fabregas, J., Sales, J., Cervantes, M., Ferrer, X., Lazcano, G., Rodriquez-Fornells, A., & Riba, J. (2016). Cocaine addiction is associated with abnormal prefrontal function, increased striatal connectivity and sensitivity to monetary incentives, and decreased connectivity outside the human reward circuit. *Addiction Biology, 22*(3), 844–856.

Verheyden, S., Maidment, R., & Curran, H. (2003). Quitting ecstasy: An investigation of why people stop taking the drug and their subsequent mental health. *Journal of Psychopharmacology, 17*(4), 371–378.

Vevelstad M., Leere Øiestad, E., Middelkoop, G., Hasvold, I., Lilleng, P., Jorunn, G., Delaveris, M., Eggen, T., Mørland, J., & Arnestad, M. (2012). The PMMA epidemic in Norway: Comparison of fatal and non-fatal intoxications. *Forensic Science International, 219* (1–3), 151–157.

Vieweg, W., Lipps, W., & Fernandez, A. (2005). Opioids and methadone equivalents for clinicians. *The primary care companion to the Journal of Clinical Psychiatry, 7*(3), 86–88.

Vigil, J., Stith, S., Adams, I., & Reeve, A. (2017). Associations between medical cannabis and prescription opioid use in chronic pain patients: A preliminary cohort study. *PLoS ONE, 12*(11), e0187795. https://doi.org/10.1371/journal.pone.0187795

Viktorin, A., Uher, R., Kolevzon, A., Reichenberg, A., Levine, S., & Sandin, S. (2017). Association of antidepressant medication use during pregnancy with intellectual disability in offspring. *Journal of the American Medical Association: Psychiatry, 74*(10), 1031–1038.

Volkow, N., Swanson, J., Evins, E., DeLisi, L., & Mei, M. (2016). Effects of cannabis use on human behavior, including cognition, motivation, and psychosis: A review. *Journal of the American Medical Association: Psychiatry, 73*(3), 292–297.

Volkow, N., Wise, R., & Baler, R. (2017). The dopamine motive system: Implications for drug and food addiction. *Nature Reviews Neuroscience, 18*, 741–752.

Vollenweider, F., Remensberger, S., Hell, D., & Geyer, M. (1999). Opposite effects of 3,4-methylenedioxymethamphetamine (MDMA) on sensorimotor gating in rats versus healthy humans. *Psychopharmacology, 143*(4), 365–372.

Volpicelli, J. R., Alterman, A. I., Hayashida, M., & O'Brien, C. P. (1992). Naltexone in the treatment of alcohol dependence. *Archives of General Psychiatry, 49*(11), 876–880.

Voorspoels, S., Coucke, V., Covaci, A., Maervoet, J., Schepens, P., DeMeyere, C., & Jacobs, W. (2002). Resurgence of a lethal drug: Paramethoxyamphetamine deaths in Belgium. *Journal of Toxicology and Clinical Toxicology, 40*(2), 203–204.

Walsh, A., Callaway, R., Belle-Isle, L., Capier, R., Kay, R., Lucas, P., & Holtzman, S. (2013). Cannabis for therapeutic purposes: Patient characteristics, access, and reasons for use. *International Journal of Drug Policy, 24*(6), 511–516.

Walsh, S., Nuzzo, P., Lofwall, M., & Holtman, J. (2008). The relative abuse liability of oral oxycodone, hydrocodone and hydromorphone assessed in prescription opioid abusers. *Drug and Alcohol Dependence, 98*(3), 191–202.

Wang, D., & Teichtahl, H. (2007). Opioids, sleep architecture and sleep-disordered breathing. *Sleep Medicine Review, 11*(1), 35–46.

Wang, Q., Yue, X., Qu, W., Tan, R., Zheng, P., Urade, Y., & Huang, Z. L. (2013). Morphine inhibits sleep-promoting neurons in the ventrolateral preoptic area via mu receptors and induces wakefulness in rats. *Neuropsychopharmacology, 38*(5), 791–801.

Wang, R., Shen, Y., Hausknecht, K., Chang, L., Haj-Dahmane, S., Vezina, P., & Shen, R. (2018). Prenatal ethanol exposure increases risk of psychostimulant addiction. *Behavioural Brain Research.* https://doi.org/10.1016/j.bbr.2018.07.030

Warner, C., Bobo, W., Warner, C., Reid, S., & Rachal, J. (2006). Antidepressant discontinuation syndrome. *American Family Physician, 74*(3), 449–456.

Watterson, L., Kufahl, R., Nemirovsky, N., Sewalia, K., Grabenaur, M., Thomas, B., & Olive, M. (2012). Potent rewarding and reinforcing effects of thesynthetic cathinone 3,4-methylenedioxypyrovalerone (MDPV). *Addiction Biology, 19*(2), 165–174.

Weil, A. (1978). Coca leaf as a therapeutic agent. *American Journal of Drug and Alcohol Abuse, 5*(1), 75–86.

Weizman, L., Dayan, L., Brill, S., Nahman-Averbuch, H., Hendler, T., Jacob, G., & Sharon, H. (2018). Cannabis analgesia in chronic neuropathic pain is associated with altered brain connectivity. *Neurology*. doi:10.1212/WNL.0000000000006293

Wellman, P. (1990). The pharmacology of the anorexic effect of phenylpropanolamine. *Drugs Under Experimental and Clinical Research, 16*(9), 487–495.

Wellman, R., Wilson, K., O'Loughlin, E., Dugas, E., Montreuil, A., & O'Loughlin, J. (2018). Secondhand smoke exposure and depressive symptoms in children: A longitudinal study. *Nicotine & Tobacco Research*, nty224. https://doi.org/10.1093/ntr/nty224

Weschules, D., Bain, K., & Richeimer, S. (2008). Actual and potential drug interactions associated with methadone. *Acute Pain, 10*(2), 101–102.

Wheaton, E., Schauer, E., & Galli, T. (2010). Economics of human trafficking. *International migration*, *48*(4), 114–141.

Whitaker, R. (2005). Anatomy of an epidemic: Psychiatric drugs and the astonishing rise of mental illness in America. *Ethical Human Psychology and Psychiatry, 7*(1), 23–35.

White, I., Altmann, D., & Nanchahal, K. (2002). Alcohol consumption and mortality: Modelling risks for men and women at different ages. *British Medical Journal, 325*(7357), 191.

White, N., Sklar, L., & Amit, Z. (1977). The reinforcing action of morphine and its paradoxical side effect. *Psychopharmacology, 52*(1), 63–66.

Wieland, D., Halter, M., & Levine, C. (2012). Bath salts: They are not what you think. *Journal of Psychosocial Nursing and Mental Health Services, 50*(2), 17–21.

Winkelman, M. (2014). Psychedelics as medicines for substance abuse rehabilitation: Evaluating treatments with LSD, peyote, ibogaine and ayahuasca. *Current Drug Abuse Reviews, 7*(2), 101–116.

Winkelman, T., Villapiano, N., Kozhimannil, K., Davis, M., & Patrick, S. (2018). Incidence and costs of neonatal abstinence syndrome among infants with Medicaid: 2004–2014. *Pediatrics, 141*(4), e20173520. doi:10.1542/peds.2017-3520

Winstock, A., & Barratt, M. (2013). Synthetic cannabis: A comparison of patterns of use and effect profile with natural cannabis in a large global sample. *Drug and Alcohol Dependence, 131*(1–2), 106–111.

Wolf, P., Roder-Wanner, U., & Brede, M. (1984). Influence of therapeutic phenobarbital and phenytoin medication on the polygraphic sleep of patients with epilepsy. *Epilepsia, 25*(4), 467–475.

Wolff, K. (2002). Characterization of methadone overdose: Clinical considerations and the scientific evidence. *Therapeutic Drug Monitoring, 24*(4), 457–470.

Woloshin, S., Schwartz, L., & Welch, H. (2008). The risk of death by age, sex and smoking status in the United States: Putting health risks in context. *Journal of the National Cancer Institute, 100*(12), 845–853.

Wolowich, W., Perkins, A., & Cienik, J. (2006). Analysis of the psychoactive terpenoid salvinorin A content in five *Salvia divinorum* herbal products. *Pharmacotherapy, 26*(9), 1268–1272.

World Health Organization. (2014a). Letter from the World Society of Intravenous Anaesthesia to the WHO Expert Committee on Drug Dependence (agenda item 6.2). *Thirty-sixth WHO Expert Committee on Drug Dependence.* Geneva: WHO.

World Health Organization. (2014b). Tobacco free initiative (TFI). Retrieved from: http://www.who.int/tobacco/mpower/tobacco_facts/en/

World Health Organization. (2018). *Global status report on alcohol and health.* Geneva: World Health Organization.

Wu, F., Parvez, F., Islam, T., Ahmed, A., Rakibuz-Zaman, M., Hasan, R., Argos, M., Levy, D., Sarwar, G., Ahsan, H., & Yu, C. (2015). Betel quid use and mortality in Bangladesh: A cohort study. *Bulletin of the World Health Organization, 93*(10), 684–692.

Yakoot, M. (2012). Phenylpropanolamine and the hemorrhagic stroke: A new search for the culprit. *Journal of Pharmacology & Pharmacotherapeutics, 3*(1), 4–6.

Yan, Y., Peng, C., Arvin, M., Jin, X., Kim, V., Ramsey, M., Wang, Y., Banala, S., Wokosin, D. L., McIntosh, J., Lavis, L., & Drenan, R. (2018). Nicotinic cholinergic receptors in VTA glutamate neurons modulate excitatory transmission. *Cell Reports, 23*(8), 2236–2244.

Yang, M., Chang, T., Chen, S., Lee, C., & Ko, Y. (1999). Betel quid chewing and risk of adverse pregnancy outcomes among aborigines in Southern Taiwan. *Public Health, 113*(4), 189–192.

Yang, M., Lee, C., Chang, S., Chung, T., Tsai, E., Ko, A., & Ko, Y. (2008). The effect of maternal betel quid exposure during pregnancy on adverse birth outcomes among aborigines in Taiwan. *Drug and Alcohol Dependence, 95*(1–2), 134–139.

Yankey, B., Rothenberg, R., Strasser, S., Ramsey-White, K., & Okosun, I. (2017). Effect of marijuana use on cardiovascular and cerebrovascular mortality: A study using the National Health and Nutrition Examination Survey linked mortality file. *European Journal of Preventive Cardiology, 24*(17), 1833–1840.

Yasaei, R., & Saadabadi, A. (2017). *Meperidine.* Retrieved from: https://www.ncbi.nlm.nih.gov/books/NBK470362/

Yau, W., Mitchell, A., Lin, K., Werler, M., & Hernández-Díaz, S. (2013). Use of decongestants during pregnancy and the risk of birth defects. *American Journal of Epidemiology, 178*(2), 198–208.

Yonkers, K., Gilstad-Hayden, K., Forray, A., & Lipkind, H. (2017). Association of panic disorder, generalized anxiety disorder, and benzodiazepine treatment during pregnancy with risk of adverse birth outcomes. *JAMA Psychiatry, 74*(11), 1145–1152.

Zaami, S., Giorgetti, R., Pichini, S., Pantano, F., Marinelli, E., & Busardò, F. (2018). Synthetic cathinones related fatalities: An update. *European Review of Medical Pharmacological Sciences, 22*(1), 268–274.

Zakzanis, K., & Young, D. (2001). Esctasy use and long-term memory loss. *Neurology, 56*(7), 966–969.

Zarate, C., & Machado-Vieira, R. (2015). Potential pathways involved in the rapid antidepressant effects of nitrous oxide. *Biological Psychiatry, 78*(1), 2–4.

Zawilska, J. (2011). "Legal highs"—new players in the old drama. *Current Drug Abuse Reviews, 4*(2), 122–130.

Zedler, B., Mann, A., Kim, M., Amick, H., Joyce, A., Murrelle, E., & Jones, H. (2016). Buprenorphine compared with methadone to treat pregnant women with opioid use disorder: A systematic review and meta-analysis of safety in the mother, fetus and child. *Addiction, 111*(12), 2115–2128.

Zehra, A., Burns, J., Liu, C., Manza, P., Wiers, C., Volkow, N., & Wang, G. (2018). Cannabis addiction and the brain: A review. *Journal of Neuroimmune Pharmacology*. https://doi.org/10.1007/s11481-018-9782-9

Zhang, S., Lee, I., Manson, J., Cook, N., Willett, W., & Buring, J. (2007). Alcohol consumption and breast cancer risk in the women's health study. *American Journal of Epidemiology, 165*(6), 667–676.

Zhao, J., Stockwell, T., Roemer, A., & Chikritzhs, T. (2016). Is alcohol consumption a risk factor for prostate cancer? A systematic review and meta-analysis. *BMC Cancer, 16,* 845. https://doi.org/10.1186/s12885-016-2891-z

Zhao, T., Li, Y., Wei, W., Savage, S., Zhou, L., & Ma, D. (2014). Ketamine administered to pregnant rats in the second trimester causes long-lasting behavioral disorders in offspring. *Neurobiology of Disease, 68*, 145–155.

Zhao, Z., Gao, Y., Sun, Y., Zhao, C., Gereau, R., & Chen, Z. (2007). Central serotonergic neurons are differently required for opioid analgesia but not for morphine tolerance or morphine reward. *Proceedings of the National Academy of Sciences, 104*(36), 14519–14524.

Zheng, X., & Hasegawa, H. (2016). Administration of caffeine inhibited adenosine receptor agonist-induced decreases in motor performance, thermoregulation, and brain neurotransmitter release in exercising rats. *Pharmacology, biochemistry, and behavior, 140*(1), 82–89.

Zimmermann, K., & Becker, J. (2016). Harmful effects of recreational ecstasy use on memory functioning. *Addiction Research & Therapy,* 7(266). http://dx.doi.org/10.4172/2155-6105.1000266

COPYRIGHT ACKNOWLEDGEMENTS

Figures 1.8, 1.11, 2.4, 3.2, 3.5, 5.1, and 5.3 from Sproule, B. (2004). *Pharmacology and Drug Abuse, 2nd Edition*. Toronto: Centre for Addiction and Mental Health. Reprinted with permission of CAMH.

Figure 1.9: D. Self, Anandamide: A candidate neurotransmitter heads for the big leagues (*Nature Neuroscience*, 2(4), 1999), 304–305, Figure 1. Reprinted with permission from *Springer Nature*.

Figure 1.10: © The Nobel Committee for Physiology or Medicine 2000. Reprinted with permission.

Figure 1.13: "Diagram of mechanism of action of the natural neurotransmitter GABA (gamma-aminobutyric acid) and benzodiazepines on nerve cells (neurons) in the brain" from H. Ashton (http://www.benzo.org.uk, 2013), Figure 1.

Figure 1.16: D. Bourne, A First Course in Pharmacokinetics and Biopharmaceutics. (https://www.boomer.org/c/p4/c07/c0705.php, 2001). Reprinted with permission.

Figure 1.18: Process of Heroin Withdrawal, from Raman-Wilms L. *Canadian Pharmacists Association Guide to Drugs in Canada. 4th Edition*. Dorling Kindersley Limited, 2014. Reprinted with permission.

Figure 2.3: International Federation of Clinical Chemistry and Laboratory Medicine (IFCC), Neurotransmitters and Their Receptors (http://www.ifcc.org/media/476986/ejifcc2004vol15no3pp061-067.pdf, 2004). Reprinted with permission.

Figure 2.10: Kosten, T., & George, T. (2002). The neurobiology of opioid dependence: Implications for treatment. *Science & Practice Perspectives*, *1*(1), 13–20. Reprinted with permission.

Figure 3.18: Northern Territory Department of Health, *The Public Health Bush Book, Volume 2* (https://digitallibrary.health.nt.gov.au/prodjspui/handle/10137/7207, 2005). Reprinted with permission.

Figure 4.21: Scholastic, *The Science of Marijuana: How THC Affects the Brain, Heads Up: Real News About Drugs and Your Body* (http://headsup.scholastic.com/students/the-science-of-marijuana, 2011). Reprinted by permission of Scholastic Inc.

Figure 5.2: K. Lattimore et al., "Selective Serotonin Reuptake Inhibitor (SSRI) Use during Pregnancy and Effects on the Fetus and Newborn: A Meta-Analysis" (*Journal of Perinatology* 25, 2005), Figure 1. Reprinted by permission of *Springer Nature*.

INDEX